Towards Better Performing Transport Networks

The performance of current transport systems is inadequate when viewed in terms of economic efficiency, sustainability, and safety. *Towards Better Performing Transport Networks* examines the tools that are necessary to effectively measure these systems and those that are required to improve them.

Utilising advanced tools of network analysis, the contributors challenge various pieces of conventional wisdom and in particular the view that intermodal transport is more environmentally benign than road transport. A broad spectrum of the approaches designed to improve performance are reviewed including regulatory reform with the aim to improve competitive pressure in the aviation and public transport sectors. Another domain covered in this book concerns technological change, in particular the potential contribution of ICT to improve transport systems.

Bart Jourquin is Professor in Computer Science and Transport Economics, Catholic University of Mons (FUCaM), Mons, Belgium. **Piet Rietveld** is Professor in Transport Economics, Free University of Amsterdam, The Netherlands. **Kerstin Westin** is Professor at the Department of Social and Economic Geography, Umeå University, Sweden.

Routledge studies in business organizations and networks

Towards Better Performing Transport Networks

Edited by Bart Jourquin,
Piet Rietveld, and Kerstin Westin

Routledge
Taylor & Francis Group

LONDON AND NEW YORK

First published 2006
by Routledge
2 Park Square, Milton Park, Abingdon, Oxon OX14 4RN

Simultaneously published in the USA and Canada
by Routledge
270 Madison Ave, New York, NY 10016

Routledge is an imprint of the Taylor & Francis Group, an informa business

Typeset in Times by Wearset Ltd, Boldon, Tyne and Wear
Printed and bound in Great Britain by MPG Books Ltd, Bodmin

British Library Cataloguing in Publication Data
A catalogue record for this book is available from the British Library

Library of Congress Cataloging in Publication Data
A catalog record for this book has been requested

ISBN10: 0-415-37971-7

ISBN13: 978-0-415-37971-7

Contents

Figures and illustrations

Figures

Map

Tables

Introduction

Performance of transport networks

Bart Jourquin, Piet Rietveld, and Kerstin Westin

Setting the scene

Transport is often regarded as a prerequisite for economic development – although there is a dispute of the direction of the relationship. Maybe economic growth has necessitated development of transport and infrastructure. Be that as it may – there is a general consensus that in order for our society to develop and for people to manage their daily lives, there has to be a functioning, well-performing transport system.

Transport can be defined as

> The movement of goods and persons from place to place and the various means by which such movement is accomplished. The growth of the ability – and need – to transport large quantities of goods or numbers of people over long distances at high speeds in comfort and safety has been an index of civilization and in particular of technological progress.
>
> (Encyclopaedia Britannica, 2004)

This definition mentions quantity and quality aspects such as volume, distance, speed, comfort, and safety. One might add performance indicators such as ease of access, external safety, sustainability, and economic efficiency.

These attributes are also recognised in the White Paper on the European transport policy (2001), which states that a modern transport system must be sustainable from an economic, social, as well as an environmental viewpoint. The common transport policy is confronted with a certain number of major difficulties. Many expressways and urban transport networks present congestion problems. In addition, transport has harmful effects on the environment and public health. Access to transport modes and transport networks is not equal to all, there are gender inequalities as transport systems were not initially developed to answer the needs of both men and women, the needs of disabled and elderly are often not fulfilled, and we also have differences in access between different social groups.

There are of course reasons for the difficulties we see today in the perform-ance of transport. Transport systems are based on networks that were historically built in a rather ad hoc way to serve the needs of their times: railway networks were essentially developed at the national level without any insight on interoperability with other countries. Roads were created, but a holistic view including land use perspectives is often missing. Nowadays, these networks exist and we have to live with them. From a long term perspective a crucial question is how to anticipate the technological possibilities and needs of tomorrow, both in terms of transport systems and land use. The current trend towards globalisation makes international transport more important than ever. The transport activities are in constant evolution and tend to become more and more complex as the delivery periods shorten. The global economy needs effective transport, and a continuous reflection is needed to best use the present networks and develop them in view of future needs.

Efficiency and sustainability may go together in certain cases. For example, improving load factors in passenger or freight transport has positive impacts on both economic and environmental directions. However, in other cases the two objectives are not easy to reconcile. This has led to extensive research programmes on how to develop our transport system so that a good balance is found between environmental and economic perspectives.

It is clear that the globalisation of the world economy is a process that started long ago (see Table I.1). Exports as a share of the world production increased from a mere 1 per cent around 1800 to 17 per cent almost 200 years later. And noticeable is that the largest leap in growth occurred as late as 1973–1998 – a growth of almost 7 per cent.

An important driving force behind this increasing interdependence of national economies has been the drastic reduction of real transport costs. For example, Table I.2 shows that for ocean shipping the real costs have decreased enormously over the past centuries.

Decreasing transport costs have contributed strongly to globalisation. On the other hand, it is clear that other forces must also have been at work. For example, institutional barriers related to borders and protectionist policies must also have played their roles. Of particular interest may be that the decrease in the real costs of ocean shipping has come to a halt over the last decades. It is probable that this has been compensated by other components of generalised costs of

Table I.1 World merchandise exports as a ratio of world GDP

Year	Exports/GDP (%)
1820	1.0
1870	4.6
1913	7.9
1929	9.0
1950	5.5
1973	10.5
1998	17.2

Source: Maddison (2001).

Table I.2 Real costs of ocean shipping (1910 = 100)

Year	Cost index
1790	376
1830	287
1870	196
1910	100
1930	107
1960	47
1990	51

Sources: Crafts and Venables (2001), Dollar (2001), Harley (1988), Isserlis (1938).

transport owing to increases in speed, frequency and reliability. Nevertheless it indicates that further decreases of transport costs cannot be taken for granted. It also implies that quality aspects of transport are becoming more and more important. The rapid growth of freight transport that takes place by air – in particular when measured in terms of value rather than tonnes – is an indication that time is more important in the generalised costs of transport than is usually thought (Hummels, 2001).

This very short sketch of long running developments in trade makes clear that as economies become richer there is a strong demand for high quality freight transport which poses a strong challenge on the transport sector. Also, it has been argued by, e.g. Taaffe *et al.* (1963) that there is a parallel evolution of political, economic, and transport systems in developing economies.

A similar story can be told on passenger transport. Domestic transport tends to grow continuously. In countries with high income levels the growth rates are modest, whereas they are very high in developing countries such as China and India. International transport tends to increase at even higher levels (Eurostat, 2004). The gradual shift from manufacturing to services as the main dynamic sectors means that passenger transport will become more important as an input for production processes. This is one of the driving forces behind the observed rapid growth of international passenger transport, in particular via the air. Another important factor explaining the growth in aviation demand is international tourism. For example, in the year 2001 international tourism reached a level of about 700 million arrivals, Europe having a share of almost 60 per cent (Hall and Page, 2002). Given that the demographic profile of the Western world is changing, with a growing number of elderly, well-educated and economically well-situated, it is reasonable to expect international tourism travel to increase.

It is clear at the same time that these strong increases in transport demand, in particular the faster modes, impose considerable threats on the sustainability of the transport sector.

Sustainability

Decoupling of the growth in emissions and economic activities is the main way towards sustainable development. For certain sectors, developments have been favourable. For example, long term trends in the EU indicate that energy consumption, leading to CO_2 emissions is growing much slower than GDP growth. However, transport is a striking exception in this development. Energy use and CO_2 emissions in transport are growing faster than the economy. As a consequence the share of energy consumed in transport compared with total energy consumption has grown considerably during the last three decades.

To understand the mechanisms behind the increase of energy use in transport the following decomposition can be used:

Energy use = (Energy use/transport volume) ×
(transport volume/GDP) × (GDP)

Given the process of globalisation sketched in Table I.1 it follows that transport volume/GDP has increased. An obvious explanation is that – as indicated above – the real generalised costs of transport are decreasing in the long run. The energy intensity in transport (energy use/transport volume) is remaining about constant. This is a striking result since during the last decades substantial technological progress has been made in improving the efficiency of energy use in transport. This means that countervailing forces must have been at work. For example, the increase in energy efficiency of engines in cars has been accompanied by the gradual increase in the weight of cars. Also there has been a gradual shift from slow to fast transport modes – in particular aviation – which implies higher energy use per kilometre travelled. Further, GDP increased substantially in the EU, although population growth itself has been modest. Thus, the major forces behind the increase of energy use in transport are the relatively high responsiveness of transport to economic growth and the occurrence of rebound effects of energy use within the transport sector that offset the potential efficiency gains that were made possible by technological development.

The above results for the EU lead to concerns on the long term environmental consequences of transport. One should be aware, on the other hand, that for a substantial number of pollutants progress has been made. For example, the phasing out of leaded gasoline in Europe and the US has tremendously reduced lead emissions. Similarly the use of catalytic converters has led a strong reduction of NO_x emissions of road transport. Thus, in other fields, outside the energy domain, large improvements have been made. The main remaining sustainability problems that are difficult to solve in the long run seem to be the local ones related to noise, accidents, etc., and the global ones related to energy use.

At the world level the situation is worse than the European situation suggests. There are two reasons for this. First, although being smaller in population size, the volume of CO_2 emissions in the USA is more than twice as high than in Europe. This means a substantial additional factor in world energy demand.

Second, of particular importance is the position of China and other developing countries with high economic growth. As indicated by WBCSD (2001), the global development of greenhouse emissions will strongly be determined by these countries if they continue to grow as they do now.

Indicators for efficiency and sustainability are needed

> Trying to run a complex society on only a single indicator like the Gross National Product is like trying to fly a Boeing 747 with only one gauge on the instrument panel. Imagine if your Doctor, when giving you a check-up, did no more than check your blood pressure.
>
> (Hazel Henderson, *Paradigms of Progress* (1993))

Indicators are quantified information which help to explain how things are changing over time. It is not only a matter of technical efficiency, but also a question of the way to effectively achieve measurable goals set by private or public actors. Historically, only a limited number of key economic indicators have been used to measure how the economy is performing – for example, output, level of employment, rate of inflation, balance of payments, etc. These figures give a general picture but do not explain the particular trends that are observed. However, they provide reasonable indicators of changes in the economy to the policy-makers and economic policy decision.

Indicators have three basic functions: simplification, quantification, and communication. Indicators generally simplify very complex phenomena in order to make them quantifiable so that information can be communicated and understood. As stated earlier, an effective transport system is an absolute need in our modern world. Industry, commerce, and services depend on it, and even social and recreational aspects of our life are made possible because of the availability of private cars. The key objective for a sustainable development is to tend to a right balance between the ability of transport to serve economic development and the ability to protect the environment and sustain quality of life, both now and in the future.

Policies aiming at enhancing efficiency and sustainability

An important challenge for our society is to reconcile the increasing demand for transport while reducing its environmental impact. About 15 per cent of all consumptive expenditures of households can be assigned to transport. The transport sector represents around 6 per cent of Europe's GDP and 6 per cent of EU employment and, over the past 30 years, goods traffic has increased by more than 75 per cent and passenger movements by more than 110 per cent.

For enhanced efficiency and quality the aim is to improve the overall cost-effectiveness and functioning of transport operations and infrastructure. Particular attention must be paid to how to integrate the respective strengths of all modes of transport in order to provide door-to-door services for both passengers and freight. A significant effort must be devoted to the reduction of congestion into networks in the coming years, but also to increase safety and security.

Table I.3, partly based on Button and Rietveld (1999) suggests a number of policies to improve efficiency and sustainability in transport. The types of measures we distinguish vary from market-based versus command and control measures. We add the distinction between direct and indirect since many measures that are not directly related to efficiency and environmental effects of transport activities have substantial indirect effects. As points of entry we use vehicle, fuel, infrastructure, traffic, and spatial structure, and a group of miscellaneous effects.

Of special importance seems to be the last element of the table, institutional change and regulatory reform. It is clear that these instruments may in the long run have very strong impacts on the performance of transport systems. For example, the liberalisation of the aviation market in the USA and Europe has led to a considerable increase of efficiency in the aviation sector in the form of lower prices and higher frequencies. At the same time, the environmental burden has increased. Another example concerns the regulatory reform of the rail and bus sector in many countries which had mixed effects on the efficiency in transport operations. The outcome is dependent on situational and geographical context, and experiences cannot readily be transferred from one country to another or from one industry to another.

Intermodal transport

It is gradually realised that intermodality may provide a key towards a better performing transport system. Car and truck will undoubtedly continue to dominate passenger and freight transport in Europe during the coming decades, but it is clear that they have their limitations and that they have to be combined with other transport modes. These limitations are obvious for passenger transport in metropolitan areas where congestion and lack of space for the car call for additional transport modes including cycling, walking, and public transport. These transport modes are not only competitors of the car, but may also be complements. For example, the principle that the car provides door-to-door transport has found its limitations in urban centres where pedestrian areas and limited or expensive parking spaces imply that the last part of the trip has to be done with another mode of transport. This calls for careful planning of parking facilities to link the car system with public transport. Also for long distance passenger transport where rail may be more attractive than the car, there is a clear need for a multimodal approach to ensure the local accessibility of railway stations. It makes little sense to carry out large investments in high speed lines when at the same time the quality of the underlying networks providing access to the stations is low. This points to the importance of working with transport planning as an integrated part of planning in general. Transport is intricately connected with all other aspects of daily life, such as housing, shopping, working and recreation, and consequently measures taken or changes made in one of these areas affects all the others.

Table 1.3 Typology of policies to address efficiency and sustainability in transport networks

	Market: direct	Market: indirect	Command and control: direct	Command and control: indirect
Vehicle	• Emission fees • Congestion charges	• Tax allowance for new vehicles	• Emission standards	• Mandatory use of low-polluting vehicles
Fuel		• Differential fuel taxation	• Phasing out of high polluting fuels	• Fuel economy standards
Infrastructure		• Compensation for intrusion at time of infrastructure construction	• Noise shields	• Bus lanes • Airport location • Motorway expansion • Railway construction
Traffic	• Kilometre charge for road use, differentiated according to environmental standard of vehicle	• Parking charges • Subsidies for less polluting modes	• High occupancy vehicle lanes	• Speed limits • Restraint on vehicle use
Spatial structure				• Restrictions on settlement densities • Location of new settlements
Others				• Institutional change • Regulatory reform

In freight transport a similar phenomenon can be observed, where rail, inland navigation and short sea shipping are attractive alternatives to the truck. But given the economies of scale in terminal operations, terminal density is limited which implies that the first and last legs of a transport chain usually have to be carried out via road. This again calls for well performing multimodal nodes. Of critical importance are the fixed costs related to the transfer from one mode to the other. These include time costs of loading, scheduling, and waiting since frequencies on rail and water are lower given the large size of the trains and barges. Due to the high costs of modal transfer the threshold for intermodal freight journeys in the European Union is about 500 km. Reducing this for example to 200 km would be a great step forward in the promotion of intermodal transport.

This simple example illustrates that enhancing efficiency can only be achieved if solutions are implemented at several levels. Indeed, better intermodal solutions need:

- technical innovative solutions to fasten transshipment operations at the terminals;
- an in-depth knowledge of demand and supply associated to a reflection on land use considerations in order to create, develop, and operate terminals at sustainable locations;
- a better technical interoperability between the different national railway networks;
- an improved legal framework on transportation considerations;
- a better convergence of the social frameworks for the different transportation modes towards the European countries;
- change of attitudes in order to bring about change of behaviour;
- integrated planning between the different sectors;
- and so on.

Book content

The challenges posed to us are not simple, and much research is still needed. This volume tries to create a small milestone for these aspects.

The contributions to the theme of transport network performance are written by researchers belonging to the Network on European Communications and Transport Activity Research (NECTAR). The first part of this volume mainly addresses the stimulation of better performances by means of regulation and various other policies. It is followed by another series of papers that discuss items related to efficiency and sustainability in transport. The book concludes with some more method-oriented contributions in which efficiency is measured by models and methods.

The first set of papers approaches efficiency and sustainability of some proposed solutions, including intermodal transport.

Political and scientific interest with regard to intermodal transport is due to its sustainable and ecological aspects. By means of a review of the literature

Kreutzberger, Macharis, and Woxenius present an overview tackling the issue of the external effects of intermodal and unimodal transport. The results of the different studies are compared to each other and common conclusions are drawn, giving a clear signal to the market about the lack of cost coverage that should be an incentive for intermodal transport to improve its quality. Moreover, from a more general viewpoint, taking into account internal and external costs, spatial and network policies are crucial.

The paper by Willigers and van Wee draws attention to the fact that literature on environmental impact of underground freight transport is very scarce. Their paper assesses the energy use and the resulting emissions from underground freight transport systems. They use an analysis method based on indirect energy in two case studies: the long distance transport of crude oil in The Netherlands and the underground distribution of packed goods in the city of Utrecht (ULS). The construction of underground infrastructure for freight transport is seen by the Dutch government as a policy measure to achieve a more sustainable transport system. The paper demonstrates that things are not so simple. However, the authors state that a positive direct effect of all the alternatives in the ULS is the shift of emissions from inside the city to its edge and to power plants; this can improve local air quality in the city itself.

An efficient transport system must also be safe. As shown by Westin, Garvill, and Marell reducing the speed is a way to improve the performance of the road system by increasing security on the roads. This paper examines the effects on speed of vehicles equipped with an Intelligent Speed Adaptation (ISA) device and the effects these devices have on the average speed in the Swedish city of Umeå. ISA systems help drivers to avoid exceeding speed limits. The obtained results tend to show that speed was reduced within the test area, and that the observed speed reduction was perceived to be positive by the participating drivers. Thus, ISA is a promising tool to improve network performance from a safety perspective.

Roson makes a link between tangible and intangible networks, starting from the observation that, even if there is competition between agents in a network market, there is also a need for interconnection between them. He shows that concepts and principles can be considered as independent from the specific type of network (Internet, transportation, water distribution, etc.). This interesting paper draws some deep theoretical insight on these concepts, to finally conclude that network economics provide general models for the analysis of imperfect competition in networked markets like transportation, water distribution, and so on. The main insight is that capacity investments have a differentiated impact for on-net and off-net flows. Whereas intra-network flows are directly affected by the increase in capacity, the influence of congestion on inter-network flows depends on both the capacity levels of the source and destination networks. In addition, network firms may compete for quality through capacity improvements.

As mentioned above, indicators are important to address transport network performance. In order to allow decision-makers to imagine various (non-)fiscal policies and measures taking into account environmental aspects, Van Mierlo *et al.* have developed Ecoscore, a rating system able to compare the environmental damages caused by different vehicles. This new approach has been especially developed for urban contexts. The authors warn about the fact that their approach is still modest in comparison with what might be done theoretically but it meets different constraints such as, for example, working with currently available data or having comparable results for different vehicles of a same category. On the basis of the sensitivity analysis, they conclude that the proposed methodology is sufficiently robust for variations of the relative contribution of each specific pollutant.

The second series of papers discuss the impact of rules and policies on the performances of networks in their constrained environment.

Button examines institutional dimensions behind the improved performance of the airline sector during the past decades, in particular with respect to the notion of barriers to entry and exit in markets. He analyses what has happened in air transportation markets since the domestic deregulation in the US. The airline market is rapidly changing and the market share of low cost carriers has increased. He uses the idea of contestable markets to explain the functioning of the current trends. The author also identifies the various forms of market fragmentation initiated by the low cost companies as well as the responses developed by the majors.

Stead and Banister show in their paper that decoupling economic growth from transport growth does not yet take place, which means that sustainable transport is still far away. They discuss the nature of travel and how decoupling can usefully be measured through volumes, distances, and efficiency. They also present possible approaches and strategies for decoupling. For example, they show the impact of land use planning policies on passenger travel distance and the impact this strategy may have on efficiency.

Enoch and Rye discuss travel plans of employers or local governments, which are aimed at reducing car use for commuting and business trips and hence improve their environmental performance. This is an example of institutional change, mentioned in Table I.3, implying a difference in definition of positions of actors, in this case the employer. A travel plan is a package of measures that can be implemented to encourage staff to choose alternatives to single-occupancy car use. This paper establishes a series of scenarios to estimate how travel plans might be more effectively introduced and supported. These models will then serve to develop the future travel plans in the UK.

The appropriate role and function of government in the regulation of the public transport sector is the topic discussed by Mouwen and Rietveld. They assess five regulatory regimes on efficiency and equity objectives of regional and local public transport authorities. They use data from 21 European cities and regions to show that competition is positively related to objectives of efficiency taken by the authorities. This underlines the importance of regulatory regimes adopted to improve the performance of transport systems, in particular public transport.

The last part of the book is more specifically related to methods and models that can help to measure and evaluate efficiency.

Nagurney and Matsypura developed a framework for the modelling, analysis, and computation of solutions to global supply chains. They model the behaviours of three decision-makers – manufacturers, intermediaries, and consumers – and obtain qualitative properties of the equilibrium product shipment and price pattern. This research extends the recent results surrounding the modelling of supply chains in network equilibrium.

The framework allows for the handling of as many countries, as many manufacturers in each country, as many currencies in which the product can be obtained, and as many retailers, as required by the specific application. Moreover, the generality of the framework allows for the demand to have almost any distribution as long as it satisfies certain technical conditions. The dynamic model, which is formulated as a projected dynamic system, provides the evolution of the product transactions between tiers of the global supply chain super network as well as the prices associated with the product at retailer and at distributor levels.

Over the last few years, the European high-speed train network has rapidly developed. Martín, Gutiérrez and Román evaluate the gain of accessibility obtained on the connection between Madrid and Barcelona. The authors use a geographic information system (GIS) to develop some synthetic indices to measure the impact on accessibility of the new line. If the new high speed line Madrid–Barcelona–French border is built, the authors conclude that Madrid, Ciudad Real, Barcelona, Segovia, Guadalajara, Valladolid, Zaragoza, Tarragona, and Lleida would become the most accessible cities in Spain. From a more general viewpoint, the project will increase regional accessibility disparities.

Kreutzberger, Konings, and Aronson point out that Pre- and Post-Haulage (PPH) is an important part of the costs in intermodal freight transport, for which they have developed a simple calculation tool. The impact of PPH costs are known to be an important question for the design of intermodal rail or barge terminals. The authors estimate the relative importance of PPH costs for distances of 5, 25, 50, and 100 km, taking into account the different typical alternative European network operations. As expected, no real general design can be proposed, as the performances depend very much on different aspects such as volumes, length of the main railway chunk, frequencies, etc., showing that the decision to create a terminal, a logistic platform or a shuttle service must be carefully studied and cannot be the simple result of a local political decision.

Bergantino, Bolis, and Canali present a methodological framework to detect the market opportunities for short sea shipping. They noticed that there is lack of empirical data that can be used to determine the operators' choices. They measure the trade-offs among service characteristics that shippers make when they evaluate the Ro-Ro option against alternative surface services. They present preliminary evidence obtained by estimating a model of forwarding agents' behaviour with respect to the maritime alternative, using adaptive conjoint data collecting methods. Reliability and frequency seem to be the key factors in the choice of the transport service alternative. Despite the fact that the outcome of the research is based on a limited sample, it confirms that the use of stated preferences can be a valid option to estimate the attitudes of operators towards the attributes of Ro-Ro freight transport markets.

Raney and Nagel present an improved framework for large multi-agent simulation of travel behaviour. For a long time, multi-agent simulations were considered to be only feasible on small networks. The authors present some new methodological insights and computer implementations of simulations on large networks, opening the way for new model possibilities. This modelling approach is promising since its immediate goal is a replacement of the traditional four-step process for transportation planning; the longer-term goal is to have an agent-based system for all aspects of urban and regional planning.

Macharis, Stevens, De Brucker, and Verbeke present a strategic assessment methodology for advanced driver assistance systems (ADAS). The partners in the research consortium include various public agencies, publicly funded research institutes, transport and insurance companies, and automobile manufacturers from ten different European Union countries. The ultimate purpose of this consortium was to improve road safety in the EU through the introduction of new technologies. Their paper focuses on sensitivity analysis and implementation challenges. The strategy selection matrix and related work intended to develop implementation strategies, provides a new framework to reflect on the complex challenge of ADAS deployment. The methodology, when applied to a number of highly ranked scenarios, was considered helpful by a number of actors involved in strategic thinking on this issue. A certain number of implementation phases were identified, which suggest fruitful avenues for business–government cooperation, especially at the European level.

Conclusion

One of the conclusions that can be drawn from this set of papers is that multimodality, although being promising and promoted, is still difficult to make a success. There are mainly two reasons for this. First, market adoption will remain a problem since generalised costs remain substantial. The second reason is that the environmental performance of multimodality is not as good as one might expect on the basis of the favourable environmental performance of the main mode (for example rail) versus the truck. This is due among other things to the detours made in multimodal transport and to the intensive use of road for pre- and post-haulage, often in already congested areas.

Another conclusion that can be drawn is that – even though substantial progress has been made in some directions – the environmental impact of transport is a matter of continuous concern. Congestion, pollution, traffic safety, and land use conflicts arise more often than ever and decoupling energy use and transport will be a major challenge. A solid assessment and evaluation of these conflicts is needed, in particular since long-term impacts of policies aiming at decoupling are hard to assess.

The challenge of tomorrow is to manage a transport system that is increasingly more global and international, and therefore hard to monitor and manage. This is partly a political issue. National governments have no doubt exerted substantial influence on transport system performance via regulatory measures and taxation, but in small countries there is less scope for intervention. This calls for the formation of geo-political institutions such as the EU to have a public sector that has sufficient power to face the power of transnational corporations and also to address problems with fiscal competition between countries.

A final point we observe is that the performance problems of today are considered to be the most urgent ones. However, demographic trends in the industrialised world, with lower fertility rates and higher life expectancy, lead to an ageing population. This means that our transport system will gradually face new performance standards related to the changing composition of the population. Given the long-term investments involved, it is advisable to start making adjustments to the transport system to meet the needs of the citizens of tomorrow.

References

Button, K.J. and Rietveld, P. (1999) 'Transport and the environment' in J. van den Bergh (ed.) *Handbook of Environmental and Resource Economics*, Edward Elgar, Cheltenham, pp. 581–592.

Crafts, N. and Venables, A.J. (2001) *Globalization in History: a Geographical Perspective*, Paper prepared for the NBER conference on 'Globalization in Historical Perspective'.

Dollar, D. (2001) *Globalization, Inequality and Poverty since 1980*, mimeo, Worldbank.

EC (2002) White Paper 'European transport for 2010: time to decide'.

Eurostat (2004) Passenger air transport 2001–2002.

Hall, C.M. and Page, S.J. (2001) *The Geography of Tourism and Recreation*, Routledge, Glasgow.

Harley, C.K. (1988) 'Ocean Freight Rates and Productivity 1740–1913: the primacy of mechanical invention reaffirmed' *Journal of Economic History*, 60: 819–841.

Henderson, H. (1993) *Paradigms of Progress.*

Hummels, D. (2001) *Time as a Trade Barrier*, mimeo, Purdue University.

Isserlis, L. (1938) 'Tramp shipping cargoes and freights' *Journal of the Royal Statistical Society*, 101: 53–146.

Maddison, A. (2001) *The World Economy: A Millennial Perspective*, OECD.

Taaffe, E.J., Morrill, R.L., and Gould, P.R. (1963) 'Transport expansion in underdeveloped countries: a comparative analysis' *Geographical Review*, 53: 503–529.

WBCSD (2001) World Business Council for Sustainable Development, Mobility 2001, Geneva.

Part I

Efficiency and sustainability in transport

1.1 Intermodal versus unimodal road freight transport

A review of comparisons of the external costs

Ekki Kreutzberger, * *Cathy Macharis,* ** *and*
Johan Woxenius***

Abstract

Intermodal transport, the combination and integration of several modes, with the use of loading units, has been said to be more environmentally friendly than unimodal road transport for the carriage of goods. The political and scientific interest in this transport system is largely due to the sustainability and ecological aspect of the intermodal transportation system. In this paper an overview is given of studies and papers that are tackling the issue of the external effects of both intermodal and unimodal transport. An overview is given of the types of external costs that were taken into account (emissions, security, noise, etc.) and the methodologies that were used to estimate the external effects and to value these effects in terms of costs. The results of the different studies are compared and conclusions are drawn.

Keywords: *intermodal freight transport, environmental performance, external costs, internalisation*

1 Introduction

Intermodal freight transport, the combination and integration of several traffic modes with the use of loading units, has often been claimed to produce less emission of harmful substances than unimodal road transport. The political[1] and scientific[2] interest in intermodal transport is largely due to this assumed ecological sustainability together with the potential to fight congestion on the roads.

Despite strong research and policy statements, a study (IFEU and SGKV, 2002) commissioned by the International Road Transport Union (IRU) and Bundesverband Güterkraftverkehr Logistik und Entsorgung (BGL) has brought the assumption of intermodal transport as being ecologically favourable into question. Cases in which intermodal road-rail transport requires more primary energy leads the IRU to recommend a transport policy not supporting intermodal transport. Also Transport en Logistiek Nederland (TLN) refers to an own study (TLN, 2002) advocating longer lorries instead of a modal shift.

Hence, the primary purpose of the article is to investigate whether published studies support the yet dominating opinion that intermodal transport is less environmentally harmful than unimodal road transport and if so, under what circumstances.

A further important point is that a stated goal of national and EU authorities is to internalise the external costs, which are the monetisation of the external effects, of all modes of transport (see, e.g. European Commission, 2001). Estimating the external costs is truly a delicate task and the effects on the competitive situation of the different modes have to be considered. If a policy would be pursued to internalise the external costs, the cost calculations underlying this policy should be reliable. A second purpose is to evaluate how the reviewed studies contribute to the knowledge of external costs.

Assuming that external costs can be accurately calculated, another issue is how they can be used for introducing fair and efficient pricing, which means that all transport assignments carry their internal and external costs. The third purpose is then to investigate what support the studies give to policy-makers and for the competition between traffic modes.

The article reviews different applied research efforts tackling the issues of the external effects of intermodal and unimodal freight transport and evaluates the results structured by the approaches presented in the theoretical framework in Section 2. Much of this kind of research is published as reports and conference papers rather than articles in scientific journals (Bontekoning *et al.*, 2003) indicating that the issue of logistics and the environment is underrepresented in scientific journals (Abukhader and Jönson, 2004). The search for reports and conference papers is a less structured process than reviewing journal publications, and the search and selection process behind this article has been somewhat pragmatic. The fact that many reports are published in national languages also means that there is a correspondence between the selected studies and the nationality of the authors.

2 Considered aspects

The policy field of external transport costs is rather complex and research results and internalisation effects are highly method dependent. Many aspects must then be distinguished and the ones influencing this study the most are listed here.

The focus of the study

The focus describes what the main subject of a study is, namely the size of external effects, possibly also their valuation to costs and benefits and even the cost coverage of social costs by taxes, charges and subsidies or even the relation between real and fair or efficient prices. Another interest could be the comparison of the transport sector with other economic sectors. The focus is of influence for the choice of economic approach.

Average versus marginal costs

Efficient prices according to welfare theory are prices based on so-called short term marginal internal and external costs.[3] Marginal approaches focus on the costs of the last additional unit of transport (vehicle, vehicle-km, ton, tonnekm, loading unit, load unit km; absolute or percentage, etc.). Marginal costs in principle differ from average ones, even though the two can be the same.[4]

The transport system aggregation level

The size of external costs depends on the envisaged transport system level. This can be the whole transport system or sub-categories, like freight and passenger transport. The external costs to 'the society' or non-participants of the evaluated traffic on the one side or transport group on the other side are smaller than if the effects to other system participants are also included (e.g. health effects of freight transport to non-participants only (like residents) and all society (residents, drivers, and passengers)). The most discussed topic in this regard is accident costs. The European research projects UNITE (Sansom *et al.*, 1999) and RECORDIT (Bacelli *et al.*, 2001; D4) consider the own risk of system participants to be internal costs, as these are accepted when deciding to use the system. The long British tradition of comparing infrastructure-related costs with revenues for the road sector by means of 'fully allocated cost' models excludes external costs internal to the transport system (Sansom *et al.*, 2001). Also, ECMT, CE Delft, and INFRAS/IWW define the own risk of system participants as external costs (Dings *et al.*, 2003). Certain costs to others, like accident damages, are not external costs as they are covered by insurance and therefore already internalised.

Another important point here is that even with an aggregate estimation of the external costs, this will not shed light on the individual modal shift decisions of companies and as such will not give an idea on the modal shift pattern on a macro-level. Indeed, at the company-level other costs and criteria are taken into account (Roson, 2003).

The system borders

The external effects can be analysed for the transport system only, or also for upstream or downstream events. Upstream events are external effects of producing something, which is used in the transport system, like petrol or vehicles. Downstream events are external effects of things that have been used in the transport system, like destroying or recycling old vehicles.

A dominating method in this domain is Life Cycle Assessment (LCA), the application of which, however, is not intended for assessing supply chains but for the full life-cycles of physical products (Abukhader and Jönsson, 2004). With some adaptations, LCA can be applied to transportation, e.g. for assessing single transport assignments or networks producing standardised services such as general cargo transport. LCA is rather easy to apply on the level of a vehicle (Van Mierlo *et al.*, 2003). Allocating the external effects to individual consignments, however, requires a number of delicate assumptions regarding, e.g. distribution between different consignments co-using transport resources, which consignment initiated the movement of the vehicle, load factors, and balances (Bäckström, 1999).

The range of external effects

The following list of typical external cost components is not complete, but nevertheless they are often the subject of research projects:

*   accidents;
*   noise;
*   air pollution;
*   climate change;
*   infrastructure;
*   congestion;
*   water pollution;
*   damage to certain ecological systems;
*   land occupation; and
*   visual intrusion.

Some of these components are of interest primarily to other system participant groups (like congestion), others primarily to non-participants (like land occupation).

The last three components are, despite their policy relevance in densely populated European regions, not included in the analysis. If it is true that land occupation of unimodal road transport per freight unit is significantly higher than that of intermodal transport (this is doubted by some authors, as we will see below), then this should be expressed in pricing schemes or by other types of political decisions.

The external cost strategy

Internalisation policies can be based on three strategies: the prevention strategy; the damage compensation strategy; and the damage recovery strategy. The first is directed towards (ex-ante) avoiding damage, the second towards compensating for realised damage, the last towards (ex-post) undoing the damage. The size of the costs and of the relation between costs and measures may differ per strategy (Boneschansker and 't Hoen, 1993).

Methods to estimate external costs

To substitute the absence of market prices, external costs are estimated in terms of shadow prices. The estimates can be direct or indirect ones, bottom-up or top-down ones, and related to political, scientific or individual targets or norms. They can also include upstream or downstream events. Some examples: CO_2 emissions are direct estimates in the light of – most often – political targets (Kyoto, European, national). The shadow prices reflect the costs to prevent or abate damage due to higher emissions.

Local emissions, noise and accidents are estimated directly or indirectly. A new indirect approach is the 'Impact Pathway Approach', which was developed and applied the first time by the ExternE project (Friedrich and Bickel, 2001), later also adopted by UNITE and RECORDIT and by many studies we reviewed here.

The methods of impact valuation

For the direct or indirect valuation of impacts alternative techniques have been developed, among which hedonic pricing, the travel cost method, contingent valuation, and the human capital approach are the most recognised.

The instruments to realise the internalisation

The instruments to realise internalisation are rather independent from the estimation of the size of effects, impacts, and monetary values. But it is useful to have the instruments in mind when thinking about estimation, since the instruments differ per strategy (as defined above). All three strategies can be realised by introducing monetary instruments such as taxes, charges, subsidies or financial compensation, which equalise the distribution of (dis)advantages between generators of traffic effects and persons who suffer or benefit from the impacts. The prevention strategy may also include non-monetary instruments such as the prohibition, the restriction or the enforcement of certain transport or traffic features. These instruments need legal frameworks, for instance a definition of who is the owner of a right or a problem. Only if the non-participant of the transport system (e.g. a resident) is owner of the right of certain residential qualities, can he or she demand financial compensation from the one who causes the quality damages. The legal framework also needs to cover the geographical scale of the problem caused. Hence, noise and local emissions can be dealt with on a community level (e.g. bans on engines running for more than three minutes at stand still), sulphur emissions on a European level, while CO_2 emissions must be negotiated globally.

The analysed modalities

The analysed modalities include unimodal road, rail, and air transport as well as intermodal road-rail and road-barge transport. In literature several comparisons on a unimodal basis were found. Dings *et al.* (2003), Forckenbrock (2001), Beuthe *et al.* (1999, 2002) and De Vlieger *et al.* (2002, 2004) are very interesting from a methodological perspective but are not incorporated in the description of studies as they do not take account of the specific settings of the intermodal transport chain. They are, however, kept in the overview (Section 4) in order to compare the other methodological steps.

All ten aspects serve as check list when reviewing the literature in the following section. The summary of Section 4 contains a table which gives an overview of all reviewed literature in relation to the included aspects.

3 Review of studies

In this section the different studies, projects and articles are reviewed. The utilised methodologies are summarised and the main results given. An overview of the reviewed papers is given at the end of the section. Here the different aspects, as discussed in Section 2, are given for each of the studies. The review covers ten studies (A–J) and starts with some supplementary information on the two critical research reports, which were already presented in Section 1.

IFEU and SGKV, 2002

The IRU/BGL study (IFEU and SGKV, 2002) focuses on the comparison between primary energy needs and CO_2 emissions of unimodal road transport and of an intermodal road-rail transport. The study shows that three of the 19 routes examined require higher primary energy need by intermodal road-rail transport (Figure 1.1.1). Otherwise in eight cases the primary energy need of intermodal transport is up to 20 per cent lower than that of road transport, in six cases it is 20–40 per cent lower and in two cases it is lower by more than 40 per cent. The best results were achieved by swap bodies and containers. If, on the other hand, CO_2 emissions are compared, the same study indicates that in two cases emissions generated by intermodal transport are higher than those generated by unimodal road transport. The rest of the study shows clearly that CO_2 emissions by intermodal transport are lower than those produced by unimodal road transport (for example: in four cases up to 20 per cent lower, in seven cases 20–50 per cent lower).

This study leads the IRU to recommend a transport policy which would not be based on a further promotion of intermodal transport. Such a conclusion represents a biased interpretation of an otherwise solid analysis. The study calculates only direct effects of only two entities, namely energy need and CO_2 emission. The dispersion of CO_2 and the impacts of energy need and CO_2 emission to society, and the valuation of impacts are not subjects of the research. The differences of environmental performance are due to:

- The type of train. Rolling road trains have clear disadvantages regarding energy use compared to trains with semi-trailers and containers.
- The length of train. Trains with ten wagons (*c.*200m) have a higher specific energy need than road. Trains with 15 wagons (*c.*300m) already have lower values. Long trains (*c.*700m) have an energy need of about 60 per cent.

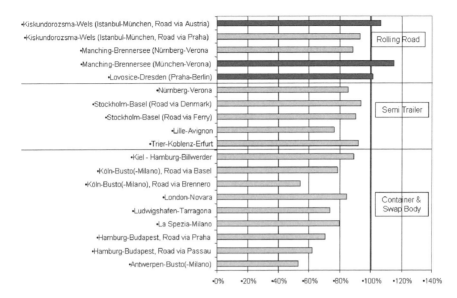

Figure 1.1.1 Primary energy consumption for every relation: intermodal transport road compared to unimodal road transport (source: IFEU and SGKV, 2002).

- The amount of pre- and post-haulage (PPH). The study concludes that for PPH 'perpendicular to the main route, the intermodal transport will be energetically disadvantageous when the total distance of PPH is more than half the distance of the direct road transport'. And if the direction of PPH 'is opposite to the main route (backwards) the intermodal transport is less favourable as soon as $\frac{1}{4}$ of the direct road transport distance is required for PPH' (IFEU and SGKV, 2002: 34–35).

The three trains with negative environmental performances have cumulative negative input characteristics: very short main modality distances (two of the three cases), longer PPH-distances than main modality distances (three of three), short train lengths (two of three) and Rolling Road trains (three of three). This allows for drawing the conclusion that average intermodal trains will always have better environmental performances (in terms of energy and CO_2 emissions) than unimodal road transport.

The negative performance of PPH is mainly due to the higher fuel consumption of lorries in local transport (48 instead of 35 litres/100 km), which is very reasonable argumentation. Less reasonable may be the fact that local road performances in unimodal road transport are considered to be short. If local parts had a comparable proportion in the entire road distance as in intermodal chains, the environmental performance of unimodal road would decrease. This reflection in any case indicates the importance of location policies.

Another important observation for conclusions from the IRU/BGL study is that reference lorries are assumed to be loaded in both directions of a round trip. In practice this is often not the case, not only because of freight imbalances (which also bother other modalities), but also because of insufficiently co-ordinated operations.

TLN, 1999

Also the report of TLN (1999) is restricted to direct effects (no dispersion, impacts or valuation). The study focuses on energy need, emissions (local and CO_2) and land occupation of three modalities: unimodal road; intermodal road-rail; and intermodal road-barge transport. The TLN cases refer to the following network and operational features: the main modality route length is 450 km, PPH for rail maritime, rail continental, barge maritime, barge continental are set at 5, 10, 5 and 20 per cent respectively. The trains have 21–28 wagons (maximal length then is approximately 400–550 m). The envisaged barges are the neo-kempenaar (32 TEU) and Europe barge (208 TEU). The report distinguishes maritime and continental flows and concludes that only the first have more favourable environmental performances. The main reason is that PPH distances are relatively short or even zero. The report therefore advocates stopping the myths about the environmental effects of a modal shift.

Even though PPH, also according to other reports, deserves much attention, most results of modality comparisons are presented on a door-to-door level. The effects of PPH are not discussed separately. On this level the global direction of results is indicated in Table 1.1.1.

Some results regarding energy need and CO_2 emissions of the TLN study diverge from those by the IRU/BGL study. The latter is more convincing in terms of methodology. The study assumes a very low fuel consumption of lorries, namely 29 litres/100 km compared to 34 litres/100 km in the IRU/BGL study. Train lengths are not varied and the reference lorry is loaded in both directions of a round trip.

Part of the TLN study is devoted to the coverage of environmental costs. This part of the study appears to be tendentious, cumulating in the conclusions that road covers 28–179 per cent of its costs, intermodal networks, on the other hand, would cover none of their environmental costs.

TLN, 2002

'Gelijke monniken, gelijke kappen' (2002) is a new TLN report on external costs rather than an update of the former one. It investigates the external costs of accidents, noise, emissions (climate and local) and infrastructure of road, rail and barge transport, including intermodal transport, and calculates the cost coverage per modality for the Dutch situation in 2002. Congestion costs are not calculated, because such costs can – in TLN's opinion – not reasonably by assigned to (road) freight transport, which must be considered to be rather a

Table 1.1.1 Environmental performance of intermodal door-to-door transport in comparison with unimodal road transport

	Rail maritime	Rail continental	Barge maritime	Barge continental
Energy need	Favourable	Non favourable	Favourable	Non favourable
CO_2	Favourable	Non favourable	Favourable	Non favourable
NO_x	Favourable	Slightly favourable	Favourable	Non favourable
SO_2 and particles	Non favourable	Non favourable	Non favourable	Non favourable
Land occupation	Non favourable	Non favourable	Non favourable	

victim than a causer of congestion. TLN concludes that road transport outside of towns has lower external costs per TEU-km than rail or barge transport, and that these costs are covered by 97–110 per cent (rail or barge only up to 26 per cent and 18 per cent respectively).

Such results differ from other studies. Most striking is the low level of rural road local and climate emissions. This is partly due to cleaner engines, but especially as a result of employing a low CO_2 shadow price, which – as TLN points out – refers to emission rights trade: 17.4 euro per ton CO_2 (instead of 166.8 euro per ton in the EC's no-trade scenario or instead of CE's value of 50 euro per ton). Also TLN's road infra and accident costs are substantially lower than in other studies. If the higher values of CE Delft or European studies were applied, TLN's road external costs would more than double and the road cost coverage would then shrink.

TLN's external rail (local and climate) emission costs are also lower than that of other studies, for the same reasons as for road. However, the cost advantages of emission trade is larger for road than for rail. Also skipping congestion calculations is in favour of road transport.

For all TLN results one should bear in mind that average variable costs have been used instead of so-called marginal costs.

Walstra et al., *1995*

The article 'Emissies van gecombineerd vervoer' (Emissions of intermodal transport) (Walstra *et al.*, 1995) concerns a case study carried out in the Dutch 'Aagrunol Project'. The aim of the case study was to compare the emissions and the energy need associated with the transport of 200 000 tons of earth by unimodal road transport with that of intermodal transport. Furthermore the study comprises a theoretical analysis of the emissions and the energy need associated with road-rail transport. The methodology consisted of using existing information about emission factors and the energy need formula (of Rijkeboer) to calculate the emissions and the energy need.

The results in the Aagrunol project made it clear that intermodal transport, though its PPH produces considerable emissions, seems to be the most environmentally friendly option regarding emissions and energy need. Furthermore the differences in the emissions between the intermodal road-barge option and the intermodal road-rail option are very small. The emissions of CO_2 are always lower with the barge option than the rail option, while the NO_x, CO, C_xH_y, and aerosol emissions are always higher.

Blinge, 1995

When developing an *Energy logistics model for system calculations of transport- and energy-supply systems*, Blinge (1995) compared transport of goods in a semi-trailer between Gothenburg and Stockholm by road and intermodal transport by use of electrically powered trains. The analysis includes PPH of 50 km,

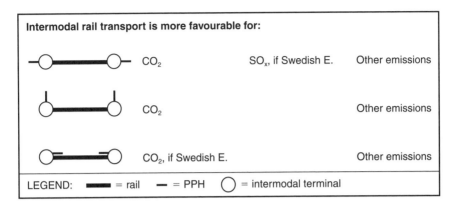

Figure 1.1.2 Energy logistics model for system calculations of transport- and energy-supply systems (source: visualisation of Blinge, 1995).

terminal handlings as well as main modality transport distance of 448 km. Three different location types of consigners/consignees were assumed (Figure 1.1.2): in prolongation of the main modality route, perpendicular to the main modality route, and along the main modality route. Electricity can be generated in different ways, namely on the basis of fossil fuel, or on the basis of the Swedish or European power plant mix (rules 3, 4 and 5 respectively of Table 1.1.2). Swedish electricity is generated by water and nuclear power and thereby involves less emissions.

Table 1.1.2 shows that CO_2 emissions are the lowest for the train, given Swedish energy. Different electricity sources imply that CO_2 emissions from trains are lower than those from lorries (rows 11 and 12), unless the shippers are located along the track (row 13). SO_x emissions of trains are lower in the combination 'Swedish electricity' and 'prolongation'. Otherwise road transport has better performances. For all other emissions, rail transport is more favourable.

In the Swedish practice the environmental performance of rail is more favourable than shown in Table 1.1.2, because the rail operator Rail Combi has an agreement with their power supplier that 'their' electricity is 'green', i.e. water or wind generated with virtually zero emissions.

The Piggyback Consortium, 1994

In the report 'The feasibility of a piggyback network for the British Isles',[5] MDS Transmodal and Servant Transport Consultants (the Piggyback Consortium, 1994) investigate how different scenarios will impact on the total external effects of transport domestically in the UK and between the UK and the Continent.[6] Four scenarios with piggyback transport are compared with a business-as-usual scenario. The total effects depend strongly on how much traffic is lifted from road to rail in the different scenarios. The scenario 'central corridor with

Table 1.1.2 Energy use and emissions including fuel generation for intermodal transport and road transport Gothenburg–Stockholm

	Energy use (MJ)	CO_2 (kg)	SO_x (g)	NO_x (g)	CO (g)	HC (g)	CH4 (g)	Part. (g)
Intermodal transport								
1 Functional unit: semi-trailer	1204	89	35	1322	369	104	28	32.9
2 Terminal handling	86	22	2	235	21	10	n	n
3 Rail transport 448 km	5850	457	2948	1453	316	27	n	21
Fossil fuel electricity								
4 Swedish electricity	2861	84	211	168	126	105	n	42
5 Western Europe electricity	4961	320	737	590	253	590	n	105
6 Terminal handling	86	22	2	235	21	10	n	n
7 To consignee	1204	89	35	1322	369	104	28	33
Total:								
8 Fossil fuel electricity	8430	679	3021	4568	1095	504	56	87
9 Swedish electricity	5441	306	284	3283	905	335	56	108
10 Western Europe electricity	7541	542	810	3705	1032	820	56	171
Road transport								
11 Prolongation case	10321	763	310	11192	2579	950	237	308
12 Road transport 448 km	8146	602	238	8828	1962	756	187	246
13 Along route case	6611	489	193	7176	1658	600	152	197

Source: Blinge, 1995.

Notes

n = negligible. Total road (dependent on location shipper/consignee towards terminal) = 11 or 12 or 13. Total rail (dependent on electricity provision): $1 + 2 + 6 + 7 + 3 = 8$ or $1 + 2 + 6 + 7 + 4 = 9$ or $1 + 2 + 6 + 7 + 5 = 10$.

German routes' assumes an 8.7 per cent market share of intermodal transport, while adding 'halved track charges' to the scenario almost doubles the market share.

The results show that each scenario decreases energy need, CO_2, SO_x, CO, HC, and NO_x emissions and accidents by 1–7 per cent compared to the business-as-usual scenario. Congestion is vaguely said to decrease on some routes, while road maintenance is the only figure priced. A modal transfer is said to save £11 million annually, however without referring to a specific scenario. Noise and local disturbances around terminals are likely to increase marginally.

It should be noted though, that the calculations were part of a project promoting infrastructure and rolling stock investments for intermodal transport and as for the IRU-funded studies, there is a risk that the analysis is biased, but in this case favouring rail and intermodal transport.

Demker et al., 1994

Also Demker *et al.* (1994) outline scenarios in the report 'Environmental effects of traffic mode choice for freight transport' and like the Piggyback consortium the calculations are based upon long-term shifts between traffic modes. The risk of bias here is related to the fact that shipping is favoured, and the authors largely take the approach that rail replaces shipping rather than road transport. The report has been criticised also for using non-favourable figures for electricity generation for rail.

One of the scenarios relates to a 25 per cent increase in rail transport between 1991 and 2015. Twelve of the additional 14 million tons are expected to be referred to intermodal transport. Full transport chains are calculated and the results show just marginal changes (-2 to $+3$ per cent) of all emissions and energy need compared to a basic scenario. Another scenario relates to an extensive transfer of goods from rail to road, however not stipulating the share of intermodal or wagonload transport. The results indicate increases for all emissions in the range of 12 to 21 per cent and an increase of energy need by 4 per cent.

NTM, 2003

In the early 1990s, the Swedish transport industry realised that they were not considered as trustworthy by their customers, who were asking for environmental effects of logistics solutions. The assumptions, calculations, and therefore results of different logistics service providers were simply too different. They then started Nätverket för Transporter och Miljön (NTM, the Network for Transport and the Environment). That is a non-profit association working for a common view and consensus on how the environmental issues of the transport sector are to be solved in order to attain a transport system that is sustainable in the long term. This means that NTM spreads knowledge on environmental issues, initiates research and development, and works for common bases of calculation of the environmental impact of transport (NTM, 2003). The basic attitude is that there is not one scientifically totally correct way of calculating environmental effects of transport activities, but an attempt must be made to do it in a consistent way across company and traffic mode borders. Their tool, NTM calc, is based upon Swedish emission data.

The Swedish intermodal operator Rail Combi published a comparison of environmental effects between Gothenburg and Stockholm in 2000 (Rail Combi, 2000), that is the same example used by Blinge. The calculation is very detailed concerning the transport chain, e.g. with real distances for different modes, including all terminal handling and marshalling operations and different loco-motives. It is based upon an earlier version of NTM calc and the primary emissions are specified and translated into an environmental cost. Since only emissions are dealt with and the train is powered by water generated electricity, the environmental costs are virtually zero.

RECORDIT, 2001

The European Commission has supported a number of studies in the field of transport and the environment. The study 'RECORDIT, deliverable 4; External cost calculation for selected corridors' (Bacelli *et al.*, 2001) and 'RECORDIT, deliverable 6; Imbalances and inefficiencies of the current pricing system' (Weibel *et al.*, 2001) calculates the external costs (global warming, noise, accidents, air pollution, and congestion) of unimodal road transport and intermodal chains on three freight corridors: Genova–Manchester, Patras–Gothenburg, and Barcelona–Warsaw. RECORDIT covers the entire range of external cost calculations, from effects to dispersion, impacts and valuation, all systematically structured by applying the 'Impact Pathway Approach'. External cost calculations include up- and downstream activities. The second report investigates the coverage of external costs by taxes, charges and subsidies in all involved European countries and compares the social costs with real transport prices.

For the route Barcelona–Warsaw, where the involved modes are road and rail for the intermodal situation, the study concludes that intermodal transport generates about 38 per cent of the external costs of all-road transport. For the route Patras–Gothenburg, where the intermodal chain is made up of road transport, short sea shipping, and rail transport, intermodal transport's external costs are 52 per cent of the external costs of all-road transport. For the route Genova–Manchester, where the chain consists of rail, barge, and short sea shipping, the external costs of the intermodal chain are 42 per cent of the external costs of all-road transport.

The study discusses points, which in regard to uncertainty of outcome deserve special attention. Table 1.1.3 is a selection of such points, supplemented by some observations by the authors of this paper.

Deliverable 6 (Bacelli *et al.*, 2001) gives an overview of so-called real costs, current costs and prices (Figure 1.1.3). The real costs are social costs without indirect costs (as overhead costs of transport). As the internal costs in the real

Table 1.1.3 Indication of some methodological features of external cost calculations and estimations of RECORDIT

Component	Effects	Type of non-internalised impacts	Valuation and points of attention
Accidents	Accident risks (mortality, light or severe morbidity)	a) Increase of WTP/WTA of others on other or same modality. b) Increase of WTP/WTA of friends on others c) Damage to rest of society.	Road: evidence flow/risk is weak. Ad a) No reliable country information (general) Ad b) Huge uncertainty Ad c) Fatalities: 10% of fatality risk value (Nellthorp, 2001) This is then to cover costs like production losses, administration costs, parts of medical costs. Not mentioned: loss of educational investments.
Air pollution	Dispersion of local emissions (11 gases)	Human health. Building materials. Crops.	Missing impacts (paper authors): Rail downstream effects Road floodlight links and nodes; Rail shunting yards; Substitution materials in buildings.
Climate change	Dispersion of greenhouse gases, e.g. CO_2	Global warming.	Calculate prevention costs to realise targets (Kyoto) Problem: there is no Europe- and sector-wide strategy to realise Kyoto targets, at all or on the most efficient way. Stock character of CO_2 in sky implies that possibly the wrong measures are taken. Conclusion: uncertainty about measures, therefore also costs.
Noise	Dispersion of noise	a) Medical costs paid by the health sector. b) Productivity loss of persons. c) Less enjoyment, more discomfort and fear.	Ad a) and b) 'Cost of illness measure', using market prices Ad c) WTP/WTA for loss of welfare. In addition WTP on the basis of house prices and surveys. Valuation: survey for (c) may suffer from unawareness, hence underestimation. Possibly high noise costs of rail recommend substitution of tread- by disc-brakes. Dispersion: noise dispersion calculated only for 'directly hit houses'.

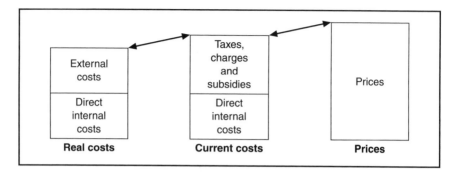

Figure 1.1.3 The relation between 'real costs', 'current costs', and 'prices' in RECORDIT (source: Weibel *et al.*, 2001: 6).

and current costs are the same, the requirement of internalisation of external costs will depend on the amount of coverage of external costs by the balance of taxes, charges and subsidies. For the three RECORDIT cases this is 89–103 per cent for the intermodal solutions and 90–101 per cent for the road solutions. The cost coverage is slightly better for road transport. This means that if cost coverage is the central criterion, and if the three cases were representative, internalisation would not improve the relative position of intermodal transport.

A comparison of current costs and prices shows that the prices cover 96–104 per cent of the intermodal current costs, whereas in the road sector they only cover 60–77 per cent. Large deficits appear to be present in all-road solutions. RECORDIT suggests a certain amount of 'non legal' actions as a cause. This pendant discussion in European politics has this year taken place around the proposal concerning social legislation relating to road transport activities.

QUITS, 1998

The QUITS project (QUality Indicators for Transport Systems), carried out by ISIS, ENEA, INISTENE, ZEW, ISI-Fraunhofer, and WHO-ECEH (ISIS *et al.*, 1998), calculates the environmental and health impacts of road and rail transport systems for the following routes: Frankfurt–Milan, Munich–Patras, Lille–London. The study calculates external costs of air pollutants, global warming, noise and accidents. The calculations are restricted to the use of transport infrastructure, that is, the supply of infrastructure is not taken into account. Also down- and upstream effects are excluded. All calculations refer to a period of one year, which is 1995, or to a single trip.

The 'Damage Pathway Approach' has been followed, which is subdivided into four stages; the first stage calculates air and noise pollutants and counts accidents. The second stage is about the measurement of the concentration of noise and pollutants at different places (dispersion). The third stage quantifies the impacts by the use of exposure-response functions, which are linear functions between concentration changes and human health impacts. The fourth stage includes the monetary valuation of the impacts. To execute these four stages, an integrated model, which consists of three inter-linked models, was employed.[7]

For the route Frankfurt–Milan (>500 km), the study concludes that air pollutants are the most important external cost for road transport; they constitute about 50 per cent of the total external costs from road transport. For rail transport, the main externality is noise and constitutes more than 50 per cent of the total external rail costs. In general each external cost (air pollutants, global warming, noise, and accidents) of road transport is much higher than for rail transport. Over a period of one year (one trip), the total external costs of road transport are about 12 times (11 times) higher than for rail transport. For both road and rail, CO_2 is the most emitted pollutant per trip, though the CO_2 emission of road transport is about six times higher than for rail transport.

For the route Lille–London (<500 km), the study concludes that over a period of one year (one trip) the noise nuisance is the highest external cost for both road and rail transport, though the monetary valuation of noise is about 12 times (1.15 times) higher for road transport than for rail transport. The external costs of noise constitute 55 and 90 per cent of the total external costs of road and rail transport respectively. When all the external effects are considered over one year (over one trip), road transport seems to have total external costs that are about 19 times (2 times) higher than rail transport. Regarding the emissions, it seems that CO_2 is the most emitted pollutant for road and rail transport. Per trip, road transport emits about 4.5 times more CO_2 than rail transport.

For the route Munich–Patras (>500 km), the figures demonstrate that over a period of one year (and also in one trip), the air pollutants form the largest external costs for both rail and road transport. They make up 42 and 50 per cent of the total external costs of road and rail transport respectively. The monetary valuation of air pollution generated by road transport over one year (per trip) is 114 times (six times) larger compared to the air pollution caused by rail transport. The total external costs of road transport calculated over a period of one year (one trip), are about 137 times (7.1 times) larger than for rail transport. Concerning the emission it appears that CO_2 is the largest pollutant for both transport modes. Road transport emits about three times more CO_2 than rail transport.

To summarise, the difference of external costs between road and rail is significantly higher than in other studies.

PETS, 1996–1999

The European research project PETS (Pricing European Transport Systems; 1996–1999) had three main objectives. First, to give an overview of the current pricing situation of passenger and freight transport; second, to analyse if those prices reflect the relevant internal and external costs; and finally, to forecast the consequences of moving to a more appropriate price level taking external constraints and developments into account. As external costs of transport, PETS focused on accident costs, congestion, noise, air, pollution, and global warming. Five corridors have been analysed in the study, but only three of them concern freight transport (the Cross-Channel Corridor, the Transalpine Corridor and the Finnish Corridor). Only the Transalpine Corridor deals with intermodal transport and rolling motorways.

PETS concluded that the appropriate level of charges is strongly dependent on the local context. Current charges can be too low in densely populated regions with a lot of traffic and too high in less busy areas. Another conclusion is that road freight vehicle taxation should be reformed and based on vehicle characteristics and distance travelled.

Summary of the reviewed literature

Table 1.1.4 gives an overview of the ingredients of the reviewed studies. The structure of the table is derived from the aspects discussed in Section 2. The ensemble of reviewed literature represents a large range of freight transport fields, policy objectives, and scientific approaches, at the same time rather the tip of the iceberg than a complete overview. Only five studies cover and discuss the whole range from effects, dispersion, impacts, valuation, calculation of social costs, and cost coverage, comparison of social costs and prices. Some studies present costs, a level which implies that the steps 'dispersion', 'impacts', and 'evaluation' actually are incorporated. In the research or publications, however, they are not explicated. Finally, there are numerous studies which focus on the effects only. Most envisaged effects or costs are average ones, including some which deal with cost coverage issues.

4 Conclusions

Calculations and comparisons of environmental performance of different freight transport solutions certainly suffer from a lack of a commonly accepted methodology. Yet, the overview of the attempts shows that intermodal transport has substantially better environmental performances than unimodal road transport. This is the case:

- already, if only 'energy use' and 'CO_2 emission' are taken into consideration;
- even more, if local emissions (except SO_x), accidents, congestion, and noise are incorporated in calculations;
- for SO_x, intermodal rail transport will only have better performances in case of very favourable conditions;
- for different kinds of commodities, such as general cargo (higher value and lower density) and also some bulk commodities;
- unless different unfavourable conditions cumulate, like:
  - very long PPH distances;

  - shippers locations along the main modality route, implying a backwards move of PPH-vehicles;
  - electricity production from non-energy-efficient fossil power plants;

- except for rolling road trains which have environmental performances comparable to unimodal road transport;
- despite the fact that important effects are excluded from any study up to now, like water pollution and related damage to ecological systems;
- despite the fact that spatial scarcity, an important entity in urban conglomerations of crowded Europe, is only partly articulated in studies;
- despite the uncertainty of research output due to the quality and availability of research data, to the range of normative points of views, and to research methodological obstacles;
- given the fact that the environmental disadvantages of nuclear electricity production are excluded from all consulted studies.

Only some studies elaborate the performance differences into internalisation and pricing policy frameworks. Such elaboration is of interest for European transport, energy and sustainability policies, as these expect the internalisation to improve the competitive position of intermodal transport. The methodology of estimating or calculating dispersion and impacts and valuating impacts to costs/benefits is complex. Results are quite method dependent, are characterised by certain amounts of uncertainty, and show larger ranges. The policy urgency would nevertheless justify careful internalisation trajectories. A point which deserves attention is that the RECORDIT study does not confirm the expectation of the White Paper that internalisation of external costs would improve the competitiveness of intermodal transport. The criterion hereby is not the height of external costs, but the coverage of external costs by the balance of taxes, charges, and subsidies is the criterion for additional internalisation actions. In general the external costs of intermodal transport are significantly lower than those of unimodal road transport, despite any uncertainty of results. For the corridors, analysed in RECORDIT, however, the cost coverage is higher for unimodal road transport than for intermodal transport. The report also observed that the prices of unimodal transport are far below the expected social (= sum of internal and external) costs. In this case the control of operational rules (like driving times) would contribute more to the improvement of the competitiveness of intermodal transport than internalisation of external costs.

Lack of cost coverage could also be an incentive for intermodal transport to improve its quality. A good example is investment into the development and implementation of disc brakes for trains, which generate less noise.

PPH is a crucial part of the success of intermodal networks and deserves much more attention since it is a burden regarding both internal and external costs. Congestion and local environmental strains are most critical in urban areas and unwise use of intermodal transport often adds to the local problems, while total external effects are lowered (Holzapfel, 2003 and Woxenius, 2003). The

Table 1.1.4 Overview of the reviewed literature

	1) Focus of study	*2) Economic approach*	*3) System aggregation*	*4) System chain*	*5) External effects*
IFEU/SGKV, 2002	E 1/5	A	N. e.	0/2	E, CC 2/10
TLN, 1999	E, V, C 3/5	A	N. e.	0/2	E, AP, CC, (C), S 5/10
Walstra *et al.*, 1995	E 1/5	A	NP, P	U* 1/2	AP, E, 2/10
Blinge, 1995	E 1/5	A	NP, P	0/2	E, AP, CC 3/10
The Piggyback consortium, 1994	E, V, C, P 4/5	A, L	NP, P	0/2	A, N, E, AP, CC I, C, O 8/10
Demker *et al.*, 1994	E 1/5	A	NP, P	0/2	E, AP, CC 3/10
NTM, 2003	E, I, V, C, P 5/5	M, A, S, L	NP, P	U, D 2/2	A, N, AP, E, CC I, C, S, O 9/10
RECORDIT, 2001	E, I, V, C, P 5/5	M, S	NP, P	U, D 2/2	A, N, AP, E, CC I, C, 7/10
QUITS, 1998	E, I 2/5	M, A	NP, P	0/2	A, N, AP, CC, I, 5/10
PETS, 1996–1999	E, I, V, C, P 5/5	M or A dep on the corridors	P	0/2	A, N, AP, CC, C 5/10
TLN, 2002	E, I, V, C, P, 5/5	M, A, S	NP, P	U 1/2	A, N, E, AP, CC, I, 6/10
Beuthe, 1999	E, I, C, V, P 5/5	M, A, S	NP, P	D 1/2	A, E, N, AP, I, C, 6/10
De Vlieger *et al.*, 2002	E, I, V, C P 5/5	M, A, L	WP/P	U, D 2/2	A, N, E, AP, CC, C, I 7/10
Dings *et al.*, 2003 (comparison of six studies)	E, I, V 3/5	M, A, S	NP, P	U/D, 2/2	A, N, E, AP, CC, I, C 7/10
Forckenbrock, 2001	E, V 2/5	A	NP, P	0/2	A, AP, CC, N 4/10

Notes:
x/x = x of x effects for each column.
N.a.b.1 = Not applicable because of aspect 1.
N. e. = Not explicated.
*For the electricity production in power plants.
**Coastal shipping.

E = Effects.
I = Impacts.
V = Valuation costs and benefits.
C = Coverage of costs.
P = Pricing and social costs.

M = Marginal.
A = Average.
S = Short run.
L = Long run.

External field consists of:
NP = Non-participants of the transport system.
P = Participants of the transport system.

U = Upstream effects included.
D = Down-stream effects included.

A = Accidents.
N = Noise.
E = Energy.
AP = Air pollution.
CC = Climate change.
I = Infrastructure
C = Congestion.
W = Water pollution.
S = Land occupation.
O = Other entities.

6) Strategy	7) Impacts	8) Valuation	9) Instruments	10) Modalities
N.a.b.1	N.a.b.1	N.a.b.1	0/5	Ro, Ra, RaPi, PPH 4/6
	N. e.	N. e.	T, Ch 2/5	Ro, Ra, RaPi, Ba, PPH, I 6/6
N. e.	O	O	0/5	Ro, Ra, Ba, PPH 4/6
N.a.b.1	N.a.b.1	N.a.b.1	0/5	Ro, Ra, PPH 3/6
P	O	ED (infrastructure maint.)	Ch 1/5	Ro, RaPi, I 3/6
N.a.b.1	N.a.b.1	N.a.b.1	0/5	Ro, RaPi, PPH, B** 4/6
P, DC, DR	IPA, O	SW, DW, OD, ED, O	T, Ch, S, C, L 5/5	Ro, Ra, Ba, PPH, I 5/6
P, DC, DR	IPA	SW, DW, OD, ED	T, Ch, S 3/5	Ro, Ra, Ba, PPH 4/6
N. e.	IPA	SW, DW,	0/5	Ro, Ra 2/6
N. e.	O	ED	T, C 2/5	Dep. on the corridors: Ra, Ro, roll. highway 2/6
P, DC, DR	O	Mixed because of multiple sources	T, Ch, S, C, L 5/5	Ro, Ra, Ba 3/6
P	O	OD, SW	Ch 1/5	Ro, Ra, Ba 3/6
DC	IPA	SW, O	Ch 1/5	Ro, Ba, R 3/6
P, DC, DR	IPA, O	All in different sources	0/5	Ro, Ra, 2/6
N. e.	O	O	0/5	Ra, Ro 2/6

P = Prevention.	IPA = Impact	SW = Stated	T = Taxes.	Ro = Road.
DC = Damage	Pathway.	willingness to pay.	Ch = Charges.	Ra = Rail ≠ RaPi.
compensation.	Approach	DW = Derived	S = Subsidies.	RaPi = Rail Piggy
DR = Damage	O = Other.	willingness to pay.	C = Compensation.	back.
recovery.		OD = Observed	O = Otherwise.	Ba = Barges.
CC = Climate		damage.	L = Legal	PPH = Pre- and
change.		ED = Expected	frameworks	post-haulage.
		damage.	discussed.	I = Innovative systems (transport units, loading units, otherwise).

possibility of using electric or hybrid vehicles for the PPH part of the intermodal chain could be a possible solution (Macharis *et al.*, 2003). Improving the resource utilisation and operational efficiency of PPH would:

- increase the market competitiveness (direct and internalised costs) of inter-modal transport;
- improve the cost coverage of external costs of intermodal transport, imply-ing that internalisation is more likely to support intermodal transport; and
- improve the tolerance for local effects in urban areas.

Also for both internal and external cost reasons, spatial and network policies are crucial. Short distances between terminals and shippers locations allow for reducing both operational and external costs of intermodal chains. The advantages of the main modalities are only to lower degrees absorbed by the disadvantages of PPH. It would be of interest, from the policy point of view, to initiate investigations about:

- long run marginal cost comparison, in order to derive more arguments for the direction to extend infrastructure network development;
- short run marginal cost comparison in European conglomerations, in order to derive more arguments for innovative urban distribution operations;
- external costs for non-traffic participants separately, as sustainability in terms of residential quality attracts more and more attention.

Acknowledgements

The authors would like to thank the Nectar cluster on integrated transport for giving us the possibility to work together on this topic. The research is partly funded by the Environmental Fund of The Swedish Association of Graduate Engineers. We also thank the referees for their very useful comments and Laetitia Vereecken for her earlier contributions to this work.

List of abbreviations

BGL	Bundesverband Güterkraftverkehr Logistik und Entsorgung
ECMT	European Conference of Ministers of Transport
ENEA	Italian Energy Agency
HGV	Heavy Goods Vehicle
IFEU	Institut für Energie- und Umweltforschung Heidelberg
IWW	Institute for Economic Policy Research (IWW) – University of Karlsruhe
INFRAS	Consulting Group for Policy Analysis and Implementation, Zürich
IRU	International Road Transport Union
ISIS	Institute of studies for the integration of systems

LCA	Life Cycle Analysis
NTM	Network for transport and environment
PETS	Pricing European Transport Systems
PPH	Pre- and post-haulage
QUITS	Quality Indicators for Transport Systems
RECORDIT	REal COst Reduction of Door-to-door Intermodal Transport
SGKV	Studiengesellschaft für den kombinierten Verkehr
TEU	Twenty Foot equivalent unit
TLN	Transport en Logistiek Nederland
UNITE	UNIfication of accounts and marginal costs for Transport Efficiency
WTA	Willingness to accept
WTP	Willingness to pay
ZEW	Zentrum für Europäische Wirtschaftforschung

Notes

* Delft University of Technology, Research Institute OTB, Thijsseweg 11, 2629 JA Delft, The Netherlands, Kreutzberger@otb.tudelft.nl and Sokreue@dso.denhaag.nl.
** Vrije Universiteit Brussel, Management School Solvay, Department of Business Economics and Strategic Management, Pleinlaan 2, 1050 Brussels, Belgium, Cathy.Macharis@vub.ac.be
*** Chalmers University of Technology, Division of Logistics and Transportation, SE-412 96 Gothenburg, Sweden, johwox@chalmers.se.
1 See, e.g. the White Paper of the European Commission (2001) and the Marco Polo programme (European Parliament, 2002/a and http://europa.eu.int/comm/transport/marcopolo).
2 For an overview on intermodal transport research, see: Bontekoning *et al.*, 2003.
3 The sum of internal and external costs are social costs. The sum of marginal internal and marginal external costs are marginal social costs. The sum of average (or total) internal and external costs are average (or total) social costs.
4 Dings *et al.* (2003) give an example: many studies consider marginal accident costs to be average ones; other ones state that accident risks decrease when traffic intensity increases, due to drivers being more alert then. Given the last point of view, the marginal accident costs are smaller than the average ones.
5 Piggyback is a term sometimes used for denoting intermodal transport based upon semi-trailers on rail.
6 UK road freight transport is dominated by semi-trailer transport but due to the limited loading profile on rail, they cannot be moved on rail without extending the infrastructure or investing in low-built rail wagons in combination with minor infrastructure adjustments.
7 The three models involve the 'Workbook on Emission Factors for Road Transport', the 'MLuS', and the 'EcoSense'.

References

Abukhader, S.M. and Jönson, G. (2004) 'Logistics and the Environment: Is it an Established Subject?' *International Journal of Logistics: Research and Applications*, Vol. 7, No. 2.

Baccelli, O. (Gruppo Clas), Black, I.G. (Cranfield University), Bühler, G. (ZEW), Capka,

40   *Kreutzberger* et al.

M. (CDV), Cini, T. (Gruppo Clas), Droste-Franke, B. (IER), Enei, R. (ISIS), Engelund, P. (Tetraplan), Handanos, Y. (NTUA), Henriques, M. (Tetraplan), Kunth, A. (Latts ENPC), Kubásek, M. (CDV), Maas, N. (TNO INRO), Seaton, R. (Cranfield University), Tamás, Á. (RT-Trans), Vaghi, C. (Gruppo Clas), Vannoni, C. (ISIS), Weibel, T.G. (Tetraplan), and Weinreich, S. (ZEW) (2001) *External cost calculation for selected corridors (deliverable 4)*, European research project RECORDIT, Brussels.

Bäckström, S. (1999) *Environmental Performance Calculation in Transport LCI – Allocation Method Design Issues, Rapport (Report) 45*, Chalmers University of Technology, Department of Transportation and Logistics, Göteborg.

Beuthe, M., Degrandsart, F., and Jourquin, B. (1999) 'External costs, facts & figures EU interurban freight traffic: a network analysis of their internalisation', web page: www.eia-ngo.com.

Beuthe, M., Degrandsart, F., Geerts, J.-F., and Jourquin, B. (2002) 'External costs, facts & figures in EU interurban freight traffic: a network analysis of their internalisation' *Transportation Research Part D*, Vol. 7, pp. 285–301.

Blinge, M. (1995) *Energilogistikmodell för systemberäkningar av transport- och energiförsörjningssystem (Energy logistics model for system calculations of transport- and energy supply systems)*, Meddelande (Message) 85, Department of Logistics and Transportation, Chalmers University of Technology, Gothenburg.

Bontekoning, Y.M., Macharis, C., and Trip, J.J. (2003) 'Is a new applied transportation research field emerging? – A review of intermodal rail-truck freight transport literature' *Transportation Research Part A – Policy and Practice*, Vol. 38/1, pp. 1–34.

Boneschansker, E. and 't Hoen, A.L. (1993) *Externe kosten van het goederenvervoer*, Instituut voor Onderzoek en Overheidsuitgaven, Den Haag.

De Vlieger, I., Int Panis, L., and Cornelis, E. (2002) *Screening CO2-emissiereductiepotentieel binnenvaart*, Studie uitgevoerd in opdracht van Promotie Binnenvaart Vlaanderen; 2002/IMS/R/182.

De Vlieger, I., Int Panis, L., and Cornelis, E. (2004) *Milieuprestaties van de binnenvaart in Vlaanderen*, Studie uitgevoerd in opdracht van Promotie Binnenvaart Vlaanderen; mei 2004.

Demker, G., Flodström, E., Sjöbris, A., and Williamsson, M. (1994) *Miljöeffekter av transportmedelsval för godstransporter (Environmental effects of traffic mode choice for freight transport)*, KFB Report 1994: 6, Stockholm.

Dings, J.M.W., Sevenster, M.J., and Davidson, M.D. (2003) *External and infrastructure costs of road and rail traffic. Analysing European studies, CE Solutions for environment, economy and technology, Delft*, commissioned by the Dutch Ministry of Transport, Public Works and Water Management.

Dings, J.M.W., Leurs, B.A., Hof, A.F. (CE), Bakker, D.M., Mijjer, P.H. (4Cast), and Verhoef, E.T. (VU) (2002) *Weg voor je geld? Toepassing van het profijtbeginsel bij de financiering van infrastructuur*, Hoofdrapport, commissioned by the Ministry of Finances, DE, Delft.

European Commission (1995) Towards Fair and Efficient Pricing in Transport, COM(95)691.

European Commission (2001) White Paper 'European Transport Policy for 2010: time to decide', Office for official publications of the European Communities, Luxemburg.

European Commission (2002) 'Proposal for a European Parliament and Council Regulation on the granting of Community financial assistance to improve the environmental performance of the freight transport system', COM (2002) 54 final, 2002/0038 (COD), Brussels.

European Parliament (2002/a) *Environmental performance of freight transport system*, texts adopted by Parliament, final edition (25/9/2002), P5_TC1_COD(2002)0038, A5-0294/2002.

Forkenbrock, D.J. (2001) 'Comparison of external costs of rail and truck freight transportation' in *Transportation Research Part A*, 35: 321–337.

Friedrich, R. and Bickel, P. (eds) (2001) *Environmental External Costs of Transport*, Springer-Verlag.

Holzapfel, H. (2003) 'Logistics in Europe in a phase of transition' paper for the *Eurolog 2003 Congress*, 12–14 June, Rome.

IFEU, SGKV (2002) *Comparative Analysis of Energy need and CO_2 Emissions of Road Transport and Combined Transport Road-rail*, IRU/BGL Energy & CO_2 Study, Geneva.

ISIS, ENEA, INISTENE, ZEW, ISI-fraunhofer, WHO-ECEH (1998) *QUality Indicators for Transport Systems (QUITS)*, Contract no. ST-96-SC-115, project funded in part by the European Commission – DGVII under the Transport RTD Programme of the 4th Framework Programme.

Macharis, C., Vandenbossche, P., and Van Mierlo, J. (2003) 'The use of electric/hybrid vehicles for the pre- and endhaulage of intermodal transport. A feasibility study' *20th International Electric Vehicle Symposium (EVS20)*, California, 15–19 November.

NTM (2003) web page: www.ntm.a.se. Accessed 15/04/2003.

Rail Combi (2000) *Miljökalkyl Göteborg-Stockholm (Environmental calculation Gothenburg-Stockholm)*, calculation published at Rail Combi's web page www.railcombi.se. Accessed 22/02/2000.

Roson, R. (2003) 'Le condizioni economiche del riequilibrio modale: un confronto tra costi percepiti e costi esterni ambientali' [Economic conditions for modal balancing: comparing perceived and environmental external costs] (with M. Meggiato), in G. Borruso and G. Polidori (eds) *I presupposti economici del riequilibrio modale nel trasporto delle merci in Italia*, Franco Angeli, Milan.

Sansom, T., Nash, C., Mackie, P., Shires, J., and Watkiss, P. (2001) *Surface Transport, Costs and Charges Great Britain 1998*, Institute for Transport Studies, University of Leeds, in association with AEA Technology Environment, Leeds.

Sansom, T., Nellthorp, J., Proost, S., Mayeres, I, Maibach, M., Niskanen, E., Quinet, E., and Schwartz, D. (1999) *The overall UNITE methodology (deliverable 1)*, European research project UNITE, Brussels and Leeds.

The Piggyback Consortium (1994) *The feasibility of a piggyback network for the British Isles*, MDS Transmodal and Servant Transport Consultants, investigation sponsored by the European Commission DGVII under the PACT (Pilot Actions for Combined Transport).

TLN (1999) *Het vergelijken van appels en peren. Pleidooi van Transport en Logistiek Nederland voor het ontmythologiseren van de milieueffecten van een modal shift*, Zoetermeer.

TLN (2002) *Gelijke monniken, gelijke kappen*, Zoetermeer.

Van Mierlo, J., Maggetto, G., Vereecken, L., Favrel, V., Meyer, S., and Hecq, W. (2003) 'How to Define Clean Vehicles? Environmental Impact Rating of Vehicles' *International Journal of Automotive Technology (IJAT)*, KSAE, SAE, isnn 1229–9138, Vol. 4, No. 2, pp. 77–86.

Walstra, J.A., Van Binsbergen, A.J., and Kroon, M. (1995) Emissies van gecombineerd vervoer, *Lucht*, No. 2, pp. 46–51.

Weibel, T.G., Henriques, M., Enei, R., Maas, N., Vaghi, C., and Schmid, S.A. (2001) *Imbalances and inefficiencies of the current pricing system (deliverable 6)*, European research project RECORDIT, Brussels.

Woxenius, J. (2003) 'Urban impact of new production philosophies for intermodal freight transport' *Logistics Solutions*, Issue 4/2003, pp. 14–21.

1.2 Environmental impact of underground freight transport

Jasper Willigers and *Bert van Wee*

Abstract

The transport sector has a large share in many environmental problems. Several new transport systems, including various forms of underground freight transport, have been proposed to reduce the environmental impact. However, literature on the life-cycle and environmental impact of such systems is very scarce, reason enough to focus this paper on the assessment of the energy use of and resulting emissions from transport systems, in which the emphasis will be on underground freight transport systems. Evaluation of the energy use and its environmental effects necessitates a complete as possible analysis of the energy use, both directly and indirectly arising from the transport process. Direct energy use is the energy necessary for actually moving the passengers or goods, in most cases the energy used by transporting vehicles. Indirect energy use results from processes like the building and maintenance of infrastructure and vehicles. Whereas direct energy use is typically calculated by sophisticated models, methods for the analysis of indirect energy use are much less developed. This paper will examine one of these methods, the process energy analysis, along with the process emission analysis, which is the process energy analysis equivalent for calculating indirect emissions of greenhouse gases (CO_2), acidifying gases (SO_2, NO_x) and other air-polluting substances (VOC, PM_{10}). The total life-time energy use and emissions are estimated using these methods in two case studies. In the first case, transport of crude oil by Dutch long-distance pipelines is evaluated, while the concern in the second case is the so-called Underground Logistic System (ULS) Utrecht concept for the underground distribution of packed goods in the city of Utrecht. This is an innovative concept that makes use of automatic guided vehicles. Each case revealed very distinct characteristics related to the proportion of direct versus indirect energy use and emission levels. Crude oil pipelines have, typically, low direct energy intensities and emission factors, and also very low indirect energy use and emissions compared to other transport modes. Contrarily, the ULS Utrecht is characterised by low direct energy and emission intensities. However, the high indirect energy use and emissions require very high transport intensities to result in a net reduction compared to the alternatives: road transport in most cases. Furthermore, the relationship between direct and indirect emissions of different substances is highly variable.

1 Introduction

Western countries are highly reliant on transport of both people and goods. The transport of goods allows countries and regions to specialise in economic activities, increasing trade volumes. The transport sector is highly influenced by the public sector and occupies a prominent position on the political agenda in many Western countries. Apart from economic reasons related to the (in)divisibleness of networks, external effects comprise a major reason for public involvement in the transport sector. External effects are the effects that users do not consider in their choices. The main external effects of transport are congestion, safety, and the environment. Congestion is often labelled as one of the diseases of Western societies, resulting in (unnecessary?) time loss and reducing livability in towns and cities. Many of these have considered several plans to reduce urban congestion, but often failed in implementing them, the congestion charge in London being a well-known exception. Among the focus groups for measures are urban goods deliveries, not only because of their share in creating intensities and their claim for road capacity, but also because vehicles loading and unloading cargo often block roads. Several of the concepts already developed in many parts of the world in the framework of city logistics include underground freight transport systems.

These underground systems have also been proposed in the context of environmental issues. The transport sector has a large share in many environmental problems. Without any drastic adaptations in transport technology and behaviour, the sector will continue to play a large role in several environmental themes (RIVM, 2000). Environmentally-friendly transport systems are now being sought to decrease the environmental load. In this context, a few years ago automated systems for underground freight transport attracted the attention of both the Dutch national and local politics. Various types of underground freight transport for reducing environmental impact have been proposed, and direct energy use of and emissions from various underground freight transport types have already been the subject of detailed studies (e.g. Van der Heide, 1999; Davis, 2000).

However, the scale of proposed infrastructural developments – including (in some cases extensive networks of) underground tubes and distribution centres – and the results of past studies (Roos *et al.*, 2000; Groot, 1991) suggest the added significance of indirect energy and emissions. However, literature on the life-cycle environmental impact of such systems remains very scarce. For these reasons, this paper will focus on the assessment of the energy use and resulting emissions of transport systems, with an emphasis on those systems for underground freight transport. The evaluation of the energy use by these systems and the environmental effects of this use will necessitate a (near to) complete analysis of the energy use, both directly and indirectly resulting from the transport process. The direct energy use is necessary for actually moving the passengers or goods, in most cases energy used by transporting vehicles, while the indirect energy use results from processes such as building and maintenance of infrastructure and vehicles.

The following section, 2, describes the policy context of direct and indirect energy use and emissions in the framework of underground freight transport. Section 3 deals with several issues related to the methods used in this research. These are the process energy analysis and the process emission analysis, which is the equivalent of process energy analysis to calculate indirect emissions of greenhouse gases (CO_2), acidifying gases (SO_2, NO_x) and other air polluting substances (VOC, PM_{10}). In Sections 4 and 5 these methods are applied in two case studies to estimate the total lifetime energy use and emissions. In the first case, the transport of crude oil by Dutch long-distance pipelines is evaluated. In the second case, the concept for the underground distribution of packed goods in the city of Utrecht, the so-called Underground Logistic System (ULS) Utrecht, is dealt with. This is an innovative concept that makes use of automatic guided vehicles. Section 6 consists of an integral discussion and Section 7 completes the paper with some concluding remarks.

2 Environmental impacts of transport: policy instruments and determinants

Environmental impact of transport depends on a number of determinants. The first is the overall volume of transport, expressed as passenger kilometres (persons) or tonne kilometres (goods). The second category is the modal split. For passengers, the subcategories are car driver, car passenger, train, bus/tram/underground, walking, cycling, aircraft and ship, while for the transport of goods, these are lorry, barge, train, ocean-going vessel, aircraft and pipeline. The third category is formed by the technology used, and the fourth is the efficiency of using vehicles (for lorries this is the load factor and for cars, trains and buses, the occupancy rate). The fifth category is the manner in which vehicles are used (speed, acceleration, and deceleration). Governments have several types of policy instruments to influence these determinants: i.e. regulations, prices, land-use planning, infrastructure planning, marketing, and information and organisation. Table 1.2.1 shows the relationship between the type of instruments and the determinants.

Table 1.2.1 shows infrastructure measures as one of several kinds of instruments. These measures can influence transport volumes, the modal split, the efficiency and use of vehicles, and behaviour. This broad spectrum of effects may explain the dominant position infrastructure measures have in many countries. In the case of underground freight transport, total transport volumes, expressed as tonne kilometres, can be influenced, as a result of changes in transport distances. Underground freight transport might also induce a modal shift, because it offers an alternative for conventional transport via road or rail, or, in some cases, via a barge. For urban networks not only might the modal split in the urban area

Table 1.2.1 Dominant interrelationships of determinants for environmental impact of transport and policy instruments

	Volume	Modal split	Technology	Use of vehicles/ efficiency	Behaviour
Restrictions	*	*	*	*	*
Prices	*	*	*	*	*
Land-use planning	*	*		*	*
Marketing		*			
Information and organisation		*		*	
Infrastructure	*	*		*	*

Source: Blok and Van Wee (1994).

be influenced in some cases, but also the mode for the trip between cities. For example, rail might become more attractive for inter-city transport than road if the urban underground freight network has a good connection to a freight railway station. Furthermore, underground freight transport can have an impact on the use of vehicles and efficiency in several ways. First, larger lorries could be used in urban underground freight transport systems, because they would not be able to enter the urban areas since underground freight transport is an alternative. Furthermore, larger lorries result in fewer vehicle kilometres and often in less energy use and fewer emissions. Second, the distribution concept, as part of the logistics concept, may be influenced. For example, point-to-point deliveries might be replaced by a concept in which lorries cover a chain of destinations in one round. The impact on behaviour is related to the distribution of vehicle kilometres by road class and related driving behaviour; this impact is also related to the use of specific (road) vehicles: i.e. distributions are influenced by the use of the underground freight system.

Table 1.2.1 does not include additional determinants relevant to the spatial aspects of impacts. For several local impacts, such as noise, high concentrations of harmful emissions and general livability impact due to driving and parked vehicles, spatial aspects (distances between the source and the receptor) are very important. The spatial distribution of transport is influenced by underground freight transport systems, so that apart from possible changes in overall energy use and emissions, a reduction in urban road traffic due to a shift to underground freight systems will have a positive effect.

Finally, with regard to transport infrastructure, a distinction can be made between the environmental effects that are directly dependent on the transport volume (the direct environmental effect) and those effects that do not depend on the transport volume in the short term (the indirect environmental effect). The most prominent example of the first is the use of fuel for propulsion; examples of the latter are the energy use of and emissions from the infrastructure related to construction and a major part of the maintenance. Direct energy use and emissions are generally assumed to be proportional to the transport volume in tonne kilometres. Therefore the expressions 'energy intensity' and 'emission factor' are often used, defined in this context as the energy use or emission divided by the transported tonne kilometres of goods. It should be noted that 'energy intensity' in the literature takes on different definitions. In research on the macro scale the term 'energy intensity' is commonly used for the energy use of an economic sector divided by the sector's economic output (Laitner, 2000; see, e.g. Wilting *et al.*, 1998). Unless stated explicitly, the terms 'energy intensity' and 'emission factor' will refer, in this paper, to the tonnekm-based definition. The direct energy intensity of transport modes is often used for comparing the environmental 'performance' of transport modes; yet, this does not include the indirect energy use. The proportion of direct and indirect effects differs greatly among transport modes. This is illustrated in a recent study (Bos, 1998), where the share of the indirect energy use in the total (= direct + indirect) energy use is shown to amount to 18 per cent for road freight transport, 45 per cent for rail freight transport and 60 per cent for inland shipping. To summarise the above, underground freight systems may influence the environmental impact of transport in several ways.

3 Methods for the integral analysis of direct and indirect energy use and emissions

In Sections 4 and 5 we will discuss the environmental effects of two types of underground freight transport: conventional crude oil pipelines and underground logistic systems. In these case studies, a life-cycle approach is applied to achieve an integral image of the environmental effects. In an environmental life-cycle analysis, the aim is to present a quantitative overview of the environmental effects of all processes going into a product's life-cycle. In transportation, life-cycle analyses have been applied by Eriksson *et al.* (1996) and Bos (1998) among others. Typically, the processes in a life-cycle can be categorised into four stages: (1) extraction and production of raw materials; (2) manufacture of the product; (3) use of the product; and (4) treatment of the product at the end of its economic lifetime. The direct environmental effect of transport forms part of the third stage in the life-cycle analysis. The other processes in both this stage and the other stages form the indirect environmental effects.

In our analysis we restrict ourselves to direct and indirect energy use, and direct and indirect emissions of the substances carbon dioxide (CO_2), nitrogen oxides (NO_x), sulphur dioxide (SO_2), volatile organic compounds (VOC), and particulate matter (PM_{10}). Before going on to the discussion, we will reflect on the methods to estimate direct and indirect energy use and emissions. By *energy use* we mean *primary* energy use – the sum of the energy use of the end user (the *secondary* energy use) and the energy lost due to processes such as the distribution and conversion of energy carriers. Other environmental effects, such as noise pollution and the use of space and safety, are not taken into consideration here, although some of these effects are amongst the most important reasons for considering underground freight transport.

Table 1.2.2 Gross energy requirement (GER) for relevant materials in the Netherlands

Materials	GER (MJ kg^{-1})	Transport
Ballast bed	0.25	Includes transport to a barge harbour
Concrete	2.5	
Sand	0.1	Includes transport to a barge harbour
Steel plates	30.2	Transport from steel mill not included

Source: Data from Bos (1998).

Direct energy use and emissions are determined by calculations according to a bottom-up approach; i.e. the overall energy use and emissions of the systems are calculated from the secondary energy use of individual pipelines and carriages. Characteristics of current pipelines in the Netherlands are used for the crude oil pipelines. A case study for a proposed network has been carried out for the underground logistic systems, not yet operational. The primary energy use and emissions are calculated from the secondary energy use, furthermore taking into account differences between energy carriers in efficiency and emission factors.

Both indirect energy use of and indirect emissions from the underground freight transport systems are calculated by means of a process energy analysis and a process emission analysis. Indirect energy use and indirect emissions, respectively, are calculated using these methods by inventorying all materials and processes that are needed to build the infrastructure and maintain it during its lifetime (see Bos, 1998; IFIAS, 1974). Energy requirements and emission coefficients are assigned to each of the necessary materials and processes. Standardised coefficients can be used for the most common materials; these values comprise the energy use or emissions of all activities necessary for extraction, manufacturing, and transportation to the Netherlands. Table 1.2.2 presents several figures that are important for the current study. The energy use and emissions from building and maintenance processes can often also be estimated from standardised values. New coefficients should be determined for very specific processes.

Process energy analysis and process emission analysis are both relatively labour-intensive methods, because they require a careful listing of materials and processes, as well as the acquisition of energy intensities and emission coefficients. The methods are therefore only feasible for use in individual infrastructure projects or clusters of homogeneous infrastructure projects. Alternative methods would be the input-output energy analysis and its equivalent, the input-output emission analysis. With these methods, the indirect energy use and emissions are calculated on the basis of an economic input-output model. These methods will require less input data, where only data are needed for the financial costs of the infrastructure project and the standardised energy intensities and emission coefficients (in this case, expressed as the energy use and emissions divided by the sectors' economic output) of the several economic sectors. This is separate from the general economic model (Bullard *et al.*, 1978, for more information on input-output energy analysis see: Wright, 1974; an example of a recent application of an input-output energy analysis is: Wilting *et al.*, 1998). However, the use of financial costs as an inter-agent in deriving energy use and emissions, and aggregation of economic activities over economic sectors, make these methods less accurate in general. Still, because of data and labour requirements, an input-output analysis may be preferred to a process analysis for large-scale projects; a relevant example of such an application is seen in Roos *et al.* (2000), who studied a country-wide network for underground automatic freight transport.

4 The direct and indirect energy use and emissions of Dutch crude oil pipelines

The first type of underground freight transport we want to discuss is formed by the conventional pipelines transporting fluids and gases, in particular, the crude oil pipelines. Conventional pipelines are used in the Netherlands on a large scale. For natural gas, and drinking and sewage water, there are country-wide networks. Most pipelines for other products such as crude oil, oil products, and chemicals run between the harbours of Rotterdam and Antwerp or between Rotterdam and the German Ruhr area. There is also an extensive pipeline network within the Rotterdam harbour area. During the last few decades the amount of fluids and gases transported by conventional pipelines for industrial use has been growing fast in comparison to the total amount of freight transported. Between 1987 and 1997 the transport volume of international crude oil pipelines[1] (expressed in tonnes) rose by 52 per cent (CBS, several editions), compared to the rise of 9 per cent for total Dutch freight transport (AVV, 1997a). A further increase in industrial pipeline transport from 57.6 million tonnes in 1995 to 65.9–68.0 million tonnes in 2020 is expected (Deelen *et al.*, 1999).

However, in contrast with other conventional means of transport, the direct energy intensity of pipelines is not well known. The statistics we found are often outdated and mostly concerned with pipelines in the United States. Therefore we carried out further research on the energy intensity of Dutch pipelines, restricting ourselves to crude oil pipelines, as these provide for most (75 mass per cent (according to AVV, 1997b)) of the pipeline transportation of industrial products and raw materials in the Netherlands. A bottom-up method, based on fluid dynamics theory, was used. The pressure differentials along a pipeline are calculated from the physical properties of the pipeline and the fluid that is transported (Mott, 2000). The Darcy equation calculates the pressure differential h as (adapted from Mott, 2000):

$$h = f \cdot L \cdot \frac{8 \cdot Q^2}{g \cdot \pi^2 \cdot D^5}$$

where:
f = a friction coefficient that depends on the turbulence in the tube,

L = the length of the tube,
Q = the fluid throughput per second,
D = the diameter of the tube,
g = the gravity acceleration, on average 9.81 ms^{-2} in the Netherlands.

The equation shows the required pressure differential per metre pipeline to largely depend on the throughput and the pipeline diameter. A strong increase in pressure differential is necessary for an increase in the transported volume per time unit. A larger tube diameter results in a sharp decrease in the required pressure differential for an equally large fluid flow. The power (energy use per second) required by the pump of a pipeline depends, linearly, on the required pressure difference and the mass of the fluid that is transported per second. The primary energy use and the emissions are derived from this secondary energy use by using national average statistics, provided by the RIVM and ECN national research institutes, on the efficiency and emissions for different energy carriers. Table 1.2.3 below summarises the energy efficiencies and emission factors used for the calculations.

The results of the calculated direct energy intensities show that large differences in energy intensities may exist between individual pipelines, especially because the transported volume per time unit and the pipeline diameter vary to a great extent. With a national average[2] of 0.10 MJ/tonnekm, the calculated energy intensities are, in general, lower than the values we found in the literature for American pipelines. These vary from 0.19 to 0.33 MJ/tonnekm, a difference in outcome that can depend on the method used – a bottom-up method in the current research versus a top-down approach in the US statistics – and on the physical characteristics of the pipelines. From the Darcy equation above, the energy intensity would appear to highly depend on the throughput and the tube diameter. The energy intensities for crude oil pipelines are much lower than the

Table 1.2.3 Energy efficiency and emission factors for energy carriers used for propulsion (1998 data)

	Diesel	Electric	Natural gas
Efficiency production/distribution	0.94	0.42	0.99
Engine efficiency	0.40	0.85–0.95	0.32
CO_2 emission (kg/GJ)	73	153	56
NO_x emission (g/GJ)	844	193	421
SO_2 emission (g/GJ)	94	52.8	<0.1
VOC emission (g/GJ)	20	2.5	175
PM_{10} emission (g/GJ)	7	2.5	<0.1

Source: Diesel: ECN (previously unpublished data), except efficiency production/distribution: based on Gijsen and Spakman (2001).
Electric: Gijsen and Spakman (2001), except VOC and PM_{10}: 2000 forecast by Geurs *et al.* (1998) and except engine efficiency: NEA and Haskoning (1993).
Natural gas: ECN (previously unpublished data), except efficiency production/distribution: based on CBS (2001).

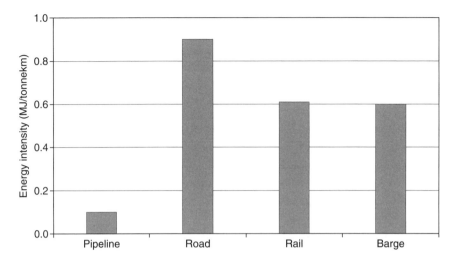

Figure 1.2.1 Average direct energy intensity for different means of transport for transporting large quantities of bulk goods over long distances (sources:
Willigers (2001), Van der Brink and Van Wee (1997)).

energy intensities of competing means of transport (see Figure 1.2.1). For fluids
other than crude oil, the energy intensity may differ from the energy intensity of
crude-oil pipelines; however, for these fluids, pipelines also have a lower energy
intensity than other conventional means of transport. Because of the lower
density of gases, the transport of gases by pipeline has a higher energy intensity
than the transport of fluids. The direct emissions due to pipeline transport are
mainly determined by the energy use. The energy carrier used is also of importance. Stationary engines are used for driving the pumps and compressors. These
may be electric engines but also combustion engines running on fossil fuels. In
general, the combustion engines lead to higher emission factors.

For the calculated energy intensity of crude-oil pipelines, we estimated a possible deviation of 31 per cent, based on the uncertainty that exists about the
extent to which the streaming velocity through the pipelines fluctuates over time.
Uncertainty is slightly higher for the emission factors; here, uncertainty about
the relative proportions of energy carriers also plays a role.

The indirect environmental effects are determined by carrying out a process
energy analysis and a process emission analysis. An initial evaluation of the
processes during the life-cycle yielded a construction process that is dominant in
energy use and emissions. The core processes for the construction of pipelines
are manufacture of tube elements, transport of tube elements, and digging operations. Together, these processes were calculated to have an indirect energy use
for the Dutch crude-oil pipelines of 3 kJ/tonnekm on average, which can be compared to the 0.10 MJ/tonnekm direct energy use mentioned above. For

Table 1.2.4 Direct and indirect energy intensity and emission factors for Dutch crude-oil pipelines

	Direct effect	Indirect effect
Energy intensity	0.10 MJ/tonnekm	5 kJ/tonnekm
Emission factor CO_2	6 g/tonnekm	0.3 g/tonnekm
Emission factor NO_x	38 mg/tonnekm	1 mg/tonnekm
Emission factor SO_2	5.3 mg/tonnekm	1 mg/tonnekm
Emission factor VOC	1.0 mg/tonnekm	0.1 mg/tonnekm
Emission factor PM_{10}	0.37 mg/tonnekm	2 mg/tonnekm

operational energy use, only cathodic protection[3] is relevant. We estimated the energy use of cathodic protection at about 1 kJ/tonnekm; however, its emissions are negligible compared to the construction stage. With respect to the low energy use of digging works, other processes such as maintenance and repairs are considered to be negligible compared to the construction stage and therefore excluded from the analyses. Altogether, the indirect energy use for crude-oil pipelines is about 5 kJ/tonnekm. Due to a lack of data, it is not possible to give an uncertainty margin for this figure. Despite the low indirect energy use, the process of emission analysis shows the indirect emissions of some substances to be relatively high compared to the direct emissions (see Table 1.2.4). For PM_{10} (particulate matter), the indirect emission even accounts for about 84 per cent of the total emission; other substances with a substantial level of indirect emissions are SO_2 (16 per cent) and VOC (9 per cent). The high indirect emission factors can be explained by the relatively high emission factors of the steel manufacturing industry in comparison to the transport sector.

5 The direct and indirect energy use and emissions of underground logistic systems

The second type of underground freight transport we examined is formed by automated systems for the underground transport of mixed cargo, in the Netherlands usually referred to as Underground Logistic Systems (ULS). The underground transport of mixed cargo has recently received much attention by both national and local governments in the Netherlands (IPOT, 2000) and by several other countries (e.g. Bliss, 2000; Taniguchi *et al.*, 2000). A ULS, as proposed in the Netherlands, is a network of totally or partially underground tubes that connect distribution centres and through which vehicles can transport standardised loads of packed goods. Most concepts use automatically guided vehicles, which are largely autonomous in deciding about their routing. In general, two applications of ULS can be distinguished, i.e. urban distribution networks and networks in industrial areas. ULS is an innovative transport concept. Although many studies, to date, have been carried out in the Netherlands on the technical and economic feasibility of different ULSs, none of these concepts have been put into practice yet. Due to the high investments that are now required for a country-wide network as originally proposed, it does not seem feasible on an intermediate-long term (Van der Heijden *et al.*, 1999).

To achieve a more realistic image of the total effect on energy use and emissions that such an underground system might have, we will discuss the possible effects of a proposed system for underground freight distribution in the city of Utrecht, the ULS Utrecht, as a case study. It is assumed that this system will consist of a city-edge distribution centre and four smaller distribution centres in the city near shopping areas, interconnected by an underground tube. For the ULS, a distinction is made between three route alternatives and two different tube diameters. The main difference between the route alternatives is the location of the distribution centre at the edge of the city. In one alternative ('Alternative 1') the distribution centre is located at a site with the possibility for rail and barge connections. In the other two alternatives the distribution centre is located at sites closer to the ring motorway. Alternative 2 is located to the northwest of the city centre – this is favourable for transport to/from the direction of Amsterdam. Alternative 3 is located to the southwest of the city centre – this is favourable for transport to/from directions other than Amsterdam (most of the goods transported to Utrecht come from the west or south, Boerkamps and Brouwer, 1999). Table 1.2.5 below shows some characteristics of the different alternatives.

For freight flows we used forecasts reported by (Boerkamps and Brouwer, 1999); for the market share we assumed that transport of all goods from outside the city of Utrecht to the central shopping area in Utrecht will be carried out by the ULS, as long as the goods are physically suitable for this.[4] This seems

Table 1.2.5 Basic characteristics of the network alternatives

Network alternative	Alternative 1		Alternative 2		Alternative 3	
Tube length (km)	6.8		7.4		6.3	
Distribution centres at city edge	1		1		1	
Distribution centres in city	4		4		4	
Tube diameter (m)	1.15	2.20	1.15	2.20	1.15	2.20
Suitable amount of freight (tonne per week in 1999)	543	1840	543	1840	543	1840
Number of vehicles*	1328	79	2120	108	1203	75
Cruising speed of vehicles (kmh^{-1})	20	20	20	20	20	20
Frontal surface vehicles (m^2)	0.36	1.60	0.36	1.60	0.36	1.60

Sources: Ettema (1999), Boerkamps and Brouwer (1999).

Note
* Due to differences in tube lengths the network alternatives require distinct numbers of vehicles to transport a similar quantity of freight per hour.

plausible, because implementation of the ULS is likely to be accompanied by legal restrictions on lorry access to local roads.

The direct energy use of underground logistic systems consists mainly of the energy use for driving the vehicles. This energy use can be calculated by integrating the energy necessary for acceleration, and compensating the roll and air friction for the duration of a ride. The acceleration and friction components of the energy use are calculated with standard physical functions (similar to Van der Heide, 1999), based on the proposed vehicle characteristics. These calculations show that because of the low speeds, the roll friction is dominant in the direct energy use,[5] despite the fact that driving in a tunnel leads to about three times the air friction of the same vehicle in open air (since the air in a tunnel has little room to flow away along a vehicle, a vehicle has to move a large air column). The energy use for acceleration is low compared to above-ground transport methods because this transport is not disturbed by other transport. In an ideal case where the underground is flat and tight curves non-existent, the ULS Utrecht can be assumed to approximate this ideal situation. Such an undisturbed transport system requires accelerating only once during a ride, resulting in a sharply decreasing energy intensity for the length of the ride.

The effect of the ULS on direct energy use consists, on the one hand, of the direct energy use of the ULS itself and, on the other, of the changes in direct energy use of the road transport as a consequence of the ULS. However, due to a lack of data we ignored possible changes in direct energy use and emissions from road transport (lorries, but also cars and vans) because of a reduction in intensities that resulted from the assumed shift of freight from road to the ULS. On the one hand, the shift may result in a decrease in energy use and emissions per kilometre due to lower congestion levels, while, on the other, the increase in speeds may result in more traffic, both due to a shift from other modes (slow modes, public transport) to cars and to induced demand (see, for example, Goodwin, 1996). The direct energy intensity of the ULS is, especially within the built-up area, low compared to the energy intensity of road transport, its major competitor. Road transport within the built-up area has a greater energy intensity than outside the built-up area because of more frequent braking and accelerating. Our calculations show the direct energy intensity of the ULS to be between 2.1 and 4.8 MJ/tonnekm for the different alternatives and tube diameters, whereas the energy intensity of road transport within the built-up area is 15.9 MJ/tonnekm. The emission factors of the ULS are low compared to the emissions from road transport. On the one hand, this is caused by the low direct energy intensity and, on the other, by the use of electric energy, which has lower emission factors than fossil fuel engines.

Figure 1.2.2 shows the effect of the ULS Utrecht on direct energy use. Here, the energy use for road transport is subdivided into transport within the built-up area and transport on the ring motorway around Utrecht. The figure shows only the values for a large tube diameter; the general picture for a small tube diameter corresponds with this, although with a somewhat higher energy intensity for the ULS. The energy use of transport on the ring motorway increases for all three of the network alternatives, because, on average, a larger distance on the motorway has to be covered to reach the distribution centre compared to directly driving to the city centre. There is a large variety of direct energy use for transport within the built-up area, because the distance from the ring motorway to the distribution centre differs per alternative. We should note here that Alternative 1 has been designed for transfer to the ULS from rail transport and inland shipping. However, making use of rail or inland shipping would probably require major adaptations at the origin of the freight transport; this is left out of the current analysis. Figure 1.2.2 shows that only one out of the three alternatives results in a net decrease in direct energy use. For this alternative the yearly direct energy use of transportation between city edge and city centre decreases by 17 per cent compared to a situation without the ULS (where this energy use is 15.4 TJ per year). Nevertheless, a shift in direct emissions takes place for all alternatives from the city centre to power plants, motorways, and roads at the edge of the city. This shift is advantageous for local air quality in the city, because the average distance between the source of emissions and locations of people is much greater for the power plant than for local road traffic, resulting in fewer health impacts (Eyre *et al.*, 1997).

The indirect energy use and emissions of the underground logistic system alternatives are calculated by the process energy analysis and process emission analysis. Energy use of construction, maintenance, and indirect operational processes, such as lighting and air conditioning, are of importance for the indirect effects. In the process of energy analysis and emission analysis a distinction is made between the construction of tubes, terminals, and vehicles. Energy use and emissions for these system components are calculated on the basis of

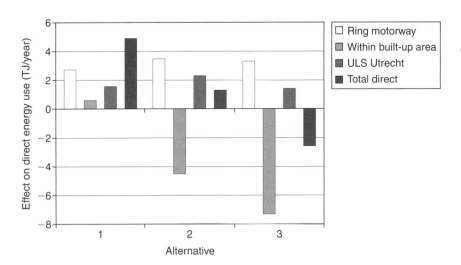

Figure 1.2.2 Effect of three network alternatives of the ULS Utrecht (large tube diameter) on direct energy use, relative to a situation without ULS.

proposed characteristics of the system: the quantity of materials needed and the projected construction activities using standardised data (see Table 1.2.2). The infrastructure is supposed to have a lifetime of 50 years, equal to the lifetime of the total project; a lifetime of 30 years is assumed for the vehicles. The secondary energy use of maintenance is expressed as a percentage of the energy use of construction; there is still a large measure of uncertainty about this relationship. The indirect energy use of the ULS Utrecht is very high compared to its effect on direct energy use, especially for the larger tube diameters. The indirect energy use accounts for 87 per cent to 94 per cent of total energy use by the ULS (without accounting for the direct effect on the energy use of road transport) for the different network alternatives and tube diameters. Such systems therefore need a large throughput of freight to compensate the indirect energy use with a possibly advantageous effect on direct energy use. For Alternative 3 with its large tube diameter (the alternative with the most favourable energy use), the amount of freight to be transported would have to be fivefold to result in a positive net effect on energy use. This is an unrealistic scenario since it is already assumed that all suitable goods will be transported via the ULS. For the emissions by ULS Utrecht the indirect emission is even greater than for the energy use. An overall decrease in emission is highly unlikely for any of the substances; possible positive effects can only be accomplished by a geographical shift of emissions: emissions of noise and pollutants in central urban areas cause a greater negative impact compared to emissions outside the built-up area.

The energy use of construction and maintenance of the tubes is dominant for a large tube diameter (see Table 1.2.6). For a system with a smaller tube diameter, this part of the energy use is much less; therefore especially the construction and maintenance of the terminals and the indirect energy use of operational activities is of importance. It should be noted that if a market share of less than 100 per cent is assumed, the share of indirect energy use in the total energy use would be even larger. However, we examined a completely underground system, whereas a partial underground system would have had a lower energy use, as it is easier to construct and in certain cases requires fewer building

Table 1.2.6 Direct and average indirect energy intensities (MJ/tonnekm) for ULS Utrecht (Alternative 3, optimistic goods flow)

	Large tube diameter		*Small tube diameter*	
Direct		2.8		4.8
Construction tubes	7.0		1.5	
Construction terminals	2.1		7.0	
Construction vehicles	0.0		0.1	
Maintenance	9.1		8.6	
Operation terminals	4.7		15.9	
Indirect		22.9		33.1
Total		25.7		37.9

materials. For direct energy use and emissions, as well as for indirect energy use and emissions, we ignored changes for road, this being the main competitor of the ULS. The shift of freight to the ULS changes the use of roads, some roads facing an increase in intensities and others, a decrease. The possible impacts of these changes on maintenance-related energy use and emissions could be non-negligible. As an illustration, Bos (1998) calculated the average indirect energy intensity for road transport in the Netherlands through a process energy analysis to be 0.460 MJ/tonnekm on average (0.123 MJ/tonnekm for vehicles and 0.337 MJ/tonnekm for infrastructure). However, as Bos (1998) indicated, the indirect energy intensity differs considerably among road types. For local roads – where the ULS has a positive effect for two alternatives – indirect effects are larger than for motorways.

The conclusions of the analyses are very clear: the amount of freight that is transported through the ULS is, even in the optimistic scenario, far too small to compensate the high indirect energy use and emissions. Although there are still significant uncertainties, the conclusions are robust with respect to the uncertainties. The uncertainty of our analyses lies mainly in the forecasts of freight volumes and the energy use for maintaining the ULS. For the latter, this has to do with the assumption of the energy use for maintaining the system being proportional to the energy use of the construction.

6 Discussion and further research

Sections 4 and 5 described an integral evaluation of two types of underground freight transport. A distinction was made between the direct and the indirect environmental effects of the transport system. This section, 6, will first discuss these two types of effects, with attention given to differences between emissions and energy use and to the location where the emissions are found. Several methodological issues are also discussed.

Direct environmental effects

The analyses in the last two sections illustrate the influence of transport infrastructure development as a policy measure, as described in Section 2. The infrastructural developments do not appear beneficial from an environmental point of view in all cases. The effect may not be similar for all different emissions. The possible effect on transport volumes is most evident for the ULS. For all of the alternatives in the case study, the distance over which the cargo is transported increases if the ULS is implemented, resulting in an increase in tonne kilometres. The transport volume in tonne kilometres appears to be dependent to a large extent on the position of the distribution centre relative to the major goods flows. Both systems have a clear impact on modal split, because they are alternatives for other transport modes: conventional pipelines for long-distance road transport, rail transport and inland shipping, and the ULS for urban road transport. Forecasting the effect of the ULS on modal split is very complex, because implementation of such systems is very likely to be accompanied by legal restrictions on lorry access to local roads. That the underground freight transport systems are fully automated and undisturbed by other traffic implies an optimal use of vehicles and the efficiency of the distribution scheme of the systems themselves. However, from the current research no information can be derived from the impact of underground freight transport on the use of vehicles or on the behaviour for the competitive or complementary transport modes. Further research into changes in transport and traffic volumes is therefore recommended.

Despite technical differences, for example, on manner of propulsion, the two types of underground freight transport distinguish themselves from other transport modes in at least two ways with respect to direct energy use. First, both systems are fully automated and undisturbed by other traffic, which results in a relatively low direct energy intensity. Second, the direct emissions caused by both systems are concentrated in a limited number of fixed locations, i.e. the location of power plants for the ULS and the location of power plants or of fixed fossil fuel engines for conventional pipelines. Other forms of underground freight transport developed worldwide often also show these two features.

These two properties of underground freight transport systems are important in the context of where emissions take place. Emissions inside a city are, in most cases, more severe than emissions in less densely populated areas, in particular, for emissions causing air pollution. The effect on the spatial distribution of transport and emissions on local environmental conditions is especially relevant for the ULS case study. Road transport in central urban areas will decrease if a ULS is implemented, whereas total transport on urban roads is expected to decrease for two out of the three network alternatives. For these two alternatives, the direct emissions from transport in the city decrease relative to the base scenario, because direct emissions due to the ULS itself take place at power plants outside of the city. This results in a positive effect on local air quality in the city. However, the favourable effect in the inner city is introduced at the cost of higher transport volumes and emissions on the city's ring motorway and of emissions released on power plant sites. Locations of emissions due to acidification are also relevant but on a much larger spatial scale.

Indirect environmental effects

Direct effects of both systems are low compared to their competitive transport modes. Indirect effects are relatively important compared to the direct effects, and are highly variable depending on the alternative chosen. Conventional pipelines have a very low indirect energy intensity, because the pipeline infrastructure is intensively used. The use of the ULS is far less intensive, resulting in an indirect energy intensity that is much larger than the direct energy intensity. To compensate the large indirect energy by a possible positive effect on direct energy use, large volumes of goods will be needed. Although our analysis only includes one particular case, it seems hardly likely that similar applications in other cities will have a positive overall effect on energy use. Applications in industrial areas probably have better possibilities for a net positive effect, because these applications typically deal with larger volumes with fewer origin–destination relationships (the fewer origin–destination relationships can reduce indirect routing via the ULS).

For both types of underground freight transport, the effect on indirect emissions is larger than on indirect energy use. As a result, whereas the indirect energy use for crude-oil pipelines is very small compared to the direct energy use, some indirect emissions are more significant for these pipelines. This is especially true for the PM_{10} emission. The reason for this is formed by the higher emission factors for the manufacturing industry compared to the transport system. Therefore, a considerable release of emissions occurs on industrial sites instead of at the infrastructure location. We recommend further research into location aspects of emissions, both for the construction and in-use phases.

Discussion on methodology

The methodology used in this paper to calculate both direct and indirect energy use and emissions can be classified as a 'bottom-up' approach. Here, the total energy use or emission of a system is calculated by aggregating the effect of all different processes making up this system. For the direct effect this allows one to calculate direct energy use and emissions when no statistical ('top-down') data is available. For the indirect effect, the use of the bottom-up process energy and emission analyses avoids aggregating processes into economic sectors (also a combination of process analysis and input-output analysis is possible, see Bos, 1998). However, the bottom-up approach has the disadvantage that a great effort is required to perform the calculations. As a result, several assumptions have been made to cope with the uncertainties that come with the system design; the most important ones will be discussed below.

First, as mentioned in Section 4 our calculation for direct energy use of pipelines yielded relatively low results compared to values found in the (US) literature, differences in methods being a possible explanation. We therefore recommend further research into direct energy use and emissions of pipelines, applying different research methods.

Second, in Section 5 we stated that due to a lack of data, we ignored possible changes in direct and indirect energy use, and emissions of road transport (lorries, but also cars and vans), because of changes in intensities resulting from the assumed shift of freight from road to the ULS. With respect to direct energy use and emission, the shift may, on the one hand, result in a decrease in energy use and emissions per kilometre on roads with reduced intensities due to lower congestion levels. However, on the other, the increase in speeds may result in more traffic, due to both a shift from other modes (slow modes, public transport) to cars and to induced demand. The increase in intensities on other roads should also be included in further analyses. Besides, changes in indirect energy use and emissions due to changes in traffic intensities on roads should be included. A further recommendation for future research is therefore a more sophisticated estimation of all changes in traffic volumes and energy use, and emissions per kilometre for ULS alternatives.

In Section 5 we also stated that assumed secondary energy use of maintenance is expressed as a percentage of the energy use of construction. However, large uncertainty still exists on this relationship, as well as on the value of the percentage. Further research into this subject is therefore recommended.

In this paper we have focused on the environmental impacts of two concepts for underground freight transport. We have explicitly not compared environmental performance of underground freight transport systems with alternatives. For suggestions on how such a comparison could be made, including several possible methodological difficulties, please refer to Van Wee *et al.* (2005).

Apart from these suggestions for further research into distinguished aspects of the possible environmental impacts of underground freight transport, the value of a comprehensive *ex ante* evaluation of all relevant aspects for policy decisions should be noted. This may be a Multi Criteria Analysis (MCA) or a Cost-Benefit Analysis (CBA), the latter being the most common in many Western countries (see the special issue of *Transport Policy* (2000) for an overview and the paper of Hayashi and Morisugi (2000), in that special issue). Such an evaluation should include financial aspects (construction costs, maintenance, and exploitation costs) but also environmental impacts (noise, emissions, effects of emissions, landscape, and livability aspects) and social aspects related to traffic in urban areas. Such an evaluation might also address questions with respect to the distribution of costs and benefits over time (using a discount rate) and over space and actor categories. Only such a comprehensive overview can provide policy-makers with information needed for decision-making.

Despite the assumptions made and the limitations of the research approach, the results of the research are shown to be rather robust. For crude-oil pipelines, both the calculated direct energy use and the top-down data from the literature are far lower than the direct energy use of competing transport modes. Furthermore, all direct emissions, except the PM_{10} emissions of crude-oil pipelines, are significantly larger than the indirect emissions. The calculated indirect energy use and emissions of the system for ULS Utrecht are considerably larger than a possible positive direct effect. It is unlikely that a possible lower energy use and emissions for the maintenance of the system and/or a possible positive indirect effect of road transport would lead to an indirect effect that is less than savings in direct energy use and emissions.

7 Concluding remarks

This study analyses the direct and indirect energy use and emissions of two types of underground freight transport: conventional crude-oil pipelines and Underground Logistic Systems (ULS), an innovative concept for the underground transport of packed goods. The construction of underground infrastructure for freight transport is seen by Dutch government as a policy measure to achieve a more sustainable transport system. We used a life-cycle approach in the current study to deal with the relationship between various determinants for environmental impact of transport and infrastructure development.

Both underground freight transport systems have been shown here to have low direct energy intensities and emission factors when compared to competitive transport modes (where energy intensity is defined as the energy use divided by the transport performance in tonnekm). However, the total effect on direct emissions also involves the effect on complementary transport modes, as shown in the case study of the proposed ULS Utrecht, where an increase in overall transport distances resulted in a net positive effect for only one out of three network alternatives. A positive direct effect of all the alternatives in the ULS is the shift of emissions from inside the city to its edge and to power plants; this can improve local air quality in the city itself.

Process energy analysis and process emission analysis were carried out to determine the indirect effect of the two underground freight transport systems on energy use and emissions. The analyses showed very distinct results for the two types of underground freight transport. Crude-oil pipelines have very low indirect energy intensities as a result of an intensive use of infrastructure. For some emissions, however, the indirect effect is substantial compared to the direct effect – particularly true for emissions of particulate matter (PM_{10}). Changes in indirect emissions and energy use are larger than in direct emissions and energy use. This conclusion holds for both types of underground freight transport and for all the emissions included in our study. A very high indirect energy use compared to its direct energy use is expected for ULS Utrecht; indirect effect is even higher for the emissions. To result in an overall positive effect on energy use and emissions, the ULS Utrecht will require extraordinarily high transport volumes.

Process energy analyses and process emission analyses require much and detailed information. Therefore uncertainty here is especially applicable to assumptions made about processes. Furthermore, the current paper focuses on a limited number of environmental effects. For a complete assessment of the environmental impacts of underground freight transport, account should also be taken of other environmental effects, such as noise pollution, use of space and safety. Finally, this study is based on the evaluation of two particular applications of underground freight transport; although these cases appear to provide a good illustration for underground freight transport in general, it cannot be excluded that other particular applications will show other characteristics.

Notes

* Urban and Regional Research Centre Utrecht, Faculty of Geographical Sciences, Utrecht University, P.O. Box 80115, 3508 TC Utrecht, The Netherlands, j.willigers@geog.uu.nl.
** Transport Policy and Logistics Section, Faculty of Technology, Policy and Management, Delft University of Technology, P.O. Box 5015, 2600 GA Delft, The Netherlands, g.p.vanwee@tbm.tudelft.nl.

1 International crude oil pipelines account for the majority of the transport volume (in tonne kilometres) of industrial pipelines in the Netherlands.
2 As an illustration: 1 MJ of energy corresponds to the heat produced by burning ca. 3 cl of diesel oil.
3 Cathodic protection prevents corrosion of steel pipelines (or other steel artefacts) by sending a low-voltage electric current through the steel pipe.
4 For the large tube diameter, about 90 per cent of all freight is suitable for transport via the ULS; for the small diameter, this is ca. 25 per cent.
5 As an alternative, the use of rail guidance in the tunnels is a possibility to lower the direct energy intensity considerably. However, rail construction would lead to higher indirect emissions that would cancel out much of the positive direct effect. This option is therefore not discussed any further in this paper.

References

AVV (1997a) *Achtergrondrapportage Vervoer-Economische Verkenningen 1997–2002*, Rotterdam: Ministerie van Verkeer en Waterstaat, Adviesdienst Verkeer en Vervoer (AVV).

—— (1997b) *Vervoer-Economische Verkenningen 1997–2002*, Rotterdam: Ministerie van Verkeer en Waterstaat, Adviesdienst Verkeer en Vervoer (AVV).

Bliss, D. 'Mail Rail: 70 years of automated underground freight transport', paper presented at 2nd International symposium on underground freight transportation by capsule pipelines and other tube/tunnel systems, Delft, September 28–29, 2000.

Blok, P. and Van Wee, B. (1994) 'Het verkeersvraagstuk' in J. Van der Straaten (ed.) *Basisboek milieu-economie*, Amsterdam/Meppel: Boom.

Boerkamps, J. and Brouwer, W. (1999) *Inventarisatie goederenstromen*, Amersfoort: DHV Milieu en Infrastructuur.

Bos, A.J.M. (1998) *Direction indirect: the indirect energy requirements and emissions from freight transport*, Groningen: Rijksuniversiteit Groningen.

Bullard, C.W., Penner, P.S., and Pilati, D.A. (1978) 'Net energy analysis: handbook for combining process and input-output analysis' *Resources and Energy*, 1: 267–313.

CBS (several editions) *Maandstatistiek verkeer en vervoer*, Den Haag/Heerlen: Centraal Bureau voor de Statistiek (CBS).

—— (several editions) *Maandstatistiek verkeer en vervoer*, Den Haag/Heerlen: Centraal Bureau voor de Statistiek (CBS).

Davis, S.C. (2000) *Transportation energy data book*, 20th edn, Oak Ridge: Center for Transportation Analysis, Oak Ridge National Laboratory.

Deelen, C., Dekker, T., and Snijders, E. (1999) *2020, Integrale verkenningen voor haven en industrie*, Rotterdam: Gemeentelijk Havenbedrijf Rotterdam.

Eriksson, E., Blinge, M., and Lövgren, G. (1996) 'Life cycle assessment of the road transport sector' *The science of the total environment*, 189/190: 69–76.

Ettema, D.F. (1999) *Ondergronds Logistiek Systeem (OLS) Utrecht*, De Bilt: Grontmij.

Eyre, N.J., Ozdemiroglu, E., Pearce, D.W., and Steele, P. (1997) 'Fuel and location effects on the damage costs of transport emissions' *Journal of Transport Economics and Policy*, 31: 5–24.

Geurs, K.T., Van den Brink, R.M.M., Annema, J.A., and Van Wee, G.P. (1998) *Verkeer en vervoer in de Nationale Milieuverkenning 4*, Bilthoven: Rijkstinstituut voor Volksgezondheid en Milieu.

Gijsen, A. and Spakman, J. (2001) *DAMES: Een bestand voor de macro-emissies van het Nederlandse elektriciteitsaanbod in 1995, 1998, 2010, 2020 en 2030*, Bilthoven: Rijksinstituut voor Volksgezondheid en Milieu.

Groot, P.J.M. (1991) *Goederenvervoer per pijpleiding*, Amsterdam: Economisch instituut voor de bouwnijverheid.

IFIAS (1974) *Energy analysis*, Stockholm: International Federation of Institutes for Advances Study (IFIAS).

IPOT (2000) *Transport onder ons: van visie naar realisatie*, Den Haag: Interdepartementale Projectorganisatie Ondergronds Transport (IPOT), Ministerie van Verkeer en Waterstaat.

Laitner, J.A. (2000) 'Energy efficiency: Rebounding to a sound analystical perspective' *Energy policy*, 28: 471–475.

Mott, R.L. (2000) *Applied fluid mechanics*, 5th edn, Upper Saddle River: Prentice-Hall.

NEA and Haskoning (1993) *Goederenvervoer per buisleiding: Een onderzoek naar de huidige en potentiële omvang van het goederenvervoer per buisleiding in Nederland*, Tilburg/Nijmegen: NEA/Haskoning.

RIVM (2000) *Nationale Milieuverkenning 5: 2000–2030*, Alphen aan den Rijn: Samson.

Roos, J.H.J., Corten, F.G.P., and Dijkstra, W.J. (2000) *Maarschappelijke baten van ondergrondse logistieke systemen*, Delft: Centrum voor energiebesparing en schone technologie.

Taniguchi, E., Ooishi, R., and Kono, T. (2000) 'Development and future perspectives for underground freight transport systems in Japan', paper presented at 2nd International symposium on underground freight transportation by capsule pipelines and other tube/tunnel systems, Delft, September 28–29, 2000.

Van den Brink, R.M. and Van Wee, G.P. (1997) Energiegebruik en emissies per ver voerwijze, Bilthoven: Rijksinstituut voor Volksgezondheid en Milieu.

Van der Heide, J. (1999) *Energiestudie OLS*, Delft: TNO Wegtransportmiddelen.

Van der Heijden, M., Iding, M., and Tavasszy, L. (1999) *Naar een landelijk netwerk voor goederenvervoer met ondergronds transport per buisleiding*, Delft: TNO Inro.

Van Wee, R., Janse, R., and Van den Brink, R. (2005) 'Comparing energy use and environmental performance of land transport modes' *Transport Reviews*, 25: 3–24.

Willigers, J. (2001) *Milieu-effecten van ondergronds goederentransport: huidige situatie en toekomstige ontwikkelingen*, Bilthoven: Rijksinstituut voor Volksgezondheid en Milieu.

Wilting, H.C., Biesiot, W., and Moll, H.C. (1998) 'Trends in Dutch energy intensities for the period 1969–1988' *Energy*, 23: 815–822.

Wright, D. (1974) 'Goods and services: an input-output analysis' *Energy policy*, 2: 307–315.

1.3 Intelligent Speed Adaptation

Increased safety through speed reduction

*Kerstin Westin, Jörgen Garvill, and Agneta Marell**

Abstract

In the period 1999–2002 the Swedish National Road Administration conducted a large-scale field test with Intelligent Speed Adaptation (ISA) in urban traffic in four Swedish cities. Approximately 5000 vehicles were equipped with different ISA systems to help prevent the drivers from exceeding speed limits. The objective of the test was to learn more about driver attitudes to ISA and how drivers use the systems, impact on road safety and environment, and the integration of the systems in the vehicles.

One of the participating cities was Umeå, where 4000 vehicles were equipped with an informative ISA device that by sound and light warned the driver when exceeding the speed limits. By involving such a large number of vehicles (approximately 10 per cent of the fleet of private vehicles in Umeå) the intention was to have a large enough car fleet equipped with an ISA device that it might be possible to determine if there were any spill over effects on speed.

In this paper results from the three-year field-test in Umeå is reported. More specifically this chapter reports on effects on speed (actual as well as self-reported speed) in vehicles equipped with an ISA device and effects on speed for the city car fleet, i.e. spill over effects. In addition, attitudes towards an ISA device are discussed.

Background

Road traffic accidents are a major cause of registered fatalities and represent the prime cause of death for persons less than 40 years old. Almost 600 people are killed annually in traffic accidents in Sweden (63 fatalities per million inhabitants), and approximately 4000 are seriously injured. The number of accidents has decreased slightly in the past 15 years, but is still considered to be unacceptably high. As a comparison, the number of accidents is higher in most other European countries, e.g. 157 per million in Greece, 129 per million in France, and 83 per million inhabitants in Germany[1] (Eurostat, 2003).

In 1997 the Road Traffic Safety Bill, based on 'Vision Zero' was passed in the Swedish Parliament. 'Vision Zero', in turn, is based on the ethical belief that it is not acceptable for people to be killed or seriously injured when moving within the road transport system. The long-term goal is that no one should be killed or seriously injured within the Swedish road transport system. The designers of infrastructure and vehicles, as well as the road-users are responsible for safety and for achieving the set goal. System designers are responsible for the design, operation, and the use of the road transport system and are thereby responsible for the level of safety within the entire system. Road users are responsible for following the rules, set by the system designers and for using the transport system. Finally the bill states that if the users fail to comply with these rules due to a lack of knowledge, acceptance or ability, the system designers are required to take the necessary further steps to counteract people being killed or injured.

The Traffic Safety Bill states that speed is the most important regulating factor for safe road traffic. The notion of a correlation between speed and risk for accidents is based on work by, for instance, Blomquist (1986), Fowles and Loeb (1995), and Graham and Garber (1984) and a consensus has evolved among researchers and transport planners that excessive speed violation is a primary problem in traffic (Fildes and Lee, 1993). In order to increase safety for unprotected road-users such as children, pedestrians, and cyclists, speed limits have been reduced to 30 km/h in many areas. Areas often targeted for such speed limits in Sweden are Central Business Districts (CBDs), residential areas, and areas just outside schools and day-care centres. Even though surveys reveal that road users generally find that 30 km/h is an appropriate speed limit in special surroundings (such as schools and day-care centres) it has been shown that, nonetheless, trespassing of speed limits occurs on such roads (Marell and Westin, 1999).

To be able to succeed in actions directed towards adherence to speed limits, the question of why individuals exceed speed limits has to be addressed. The issue of weak correlations between attitude and actual behaviour is extensively discussed in many domain-specific settings (e.g. traffic psychology, purchase behaviour, and environmental concern). As a starting point of analysis Ajzen and Fishbein's theory of reasoned action (Ajzen and Fishbein, 1980) and the later developed theory of planned behaviour (TPB) (Ajzen, 1985) has often been used. The correlation between attitude and behaviour is, however, often found to be very low. Rothengatter (2002) provides two explanations for the observed low correlation. First, Rothengatter states that when TPB is applied to test attitude behaviour consistency, the measure of behaviour is usually behaviour in the past and not, as the theory stipulates, intentions about future behaviour, i.e. intended behaviour. Second, the measure of actual behaviour is often an approximation of actual behaviour, and not actual behaviour. Another equally important reason for low correlation might be that speeding behaviour is multiple determined and that attitudinal factors, contextual factors, and habits are all important in explaining speeding behaviour. For example, Haglund (2001) found that drivers' choice of speed is influenced by a number of interrelated factors, such as road factors, other road users, and enforcement. Furthermore, drivers' own judgements of what is an appropriate speed were also important. However, research also indicates that there is an interaction between attitudes and contextual factors (Stern, 2000) and between attitudes and habits (Triandis, 1977, 1980; Verplanken and Aarts, 1999) such that the stronger the contextual factors or the habit, the less the influence is from attitudes on behaviour. Since most driving behaviour is repeated in similar contexts and drivers adapt to other drivers' behaviour and to the road conditions, it is reasonable to assume that speeding behaviour to a large extent is determined by habit and by contextual factors. This might explain why drivers exceed speed limits despite a positive attitude towards keeping them and despite the awareness of a correlation between speeding and risk for accidents.

Rothengatter (2002) suggests that studies of the relationship between contextual factors and the attitude behaviour correlation might link the attitude theory better to traffic psychology. For example, he argues that behaviour not accepted by the driver in one task environment might be accepted when the environment is changed. This means that it is important to create traffic environments that are perceived as positive and that generate the desired behaviour. Moreover, from studies of drivers and the traffic system it is sometimes argued that drivers influence the behaviour of one another (e.g. Åberg *et al.*, 1997; Manstead *et al.*, 1992). Åberg *et al.* (1997) argue that drivers adjust their own speed to their estimates of the driving behaviour of other drivers. Following this reasoning, a spill over effect from one groups' change of behaviour can be expected. In this case a more positive attitude to an ISA device is assumed to lower speed among the test drivers that in turn will lead to a change in behaviour among drivers not participating in the test.

The purpose of this paper is to report on drivers' speeding behaviour as a result of a trial with Intelligent Speed Adaptation (ISA). More specifically, the effects on speed after installing an Electronic Speed Checker (ESC) in 10 per cent of the car fleet are discussed, and both effects on test drivers as well as on non-test drivers are discussed. Both actual and self-reported measures of speed are presented. As studies by Corbette (2001) find a moderate correlation between actual and subjective speed, and Haglund and Åberg (2002) find that consistency between actual and reported speed limits varies between roads with different speed limits, both actual and self-reported measures are reported for robustness purposes. Moreover, attitudes towards an ISA device and to adherence of speed limits prior to and after installation are presented.

ISA trial in Sweden

Speed limits are often exceeded in urban traffic in Sweden. Police surveillance has been a common tool to increase adherence to speed limits. It has been efficient, but very costly to maintain and hence sporadic. Another recently used method in Sweden is speed cameras, which are placed at specific spots (such as a pedestrian crossing or at some point of a road segment with a history of speed exceeding). Speed cameras have been shown to reduce speed, but the negative aspect is that they are stationary and have a geographically very limited effect. A different type of speed reducing measure has been physical obstacles on the road, such as elevated pedestrian crossings, bumps, and circulation places. However, drivers do not appreciate such physical measures. These obstacles can cause damages to cars, they can cause difficulties for emergency vehicles (ambulance, fire brigade, etc.), and in winter these obstacles can reduce access for snow-clearing vehicles. An alternative to physical measures is different applications of ISA. ISA aims at adjusting speed (keeping speed limits) by means of electronic equipment in the vehicles, instead of by physical measures on the road, or police surveillance.

In the period 1999–2000 the Swedish National Road Authority launched a large-scale trial involving ISA in urban areas. Approximately 5000 vehicles in four different cities were equipped with warning, informative or supportive[2] systems to help the drivers keep to the speed limits. Participation in the project was voluntary. The primary objective of the test was to evaluate the effect on road safety and the drivers' acceptance of and attitudes to ISA. More specifically the aim of the trial was to obtain knowledge on (i) driver attitudes towards different ISA applications; (ii) driver usage of ISA, i.e. driver behaviour; (iii) impact on road safety and the environment; (iv) integration of the systems in the vehicles; and (v) prerequisites for road informatics on a large scale.

A warning ISA was tested in Umeå,[3] where some 4000 vehicles were equipped with an Electronic Speed Checker (ESC), a device that with sound and flashing light warned the driver when she or he was exceeding the current speed limit. In Borlänge, 400 vehicles were equipped with an informative ISA that used audible and visual warnings for breaches of the current speed limit, and in addition a display that informed the driver about the current speed limit. In Lund a system was tested that supported the drivers' speed

Map 1.3.1 Cities participating in ISA.

adaptation through an 'active accelerator', which meant that when the drivers had reached the legal speed limit a counter pressure was applied to the accelerator. The Lund trial encompassed 290 vehicles. Finally, in Lidköping, 150 vehicles were equipped with an informative system and 130 vehicles with active accelerator.

ISA in Umeå – Smart Speed

In order to measure whether ISA had any influence on the overall speed in the cities and on traffic safety, a large number of vehicles in the trial were necessary. The most extensive test, in terms of number of participants, was carried out in Umeå, Sweden. The focus of the Umeå-test – called Smart Speed – was to investigate spill over effects when a large part (10 per cent) of the vehicle fleet was equipped with ISA. The ISA-device tested in Umeå was an in-vehicle electronic speed surveillance device mounted on the vehicle's dashboard, a so-called Electronic Speed Checker (ESC). The function of the ESC was to inform the driver when he/she exceeded a speed limit. The ESC was activated by roadside radio transmitters, and linked with the vehicle's speed metering system. If the vehicle's speed exceeded the value (the current speed limit) received from a roadside transmitter, the ESC signalled this with a flashing red light and intermittent sound. Approximately 100 road segments in the urban area were included in the field study. The selected road segments represented the different speed limits 30, 50 and 70 km per hour.

The ESC could be installed in a majority of cars from model 1989 onwards. Out of 42 000 private vehicles in Umeå, 15 500 were found to be suitable for installation of the ESC. Apart from technical problems a drop-out was also due to problems finding the owner's address, the owner had sold the car, etc. 13 852 car owners were contacted by phone (1700 could not be reached), 11 971 (85 per cent) answered questions regarding the trial, and 5441 (40 per cent) agreed to participate in the trial. Out of these 5441 drivers, 3564 in the end came to have an ESC installed in their car; the drop-out was caused by further technical problems, or the drivers changed their mind about participating. In addition, 315 buses, trucks, and company cars were equipped with an ESC.

The drivers participating in the trial answered questionnaires on several occasions, the first questionnaire at the time they were recruited to the trial – recruitment questionnaire. The questions concerned some characteristics of the driver (age, sex, annual mileage, and type of car), evaluation of different ISA-applications, and questions on attitudes to speed and risk. A second questionnaire was answered prior to the installation of the ESC, and the questions concerned expectations of driving with an ESC (pre-test questionnaire). After having tested the ESC for a month another questionnaire was answered, with questions regarding the initial experiences (short-term questionnaire). These questions were repeated after six months of driving, after one year (medium-term questionnaire), and finally after two years of testing the ESC[4] (long-term questionnaire). In addition, in-depth interviews were carried out with ten drivers. A panel of 335 drivers took part in all interviews. The results presented here are based on this group and the surveys carried out after one month (short-term effects), after one year (medium-term effects), and after two years (long-term effects).

Participating drivers – who were they?

In the end 25 per cent of the contacted car owners entered the test, and had an ESC installed. The group that chose to participate was not fully representative of drivers in general. First, the technical conditions connected with the ESC excluded drivers with older cars, certain owners of special models, etc. Second, cars are more often registered to men than to women; in Sweden 68 per cent of all cars are registered to a man. In the sample (13 852 car owners) the percentage of men was 79, and in the trial 81. An explanation as to the difference of the national number is the limitation to cars of year 1989 or later – women often have older cars, especially in two-car households.

There were also differences between the drivers who chose to participate and those who decided not to participate. The drivers who chose to participate were older than those who did not participate, they had older cars (on average seven years compared to six years for non-participants), and the older test drivers stayed with the trial for a longer period of time than the younger ones. Participants and non-participants were compared with regard to their perceived moral obligation to keep the speed limits, perceived demands from traffic pace, perceived relation between speed and risk, perceived difficulty to keep to the speed limits, and with regard to how often they exceeded the speed limits. Participants agreed more strongly than non-participants with the statements that it is a moral obligation to keep to the speed limits within the city and that there is a strong relation between speed and risk for accidents. Participants perceived it as more difficult to keep to the speed limits and indicated that they exceeded the speed limits more often compared to non-participants (for more details see Eriksson *et al.*, 2003; Garvill *et al.*, 2002).

Results

The Smart Speed trial in Umeå involved almost 3600 private cars, and just over 400 commercial vehicles and city buses. At the beginning of the year 2001 there were 42 733 passenger cars registered in Umeå (Statistics Sweden, 2001), which means that approximately 8 per cent of the vehicle fleet was participating in Smart Speed and had an ESC installed. A hypothesis was that if a sufficient number of cars had an ESC installed – and provided that the drivers of these cars complied with the speed limits – it would be possible to register a spill over effect. The ESC-equipped cars would work as 'speed reducers' in the traffic. To test this hypothesis, average speed was measured in 1999 before the trial started, and during the trial in the years 2000 and 2001.

In the Umeå test two different measures of speed-reduction were used; actual or registered speed reduction, and perceived reduction of speed. Actual speed measurements were made within as well as outside of the trial area. All in all measurements were made in 106 points, divided on 16 road types and 53 road sections (both directions), and in order to calculate speed at peak hours, low traffic, and medium traffic the measurements were made during a continuous week. Measuring was made in the middle of each link, and 10 m before an intersection.

The exposure/penetration of Smart Speed cars varied from 5 per cent on large streets to 14 per cent on certain local streets, and the average exposure was 7 per cent. The measurements also show a reduction of average speed on most links within and outside the trial areas (cf. Figure 1.3.1). On for instance local roads in central areas of the city with 50 km/h speed limit a reduction of average speed of 1.2 km/h (all vehicles) was registered within the trial area, and 0.9 km/h outside the trial area. On roads limited to 30 km/h the reduction varied from 0.3 to 0.9 km/h, and the largest reduction was noted on local streets. As is indicated in Figure 1.3.2, average speed increased on some links: within the test area on 70–50 transitions average speed for all vehicles increased by 2 km/h, while a

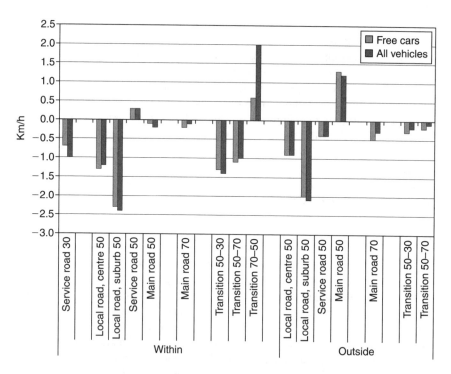

Figure 1.3.1 The difference in average speed (km/h) for private cars per road environment in Umeå throughout the day between autumn 1999 and autumn 2002, free vehicles and all private cars on links (source: SNRA, 2002).

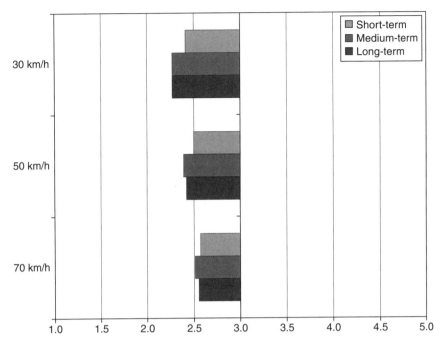

Figure 1.3.2 The test drivers' perception of changes of their own speed with an ESC in the car. Measured on a 5-point scale, where 1 = major decrease, 3 = no change, and 5 = major increase.

decrease by 0.1 km/h was registered outside the test area. A certain lowering of speed can also be noticed in the measurement located 10 m before an intersection.

All in all, links and sections taken together, a small but systematic reduction of average speed for free vehicles[5] could be established, and these results can be derived from the ISA trial (Swedish National Road Authority, 2002), and the hypothesis of a spill over effect from ISA vehicles can be supported by speed measurements.

Test drivers' perception of speed

As interesting as actual speed measures is the question whether the test drivers did perceive that they had lowered their speed. The test drivers (335 drivers) perceived that their speed had been affected during the trial. The drivers were asked whether their speed had increased or decreased on 30, 50 and 70 km/h roads respectively, and these questions were asked after one month of participation (short term), after approximately one year (medium term), and after two years (long term). As indicated in Figure 1.3.2 the drivers stated that their speed

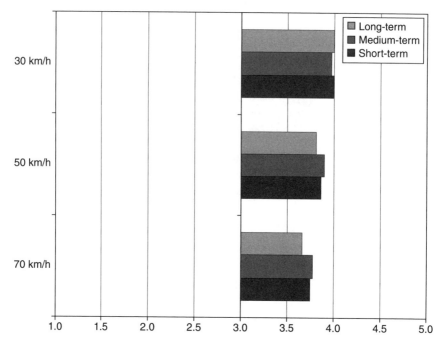

Figure 1.3.3 The test drivers' perception of whether it has become easier or more difficult to keep to speed limits with an ESC in the car.

had decreased on all speed limits. The reduction was larger on 30 and 50 km/h roads at the long-term measurement compared to the short-term measurement ($p < 0.05$). Further, the reduction was also larger on 30 km/h roads than on 50 km/h roads, and larger on 50 km/h roads than on 70 km/h roads ($p < 0.05$).

The test drivers were asked if they thought it had become easier or more difficult to keep to the speed limits 30 km/h, 50 km/h and 70 km/h when having an ESC in the car.[6] The general opinion was that it had become easier to keep to the speed limits in the test area (see Figure 1.3.3). The largest effect was noticed on 30 km/h roads, slightly less effect on 50 km/h roads and least effect on 70 km/h roads. The effect remained unchanged throughout the test period, i.e. perceived as large at the end of the test as in the early phase.

Finally, the drivers were asked how often they exceeded the speed limits 30, 50 and 70 km/h in urban traffic with 10 km/h or more.[7] Here a comparison is made between the drivers' perception of speed violation before the installation of the ESC and their perception of violations during the test period. As shown in Figure 1.3.4, speed limits on 30 km/h roads were exceeded to the least extent, and on 70 km/h roads to the largest extent. The speed limits 30 and 50 km/h respectively, were exceeded more often before the ESC was installed in the car compared to when the drivers were driving with an ESC. There is no change

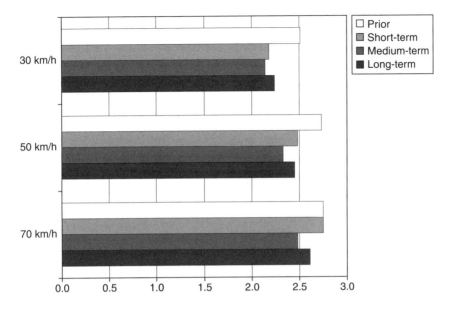

Figure 1.3.4 How often the test drivers exceeded speed limits before and during the test.

from prior to the test and the short-term survey in how often speed is exceeded on 70 km/h roads; however, we notice a significant decrease in trespassing of speed limits by the medium-term and long-term measure ($p < 0.001$).

A comparison between how men and women perceived speed and trespassing of speed limits shows no differences with regard to how easy or difficult it was to keep to the limits. Nor were there any differences between how often men and women reported that they exceeded different speed limits by 10 km/h or more. Further, there were no differences between the age groups (18–44 years, 45–64 years, and 65 years and older) with regard to how easy or difficult it was to keep to the limits. However, we notice that the age group 65 years and older reported that they exceeded the 70 km/h limit less often than the group 18–44 years reported ($p < 0.05$).

The results show that the drivers perceive that it has become easier to keep to set speed limits in urban traffic with an ESC, that they perceive that their speed has been reduced, and the drivers also report less trespassing of speed limits. The effects are most noticeable on 30 km/h roads, and least noticeable on 70 km/h roads.

The experience of driving with an ESC

In order to examine if the ESC affected driving in a positive or negative way, and if this experience changed over time, the drivers were asked to compare driving before and after having the ESC installed.[8]

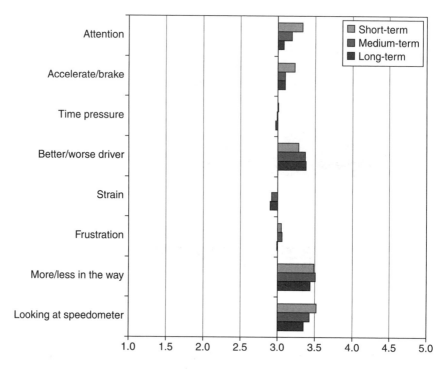

Figure 1.3.5 The drivers' perception of driving with an ESC compared to prior to having an ESC.

As indicated in Figure 1.3.5, the drivers perceived that at the short-term survey it took more attention to drive with an ESC, but this effect decreased over time. By the long-term survey there was no significant change compared to the situation prior to driving with an ESC. It was also perceived that initially one had to be more active with accelerating and braking, but this effect had disappeared by the medium-term and long-term survey. There was no change in time pressure or frustration. One effect was noticeable throughout the whole test period; the drivers felt more 'in the way' of others when driving. A positive effect was that the drivers perceived that they had become better drivers after having an ESC installed in the car, and also that the strain of driving decreased during the test period.

The younger drivers, 18–44 years, had a slightly less positive evaluation of driving with an ESC. The group 18–44 years stated, to a higher extent than did the group 65 years and older, that they perceived higher time pressure and frustration driving with an ESC in the car compared to prior to the test. The younger group also felt that driving had become more strenuous than did the drivers 45 years and older. The age group 65 years and older to a larger extent than the group 18–44 years, perceived that they had become better drivers after having an ESC installed in their car. However, the oldest group felt that they were more in the way of others than did the other age groups (p < 0.05). Women perceived to a larger extent than men did, that their attention had increased and that they had to accelerate and brake more often after having an ESC in the car (p < 0.05). No other gender differences were noted.

Attitudes towards keeping to speed limits

The test drivers were asked to what extent they agreed to a number of statements concerning negative consequences of keeping to the speed limit. They were asked these questions before having the ESC installed in their car, as well as at the medium-term and at the long-term questionnaire. The result, shown in Figure 1.3.6, reveals that drivers had changed their opinion about the negative consequences of keeping to speed limits for five out of seven statements after driving with the ESC. In the long term, compared with prior to installing an ESC, the drivers agreed, to a significantly lower degree, with statements that they exceed speed limits because other drivers do, that if they keep to the speed limit other drivers can engage in reckless overtakes, keeping to the speed limits

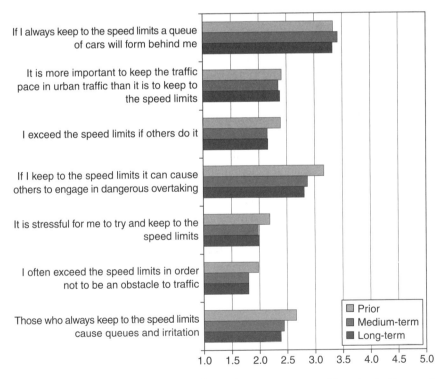

Figure 1.3.6 Test drivers' evaluation of negative consequences of keeping to the speed limits in urban areas. The evaluation is made on a 5-point scale ranging from 1 = totally disagree to 5 = totally agree.

is stressful, they exceed the speed limits since they do not want to be an obstacle, and that drivers who keep to the speed limits often create queues and irritation in traffic ($p < 0.001$). No change over time is noted for two of the statements; if they keep to the speed limits a queue behind them is created and it is more important to adjust to the traffic pace than keeping to the speed limits.

There are differences between different age groups and between men and women with respect to the evaluation of the negative consequences of keeping to the speed limit. Young test drivers did to a higher extent than older drivers agree that they exceed speed limits if other drivers exceed them. Elderly test drivers on the other hand, agreed to a higher extent than young drivers that if they keep to the speed limits a queue will occur behind them, if they keep to the speed limits other drivers might engage in reckless overtaking, and that drivers who always keep to the speed limits create queues and irritation ($p < 0.05$). Men agreed to a higher extent than women with the fact that it is more important to follow the traffic flow than the speed limits, that they drive faster than the speed limit if others do, that they often speed as they do not want to be an obstacle, and that drivers who keep to the speed limits create queues and irritation ($p < 0.05$).

Traffic safety

Statistics on accidents (reported to hospitals) during the period 1998–2001 do not show any significant change from 1998 to 2001. The number of injured (in the test area) decreased from 555 to 543, a change that was not significant. However, in the same period 1999–2001, the number of accidents involving injury to persons in urban areas in Sweden as a whole increased by 3 per cent compared to the previous three-year period, and the number of fatalities and seriously injured increased by 7.3 per cent. This means that the serious consequences have increased more than the number of accidents. In conclusion, the number of injured and fatalities did not change in Umeå during the test period, while the trend in the whole of Sweden was a 7 per cent increase.

In addition, a study on serious and non-serious traffic conflicts, i.e. incidents almost leading to an accident, showed that the number of serious conflicts decreased by 54 per cent during the test period. The total number of conflicts decreased by 68 per cent. Partly this substantial reduction can be explained by the introduction of pedestrian precedence during this period, but also the large number of ISA equipped vehicles are likely to have been a contributing factor.

Concluding remarks

The purpose of this paper was to report on drivers' speeding behaviour as a result of an ISA trial. Measures of both actual speed and self-reported speeding behaviour have been presented.

The results show that speed was reduced within the test area. First, the self-reported speed indicates that drivers who installed an ISA device did change their behaviour and lowered the speed. Second, apparently a penetration of 8 per cent of ESC equipped vehicles was sufficient to achieve a spill over effect on the traffic fleet. Self-reported speed behaviour indicates that speed was lowered within the test area, especially on roads with low speed limits. For example, a larger speed reduction was found on roads with 30 km/h than on roads with 50 km/h. Moreover, the effect was larger in the long run than in the short run, indicating that the effect is not only a short-term reaction of testing the ESC. In the same vein, drivers indicate less speeding violations after installing an ESC in the vehicle.

Drivers supported the perception of lower speed by indicating that they perceived it to be easier to keep to speed limits with an ESC in the vehicle and that installing and driving with an ESC made them better drivers.

As speeding is one major factor in explaining car accidents and consequently explaining injuries in traffic, lowering speed is important for increased safety. The Umeå trial has shown an actual decrease in speed within the test area. Moreover, drivers also report on lower speed and less speed violation occasions. In conclusion, the ISA device – ESC – is perceived as helpful in reducing the number of speeding occasions as well as in lowering the general speed.

It should be noted that some of the spill over effects might be a result of increased congestion and shorter distances between vehicles. However, the speed measures are made in Umeå where, in general, congestions are rare. But even if some of the effects are attributed to congestions there is support that a lowered speed and a calm traffic pace was the result of the ISA trial.

Notes

* Transportation Research Unit, Umeå University.
1 Refers to the year 2002.
2 A warning system indicated by light and sound that the current speed limit was being exceeded. An informative system in addition to sound and light also gave information on prevailing speed limits. In the supportive system a counter pressure in the gas pedal made it more difficult to exceed the current speed limit.
3 Umeå is situated in the north of Sweden, with snowy and icy roads in the wintertime. The city itself has a population of about 70 000, with a further 30 000 living in the surrounding area.
4 Drivers of trucks, buses, and company cars were also interviewed.
5 Free vehicles indicates vehicles that arrive within a time gap of at least five seconds, that is the drivers' choice of speed is not affected by cars ahead (no queues).
6 The valuation was made on a 5 point scale, where 1 = very difficult, 3 = no change, and 5 = very easy.
7 The valuation was made on a 6 point scale, where 1 = Never, 2 = Very seldom, 3 = Seldom, 4 = Sometimes, 5 = Often, and 6 = Very often.
8 The valuation was made on a 5 point scale, where 1 = much less/much worse, 3 = no change, and 5 = much more/much better.

References

Åberg, L., Larsen, L., Glad, A., and Beilinson, L. (1997) 'Observed vehicle speed and drivers' perceived speed of others' *Applied Psychology: An international Review*, 46, 3: 287–302.

Ajzen, I. (1991) 'The theory of planned behavior' *Organizational Behavior and Human Decision Processes*, 50: 179–211.

—— (1985) 'From intentions to actions. A theory of planned behaviour' in J. Kuhl and J. Beckman (eds) *Action-control from cognition to behaviour*, Heidelberg.

Ajzen, I. and Fishbein, M. (1980) *Understanding Attitudes and Predicting Social Behavior*, Prentice Hall, Englewood Cliffs, NJ.

Blomquist, G. (1986) 'A utility maximization model of driver safety behavior' *Accident Analysis and Prevention*, 18371–18375.

Brehmer, B. (1994) 'Psychological aspects of traffic safety' *European Journal of Operational Research*, 75: 540–552

Comte, S., Wardman, M., and Whelaan, G. (2000) 'Drivers' acceptance of automatic speed limiters: implications for policy and implementation' *Transport Policy*, 7: 259–267.

Corbett, C. (2001) 'Explanations for understating in self-reported speeding behaviour' *Transportation Research Part F*, 4: 133–150.

Eriksson, L., Garvill, J., Marell, A., and Westin, K. (2003) 'Långtidseffekter av ISA – att köra med Fartkollare' (Long-term effects of ISA and driving with an ESC), TRUM Rapport 2003: 1, Umeå universitet.

Eurostat (2003) Energy & Transport in Figures 2003, European Commission, Directorate-General for Energy and Transport.

Fildes, B. and Lee, S. (1993) 'The Speed review: Road Environment, Behaviour, Speed Limits, Enforcement and Crashes' Federal Office of Road safety, Report CR127, Department of Transport and Communication, Canberra.

Fowles, R. and Loeb, P.D. (1995) 'Effects of policy-related variables on traffic fatalities: An extreme bounds analysis using time-series data' *Southern Economic Journal*, 62: 359–366.

Garvill, J., Marell, A., and Nordlund, A.M. (2003) 'Effects of increased awareness on choice of travel mode' *Transportation Research Part F*, 6: 37–43.

Garvill, J., Marell, A., and Westin, K. (1999) 'Umeåtrafikanters inställning till trafiksäkerhet och trafiksäkerhetshöjande åtgärder' (Umeå-drivers' perception of traffic safety and safety increasing measures), TRUM-Report, 1999: 01, Umeå university.

—— (2002) 'Factors influencing drivers' decision to install an Electronic Speed Checker in the car' *Transportation Research, Part F: Traffic Psychology and Behaviour*, 6: 37–43.

Graham, J. and Garber, S. (1984) 'Evaluating the effects of automobile safety regulation' *Journal of Policy Analysis and Management*, 3: 206–224.

Haglund, M. (2001) 'Speed Choice. The Driver, the Road and Speed Limits', Uppsala Dissertations from the Faculty of Social Sciences 108.

Haglund, M. and Åberg, L. (2001) 'Speed choice in relation to speed limits and influences from other drivers' *Transportation Research Part F*, 3: 39–51.

Manstead, A.S.R., Parker, D., Stardling, G., and Baxter, J.S. (1992) 'Perceived consensus in estimates of the prevalence of driving errors and violation' *Journal of Applied Social Psychology*, 22, 7: 509–530.

Marell, A. and Westin, K. (1999) 'Intelligent transportation system and traffic safety – drivers perception and acceptance of electronic speed checkers' *Transportation Research Part C*, 7: 131–147

Rothengatter, T. (2002) 'Drivers' illusions – no more risk' *Transportation research Part F*, 5: 249–258.

Stern, P.C. (2000) 'Toward a coherent theory of environmentally significant behaviour' *Journal of Social Issues*, 56: 407–424.

Swedish National Road Authority (2002) 'Intelligent Speed Adaptation (ISA) – results of large-scale trials in Borlänge, Lidköping, Lund and Umeå in the period 1999–2002' Publication 2002: 89 E.

Triandis, H.C. (1977) *Interpersonal behavior* Monterey, CA: Brooks/Cole.

—— (1980) 'Values, attitudes and interpersonal behavior' in H.E. Howes Jr and M.M. Page (eds) *Nebraska Symposium on Motivation, 1979*, Lincoln, NE: University of Nebraska Press.

Verplanken, B. and Aarts, H. (1999) 'Habit, attitude, and planned behavior: Is habit an empty construct or an interesting case of goal-directed automaticity?' *European Review of Social Psychology*, 10: 101–134.

Zaidel, D.M. (1992) 'A modelling perspective on the culture of driving' *Accident Analysis and Prevention*, 24: 585–597.

1.4 Peering and investments in interfaced networks

*Roberto Roson**

1 Introduction

Networks, both physical and intangible, constitute a complex economic environment. Market interactions, within a network, are typically characterised by a mixture of cooperation and competition, complementarity and substitution. Agents in a network market are subject to competitive pressure, but at the same time need to be interconnected to each other.

Recent contributions in the 'network economics' field have stressed that these markets share key economic characteristics (e.g. Economides, 1996; Shy, 2001), and analytical models can be usefully developed to explore these features, while abstracting from the specific type of network under examination. In other words, network economics provides general theoretical models for the analysis of imperfect competition in networked markets such as transportation, Internet and other telecommunications, gas, oil, electricity and water distribution, and so on.[1]

A major benefit of this methodology is the possibility of transferring concepts and principles from one field to another, possibly taking advantage of advances achieved in the analysis of specific policy issues. From this point of view, the surge of the 'new economy' in the 1990s, associated with the wave of privatisations in public utilities (Newbery, 2004), have triggered substantial interest on issues like network access regulation, foreclosure, market entry, and incentives. In my opinion, mainstream transport economics has not yet fully acknowledged the potential of such a truly interdisciplinary approach, although some useful cross-fertilisation (e.g. between transportation and telecommunications) is sometimes recognised.

This chapter follows this approach in examining the consequences, in terms of network expansion and growth, of a specific regime of network access, sometimes known as 'peering' (in the Internet), or 'bill-and-keep' (in telephony). Under this settlement, all traffic destined to the customers of a network provider is accepted without imposing any access fee, whereas all outgoing traffic is routed freely on external, interfaced networks.

In the Internet, peering schemes traditionally regulate the exchange of data packets between backbone operators of similar size. Peering has been advocated within the Federal Communications Commission as an efficient instrument to regulate access between telecommunications networks (DeGraba, 2000, 2002; Wright, 2002).

In transportation networks, peering schemes can be observed in different contexts, although they are not normally called this way. International railway transportation, for example, requires the use of railway infrastructure owned and maintained by different (national) operators. Since transportation services are usually sold by a single (home) operator, some clearing between payments for outgoing and incoming traffic would be necessary. A peering agreement may be said to exist if no monetary compensation takes place, and free access is reciprocally granted. Such a case could also emerge in air transportation (e.g. between airlines within an 'alliance'), or between operators of toll highways, whenever the car drivers do not need to make separate payments for entering different segments of a network during a journey.

Some papers have addressed the relationship between peering schemes and the incentives for investment in network capacity (e.g. bandwidth, road or railway capacity). In particular, Little and Wright (2000) show that if regulation forbids settlement payments between firms, there will be under-investment in capacity and under-pricing of usage. This is because the absence of an access fee allows outside users to free-ride on the improved quality (reduced congestion) of accessed networks. To overcome these problems, operators that are net providers of infrastructure should be allowed to charge operators that are net users. The first-best outcome is achieved if settlement fees are set at the incremental cost of capital provided.

This and other models found in the literature are typically stated as two (or three) stage games: capacity levels are chosen first, and conventional market competition follows (assuming reciprocal free access). In this chapter, I propose a model, which retains this type of approach, but adopts fairly general assumptions about some key functions, like utility and cost functions, with the aim of highlighting the critical factors affecting the amount of capacity investment.

In my model, the utility of a representative consumer is supposed to be influenced by two distinct elements: 'on-net' and 'off-net' traffic flows. The former involves the use of a network infrastructure owned by a single 'home' operator, whereas the latter involves the sharing of some external infrastructure.

These two elements are considered separately, because it is possible that an investment in capacity affects the two networks asymmetrically: a higher capacity directly affects the on-net flows, whereas off-net flows are affected only through the interaction between capacity of the source network and capacity of the destination network. Even if external consumers may benefit from investments in the home network, the impact of quality improvements may be stronger within the network in which the capacity has been expanded. This means that network operators may compete in quality through capacity investment (as in Valletti and Cambini, 2002).

The market equilibrium is characterised by externalities and consequently it is not, in general, socially efficient. The model is aimed at highlighting the role played by some factors in determining the *sign* of the externalities (a negative externality implies over-investment, a positive externality implies under-investment), as well as their magnitude.

The work is organised as follows. Basic assumptions of the model are set out in the next section. In the subsequent sections, alternative model versions are presented and discussed, mainly differing in terms of pricing and consumers' mobility hypotheses. As usual, a final section summarises the main findings and draws some concluding remarks.

2 Basic assumptions

There are two groups of consumers, initially connected to two networks, called 1 and 2. The number of consumers in each group is normalised to one. All consumers have the same characteristics, and derive utility from the consumption of on-net and off-net network services (telephone calls, data exchange, goods or passengers transportation), in the following way:

Assumption A1. A representative consumer connected to network i derives utility from consumption of on-net services q_i and off-net services q_{ic}, through a sub-utility function $U(q_i, q_{ic})$, having the following properties:[2]

$$\frac{\partial U}{\partial q_i} = U^{qi} \geq 0 \, \frac{\partial^2 U}{\partial q_i^2} = U^{qi,qi} \leq 0$$

$$\frac{\partial U}{\partial q_{ic}} = U^{qic} \geq 0 \, \frac{\partial^2 U}{\partial q_{ic}^2} = U^{qic,qic} \leq 0 \qquad [1]$$

$$\frac{\partial^2 U}{\partial q_i \partial q_{ic}} = U^{qi,qic} = 0 \quad i \in \{1, 2\}$$

Assumption A2. The supply of network services gives raise to two kinds of cost: constant production costs, which can be normalised – without loss of generality – to zero, and congestion costs, which are different for the two types of flows:

$$C_i = C_i(k_i, q_i, q_{1c}, q_{2c}) \quad C_c = C_c(k_1, k_2, q_1, q_2, q_{1c}, q_{2c})$$

$$\frac{\partial C_-}{\partial k_-} = C_-^{k-} \leq 0 \, \frac{\partial C_-}{\partial q_-} = C_-^{q-} \geq 0 \qquad [2]$$

Assumption A3. Consumers in each group i are assumed to maximise:

$$V_i = U_i(q_i, q_{ic}) - p_i q_i - p_{ic} q_{ic} - C_i(\cdot) q_i - C_c(\cdot) q_{ic} \qquad [3]$$

while taking the congestion costs as independent from the individually chosen quantity levels. This implies the following optimisation conditions:

$$U_i^{qi} = p_i + C_i(\cdot) \quad U_i^{qic} = p_{ic} + C_c(\cdot) \qquad [4]$$

On this type of setting, we now analyse some model variants.

3 Two-parts tariffs, captive consumers

Consider first a situation in which every consumer is connected to one network, but switching to the alternative network is impossible. For example, customers of transportation services are physically located nearby some transport infrastructure, and their initial location cannot be easily changed.

There is perfect information about cost and demand characteristics, and each provider applies a two-part tariff (a fixed fee and a price per consumed unit). A standard result, which I recall here without demonstration, states that a profit-maximising supplier will then charge a marginal cost price (in this case, zero[3]) and a fixed fee, which fully expropriates the representative consumer of her surplus.

Since social surplus coincides with total profits, the choice of capacity investment (independently done by the two providers) will be efficient in the absence of pecuniary externalities, that is, if an increase in a network capacity does not affect the other operator's profits. If, for example, expanding the capacity in a network creates positive effects for the external consumers (e.g. benefiting from reduced congestion in off-net calls), the other network operator may be able to increase the fixed fee. This positive spillover would not be internalised by the investment-making operator, who may then select a network capacity level lower than the socially optimal one (e.g. when marginal investment costs are strictly increasing).

To verify if this is the case, it is important to make a preliminary observation.

Proposition P1. The volume of on-net and off-net traffic changes in opposite ways, when capacity is increased in the external network. As a consequence, the (gross) utility of the representative consumer may either increase or decrease (or stay constant), depending on how the two types of services are weighted in the utility function. (Proof: see the appendix in this chapter)

For example, if k_2 is expanded, we could observe a reduction of congestion costs for off-net calls, raising the inter-network traffic. If k_1 is left unchanged, this creates an extra pressure on network one, raising congestion costs for intra-network calls. It is not difficult to build specific examples in which this *induced congestion effect* reduces the utility of consumers linked to network one.[4]

In general, we cannot rule out the possibility that an increase of capacity k_2 reduces q_{1c} flows. This may happen when q_2 increases so much that congestion costs for the inter-network calls are higher, despite the larger capacity. However, even in this case, q_{1c} and q_1 would move in opposite directions.

On the whole, the effects of an expansion of k_2 on the different traffic flows can be obtained through differentiation of first order conditions, which can be expressed in matrix form as:

$$
\begin{bmatrix}
sq_1 & c_1^{q1c} & c_1^{q2c} & 0 \\
c_c^{q1} & sq_{1c} & c_c^{q2c} & c_c^{q2} \\
c_c^{q1} & c_c^{q1c} & sq_{2c} & c_c^{q2} \\
0 & c_2^{q1c} & c_2^{q2c} & sq_2
\end{bmatrix}
\cdot
\begin{bmatrix}
q_1^{k2} \\
q_{1c}^{k2} \\
q_{2c}^{k2} \\
q_2^{k2}
\end{bmatrix}
=
\begin{bmatrix}
0 \\
-c_c^{k2} \\
-c_c^{k2} \\
-c_c^{k2}
\end{bmatrix}
\qquad [5]
$$

where $sq_x = -(U^{qx,qx} - c_x^{qx}) > 0$ (because of second order conditions associated to [4]).

Here, the right hand side vector expresses the direct effect of a capacity expansion on congestion costs. The matrix on the left hand side, instead, accounts for the systemic effect of changes in the traffic flows.

4 Linear pricing, captive consumers

The situation in which the network providers use a simple price per unit of traffic, instead of a two-parts tariff, can be considered as a simple variant of the case discussed above.

Two key observations are necessary here. First, linear pricing fails in fully expropriating the consumer surplus. This means that, generally speaking, a network operator cannot fully internalise, in terms of profits, all the benefits of an investment in capacity. As a consequence, the level of investment in network capacity will tend to be lower than the socially optimal one.

Second, even if linear pricing is an imperfect device to extract the consumer surplus, it remains true that more profits can be achieved if the consumer surplus increases. To see this, consider the f.o.c. in [4] and suppose that an investment in capacity has reduced the congestion cost $C(\cdot)$ for one type of service (on- or off-net). To restore the equality, we must observe an increase in the price, and/or an increase in the quantity (reducing the marginal utility). In both instances, profits increase.

Combining these two elements, we can conclude that investments in capacity are associated with two types of externalities. One positive externality affects the consumers, and a second externality affects the operator in the interfaced network. The latter may either reinforce or weaken the first effect. The conditions determining the direction of the secondary externality are the same as those discussed in the previous section.

5 Two-parts tariffs, endogenous market shares

Suppose that network services are horizontally differentiated and the consumers may change provider, on the basis of utility differentials and preference parameters. If consumers are homogeneously distributed in terms of absolute preferences, we can adopt a standard Hotelling-type competition framework, and compute the market shares in the following way (ruling out the possibility of a corner solution with zero customers):

Assumption A4. Let the market size α for the operator i be determined by:[5]

$$\alpha_i = 1 + \mu(V_i - V_j) > 0 \quad i, j \in \{1, 2\} \tag{6}$$

where μ is a parameter, measuring the intensity of competition (degree of service differentiation).

In this setting, network congestion may change because more or less customers are connected to a network (as in Baake and Mitusch (2002)), even if the traffic generated by each single consumer does not change. Congestion costs may then be expressed as:

$$C_i = C_i(k_i, \alpha q_i, \alpha q_{1c}, (2 - \alpha)q_{2c})$$

$$C_c = C_c(k_1, k_2, \alpha q_1, \alpha q_{1c}, (2 - \alpha)q_{2c}, (2 - \alpha)q_{2c}, (2 - \alpha)q_2) \tag{7}$$

where $\alpha_i = \alpha$ and $\alpha_j = [\alpha_i + \alpha_j] - \alpha_i = 2 - \alpha$. To keep the model tractable, as well as to isolate this effect from the one discussed in the previous sections, the following hypotheses are introduced:

Assumption A5. For small variations in capacity levels, individual traffic demand does not change:

$$\frac{\partial q_i}{\partial k_i} = \frac{\partial q_i}{\partial k_j} = \frac{\partial q_{ic}}{\partial k_i} = \frac{\partial q_{ic}}{\partial k_j} = 0 \quad i, j \in \{1, 2\} \tag{8}$$

Assumption A6. The impact of additional traffic on congestion costs does not depend on the traffic type:

$$\frac{\partial C_i}{\partial q_i} = \frac{\partial C_i}{\partial q_{ic}} = \frac{\partial C_i}{\partial q_{jc}} = C_i^t$$

$$\frac{\partial C_c}{\partial q_i} = \frac{\partial C_c}{\partial q_j} = \frac{\partial C_c}{\partial q_{ic}} = \frac{\partial C_c}{\partial q_{jc}} = C_c^t \quad i, j \in \{1, 2\} \tag{9}$$

Considering again two-part tariffs, implying the expropriation of consumer surplus, the incentives for the expansion of network capacity continue to be influenced by the cross effect of a capacity increase on profits, which can be expressed here as:

$$\Pi_i = \alpha_i V_i \Rightarrow \frac{\partial \Pi_i}{\partial k_j} = \mu(V_i^{kj} - V_j^{kj})V_i + \alpha_i V_i^{kj} \tag{10}$$

To evaluate [10], the effects of some additional capacity on the consumer surpluses must be computed first. These can be obtained by solving the following system:[6]

$$V_j^{kj} = -q_j(C_j^t + C_j^t(\mu(V_j^{kj} - V_i^{kj})(q_j + q_{jc} - q_{ic}))) -$$

$$q_{jc}(C_c^t + C_c^t(\mu(V_j^{kj} - V_i^{kj})(q_j + q_{jc} - q_{ic} - q_i)))$$

$$V_i^{kj} = -q_i(C_i^t(\mu(V_i^{kj} - Vj_i^{kj})(q_i + q_{ic} - q_{jc}))) -$$

$$q_{ic}(C_c^{kj} + C_c^t(\mu(V_i^{kj} - V_j^{kj})(q_i + q_{ic} - q_{jc} - q_j))) \tag{11}$$

The solution of [11] is rather messy. To ease its interpretation, let us consider a situation in which: $q_1 = q_2 = q$ and $q_{1c} = q_{2c} = q_c$. In this case, the solution of [11] simplifies to:

$$V_j^{kj} = -\frac{C_j^{kj}(q + C_i^t q^3 \mu) + C_c^{kj} q_c \Psi}{\Psi} > 0$$

$$V_i^{kj} = -\frac{C_j^{kj} C_i^t q^3 \mu + C_c^{kj} q_c \Psi}{\Psi} > 0 \qquad [12]$$

where $\Psi = 1 + C_1^t q^2 \mu + C_2^t q^2 \mu > 0$.

Subtracting these two equations, we can see that the variation in the utility differential is strictly positive:

$$V_j^{kj} - V_i^{kj} = -\frac{C_j^{kj} q}{\Psi} > 0 \qquad [13]$$

The meaning of [13] is rather straightforward. When capacity in a network is expanded, this network attracts consumers. In this way, some additional congestion reduces the initial benefits of a larger capacity, but at the same time few customers remain in the other networks, which also experience less congestion.

The numerator accounts for the direct effect of a capacity expansion on intra-net calls, which matters only for those consumers attached to the improved network. The denominator accounts instead for a smoothing effect, due to the shifting of customers. Indeed, this term is increasing in the parameter μ: a higher degree of mobility in the consumers implies a lower differential advantage, obtained by the capacity increase.

This result does not depend on the hypothesis $q_1 = q_2 = q$ and $q_{1c} = q_{2c} = q_c$, which is a sufficient but not a necessary condition. To see this, consider the position of the marginal consumer, who is indifferent in terms of network membership. Her utility, when connected to network i, must be the same as her utility, when connected to network j:[7]

$$\bar{U}_i - C_i(\cdot)q_i - C_c(k_j,.)q_{ic} = \bar{U}_j - C_j(k_j,.)q_j - C_c(k_j,.)q_{jc} \qquad [14]$$

From this situation of balanced utility, suppose that capacity in network j is augmented. Both left and right hand sides of [14] would then change, possibly breaking the equality. There is a direct effect here due to the larger capacity on congestion costs, and an indirect effect, due to the induced changes in the market shares. The indirect effect is of second order, however, and does not affect the sign of the variation in utility differentials.

In other words, to make sure that the marginal consumer switches to network j, when capacity in this network is increased, the following requirement must be met:

Assumption A6: Let $-C_j^{kj} q_j > -C_c^{kj}(q_{ic} - q_{jc})$ $i, j \in \{1, 2\}$.

This condition is, of course, satisfied when $q_1 = q_2 = q$ and $q_{1c} = q_{2c} = q_c$, since the right hand side would be zero. It would also be satisfied if the switching consumers do not significantly change their demand for *off-net* services, after having changed their provider. Now we can state the following:

Proposition P2. Under assumption A6, an increase in capacity for a network benefits the consumers directly connected to this network, as well as the external consumers, connected to the interfaced networks. However, the welfare gain is larger for the consumers belonging to the network in which the capacity expansion takes place.

Coming back to equation [10], notice first that an increase in the capacity of an external network affects the profits in two opposite ways: some customers are lost (attracted by the outside network), but the remaining ones enjoy a higher potential surplus (which is actually fully extracted by the home network provider). Therefore, as in the first model, the sign of the externality cannot be determined a priori.

One could conjecture that a lower degree of service differentiation, or a higher degree of consumers mobility, boosts the 'business stealing' mechanism and makes the sign of [10] negative (remember that this would bring about over-investment in capacity). This is only partly true, though, as can be seen by plugging [12] into [10]:

$$\frac{\partial \Pi_i}{\partial k_j} = \frac{C_j^{kj} q (1 - C_i^t q^2) \mu - C_c^{kj} q_c \Psi}{\Psi} \qquad [15]$$

Here, the denominator is positive. The numerator is given by the algebraic sum of two terms. The second one is positive, but the first one, which is weighted by μ, has an ambiguous sign. However, for a sufficiently large C_i^t, even this element is positive. This case, emerging when congestion is high for internal calls within network i, is characterised by positive cross-effects on profits (and, consequently, under-investment in capacity, despite the fact that firms use capacity investments to compete in quality). This happens when customers of network i experience a significant reduction in the on-net congestion, due to the shrinking of their network group size. This positive externality adds to the one associated with lower congestion costs in the inter-network calls (last term in the numerator of [15]).

6 Conclusion

Networks are built, expanded, operated, and maintained in different ways. Until recently, most network infrastructure, especially in transportation, was built and controlled directly by public authorities. As a consequence, regional development and other policy objectives were the primary determinants of centralised investment planning. The liberalisation of many network industries has changed the picture somewhat, and now many investment decisions are driven by economic incentives of individual operators, competing in the market. These incentives depend, in turn, on the regulatory regime and the specific characteristics of each industry.

This chapter has focused on the incentive implications, in terms of network capacity expansion, of a special access mechanism (peering) that can be applied, freely or through a regulator, between interfaced networks.

The main insight is that capacity investments have a differentiated impact for on-net and off-net flows. Whereas intra-network flows are directly affected by the increase in capacity, the influence of congestion on inter-network flows depends on both capacity levels of the source and destination networks. Outside users, having access to a capacity-improved network, typically experience a reduction in the cost of off-net services, but at the same time congestion may increase in their home network, raising the cost of on-net services.

In addition, network firms may compete in quality, in this case through capacity improvements. Even if a firm loses customers, when a competitor network expands its capacity, the remaining customers can benefit from reduced congestion.

To better understand the nature of investment incentives, we identified a set of market externalities. When investment in capacity produces positive spillovers for outside firms and customers, the investing firm does not internalise all the benefits, and the investment level tends to be lower than the socially optimal one. The opposite case emerges when the externalities are negative.

Competition in quality ('business stealing') generates negative spillovers (= over-investment), but direct and indirect reductions of congestion work in the reverse direction (= under-investment).

All these factors may be more or less important in the various networks in which peering access schemes are applied. For example, the business stealing effect may not be relevant for the case of interconnected regional transportation networks. In this case, if customers do not value domestic and interregional transport services very differently, peering is likely to induce lower levels of investments. On the contrary, customers can easily switch provider of mobile phone services. In this other case, network capacity is an instrument of market competition, and 'excess' investment is likely to be observed.

Appendix

Proof of Proposition P1

Consider the f.o.c. associated with quantity q_1:

$$U_1^{q1} - C_1(k_1, q_1, q_{1c}, q_{2c}) = 0 \qquad [\text{A1}]$$

Differentiate with respect to k_2, and explicit q_1^{k2}:

$$q_1^{k2} = \frac{C_1^{q1c} q_{1c}^{k2} + C_1^{q2c} q_{2c}^{k2}}{U_1^{q1,q1} - C_1^{q1}} \qquad [\text{A2}]$$

The denominator is negative if [A1] identifies a maximum. On the numerator, cost derivatives are positive, by assumption. On the other hand, derivatives of off-net traffic quantities must have the same sign ($sign[q_{1c}^{k2}] = sign[q_{2c}^{k2}]$), because these are determined on the basis of the same level of congestion cost, C_c,

and marginal utilities are monotonically non-decreasing. Therefore:
$$sign[q_1^{k2}] = -sign[q_{1c}^{k2}].$$

Q.E.D.

Notes

* Dipartimento di Scienze Economiche, Università Ca'Foscari de Venezia, Cannaregio 873, Venice, Italy. E-mail: roson@unive.it.
1 Often, the network concept is also used to illustrate vertical relationships among firms in productive processes, especially in terms of access to 'essential facilities' (Rey and Tirole, 2003).
2 In the following, superscripts will be used to indicate derivatives.
3 Alternatively: the service provider bears the congestion, and charges the marginal congestion cost.
4 This is the case, for instance, when the utility is linear logarithmic in consumption of the two services, and congestion functions are expressed as the inverse of the difference between total capacity and total traffic.
5 So far, the number of consumers connected to each network (a constant) was normalised to one. Here, this number is variable, but it is still one if the utility differential is zero. Consumers choose their provider on the basis of the sub-utility function V and of some other subjective preference parameters, related to the identity of the provider but independent from the price/quantity characteristics of each network.
6 Basic utility functions $U(\cdot)$ do not appear in [11] because of Assumption A5. However, even without A5, they would not appear because of the envelope theorem.
7 The parameters $\bar{U}$ in [14] comprise quantity-dependent utilities U and subjective preference parameters. Both terms are constant, as they depend neither on market shares, nor on capacity levels.

References

Baake, P. and Mitusch, K. (2002) *Competition with Congestible Networks*, Mimeo, Humboldt and Technical University, Berlin.

DeGraba, P. (2000) *Bill and Keep at the Central Office as the Efficient Interconnection Regime*, OPP Working Paper #33, Federal Communications Commission.

DeGraba, P. (2002) 'Bill and Keep as the Efficient Interconnection Regime?: A Reply' *Review of Network Economics* 1: 60–64.

Economides, N. (1996) 'The Economics of Networks' *Journal of Industrial Organization* 14: 673–699.

Little, I. and Wright, J. (2000) 'Peering and Settlement in the Internet: an Economic Analysis' *Journal of Regulatory Economics* 18: 151–173.

Newbery, D.M. (2004) *Privatising Network Industries*, CESifo Working Paper n. 1132.

Rey, P. and Tirole, J. (2003) 'A Primer on Foreclosure' in M. Armstrong and R.H. Porter (eds) (2006) *Handbook of Industrial Organization*.

Shy, O. (2001) *The Economics of Network Industries*, Cambridge University Press.

Valletti, T. and Cambini, C. (2002) *Investment and Network Competition*, Mimeo, Imperial College, London and Politecnico di Torino.

Wright, J. (2002) 'Bill and Keep as the Efficient Interconnection Regime?' *Review of Network Economics*, 153–159.

1.5 Environmental vehicle rating system

Joeri Van Mierlo,* Jean-Marc Timmermans,*
Peter Van Den Bossche,* Gaston Maggetto,*
Vincent Favrel,** Sandrine Meyer,** and
Walter Hecq**

Abstract

A rating system, used to compare the environmental damage caused by vehicles, in order to allow decision-makers to draw (non-)fiscal policies and measures taking into account their impact on the environment, is analysed and evaluated.

The analysis of rating systems comprises the study of the effects on numerous receptors such as ecosystems, buildings, and human beings (e.g. cancer, respiratory diseases, etc.) caused by different types of pollutions (acid rain, photochemical air pollution, noise pollution, and global warming, etc.).

The methodology described, known as Ecoscore, is based on a Life Cycle Assessment (LCA) approach which considers the contribution of emissions to certain types of damage (e.g. by using the Exposure-Response damage function). Total emissions include oil extraction, transport and refinery, fuel distribution, and electricity generation and distribution (Well-to-Wheel approach). Emissions due to the production, use, and dismantling of the vehicle (Cradle-to-Grave approach) could be considered as well.

Assessment is made possible by normalising the different types of damage. A reference value assigned to a predetermined reference vehicle is defined as a target value (the normalised value thus determines a kind of 'distance to target' consideration). The contribution of the different normalised types of damage to a single value, Ecoscore, is based on a panel weighting method.

This new approach has been especially developed for the evaluation of the environmental damage caused by vehicle emissions in an urban context, such as the Brussels Capital Region and differs in that option from other methodologies. Additionally this methodology does not only consider conventional vehicles, but it can also assess all alternative fuels and propulsion systems with new vehicle technologies, such as electric and hybrid vehicles.

A detailed description of the methodology itself can be found in reference [1]. In this paper the methodology is summarised and illustrated by some examples of Ecoscore calculation. Additionally new recent amendments of the methodology are highlighted. Finally, a sensitivity analysis demonstrates the robustness of the Ecoscore model.

Keywords: *Environmental assessment tool, vehicle emissions, alternative fuels, electric and hybrid vehicles, clean vehicles, road vehicles, ecoscore, LCA, decision support tool, emissions, energy*

1 Introduction

The transport sector is a huge source of polluting emissions that have a direct and indirect impact on many environmental receptors (human beings, buildings, climate, etc.). The pollution caused by transport is important especially in urban areas. This can be explained by the combined presence of a large number of pollution sources (different modes of transport and heating systems) on the one hand, and a high concentration of receptors (people and buildings) on the other.

Studies carried out under the auspices of the European ExternE project [2, 3], assessing the external costs of both the energy and the transport sector, have shown that emissions from road transport have very important local effects. The yearly effect of transport in the Brussels Capital Region is estimated by the CEESE [4] at €774 million.

One of the measures to improve the air quality – whether on the local, regional or global level – as well as to diminish noise exposure and to reduce energy consumption, involves the introduction of new technologies into fleets of road vehicles. New technologies (such as advanced engines, management systems, tailpipe emissions clean-up devices, etc.) are emerging as a result of more demanding emission directives imposed on conventional petrol and diesel vehicles.

Driving systems such as fuel-cell powered and hybrid- or battery-powered electric vehicles are worthwhile alternatives. Also, several different fuels (LPG, CNG, alcohols, biodiesel, hydrogen, etc.) are being considered as possible fuel options for the future.

The introduction of clean innovative vehicle technologies, which can contribute to a large reduction of harmful exhaust gases, would facilitate the achievement of the Kyoto objectives (GHG emissions abatement) for Belgium and other countries. Other advantages offered by the introduction of clean innovative vehicle technologies are the reduction of energy reliance on fossil fuels and the shift towards the adoption of a sustainable development in the field of transport.

Both decision-makers and consumers are confronted with a difficult choice when dealing with vehicles that are not yet spread on a large scale. Reasons for this are the lack of appropriate information on available techniques, their cost, their environmental impacts, and the compulsory infrastructure (e.g. refuelling stations or battery charging stations).

A Brussels 'Air' ordinance [5], stipulates that in the coming five years at least 20 per cent of the vehicles belonging to institutions and administrative services under the Brussels Capital Region supervision will have to be 'clean', but the remaining question is: 'What are Clean Vehicles?'

In this respect the Brussels Capital Region commissioned a study entitled

'Clean Vehicles' via the Brussels Institute for the Management of the Environment (BIME). The Vrije Universiteit Brussel (ETEC) and the Université Libre de Bruxelles (CEESE) carried out a joint study programme. Some of the results of the 500-page final report [6] will be highlighted in this paper. The results of the study are also used for a new ordinance published in the official journal of Belgium [7].

New research projects are commissioned by the Flemish government with the aim to compare the Ecoscore methodology with the European Cleaner Drive project [8] and to evaluate the usability of the developed Ecoscore in order to apply policy instruments (taxation, incentives, awareness raising campaigns, etc.) favouring cleaner vehicles [9].

2 Methodology

A number of projects have focused on the problem of establishing an environmental indicator adapted to all road vehicles. This is, for example, the matter of the list of 'clean vehicles' developed by the 'Verkehrsclub Deutschland' [10] and used in Germany, Switzerland, and Austria; the 'Green Book' edited in the USA by ACEEE [11] or the 'Ecolabelling' carried out for the Flemish Region [12] as well as the European Cleaner Drive project [8].

The methodology presented in this paper is based on a Life Cycle Assessment (LCA) approach which defines an approach to decision-making or to a method for the structuring and aggregation of environmental and economic effects. This approach not only enables the associated effects to be ordered at the different stages in the life of a product or a service but also provides an aggregation system in the assessment of the overall balance of the product or service.

LCA has undergone numerous developments in recent years [13]. It has the advantage of being standardised (ISO 14040 Series), and in particular has already found applications in the case of road vehicles [14, 15, 16]. In these applications, LCA is mostly employed as an analytical environmental tool for industry. The study presented in this paper is more 'consumer oriented' because most of the environmental burdens take place throughout the stage of the vehicle use.

Furthermore, some studies mainly concern a generic vehicle or average production processes which don't facilitate any choice for the consumers. That is the reason why this study develops a methodology for a per-model applicability.

The Ecoscore methodology comprises a 'five-step scheme', similar to that used in LCA of products. These steps are in fact the answers given to the five following questions:

- 'Which pollutant emissions are associated to the vehicle to assess?' (inventory)
- 'Which types of damage are these emissions contributing to?' (classification)
- 'Which values are to be attributed to this damage?' (characterisation)

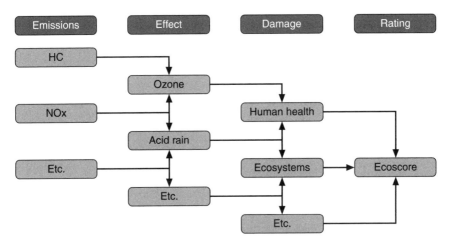

Figure 1.5.1 One single value for the environmental impact rating [1].

• 'Is this damage important in comparison with those of a reference vehicle?' (normalisation)
• 'How important is a type of damage in comparison with another?' (weighting)

Figure 1.5.1 illustrates the methodology resulting in one single end-score.

Emission inventory

To be able to compare alternative vehicle technologies, it is not only necessary to compare direct tailpipe emissions (Tank-to-Wheel), but also the indirect emissions due to fuel refinery or electricity production and distribution (Well-to-Tank).

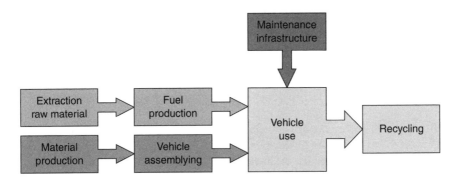

Figure 1.5.2 One 'Cradle-to-Grave' overview [1].

This Well-to-Wheel approach involves tailpipe emissions, oil extraction, transport and refining, fuel distribution, and electricity generation and distribution. Emissions due to the production, use, and dismantling of the vehicle (Cradle-to-Grave approach) are not included in the model due to the 'consumer oriented' approach but also due to the lack of data for each vehicle model.

Tank-to-Wheel direct emissions

Data availability is a very important factor to consider and is usually restricted especially for vehicles using alternative fuels or propulsion systems.

The COPERT/MEET methodology [17, 18] was found not to be adequate enough for all new alternative fuels.

For this reason the Ecoscore methodology is only based on type approval emissions (CO, HC, NOx, and PM) and emissions depending on fuel consumption (CO_2, SO_2). CH_4 is calculated out of the HC emissions and N_2O as a function of CO_2 emissions.

However, in practice, real vehicle emissions are mostly much higher than the emissions measured at the type approval due to ageing, bad engine and catalyst tuning and/or to differences in driving dynamics. In fact, real-life emissions ($E_{real\ life}$) may be two, three or even 30 times higher than those set in the emission directives (E_{reg}) [19].

For a robust model these influences should be taken into account according to function of different vehicle classes and age, etc. Through lack of this detailed information for each vehicle model only type approval data is used and should be seen as an optimistic approach.

Well-to-Tank indirect emissions

Indirect emissions are related to the extraction and transportation of raw materials as well as to the production and transformation and distribution of energies consumed (fuel or electricity). This Well-to-Tank approach is required especially when comparing different alternative fuels and propulsion systems (particularly in the case of electric vehicles), since there can be large differences in the emissions related to the production process of fuels and electricity.

The emissions corresponding to electricity production are a function of the type of power station (nuclear, coal, gas, air wind, hydro, etc.) and the relative share of each power station to the energy consumption. Using an average electricity production mix as a basis seems at first sight to be an acceptable approach. However, electric vehicles can be charged at night, when the main sources of electricity generation are the base stations, which are different from the 'average' power station, the latter also including old power plants and peak units. If the market share of electric vehicles would increase in the next ten years, it is necessary to consider the investment policy of the electricity production companies. The main Belgian electricity company, Electrabel, invests mainly in renewable energy or Combined Cycle Gas Turbine (CCGT) with low emissions and a high level of efficiency (55 per cent). Since 2003 the electricity market in Europe is on the path of a complete deregulation and consumers are already or soon will be able to buy emission-free electricity (Dutch wind energy or Swiss hydro-energy, etc.). Electric vehicles charged with these sources of electricity will consequently be virtually emission-free. However it is very difficult to attribute a particular energy use of an appliance (i.e. an electric vehicle) to one particular power plant. Therefore the average electricity generation mix is used and should be seen as a pessimistic case scenario for electric vehicles.

Table 1.5.1 [18, 20] summarises the indirect emissions for different types of fuel and the Belgian electricity mix. As can be noticed the bio-fuels related emissions are high due to the related agricultural processes. The indirect emissions of CH_4, which is a greenhouse gas, are high in the case of CNG vehicles. Although the indirect emissions related to electricity production seem to be high, electric vehicles have no tailpipe emissions as is the case for the other types of vehicles. Emissions due to electricity generation decreased considerably the last five to ten years (see Table 1.5.1). The energy used per km for non-electric vehicles can be calculated from the fuel consumption (FC) and the energy content of the fuel. The consumption of electric vehicles is often expressed directly in kWh/km. The indirect emission can easily be calculated on the basis of this energy consumption and Table 1.5.1.

Since refinery plants and power stations are mainly located far away from densely populated areas, their effects on human health are inferior to the effects of direct tailpipe emissions (cf. difference in the dispersion ways). One gram of particulate matter (PM) emitted by a diesel car in a crowded city will be markedly more harmful to human health than one gram of particulate matter

Table 1.5.1 Indirect emissions for Belgium (mg/kWh)

	CO	NMHC	CH₄	NOx	PM	CO₂	SO₂
Reference	18.4	761.4	62.6	151.9	8.6	33 100	236.2
Petrol	18.4	761.4	62.6	151.9	8.6	33 100	236.2
Diesel	16.6	315.4	56.5	129.6	3.6	24 500	174.2
Bio-fuel	493.2	280.4		871.9	66.6	108 700	245.5
CNG	5	99	805.3	38.2	2.9	14 800	60.8
LPG	14.8	202.7	58	116.3	5.4	21 600	114.1
Electricity Renewable	0	0	0	0	0	0	0
Electricity Belgian Mix 2001	60.1*	44*	1.75	440	36	290 000	420
Electricity CCGT 1995	78	129	266	495	0	447 500	0
Electricity Belgian Mix 1995	60.1	44	865	1041.8	97.9	339 500	1920

Note
* No new data available, data of MEET 1995 are used.

emitted out of a chimney far away from the residents. To take this into account in calculating the total emissions related to health effects, some references such as [11] introduce a weighting factor (e.g. 50 per cent). See equation [1].

$$E_{total} = E_{direct} + w_{ind.} \cdot E_{indirect} \qquad\qquad [1]$$

The following factors were selected on the basis of a specific study on damage to buildings in the Brussels Capital region [4], in which emissions dispersion calculations and exposure-response assessments were carried out: 1 for HCs and NOx; to 0.4 for SO_2; to 0.1 for CO and particles. Contrary to health effects, no weighting is authorised for overall damage like global warming since every gram of CO_2 makes the same contribution to this effect.

Noise pollution

In the Brussels Capital region 28 per cent of the inhabitants are exposed to sound levels higher than 65 dB(A). The WHO considers that a daytime sound level of 50 dB(A) $L_{Aeq,8h}$ is irritating. On the basis of an enquiry 43 per cent of the population judges the noise caused by traffic to be too high [21].

Classification

The second stage of the 'Ecoscore' methodology consists in classifying the different emissions assessed according the categor(y)(ies) of damage to which they contribute.

As already mentioned only type approval and fuel consumption depending emissions are considered (see Table 1.5.3).

Table 1.5.2 Classification of the studied atmospheric pollutants per category of damage

Effects	Pollutants
Human health	
Carcinogenic effects	VOC (1,3 Butadiene; Formaldehyde; HAP (Benzo(a)pyrene; Benzo(a)anthracene; Dibenzo(a)anthracene)
Respiratory effects (organic components)	VOC (NMVOC; methane)
Respiratory effects (inorganic components)	CO, Particles, TSP (Total Suspended Particles), NOx (in NO_2 equ.), SO_2
Greenhouse effect	CO_2, CH_4, N_2O
Eco-systems	
Ecotoxicity	VOC (Benzene; Toluene); HAP
Acidification	NOx (in NO_2 equ.), SO_2
Buildings	Particles (PM10), SO_2
Noise	Noise [in dB(A)]

Table 1.5.3 Characterisation and classification of different effects and damages

Damage categories	Emission	Unit	Contribution damage factors
Global Warming	CO_2	GWP	1
	CH_4	GWP	23
	N_2O	GWP	296
Respiration and Cancer	HC	Daly/kg	6.46E-07
	NOx	Daly/kg	8.87E-05
	CO	Daly/kg	7.31E-07
	PM	Daly/kg	9.78E-06
Acidification	NOx	PDF.m².y/kg	5.713
	SO_2	PDF.m².y/kg	1.04
Buildings	SO_2	€/kg	8.3
	PM	€/kg	259
Noise			1

Characterisation

The next step of the assessment consists of calculating the contribution rate of the incriminated pollutants in each category of damage.

To evaluate the damage rate in each category, the calculated level of emissions, expressed in [g/km] or in [g/kWh], is multiplied by a damage factor $\delta_{i,j}$ (see equation [2]):

$$D_{i,j} = \delta_{i,j} \cdot E_{j,total} \qquad [2]$$

where:
- $D_{i,j}$: the partial damage of the category i, associated to the pollutant j;
- $\delta_{i,j}$: the damage factor of the category i, linked to the pollutant j;
- $E_{j,total}$: the total emissions due to pollutant j.

The damage factors δ_{ij} are illustrated in Table 1.5.3.

For each category of damage, the factors δ_{ij} have representative units:

- Damage of greenhouse gas emissions (in CO_2-equivalent) is expressed in Global Warming Potential (GWP).
- The deterioration cost of buildings is expressed in €/kg [4].
- The noise pollution is expressed in dB(A).
- Damage from acidification and eutrophication are characterised by observing their effects on plants. From these observations the probability to find a specific plant in the area studied can be determined. This is called the Probability Of Occurrence (POO), which can also be translated into Potentially Disappeared Fraction (PDF = 1-POO). For a certain period of time and a definite region, damage from acidification and eutrophication is expressed in PDF·m²·yr [22].

- Damage analysis links health effects to DALYs (Disability Adjusted Life Years), using estimates of the number of Years Lived Disabled (YLD) and Years of Life Lost (YLL). The core of the DALY system is a disability weighting scale. The scale lists many different disabilities and scores them between 0 and 1 (0 meaning being perfectly healthy and 1 meaning death).[1] This system allows calculating the number of DALY if one knows how many people in the area studied, Europe for instance, are exposed to a certain background concentration of toxic substances in air, drinking water, and food [22].

The total damage Q_i of a given damage category i is obtained by adding partial damage $D_{i,j}$ related to every single concerned pollutant.

$$Q_i = \sum_j D_{i,j}$$ [3]

The damage factors are characterised by uncertainties. In order to cope with these uncertainties a balanced time perspective (Hierarchist) is chosen for the human health damage and the damage to ecosystems, as described in the Eco-Indicator 99 methodology [22]. This Hierarchist perspective results from a consensus among scientists which determines inclusion of effects. The perspective lies between a long-time perspective (Egalitarian: even a minimum of scientific proof justifies inclusion) and a short-time perspective (Individualist: only proven effects are included).

The calculation of a GWP is based on the radiative efficiency (heat-absorbing ability) of the gas relative to the radiative efficiency of the reference gas (carbon dioxide), as well as the removal process (or decay rate) for the gas relative to the reference gas over a specified time horizon. Also in calculating GWPs there are elements of uncertainty. The radiative efficiencies of greenhouse gases do not necessarily stay constant over time (as calculated in GWPs). The lifetime of a greenhouse gas (used in GWP calculations), particularly carbon dioxide, is also subject to uncertainty. Various natural processes cause many greenhouse gases to decompose into other gases or to be absorbed by the ocean or the ground. For the purposes of calculating 'CO_2 equivalent' units for this research, 100-year GWPs are used [23].

Normalisation

By normalising the damage of each category it becomes possible to compare damage caused by the vehicle to be assessed with a reference case and to determine what type of important or, on the contrary, restricted effects this vehicle can have.

The normalised damage is calculated for every category of damage i, on the basis of equation [4]:

$$q_i = \frac{Q_i}{Q_{i,ref}}$$ [4]

where:

- q_i: the normalised damage of category i;
- Q_i: the damage of category i associated to the vehicle to be assessed;
- $Q_{i,ref}$: the damage of category i associated to a vehicle of reference.

As reference, the damage associated with an imaginary passenger car corresponding to the Standard Euro IV for petrol vehicles is considered. For light duty vehicles the reference values correspond to the Standard Euro IV required for medium-sized diesel cars (1305–1760 kg).

For CO_2 emissions the value of 120 g/km is taken as reference for passenger cars, as this value is the objective the automobile industry, ACEA, has accepted to aim at in the European Union. The indirect emissions can also be calculated from these target values since they are proportional to the fuel consumption and consequently to CO_2 emissions.

For SO_2 emissions, the reference level is based on the content of 50 ppm of sulphur in the petrol or diesel forecasted from 2005 on.

A level of 70 dB(A) has been chosen as a reference.

Weighting

The final step of the methodology consists of weighting the normalised damage before adding them to an environmental score or rating.

$$Rating = \Sigma \alpha_i \cdot q_i \qquad [5]$$

With:

- q_i: the normalised damage of category i;
- α_i: the weighting factor of the damage of category i.

This is a feature of the methodology that allows giving more weight to issues that decision-makers prefer to be more essential than others.

The weighting procedure is executed based on a stakeholder expert panel procedure. Starting from other weighting systems (e.g.: IFEU [10], Green Car [11], and Ecolabel [12]) a proposal for the weighting factors has been formulated by the research consortium in close collaboration with the expert group.

A specific weighting system for the Brussels Capital Region seems to be required, given the specificity of this largely urbanised region where environmental priorities can diverge very much from those of a country or a continent.

In terms of weighting, the 'Ecoscore' is very much concerned with the effects on health: they account for some 50 per cent of the total which is comparable to the other weighting systems, except for the IFEU model [10].

The effects linked to the climate change are granted with as much as 25 per cent. This weight seems lower than in other models such as the Green Car [11], the IFEU [10] or Ecolabel [12] that gave a weight of more than 40 per cent to this item. This difference results in fact from the specificity of the 'Clean vehicle' study that is made in an urban context.

The remaining 25 per cent are distributed among the effects on ecosystems (10 per cent), the noise pollution (10 per cent), and damage to buildings (5 per cent).

Transparent results

For communication use to the general public the results of the above-described scientific model are converted to an easy to understand number. The results of the above-described methodology equals zero when there are no emissions and turns out to be very high, up to 700 and more, the higher the emission of the considered vehicle are. For communication purposes the rating is transformed to a score between 0 and 100, where zero means an infinitely polluting vehicle (worst) and 100 indicates an emission free vehicle (best). This approach yields no negative scores since these would be quite confusing for the general public. This conversion can be done with equation [6]

- Rating $= 0$ $\rightarrow 100$
- Rating $= 100$ $\rightarrow 50$
- Rating $=$ infinitive $\rightarrow 0$

$$EcoScore = 100e^{-0,0069.Rating} \qquad\qquad [6]$$

3 Results

To illustrate the methodology some examples are calculated. Cars with different fuel types and propulsion systems were selected. Various engine capacities and vehicle sizes were evaluated to have an idea of the best and worst vehicles.

The Ecoscore of 24 different vehicles is represented in Figure 1.5.3 and compared with the reference vehicle which has an Ecoscore of 50 (dashed line). Light shaded columns (on the left) indicates a good environmental score and dark shaded columns (on the right) corresponds to high polluting cars.

In a Brussels context (Belgium), a good environmental impact rating (Ecoscore) can be seen for the electric car (Peugeot 106 electric) in comparison with other technologies. Also hybrid-petrol, CNG and LPG vehicles have good Ecoscore and are mostly better than the reference vehicle (EURO IV). Most petrol and diesel vehicles examined cannot be considered as clean (in comparison with the reference) since they have a lower Ecoscore than the reference vehicle. Small and light petrol vehicles score well due to their low fuel consumption. The Ecoscore of 'conventional' EURO IV vehicles is much better than EURO III vehicles. Due to the high NOx and PM emissions in comparison with petrol vehicles, diesel vehicles have bad Ecoscore. The worst scores (out of 2000 evaluated EURO III vehicles) match up to heavy vehicles with large engine capacities.

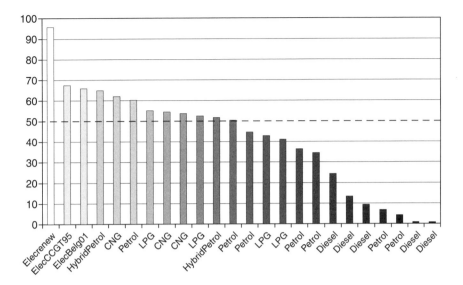

Figure 1.5.3 Some examples of the converted Ecoscore screening (Belgium–Brussels situation).

If these results are examined in more detail by evaluating the distinguished types of damage, the following conclusions can be formulated. In general, due to their highly efficient propulsion system, electric, hybrid, and diesel powered vehicles contribute less to global warming than CNG, LPG, and petrol driven vehicles. Concerning health damage, the diesel vehicles have a very bad effect (due to high NOx and PM emissions), and CNG vehicles score best. Electric, hybrid and LPG vehicles also have a very good health score. In the case of acidification, NOx emissions bring the diesel vehicles into very bad position and their PM emissions contribute greatly to the damage of buildings. In the future new NOx clean-up devices and PM filters may bring down the damage to health of diesel vehicles. Noise pollution is very low in the case of electric and hybrid vehicles.

4 Sensitivity analysis

To be able to validate the robustness of the model a sensitivity analysis was carried out. This analysis is very important due to the fact that the data used to calculate the Ecoscore are characterised by uncertainties as well as variations (e.g. real life emissions versus type approval emissions).

Influence of the characterisation

The most interesting sensitivity analysis is the influence of the value of each pollutant on the resulting Ecoscore. This was achieved by doubling the

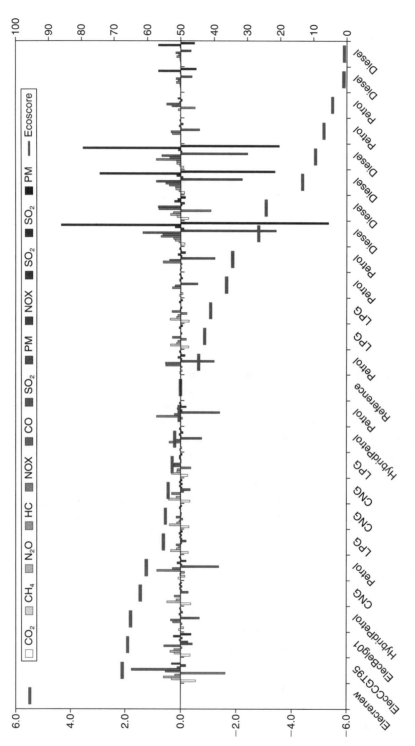

Figure 1.5.4 Influence of the characterisation.

contribution of each individual pollutant and calculating the difference on the Ecoscore.

In Figure 1.5.4 the right vertical axis indicates the value of the Ecoscore (marked with a flat line). The left vertical axis indicates the difference on the Ecoscore caused by the doubling of the respective contribution of the pollutant (marked with a column).

The value of the left axis should be added or subtracted from the Ecoscore result on the right axis (remark: different scales) to find the new Ecoscore when doubling the contribution of a pollutant.

One can conclude that a doubling of the contribution has no significant influence on the final ranking of the evaluated vehicles. For certain diesel vehicles the influence becomes noticeable for PM and SO_2 emissions.

Influence of the ω_{ind} factor

The influence of the ω_{ind} factor (see equation [1]) on the end result was evaluated by comparing the methodology as described above with the results obtained by treating the direct and indirect emissions equally ($\omega_{ind} = 1$).

Figure 1.5.5 shows that there is no significant influence on the comparison between the different vehicle types. Nevertheless one can see that the Ecoscore for all diesel vehicles has become better (increased). This can be explained by the greater proportion of direct emissions of a diesel compared with other types, in the Ecoscore methodology.

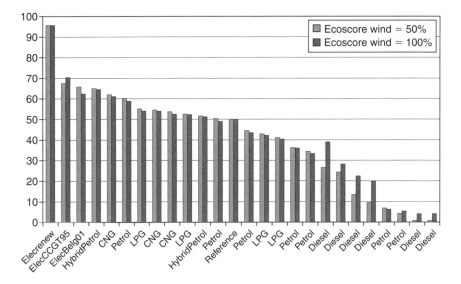

Figure 1.5.5 The influence of the ω_{ind} factor.

Influence weighting system

To assess the influence of the weighting system chosen by the expert panel the Ecoscore is calculated when each category of damage contributes for 100 per cent. Figure 1.5.6 illustrates the results when respectively only global warming should be assessed, only health effects, only the damage to ecosystems, only the damage to buildings, and only noise is taken into account. The new Ecoscore is compared with the Ecoscore when all the damage categories are considered and weighted on the basis of the weighting system as described above. When only taking into account global warming, diesel vehicles receive much better environmental rating, due to their lower CO_2 emissions, and vice versa, when comparing health damage.

5 Discussion

Adaptation of the methodology to heavy vehicles

The Ecoscore methodology had to be adapted before it could be used to evaluate the environmental damage of heavy duty vehicles and buses. Type approval tests for heavy vehicles are based on consumption and emission tests of the engine and not of the vehicles.

For this reason the model was changed: direct and indirect emissions of heavy vehicles were evaluated separately following the 'Ecoscore' approach. Within some damage categories emission data of engines are expressed in g/kWh, whereas emissions linked to vehicles are expressed in g/km. The two

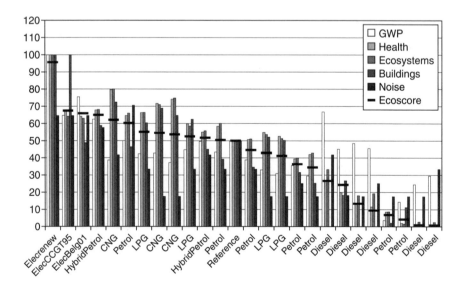

Figure 1.5.6 Influence of the weighting of effects.

different scores were then integrated into one single score by weighting the score related to indirect emissions with the ω_{ind} factor.

Potential improvements

At its current stage of development, the Ecoscore ignores real traffic conditions (driver behaviour, impact of traffic circulation measures (e.g. roundabouts)).

Concerning the methodology, the study might, in the future, extend the LCA to production and recycling of vehicles (Cradle-to-Grave).

On a practical point, the 'Ecoscore' methodology applied to 'conventional' vehicles is based on emission levels identified in approval tests, while for vehicles 'newly developed' (e.g. some vehicles running on CNG, electric and hybrid vehicles, and vehicles with fuel cells) it is sometimes based on real data resulting from practical tests. It is clear that data collected from standardised tests should not be compared to data from real traffic, otherwise the methodology could become biased in favour of the technologies already available on the market.

The current database does not include fuel-cell vehicles. Policy-makers and the vehicle industry have high expectations of fuel-cell powered vehicles to reduce (or eventually solve) the environmental problems of the transport sector (and in the long term also the dependency on fossil fuels). However, given the goal (and horizon) of the research project on which this paper is based, fuel-cell vehicles have not been included. Additionally many hydrogen production pathways are being investigated at the moment. Currently it is not possible to define the corresponding Well-to-Tank emissions for all required pollutants in the model. When data will become available, the model can easily be extended to fuel-cell vehicles.

Finally it would be interesting to include noise in the Well-to-Tank analysis. In this article, under the heading 'Noise pollution', noise is only considered from the vehicle and not from the fuel production process.

Context of the analysis and further work

To meet the administrative requirements of the Brussels Capital Region, the 'Ecoscore' has been completed by a technical and economic analysis of vehicles, in order to include into the study important aspects such as refuelling, range, or eventual additional costs linked to the choice of a clean vehicle.

Thanks to this complementary analysis, the 'Ecoscore' could be resituated in a more practical context in order to help the consumer in choosing a suitable clean vehicle.

An improved 'Sustainable transport score' should integrate the following interdisciplinary aspects:

• an analytical approach of the environmental Life Cycle Assessment (LCA), with particular attention devoted to improving the assessment of the environmental impact of road transport on ecosystems and biodiversity;

- a conventional economic assessment (costs, public economic incentives or taxes, externalities, etc.);
- market research methodologies (interviews, focus groups, survey, conjoint analysis, and stakeholders panels).

The economic and socio-economic aspects will be incorporated with the environmental LCA in order to have a set of three complementary scores (a 'Socioscore', an 'Ecoscore', and an 'Econoscore'). These scores will then be expressed in a 'sustainable transport score', complemented by a qualitative assessment taking into account factors that cannot be expressed through quantitative figures only.

6 Conclusions

The proposed methodology is based on the development of an indicator that allows assessing, on a scientific and adjustable basis, the environmental damage caused by individual vehicles, whatever their type, their mode of propulsion or their energy use.

This approach is still modest in comparison with what might be done theoretically but it meets different constraints such as, for example, working with currently available data or having comparable results for different vehicles of a same category.

As for the weighting of the different damage categories considered, this methodology is focused in particular on nuisance occurring in urban areas by allocating greater weight factors to health effects.

From a practical viewpoint, the 'Ecoscore' indicator makes it possible to compare the different available vehicles on the (Belgian) market and to define an adequate policy for the acquisition of future vehicle fleets.

Finally on the basis of the sensitivity analysis, one can conclude that the proposed methodology is sufficiently robust for variations of the relative contribution of each specific pollutant.

Acknowledgements

This article is based on the 'Clean vehicles' research project [6] jointly developed by the 'Université Libre de Bruxelles (CEESE)' and the 'Vrije Universiteit Brussel (ETEC)' on behalf of the Brussels Capital Region via the 'Institut Bruxellois pour la Gestion de l'Environnement (IBGE)'.

Notes

* Vrije Universiteit Brussel, ETEC-tw-VUB, Pleinlaan 2, 1050 Brussels, Belgium, joeri.van.mierlo@vub.ac.be.
** Univ. Libre de Bruxelles, CEESE-ULB, av. Jeanne 44 CP 124, 1050 Brussels, Belgium.
1 Example: Carcinogenic substances cause a number of deaths each year. In the DALY

health scale, death has a disability rating of 1. If a type of cancer is (on average) fatal 10 years prior to the normal life expectancy, one counts 10 lost life years for each case. This means that each case has a value of 10 DALYs.

During a summer smog period, many people have to be treated in hospital for a number of days. This type of treatment in a hospital has a rating of 0.392 on the DALY scale. If the hospital treatment lasts 0.01 years on average (3.65 days), each case is weighted 0.004 DALYs.

References

[1] Van Mierlo, J., Maggetto, G., Vereecken, L., Favrel, V., Meyer, S., and Hecq, W. (2003) 'Comparison of the environmental damage caused by vehicles with different alternative fuels and drive trains in a Brussels context' Proceedings of the Institution of Mechanical Engineers Part D – *Journal of Automobile Engineering*, I MECH E, SAE and IEE, isnn 0954-4070.

[2] European Commission, Directorate-General XII, Science, Research and Development, JOULE (1995) 'Externalities of Fuel Cycles 'ExternE' Project. Report number 2, Methodology', EUR16521, Luxembourg.

[3] European Commission, Directorate-General XII, Science, Research and Development, JOULE (1998) 'Externalities of Fuel Cycles "ExternE" Project. Report number 7, Methodology, 1998 update', EUR16521, Luxembourg, 518 pp.

[4] Favrel, V., Pons, T., Maréchal, K., Claeys, P., Ferdinand, C., and Hecq, W. (2001) 'Mobilité durable en Région bruxelloise: Analyse des impacts sur l'environnement – Evaluation des externalités physiques et monétaires', final report, SSTC MDDD012, Centre d'Etudes Economiques et Sociales de l'Environnement, Université Libre de Bruxelles, Aug. 2001, 68 pp. + Annexes.

[5] Ch. Picque, Minister-President, Article 22 of the Ordinance of March 25 1999 of the Brussels Capital Region concerning the evaluation and improvement of the quality of the air (published in the Official Journal 24.06.1999) pp. 23861–23868.

[6] Van Mierlo, J., Favrel, V., Meyer, S., Vereecken L., et al. (2001) 'Schone Voertuigen (Clean Vehicles)', Final report, VUB-ETEC, ULB-CEESE, 500 pp.

[7] Article of the Official Journal of Belgium, MONITEUR BELGE – BELGISCH STAATSBLAD of 26.09.2003, [C – 2003/31374] N. 2003–3728, 2nd edn; pp. 47484–47493.

[8] Hill, N., Haydock, H., and Saynor, B., 'Cleaner Drive – Development of an EU environmental rating methodology', AEA Technology, UK, http://www.cleaner-drive.com/, July 2002.

[9] Van Mierlo, J., Timmermans, J.-M., et al. 'Bepalen van een EcoScore voor voertuigen en toepassing van deze EcoScore ter bevordering van het gebruik van milieuvriendelijke voertuigen', AMINAL project.

[10] Auto-Umweltliste 1999/2000, VCD, Bonn, 1999.

[11] DeCicco, J., Thomas, M., and Kliesch, J. (2000) 'ACEEE's Green Book', Washington, 2000, 61 pp.

[12] Govaert, L. (2001) 'Emissielabelling nieuwe personenwagens', Final report, VITO, AMINAL project, 2001/ETE/R/056, juli 2001, 23 pp.

[13] Consoli, F., et al. (1993) 'Guidelines for Life-Cycle Assessment: a "Code of Practice"', SETAC, pp. 51–54.

[14] Lewis, C.A. and Gover, M.P. (1995) 'Life Cycle Analysis of motor fuel emissions',

European Commission, Proceedings of the workshop on 27–28 November 1995 at ULB-Brussels, 14 pp.

[15] Davison, P. (1999), 'Life-cycle emission analysis of fuel use', European Commission, Transport Research COST 319.

[16] Nicolay S., *et al.* (2000) 'A simplified LCA for automotive sector: comparison of ICE (diesel and petrol), electric and hybrid vehicles', SETAC, 8th LCA Symposium for Case Studies, Brussels, pp. 97–105.

[17] Keller, M. and de Haan, P., 'Intermodal Comparisons Of Atmospheric Pollutant Emissions', MEET project, deliverable no. 24, EC Contract No. ST-96-SC.204, INFRAS, Berne, Switzerland, October 1998.

[18] Joumard, R. (1999) 'Methods Of Estimation Of Atmospheric Emissions From Transport: European Scientist Network And Scientific State-Of-The-Art', Final report, LTE 9901 report, action COST 319, Institut National de Recherche sur les Transports et leur Sécurité (INRETS), France, March 1999, 83 pp.

[19] Van Mierlo, J., Van de Burgwal, E., *et al.* (2002) 'Invloed van het rijgedrag op de verkeersemissies: kwantificatie en maatregelen', Vrije Universiteit Brussel, TNO, AMINAL project.

[20] Becquaert, A. 'Productie Milieurapport 2001', Electrabel, mei 2002.

[21] BIM (1998) 'De strijd tegen geluidshinder in een stedelijke omgeving voor het Brussels Hoofdstedelijk Gewest'.

[22] Goedkoop, M. and Spriensma, R. (2000) 'The Eco-Indicator 99, A damage oriented method for Life Cycle Impact Assessment, Methodology report', PRé Consultants, 2nd edn, 103 pp. + Annexes; April 2000, 103 pp. + appendices.

[23] Intergovernmental Panel on Climate Change, Climate Change 2001: The Scientific Basis. Summary for Policy-makers (Cambridge, UK:Cambridge University Press, 2001).

Part II

Regulation and policies to stimulate better performance

2.1 Is the debate over the contestability of airline markets really dead?

Kenneth Button

*

Introduction

The liberalisation of the US domestic air-freight market in 1977, and the more well-known liberalisation of the US domestic passenger market the following year, attracted considerable academic attention. The move from a highly regulated industry to one characterised by essentially free entry and exit provided economists with a rare chance to study a dramatic transformation in market conditions that would not be excessively muddied by other policy changes.[1] Since that time there have been other regulatory reforms that have offered somewhat similar opportunities, but analysis has often been clouded by reforms being staggered over a large number of years, as in the case of the European Union, or only applying to a relatively small market, as with New Zealand and Australia.

The timing of the liberalisation of the US market was largely motivated by the macroeconomic need to bring prices down in an inflationary economy where unemployment was high and conventional Keynesian and monetarist policies provided only conflicting economic recommendations. They were the days of 'stagflation'. The position that deregulation would lower the costs of air travel was premised on the intellectual arguments that the rate-of-return controls of the time had largely been captured by the airline industry. This was leading to X-inefficiency and rent seeking by those supplying inputs into the industry (e.g. labour). The line of argument was supported by empirical evidence of lower fares under more liberalised conditions gleaned from comparing intra-state unregulated fares with inter-state regulated fares on similar types of route.

The notion put forward at the time by some members of the Civil Aeronautics Board (CAB) overseeing regulatory policy was that a free market would naturally be broadly contestable, and thus not in need of regulation. This was not, however, a position held by all members. Indeed, retrospective observations by its Chair at the time of deregulation, Alfred Kahn (1988), highlight the role that he felt conventional competitive pressures would play in the absence of significant economic regulation. Indeed, he felt that some residual controls may be needed to limit potential oligopoly distortions.

The idea of contestability, essentially the power of potential market entry, and *de facto* latent competition, to limit the rent seeking or X-inefficiency tendencies of incumbents in the market, however, did play a significant role in several subsequent deregulatory debates. It, for example, was a frequently cited justification for the deregulation that took place in many European countries, and the term regularly appeared in arguments for market liberalisation within the larger European Union structure. The linked notion of competing 'for' markets rather than 'within' markets is the foundation for many current subsidisation systems, and for the spectrum auctions that have taken place in the communications field.

William Baumol's Presidential Address to the American Economic Association, and the subsequent publication of *Contestable Markets and the Theory of Industry Structure* (Baumol *et al.*, 1982), brought the concept of potential competition to the fore with a bang. However, the 'uprising in industry theory' that some felt the development of contestable market concepts heralded (Baumol, 1982) has somewhat petered out.[2] This is perhaps most pronounced with regard to the air transport industry where it initially attracted considerable academic attention and public policy debate.

Initially there was some evidence of contestable forces at play in the US airline market. Early supporters of the importance of contestability forces pointed to how, after deregulation, actors seemed to be following a path broadly in line with what they had predicted (Bailey and Panzar, 1981). They pointed out that, 'in some ways the airline industry presents a particularly close approximation to contestability' (Bailey and Baumol, 1984: 128).

But by the mid-1980s, this position had been tempered. Indeed, in a retrospective written only four years after the publication of the primary text on the subject, its authors came to the conclusion 'We now believe that transportation by trucks, barges and even buses may be more contestable than passenger air transportation' (Baumol and Willig, 1986: 24). And those who never enthused about the airline industry being inherently contestable were content to reflect that 'airline competition can be explained well by established concepts of market structure and entry' (Shepherd, 1984: 585).

The objective here is to look back on what has happened in air transportation markets in the years since the domestic deregulation in the US, with something of a focus on the European situation. It seeks to see just how useful the idea of contestable markets is in explaining the functioning of the current airline market, and whether there are valid insights to be gained from ideas of external competition in the construction and implementation of air transportation policies. It basically asks whether it is time to take down again the yellow and crisp pages[3] of *Contestable Markets and the Theory of Industry Structure*, or to leave them to decay on the bookshelf. In other words, to see if the concept of contestability is simply an intellectual curiosum, or whether its advocates were seers ahead of their time.

Contestable markets: an aide-mémoire

The concept of contestable markets can be traced back in spirit, if not in name, to the work of the nineteenth century English economist Edwin Chadwick

(1859). He drew attention to the possibility of competition for the market as well as competition in the market. In other words, those who already supply goods or service do not just consider those in direct competition with them at the time but also the possibility of new suppliers emerging to challenge them. But it was not until 1981 when, in his Presidential Address to the American Economics Association, William Baumol (1982) sought to shift the focus of thinking about industrial structure away from concern with internal competition to the matter of external competition, that it gained a major hold on academic thinking. Or at least there was a major debate about the subject.

Much of traditional anti-trust and industrial regulatory policy of the early part of the twentieth century had, following in the traditions of Alfred Marshall, focused on degrees of actual competition in markets. Concentration ratios, and then the Hiefindahl-Hirshman index, reigned supreme in anti-trust cases as well as the confines of academic libraries. It is only comparatively recently that any significant interest has been taken in matters of barriers to entry (most notably by Bain, 1956), and even later in notions of barriers to exit (Caves and Porter, 1976) and in mobility among parts of the market (Caves and Porter, 1977). These elements of theory, while gaining a limited academic audience, did not really permeate mainstream thinking amongst industrial organisation experts, or anti-trust debates, and certainly were seen as largely peripheral to economic policy-making and legal rulings.

The interest in the role of ultra-free market entry that emerged in the 1980s stemmed in part from a growth in the influence of the Chicago School of economists. This saw virtue in all forms of competition as a natural mechanism to limit monopoly exploitation, and also saw major dangers of capture by administrators, or by the 'regulated industry', in institutional regulation.[4] The difficulties inherent in applying the regulatory tools of the day, combined with empirical evidence that welfare objectives were not being achieved, only helped efforts to seek a less interventionist approach. But it was also a time of significant structural change in many economies as service industries grew in significance. Many of these were network industries. There was an emerging appreciation that these types of industry may have somewhat different features to most of those that had been the initial subject of economic regulation (Economides, 1996).

The idea of potential competition playing a more powerful role than had previously been thought, therefore, came at an opportune time when there was concern over the traditional public interest approach to regulation, both in terms of the usefulness of the instruments used and in terms of its objectivity. In particular, contestability theory allows a move away from simply assuming that a strong market presence is the same as market power.

In terms of strict definitions Baumol and Willig (1986: 9) state:

> We define a perfectly contestable market as one that is accessible to potential entrants and has the following two properties: First, the potential entrant can, without restriction, serve the same market demands and use the same productive techniques as those available to the incumbent firms . . . Second

the potential entrants evaluate the profitability of entry at the incumbent firms' pre-entry prices.

One can consider the implications of these features in terms of a comparison with perfect competition and monopoly. Table 2.1.1 sets out some of the main differences between the straw-man of perfect contestability, and perfect competition and monopoly. As can be seen, one implication is that perfect competition is a singular case of perfect contestability.[5] It is when all of the potential competition is actually within the market.

Just as perfect competition is seen as a benchmark in many cases, as well as being a descriptive approximation, in others perfect contestability serves a similar role. The outcome of perfect contestability is identical to that of a perfectly competitive market with welfare maximisation attained – Pareto conditions are met. This strong form of the concept, however, is also partnered with weak contestability. This imperfect form of contestability involves a market structure that is approaching that of perfect competition but not all conditions are met. In some ways it is akin to Bain's concept of workable competition in that in a regulatory sense, while it does not optimise a situation, it is preferable to attempting to go further through government intervention.[6]

The driving force towards an incumbent offering lower prices in a contestable environment is the fear of hit-and-run entry rather than competition per se. If there are no scale effects this leads to marginal cost pricing – the standard Pareto outcome. Where there are scale economies, the incumbent must set a price equal to the intersection of the market demand curve and average cost to deter hit-and-run entry and to maximise welfare subject to a budget constraint. This, however, raises potential problems of market stability as discussed later.

The implication of this is that the aim of utility maximising regulators should be to adopt policies that enhance contestability through facilitating ease of market entry and exit where there are few sunk costs. But it also means that there may be a need to develop strategies to deal with situations where there are

Table 2.1.1 Competitive, contestable, and monopoly markets

Feature	Perfect competition	Perfectly contestable	Monopoly
Profit maximisation	Yes	Yes	Normally
No barriers to entry/exit	Yes	Yes	No
Perfect mobility of inputs	Yes	Yes	No
Ubiquitous information	Yes	Yes	No
Large number of firms	Yes	Maybe	No
Homogeneous product	Yes	Maybe	Yes
Firms confronted by same cost functions	Yes	Yes	Yes
U-shaped average cost functions	Yes	Maybe	Maybe
Profits	Normal	Normal	Monopoly rent

sunk costs involved – e.g. through competition for the market in the form of leases and auctions. The latter situation has attracted a lot of attention in fields such as communications and energy where traditional rate-of-return regulations of monopolies or public ownership have been replaced in many countries by periodic auctions for the right to supply. The academic literature on optimal auction theory has enjoyed a marked resurgence since Baumol set out his ideas on contestability. One of these strands has to do with the allocation of airport landing and take-off slots but this is not explored here.

Looking back on the theoretical debates

The publication of *Contestable Markets and the Theory of Industry Structure* was accompanied by a series of detailed critiques and evaluations. Many of these papers were review articles in the premier academic economics journals, and by leading microeconomists (including a number who subsequently were awarded Nobel Prizes) and industrial organisation specialists. These in turn brought forth a series of complementary papers offering refinements and extension of contestability concepts as well as rebuttals (e.g. Baumol *et al.*, 1983). It is not easy to offer a blow-by-blow account of the debates. Indeed, it is well beyond the aim and needs of this paper to do so. Rather a number of brief comments are offered on some of the developments in the theory that took place in the 1980s, and then this is followed by considering some of the difficulties and questions that have been posed by those who are less than convinced. There is no claim of completeness[7] and there is an inevitable blurring of the material at times.

Refinements to the theory

The 1980s spawned an industry of writing about various forms of contestability, and of empirical and simulation studies seeking markets that seemed to meet the underlying criteria. On the theoretical front, considerable efforts were put into defining structures where a contestable market would be sustainable. A number of papers explored the need for Ramsey prices to sustain a multi-product natural monopoly and came up with alternatives that suggest Ramsey prices are only one possibility (Sharkey, 1981; Spulber, 1984). This line of work was subsequently extended by Mirman *et al.* (1985b) who defined conditions under which Aumann-Shaply prices would be sustainable.

There were also contributions that sought to extend the scope of the theory. Quirmbach (1986), for example, looked at vertical integration by an upstream monopolist into a competitive downstream industry and found welfare gains if the upstream markets were perfectly contestable. Work on international trade includes that of Helpman and Krugman (1989) that looked at the implications of increasing returns to scale within a firm in a contestable market framework. This removed the need for defining specific business behaviour for the oligopolies involved.

Economies of scale were refined in the initial analysis of network industries and this brought forth a plethora of studies that sought to examine the nature of economies of scope and density. These theoretical and empirical studies covered a number of industries but were particularly prominent in looking at the economic features of the multi-product outputs of linear and hub-and-spoke systems of airline services. Bittingmayer (1985), for example, constructed and estimated a model based on operating costs of airlines. Caves and others sought to develop econometric models that allowed for the separation and quantification of these various forms of economy (e.g. Caves *et al.*, 1983).

A final area of development involved looking at the strategic games that actors in a contestable market might play. As Baumol and Willig (1986) point out, in its pure form contestability with its assumptions of no sunk costs and no irreversible commitments necessary for entry is immune from matters of strategic behaviour by firms. However, there are good reasons to see what sort of games dynamic monopolies and oligopolies yield, or do not yield, and if outcomes are consistent with contestability features.

Baumol and his colleagues essentially used a partial equilibrium, neo-classical framework for the basis of their work. This makes use of very simple reaction functions. Basically it involves a Nash-equilibrium in a price-setting game without pre-commitments (Mirman *et al.*, 1985a) and where the supply schedules comprise the strategic sets. As sunk costs approach zero, then when incumbents have short-term sticky prices, contestability will produce equilibrium. Such outcomes do, however, seem sensitive to the price-setting assumptions. Games played where output is taken as given (quantity sustainable games), for example, generate results different to those suggested by contestability theory (Kreps and Scheinkman, 1983). Another framework, developed by Dasgupta and Stiglitz (1988), shows that an incumbent can earn super-normal economic profits over a potential rival without fear of market entry when it has some form of strategic advantage, however limited this advantage is. Stiglitz (1981) considered the response of incumbents to the threat of market entry and showed that they may engage in a variety of defensive actions to deter entry that may actually harm consumers.[8]

Some criticisms of the theory

The critics of contestability theory per se have focused on a number of issues such as whether contestability is logically possible, whether the theory is robust and what happens if uncertainty is introduced into the analysis.[9]

Much of the critical debate has centred about the issue of exactly what is meant by 'sunk cost' (Schwartz, 1986; Dasgupta and Stiglitz, 1988; Spence, 1983; Weitzman, 1983; Brock, 1983). A major difficulty is to think of situations where there are scale effects (e.g. in the form of scope and density) that do not involve some form of sunk cost.[10] The potential hit-and-run effect of contestability depends upon strong assumptions concerning the time it takes incumbents to react, and the responsiveness of demand to price changes due to market entry.[11] The model also assumes that potential entrants only look at the prevailing market prices. In fact, prices are quite easily changed by incumbents. Indeed critics, again returning to the lack of a sophisticated model of potential inter-action between firms engaged in the market and potential activists, argue that potential entrants are more inclined to take cognisance of oligopoly interactions anticipated to prevail post entry.

In the context of weak contestability, there are issues about appropriate lags for cost recovery, and also the degree of recovery – essentially how sunk costs should be defined. There are a number of modelling options and, for example, Schwartz and Reynolds (1983) make the assumption that it is an all-or-nothing entry with zero recovery before a certain time and full recovery thereafter. In this case the exit lag is akin to the classic Marshallian short period but it is not transparent that this is the only option.

The policy recommendations put forward by supporters of the contestable theory proposition have also not been accepted by all. In particular, the notion that when markets are not sustainable or there are sunk costs, there should be, following Demsetz's (1968) approach, long-term contracts to supply – a sort of periodic property rights allocation – is seen to pose problems. The nature and length of such contracts are viewed as essentially arbitrary. The method of awarding them through mechanisms such as auctions are themselves far from perfect, and embrace such problems as non-welfare maximising strategic behaviour and matters of incumbent advantage. They may also involve signific-ant transactions costs. Enforcement and quality control can pose problems, and such contracting can tie-in a technology at times of rapid technical change. Indeed, with uncertainty about contract renewal there is limited incentive for innovation on the part of suppliers.

Critics have also questioned the methodology used in some of the empirical studies of contestability. The experimental economics work of Coursey *et al.* (1984) purported to find some evidence of a hit-and-run deterrent effect, but Harrison and McKee (1985) point to the fact that the experiments do not contain a key feature of a contestable market. The work assumes simultaneous price setting by the actors rather than having a response price lag affecting the incum-bent that an entrant may exploit. It also means that the entrant does not know the entry price because it has yet to be determined. What these experiments seem, therefore, to examine are more conventional oligopoly interactions.

Equally there have been questions raised about the validity of more conven-tional, econometric based studies, including some on airlines. A major problem in such work is the inability to strictly incorporate potential entry. There are also debates, to which we return below, about the exact interpretations that can be put on the studies that have attempted to incorporate what amount to judgemen-tal potential competitive variables (Schwartz, 1986).

The empirical evidence on airlines

Testing directly for the existence of contestability, and for the power of potential competition, is not possible. Quantifying potential competition is by definition not possible – potential competitors only reveal themselves when they become actual competitors. What evidence there is often tends to rely upon anecdotal evidence from case studies and interviews of managers, or other actors in the market. Where there has been econometric work this has been of an indirect kind. It has usually compared situations where a priori reasoning suggests that there are few sunk costs to those where there are such costs. Sometimes it has involved exploring situations where there is actual competition and those where in theory, because of limited barriers to entry, it could take place. These studies have involved looking at a number of industries but the focus here is on air transportation.

The 1978 Airline Deregulation Act in the US, combined with excellent official data in the form of a 10 per cent ticket sample, provided the basis for several innovative econometric studies.[12] These were further stimulated by the initial views of Baumol and his co-workers that the airline market represented one where contestable forces would play a key role.[13] It should be remembered that contestability was not the only theory that was being looked at at that time, and advocates needed evidence to support their a priori case.

There are essentially four ways in which one can go about testing whether the airline market became contestable after deregulation. On deregulation, it would be anticipated that initially considerable entry to the market (or more strictly the threat of such entry that may or may not have been realised) and exit from it would take place at both the industry and the city-pair levels of aggregation. Following the theory, the resultant industry should have adopted a cost-minimising structure. This would be coincidental with the absence of persistent super-normal profits. Finally, pricing behaviour in the industry should be insensitive to the number and size of competitors on any particular route because potential entry would take the place of actual competition where the latter failed to materialise. Much of the empirical work, for reasons of both data availability and ease of analysis, has focused on this last issue of pricing and studies in this vein are dealt with in more detail later.

Much of the initial work looked at the conditions that may limit market entry and exit rather than entry and exit per se. Essentially they sought to highlight any sunk costs that may impede entry or exit (see Table 2.1.2).

A number of pricing studies highlighted the imperfections of contestability, giving only support at best to the weak contestability hypotheses. They found the markets examined had some potentially competitive elements, but did not exhibit prices comparable to those that actual competition would generate. Call and Keeler (1984) found a positive link between market concentration and profit of airlines indicating that potential competition was not always generating normal profit levels. Additionally, when there was market entry they found that incumbents responded by cutting their fares, an action not consistent with them previously having contestable pressures on them. Taking a somewhat different methodological approach, Morrison and Winston (1987) do find that potential market entry can limit the actions of incumbents, but that this effect only becomes significant when the number of potential entrants exceeds three.[14] Work

Table 2.1.2 A sample of empirical studies of contestable markets in US airline services[15]

Study	Method	Findings
Bailey and Panzar (1981)	Looked at city-pair markets fares before and immediately after deregulation.	Actual competition from trunk carrier checked local carriers' fares on routes of under 400 miles and potential competition for longer routes.
Graham *et al.* (1983)	Related a number of indicators to market concentration in a series of regressions.	A positive relationship between fares and market concentration went against the contestability hypothesis.
Bailey *et al.* (1985)	Used simultaneous equation system focusing mainly on fares.	Found some evidence of weak contestability immediately after deregulation. Carriers only reduce fares after actual market entry.
Moore (1986)	Compared coach fares in 1983 and 1976 in a regression analysis.	Fares were lower in markets with more carriers going against contestability theory.
Morrison and Winston (1986)	Used 1983 data to look at welfare situations with a regression analysis.	Difference between actual and welfare was 0.44 cents per mile less with actual competition and 0.15 cents with potential competition.
Strassman (1990)	Applies a systems approach to the inter-action between prices, entry and concentration using 1980 data over 92 heavily travelled city-pair markets.	Barriers to market entry are found and the market is found not to conform to contestable criteria. Actual competition is seen as a more potent check on market power.
Leigh (1990)	Uses profit data from 1978 to 1986 and focused mainly on the impact of hub-and-spoke operations.	Hub-and-spoke operations offer a degree of market power. Market entry and exit does not conform to patterns consistent with contestability.
Morrisson (2001)	Examines the implications of the actual presence of Southwest Airlines on air fares offered by other carriers over a series of routes in 1998.	It was found that actual competition from Southwest produced aggregate fare savings of $12.9 billion and that potential and adjacent competition produced a savings of $9.5 billion.

by Moore (1986) found that there had to be five or more carriers on a route for there to be any downward pressure on fares; it was only then that airlines began to ignore strategic considerations of the behaviour of their competitors and embark on price wars.

Using data embracing a slightly later period (1978–1986) Leigh (1990) offers confirmation that there was a degree of market dominance associated with the hub-and-spoke structure of routes that had evolved by that time.[16] Bailey *et al.* (1985) found in the fares airlines charge sensitivity to the income levels of travellers (suggestive of an ability to price discriminate), and also that incumbent suppliers moved fares down to meet competition only when a rival actually entered the market. These typical monopoly markets were found to have fares 6 per cent higher than those with two equal sized competitors, and 11 per cent higher than markets with four equal sized competitors.

While there were inevitable caveats attached to the idea that deregulation had produced a contestable air transport market in the US, an examination of the empirical analyses a decade or so later did allow Baumol to conclude:

> In short, in terms of the airlines' case we can infer that market forces through the pressures of competition, both actual and potential, have done a commendable if imperfect job in protecting consumer interests.
>
> (Baumol and Willig, 1986)

This was not, however, an interpretation shared by all. Alfred Kahn (cited in Labich, 1986), for instance felt:

> (T)he number of carriers in a market is the main factor in keeping prices down. If carriers in a city are reduced from two to one, I get worried. The possibility that other carriers might come in is not sufficient protection for consumers.

From this one may conclude that, whilst deregulation did generate economic gains for US air travellers, it was only partly due to the power of potential competition. That the US air transport market proved such a disappointment for those thinking deregulation would naturally unleash the power of potential competition may be due to a number of factors other than a true reflection of the long-term situation.

First, the incumbent airlines seem to have enjoyed a first mover advantage, a legacy effect. This may be seen in terms of economies of experience, but may also be a reflection of the inventiveness of airline management when freed from the constraints of rate-of-return and other regulations. Along the lines suggested by Stiglitz, they effectively built up barriers by initiating the need for potential competitors to incur fixed costs. The development of frequent flyer programmes by American Airlines is one example of this. Airlines also formed alliances, and acquired feeder carriers, that made network entry by others costly. But the incumbents also had the advantage of already having considerable numbers of slots at key airports that were not easy to replicate by new airliners, and acted as constraints to existing airlines moving into others' territories.

Second, by developing computer reservation systems, and with this yield management,[17] they were able to extract extra consumer surplus from customers in the form of economic rent. This provided a flow of cash that allowed the possibility of predatory activities, either in terms of a price or quantity response, should the need arise.[18]

Third, contestability theory focuses almost exclusively on the cost side of an industry, and on market structures, and gives relatively little attention to demand. One thing that the early years of US domestic deregulation seemed to indicate was that there are benefits of what Levine (1987) calls 'economies of market presence'. In other words revenue goes up faster than the size of the network served.[19] A larger network affords potential users a wider choice of destinations from a single carrier. This makes small-scale entry difficult. The formation of alliances, and subsequently strategic alliances, offering near seamless services amongst their members reinforced the difficulties of viable market entry. This advantage is magnified when linked to frequent flyer programmes because of the larger choice of destinations available for redeemed miles.

Have the barriers to contestability been reduced?

Much of the analytical work exploring market structures in the airline sector related both to a period somewhat distant in the past, and to the US domestic market. If one believes in generic market structures then the latter may not be such a major problem but there are nevertheless important peculiarities regarding, for example, airport access inherent in the US situation. Perhaps more important is that there have been significant changes, institutional and technological, in Europe and elsewhere since the 1980s when most of the empirical studies of US airline markets were conducted or which form the data points for later studies.

The European market was in part deregulated with at least some support for the conviction that contestable forces had a degree of influence. The European deregulation took the form of a series of 'Packages' introduced in 1987, 1989, and 1992 that by 1997 led to an internal market similar to that in the US (Button, 2004). Institutional constraints on pricing and market entry have been removed save for quality controls for safety and environmental reasons. Over the past 25 years there has also been a major shift away from public ownership of airlines coinciding with lighter control of the sector. The early studies of the deregulated US market showed significant consumer gains and these have been retained. Equally, analysis of the European market after its more gradual and phased liberalisation shows that overall air travellers have benefited.

The prospect of the European market becoming even moderately weakly contestable after liberalisation was, however, questioned by some people. Barrett (1992) pointed to a number of major impediments to strong contestability ranging from airport domination by incumbents to predatory behaviour and ground handling monopolies.[20] Indeed, the initial evidence was of significant and continuing market entry coupled with falling fares (Figure 2.1.1). These are features that do not reflect the characteristics of a contestable market where the lack of supra-normal profits offers no incentive for entry. Whether barriers still limited the operation of weakly contestable forces in the early years, and if so to

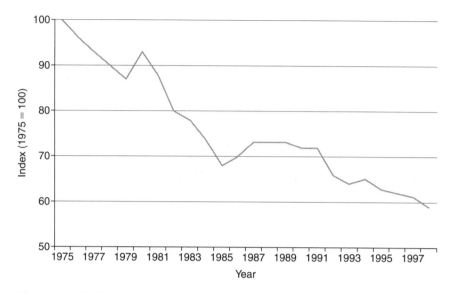

Figure 2.1.1 Decline in real fares in Europe (source: Based on Association of European Airlines data).

what degree, is now perhaps becoming a little clearer, if far from transparent. The issue is whether the picture that emerged in the 1990s was one of transition rather than one that represents the long-term structure of the sector. And if the former, where does it end?

The situation has in fact changed somewhat in recent times. Initially, the incumbent European 'flag' carriers enjoyed a degree of monopoly power from their inherited slots at large airports, and their retention of air service agreement rights on extra-European Union routes. Subsequently, the large air carriers (as represented by carriers belonging to the Association of European Airlines) have failed to earn a long-term rate of return commensurate with full cost recovery. Figure 2.1.2 provides details of operating margins for the major European carriers, the major US carriers and the global market. It is clear that over the long-term a positive margin has not been earned. More important, given the opportunity cost of investment the return is below that which may be expected (in the order of 4–6 per cent or more).[21] This does not support the idea that the industry is extracting large amounts of economic rent and the openness of the sector, and the demonstrable extent of market entry and exit, would suggest X-inefficiency is now limited.

There is also evidence of significant changes in the nature of the services being offered, the types of airlines offering them, and the business models being employed. In particular there has been a significant growth in the market share of no-frills, low cost carriers (Figure 2.1.3). These are becoming very prominent on routes of 1000 to 1200 kilometres that allow for high utilisation of aircraft

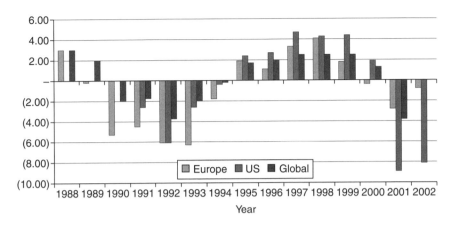

Figure 2.1.2 Operating margins of airlines after interest as a percentage of operating revenue.

Note:
The US data refer to airlines that are members of the ATA and the European data to airlines that are members of the AEA (financial years). The global data are from Boeing Commercial Airplanes.

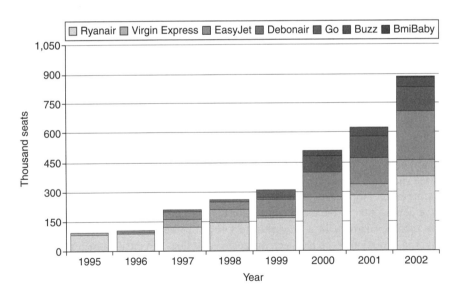

Figure 2.1.3 Growth of no-frills carriers (source: Association of European Airlines).

and for rapid turnarounds at airports. There are a variety of business models that have emerged but they are significantly different to those of the traditional full-service carriers that were the mainstay of the European market under regulatory structures.

The situation may reflect a number of influences but the aim in this chapter is to see if there is any indication of changes that could lead to greater ease of market entry and exit and, *ipso facto*, to more contestable market conditions. In doing so, it reworks some of the older themes but also adds some new ones.

Information

The importance of information in terms of market structures has long been appreciated. Control over information can constitute a major barrier to others entering a market. As technology has changed so has the nature of information flows. The advent of the Internet and the web has opened up the market for information that was formerly largely the domain of the large air carriers, and subsequently global distribution systems (GDSs). Historically, the computer reservations systems (CRSs) generated both a direct beneficial affect for airlines associated with them or owning them by the way information was displayed, and indirect halo affects through the way this information was read by travel agents who were generally remunerated in ways favourable to particular carriers.

The situation in Europe, where systems were not developed by individual airlines, and where union actions came early, never did favour specific carriers to quite the same extent as in the US when many of the early studies of contestability were undertaken. In the US, computer reservation systems were often owned by individual carriers (e.g. Sabre linked to American Airlines). Legislation in Europe largely removed the direct display bias that existed, and travel agent commissions have declined in many European markets. Additionally, the four major global distribution systems that now exist are accessible to all carriers.

But other factors are now perhaps even more important. Many of the no-frills carriers in Europe sell their tickets almost exclusively through their own websites or by direct telephone services. But even potential travellers that use the traditional carriers now have the ability to compare fares on a variety of websites such as Travelocity and Expedia. The airlines themselves are also making information more accessible through their own web links, and there is cooperative action such as the establishment of Opodo that offers cheap seats on flights by member carriers in a way akin to Orbitz in the US. Consequently, control over information flows has been dissipated and does not create a major barrier to either market entry to or exit from a route.

Hub control

The older European airlines, because the majority of their traffic was international and controlled through bilateral air service agreements, never had the

Table 2.1.3 Flights by the three lead carriers at US and European airports

Airport	Carrier 1	Carrier 2	Carrier 3
Top 10 US airports ranked by passengers			
Atlanta	Delta 73.7%	AirTran 14.6%	American 2.3%
Chicago	United 47.0%	American 38.6%	Delta 2.2%
Los Angeles	United 30.8%	American 19%	Southwest 13.8%
Dallas/Fort Worth	American 63.2%	Delta 25.7%	United 1.6%
Denver	United 53.3%	Frontier 15.1%	Great Lakes 12.2%
Phoenix	America West 51.1%	Southwest 27.7%	United 3.6%
Las Vegas	Southwest 39.6%	America West 20.3%	United 8.7%
Houston	Continental 82.7%	America West 3.4%	Delta 3.0%
Minneapolis	Northwest 80.3%	American 3.6%	Delta 2.9%
Detroit	Northwest 79.4%	American 3.8%	Delta 2.8%
Top 10 European airports ranked by passengers			
London Heathrow	British Airways 41.6%	bmi 12.1%	Lufthansa 4.8%
Frankfurt	Lufthansa 59.4%	British Airways 3.6%	Austrian 2.9%
Paris Charles de Gaulle	Air France 56.6%	British Airways 5.15%	Lufthansa 4.9%
Amsterdam	KLM 52.2%	Transavia 5.5%	easyJet 4.3%
Madrid	Iberia 57.0%	Spanair 12.7%	Air Europa 7.1%
London Gatwick	British Airways 55.1%	easyJet 12.8%	flybe British European 5.6%
Rome	Alitalia 46.2%	Air One 10.0%	Meridiana 3.9%
Munich	Lufthansa 56.8%	Beutsche BA 6.6%	Air Dolomiti 6.5%
Paris Orly	Air France 64.2%	Iberia 8.2%	Air ittoral 3.6%
Barcelona	Iberia 48.5%	Spanair 9.4%	Air Europa 5.5%

Source: Airline Business June 2003.

opportunity to gain the control over hub airports that some of their US counterparts did. Nevertheless, the traditional flag carriers did and often continue to control large numbers of slots at major and congested European airports (Table 2.1.3). The usefulness of this power in preventing others entering markets has, however, waned in many cases. The European Union has actively pursued a policy of seeking to allow other airlines into these airports, for example by reallocating little used slots or through actions when airlines merge to limit the market power of the merged entity. In other cases, as with Sabena, former flag carriers have failed and slots have become available for other airlines.

More important has been the growth in the role of second and third tier airports. These often have spare capacity and serve local regional markets as well as offering a degree of competition to the larger hubs. As Pryke (1991) pointed out, a fundamental difference between the US and the European air transport markets is that the latter has few long routes that are amenable for hub-and-spoke operations. This means that the economies of scope and density[22] that such networks can generate are limited and on-lining is less important. There is effectively more opportunity for point-to-point services to compete.

In consequence, airports around London, such as Luton and Stansted, have become bases for easyJet and Ryanair to offer competing services with

Heathrow to continental Europe. Equally, Frankfurt–Hahn, Stockholm–Skavsta, Paris–Beauvais and Brussels–Charleroi have become focus airports in Continental Europe that compete with established 'gateway' hubs. The impact on the established carriers has in some cases been in terms of taking traffic directly – a pure competitive situation. But there is also evidence from statements by airline executives that it has resulted in incumbents getting lower yields, and by implication lower fares, on routes where there is still no actual competition. This, however, may not be a contestable situation because there is also competition between routes as well as for routes, particularly for leisure traffic. Unlike the US there have been no serious academic efforts to rigorously test for the impacts of potential competition.

Aircraft economics

Low cost carriers in the US demonstrated the cost advantages of utilising standard fleets. These benefits include greater flexibility in crew scheduling, discounts in purchasing, and the need to hold smaller inventories of spare parts and aircraft. The US low cost carriers often in the past sought to keep costs down by buying or leasing older equipment, trading off lower capital costs against higher maintenance costs. Problems of inadequate cash reserves, however, sometimes led to rapid exit and laid them open to predatory behaviour by incumbent airlines. The European no-frills carriers, however, have tended to follow the example of many established European charter carriers and invested in more modern equipment. The ability to lease out this equipment and (in a wet lease) crew gives added flexibility to operations and makes entry to routes relatively easy.

The use of standardised equipment, or at least compatible equipment based around a single aircraft model, has significant advantages in the intra-European context where the major route lengths are considerably shorter than in the US. It allows, in particular, for the development of radial networks based around a series of focus airports. The lack of the need for on-line services makes for a less structured use of a fleet and allows for a much higher utilisation of capital. Networks in this context are little more than a series of point-to-point services of roughly equal length focused about an airport.

Loyalty programmes

Frequent flyer programmes were initiated in the US to give regular customers a retrospective bonus and thus retain their business. The more a customer flew with a single airline the larger this bonus became and the more varieties it took (e.g. confirmed up-grades to higher classes of services and companion travel tickets as well as 'free flights'). The airlines also found it advantageous to sell these bonus miles to hotels, car rental companies, telephone companies, etc. so that they could use them as loyalty incentives to their customers. Indeed for many US airlines this has been a highly profitable element of their activities.

As airlines have recently contracted their services in light of events in the US, the SARS epidemic, and generally depressed economies, and have sought to get higher load factors, so the value of these bonuses have been deflated. Some airlines have also increased the number of miles required for redemption and tightened the time periods when they may be redeemed. This has meant the lack of a frequent flyer programme has become less of a barrier to market entry. In addition, if a new entrant did wish to offer loyalty payments then it can buy its way into a programme operated by an incumbent. But perhaps more fundamentally, the fare savings that some potential no-frills entrant airlines can offer outweigh any gains that frequent flyer miles provide. Basically retaining cash by taking a lower fare gives a person an almost infinite choice of expenditures compared to the limited options offered by a frequent flyer programme.

Alliances

Alliances were initially formed to generate additional economies of market presence and enhance the revenue flow of participants. Strategic alliances have emerged to take this concept further. The evidence from the major North Atlantic alliances (Star, oneWorld and Sky Team) is that there are benefits to participants. The rapid expansion of Sky Team indicates the importance larger airlines attach to alliances. The evidence is not always so clear for alliances that are euro-centric. The annual survey of alliances by *Airline Business* reveals considerable instability with numerous route-based alliances being transitory. Being outside of an alliance for intra-European carriers seems to be much less important than perhaps it was thought in the past, and indeed seems to confirm the experiences of US low cost carriers, many of which have no, or very limited programmes.

Cost structures

Market entry and subsequent durability generally means that a newcomer has costs lower than the incumbents. One of the major cost innovations in the provision of air services is the unbundling that is taking place and the new business models that many no frills carriers in Europe are adopting. As seen in the list below setting out the features of no frills carriers, such airlines are pursuing an entirely different approach to supplying their services compared to the conventional carriers.

- They often focus their operations on under-utilised secondary airports close to the key European metropolitan areas. For example, Ryanair has focused its services around Paris (Beauvais), Brussels (Charleroi), and London (Stansted and Luton airports).
- There is one class of service with dense seat configurations and minimum cabin crew.
- Some unbundle services and effectively charge extra for anything other than the flight.

- They negotiate hard with airports to obtain the portfolio of services that they wish.
- There is no flexibility in the tickets that they sell.
- They keep their distribution costs low (e.g. by not using GDSs) and largely rely on the Internet and call centres for their business.
- Many use new aircraft that enables short term drains maintenance costs to be delayed until business has been built up.
- They provide a very limited range of point-to-point services.
- Inputs are used intensively, e.g. making full use of the 900 hours cabin crew flying hours limit.
- Employees' remuneration is often in part in stock option. This releases liquidity for expansion but can pose labour relations problems if share prices do not grow as forecast.

Whilst there were low cost carriers operating in the US in the period immediately after deregulation, and airlines such as jetBlue and Southwest are taking an increasingly large market share, in several respects they differ in their approach to many of the new European airlines. More importantly, the airlines that have formed the basis of past US empirical studies have tended not to reflect the degree of unbundling that has emerged in recent years in some segments of the European market. The unbundling has involved outsourcing some activities and simply not offering others (Figure 2.1.4). This makes it both easier to enter markets and also to leave them.

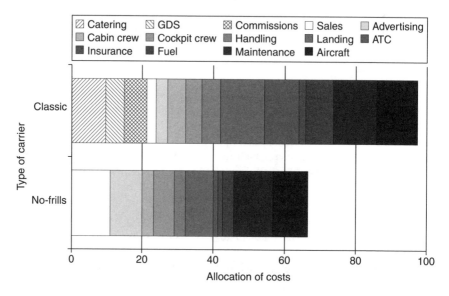

Figure 2.1.4 Typical cost differences on a flight stage between a no-frills and a full service carrier (source: Button (2004)).

Extra European Open Skies policies

Since 1979, but more strenuously in the 1990s, the US has sought to develop liberal air service agreements with its air transport trading partners. Many European states, including the Netherlands and Germany, have signed such agreements whilst others, such as France, have similar arrangements. Recent agreement amongst EU member states has allowed the Union to negotiate external air transport rights that are leading to such things as a transatlantic Open Skies and are reinforcing this pattern.

While this extra-European trend does not directly affect intra-European air transport it does introduce competition into routes traditionally served by flag carriers. Removal of protection on these routes removes the ability of incumbent carriers to spread costs over a large range of services, some of which may generate revenues that could be used in a variety of ways to protect routes within Europe.

Policy implications

There are, therefore, signs that many of the impediments to free entry and exit to European air service markets highlighted a decade or so ago by Barrett and others are now weakening if not entirely vanishing. If the European air transport market is indeed more contestable than was thought in the early 1990s, or at least circumstances have changed to make it more contestable, then this has implications for public policy. The issues really revolve around the degree of contestability that exists, or perhaps more accurately, is emerging, and whether the market is sustainable if it is contestable.

If the air transport market were inherently contestable, or at least contestable to an extent akin to workable competition in the competition literature, then this would argue for ensuring that other institutional barriers to market entry and exit are minimised. The various actions of the European Union in recent years have removed many barriers but some still remain. Competition policy still acts to limit mergers with the intent of serving the public interest by restricting potential Harburger losses and X-inefficiency associated with monopoly power. What it may also be doing is limiting scope and density economies that may further reduce costs of offering network services and in so doing distort incumbent's cost structures vis-à-vis potential entrants. Actual entry may thus occur when it is not fully economically efficient.

On the other hand, there are still remnants of control exercised by incumbent carriers, and in particular their access to heavily congested airports where slots are largely allocated on grandfathering principles. A more rapid movement to such mechanisms as secondary slot trading with money transfers (only allowed in the UK), scarcity pricing, and/or auctions would reduce some of these problems. There are also some complementary activities that incumbent airlines may use as barriers and these range from provision of ground handling long-term contracts over check-in facilities, to control over some aspects of airport access. These are only very slowly being removed.

Perhaps a more fundamental issue is what sort of industry would emerge if policies did force ultra-free entry and exit. There are a number of potential cost structures discussed in Baumol *et al.* (1982) where an equilibrium cannot be sustained. There are also other theories based around the strategic behaviour of firms suggesting that under some conditions there may be market instability, and in particular an empty core may emerge (Button, 1996).[23] In this case normal profitability could not be sustained for a long period. Indeed, the data in Figure 2.1.1 would suggest the possibility of this being an issue.

While the lack of a core, essentially a lack of any competitive equilibrium, may in many cases be a function of imperfections in markets that do not allow the full forces of contestability to be felt, it may in others be a reflection of the underlying cost and demand structures of the industry. If the latter,[24] and it would require much more analysis for this to be confirmed, then there may be a need for some form of regulation to prevent violent market fluctuations and, in the long term, inadequate market supply. The forces of contestability would push fares down to short-run marginal costs with airlines incapable of full cost recovery. Following Chadwick and Baumol, contestability theory would in these circumstances offer support for some method of auctioning of leases for routes (similar to that used in London for bus route allocations and for communications spectrums) on parts of the airline network. The competition would thus be for market access rather than for supplying within the market.

Conclusions

The emergence of a theoretical foundation for reforming economic regulation was important in the 1980s. There were manifest problems with the existing regime of controls not only in terms of the way the portfolio of instruments were being used, but more broadly with the overall efficiency of the highly bureaucratic structure of the system. There were also new ideas about market structures that sought to embody potential competition within a neo-classical framework where market concentration was evident. What is perhaps surprising is that it took so long to attempt to do this, as Joe Bain (1949) once commented, '[T]o argue that sellers in concentrated industries deliberately disregard the consequences of threatened entry would picture them as unbelievably stupid'.

The practical matter addressed here is whether the theory of contestable markets that emerged in the 1980s has some relevance to modern air transport markets. Early analysts largely questioned this but their views and findings related to a time of transition in the air transport industry. There have been significant developments since that time, and in particular a series of policy measures and market induced changes have modified the nature of the market. There would seem to be some evidence that former barriers to market entry and exit are now less than a decade or so ago. If so, then there is a case for re-examining some of the arguments put forward by William Baumol and his colleagues. But as a final caveat, it is always worth reflecting on the inventiveness of businessmen to devise schemes to retain monopoly power when all about them think that competitive forces are about to dominate.

Notes

* Professor of Public Policy, School of Public Policy, George Mason University (MS 3C6), Fairfax, VA 22030,USA, Email: kbutton@gmu.edu
1 In fact the 1978 Airline Deregulation Act did involve some phasing in of change, and its impacts were affected by a severe downturn in the US economy, but in contrast to many other regulatory changes it did represent a relatively clean break.
2 Although many of the concepts or 'language' inherent in this work remain in the vocabulary of economists and business strategists and provide what was largely lacking before the publication of *Contestable Markets and the Theory of Industry Structure* namely a common grammar for debate and discussion when dealing with the cost structures of multi-product firms.
3 The deteriorating quality of most copies of the original volume is probably as much due to the poor quality of the paper used in printing as to underuse.
4 Other influences included appreciation that allocative inefficiency may not be the only, or indeed the major, loss from monopoly power. A number of papers had emerged, for example, from the mid-1960s considering the costs of X-inefficiency that can accompany an industry subjected to rate-of-return regulation.
5 'The notion of contestable markets offers a generalisation of the notion of purely competitive markets, a generalisation in which fewer assumptions need to be made to obtain the usual efficiency results' (Baumol *et al.*, 1982: xix).
6 Keeler (1991) argues that the US domestic airline market was in the late 1980s workably competitive, although he put the credit down to traditional competitive pressures.
7 There is also minimal discussion here of the large number of empirical studies that have relevance to the debates over contestability. These studies cover a wide range of industries and extend well beyond the airline industry. The timing of the debates over contestability coincided with a number of significant developments in estimation procedures. For example, more flexible forms of cost and production functions (e.g. trans-log models) came into widespread use with accompanying estimation procedures and computer software, as did techniques that offered some insights into X-efficiency (e.g. stochastic frontiers). There were also important developments in programming with refinements to techniques such as data envelopment analysis. In some cases these techniques had a direct relevance for examining contestability hypothesis whilst in others some tweaking was needed (e.g. applying a Box-Cox transformation to outputs when looking at multiple product firms in a trans-log framework).
8 As Dasgupta and Stiglitz (1998: 571) put it subsequently, 'Indeed while potential competition might alter behavior – firms might undertake greater capacity expansion, invest in more durable machines, engage in a host of other *entry deterrence* [italics in original] – welfare might not be increased relative to what it would have been in the absence of competition; a fortiori there was no presumption that potential competition ensured any kind of (constrained or unconstrained) optimum'.
9 There have also been semantic debates about the appropriateness of the term 'contestability' (Shepherd, 1984), but we leave such matters for the linguists to cogitate over.
10 Although Schwartz (1988: 38) does concede 'that contestability proponents offer a valuable insight: fixed costs need not be sunk costs'.
11 Basically contestability assumes that if the response time for an incumbent to react to market entry is t and the period for which the potential entrance costs would be sunk is τ, after which the investment is costless reversible then $t > \tau$. Demand also

responds instantly to price changes or differentials, if this is not so then entrants cannot earn a full return on their investment which would deter market entry.

12 As Beesley (1986) puts it: 'It is generally agreed that this upswell of theorising breeds a great skepticism about, and at the same time a desire for, empirical work which might underpin it'.

13 For example, '[I]t is highly plausible that air travel provides real examples of contestable markets' (Baumol *et al.*, 1982: 7) and again, '[I]n some ways the airline industry presents a particularly close approximation to contestability' (Bailey and Baumol, 1984: 128).

14 They conclude, '[A] combination of some version of the dominant firm model and imperfect contestability seems to characterise competition in the deregulated airline industry'.

15 Sinha (1986) offers comments on a more limited number of early empirical studies of the US airline industry.

16 'In particular, analysis of the data supports the proposition that the development of hub-and-spoke networks provides carriers with the opportunity to exercise a degree of market power over exiting competitors and to erect barriers to entry of potential new ones – both things that the pure contestability model assumed they could not' (Leigh, 1990: 55).

17 It can be argued that the very ability to price discriminate implies a significant degree of market power that runs against any notion that strong contestability was a force. There are, however, counterviews that price discrimination does not in itself imply market power (Levine, 2002).

18 This effectively represents a Tullock rent seeking loss as suppliers use excess earning to protect market share by lobbying, advertising, etc.

19 There is much talk in the airline industry of the 'S-curve' effect – revenues go up much faster than market share once a critical level of market share has been reached. There seems very limited rigorous analysis of the phenomenon.

20 Barrett listed the impediments under two headings, Structural (hub airport dominance; ground handling monopolies; computer reservation system bias) and Strategic (mergers; pricing policy). We look at a wider range of issues.

21 Estimating a viable long-term operating margin is highly subjective and depends on factors such as capital-equity ratios and the cost of equity capital.

22 Scale economies stem simply from the ability to spread fixed costs over a larger level of output and are mainly independent of the form of network that is operated. Economies of scope reflect the ability to spread costs by offering a range of services and economies of density from being able to maximise the use of equipment, etc. This type of economy can particularly be enjoyed with the hub-and-spoke style of network that is often adopted by larger air carriers. The technical distinction between economies of scale and scope can be seen by reference to the following equation where C denotes cost and Q is output. Economies of scope are assessed as:

$$S = \{[C(Q^1) + C(Q^2)] - C(Q^1 + Q^2)\}/\{C(Q^1 + Q^2)\}$$

Where, $C(Q^1)$ is the cost of producing Q^1 units of output one alone, $C(Q^2)$ is the cost of producing Q^2 of output two alone, and $C(Q^1 + Q^2)$ is the cost of producing Q^1 plus Q^2. Economies of scope exist if $S > 0$. There are economies of scale if C/Q falls as Q expands.

23 Although contestable market advocates admit there 'may well exist a more fundamental and unifying approach which encompasses both views' (Baumol *et al.*, 1982: 198), they find it difficult to see how coalition theory fits within their framework.

24 Interestingly EU legislation does allow for market intervention to impose fare floors or market entry controls should it be felt the air transport market had become too competitive.

References

Bailey, E.E. and Baumol, W.J. (1984) 'Deregulation and the theory of contestable markets' *Yale Journal on Regulation*, 1: 111–137.

Bailey, E.E. and Panzar, J.C. (1981) 'The contestability of airline markets during the transition to deregulation' *Law and Contemporary Problems*, 44: 125–145.

Bailey, E.E., Graham, D.R., and Kaplan, D.P. (1985) *Deregulating the Airlines*, Cambridge MA, MIT Press.

Bain, J.S. (1949) 'A note on pricing in monopoly and oligopoly' *American Economic Review*, 39: 448–452.

Bain, J.S. (1956) *Barriers to New Competition*, Cambridge MA, Harvard University Press.

Barrett, S.D. (1992) 'Barriers to contestability in the deregulated European aviation market' *Transportation Research A*, 26: 159–166.

Baumol, W.J. (1982) 'Contestable markets: an uprising in the theory of industry structure' *American Economic Review*, 72: 1–15.

Baumol, W.J. and Willig, R.D. (1986) 'Contestability: developments since the book' *Oxford Economics Papers*, 38: 9–36.

Baumol, W.J., Panzar, J.C., and Willig, R.D. (1982) *Contestable Markets and the Theory of Industry Structure*, New York, Harcourt, Brace, Jovanovich.

Baumol, W.J., Panzar, J.C., and Willig, R.D. (1983) 'Contestable markets: an uprising in the theory of industry structure: reply' *American Economic Review*, 73: 491–496.

Beesley, M.E. (1986) 'Committed sunk costs and entry to the airline industry. Reflections on experience' *Journal of Transport Economics and Policy*, 20: 173.

Bittlingmayer, G. (1985) 'The economics of a simple airline network', mimeo.

Brock, W.A. (1983) 'Contestable Markets and the theory of Industry Structure': a review article *Journal of Political Economy*, 91: 1055–1066.

Button, K.J. (1996) 'Liberalising European aviation: is there an empty core problem?' *Journal of Transport Economics and Policy*, 30: 275–291.

Button, K.J. (2004) *Wings Across Europe: Towards an Efficient European Air Transport System*, Ashgate, Aldershot.

Call, G. and Keeler, T.E. (1984) 'Airline deregulation, fares, and market behaviour: some empirical evident' in A.F. Daughety (ed.) *Analytical Studies in Transport Economics*, Cambridge, Cambridge University Press.

Caves, D.W., Christensen, L.R., and Tretheway, M.W. (1983) 'Productivity performance of US trunk and local service airlines in the era of deregulation' *Economic Inquiry*, 21: 312–334.

Caves, R.E. and Porter, M.E. (1976) 'Barriers to exit' in R.T. Masson and P.D. Qualls (eds) *Essays in Industrial Organization in Honor of Joe S. Bain*, Cambridge MA, Ballinger.

Caves, R.E. and Porter, M.E. (1977) 'From entry barriers to mobility barriers' *Quarterly Journal of Economics*, 91: 241–261.

Chadwick, E. (1859) 'Results of different principles of legislation and administration in Europe; of competition for the field, as compared with the competition within the field of service' *Journal of the Royal Statistical Society*, p. 381 ff.

Coursey, D., Issaac, R., and Smith, V. (1984) 'Natural monopoly and contestable markets; some experimental results' *Journal of Law and Economics*, 27: 91–113.

Demsetz, H. (1968) 'Why regulate utilities?' *Journal of Law and Economics*, 11: 55–65.

Dasgupta, P. and Stiglitz, J.E. (1988) 'Potential competition, actual competition, and economic welfare' *European Economic Review*, 32: 569–577.

Economides, N. (1996) 'The economics of networks' *Econometrica*, 56: 165–185.

Fawcett, S.E. and Farris, M.T. (1989) 'Contestable markets and airline adaptability under deregulation' *Transportation Journal*, 29: 12–24.

Graham., D.R., Kaplan, D.P., and Sibley, D.S. (1983) 'Efficiency and competition in the airline industry' *Bell Journal of Economics*, 14: 118–138.

Harrison, G. and McKee, M. (1985) 'Monopoly behavior, decentralized regulation and contestable markets: an experimental evaluation' *Rand Journal of Economics*, 16: 51–69.

Helpman, E. and Krugman, P.R. (1989) *Market Structure and Foreign Trade*, Cambridge University Press, London.

Kahn, A.E. (1988) 'Airline deregulation – a mixed bag, but a clear success nevertheless' *Transportation Law Review*, 16: 15–27.

Keeler, T.E. (1991) 'Airline deregulation and market performance: the economic basis for regulatory reform and lessons from the US experience' in D. Banister and K.J. Button (eds) *Transport in a Free Market Economy*, London, Macmillan.

Kreps, G. and Scheinkman, J. (1983) 'Quantity precommitment and Bertrand competition yield Cournot outcomes' *Bell Journal of Economics*, 14: 326–338.

Labich, K. (1986) 'The show down at Eastern Airlines' *Fortune*, 113(7): 40–42.

Leigh, L.E. (1990) 'Contestability in deregulated airline markets: some empirical tests' *Transportation Journal*, 30: 49–57.

Levine, M.E. (1987) 'Airline competition in deregulated markets: theory, firm strategy and public policy' *Yale Journal on Regulation*, 4: 393–494.

Levine, M.E. (2002) 'Price discrimination without market power' *Yale Journal on Regulation*, 19: 1–36.

Mirman, L.J., Tauman, Y., and Zang, I. (1985a) 'Monopoly and sustainable prices as a Nash equilibrium in contestable markets' *Issues in Contemporary Microeconomics and Welfare*, 328–339.

Mirman, L.J., Tauman, Y., and Zang, I. (1985b) 'Supportability, sustainability and subsidy-free prices' *Rand Journal of Economics*, 16: 114–126.

Moore, T.G. (1986) 'US airline deregulation; its effects on passengers, capital and labor' *Journal of Law and Economics*, 29: 1–28.

Morrison, S.A. and Winston, C. (1987) 'Empirical implications and tests of the contestability hypothesis' *Journal of Law and Economics*, 30: 53–66.

Morrison, S.A. (2001) 'Actual, adjacent, and potential competition: estimating the full effects of Southwest Airlines' *Journal of Transport Economics and Policy*, 35: 239–256.

Pryke, R. (1991) 'American deregulation and European liberalization' in D. Banister and K.J. Button (eds) *Transport in a Free Market Economy*, London, Macmillan.

Quirmbach, H. (1986) 'Vertical integration: scale distortions, partial integration, and the direction of price change' *Quarterly Journal of Economics*, 101: 131–147.

Schwartz, M. (1986) 'The nature and scope of contestability theory' *Oxford Economics Papers*, 38: 37–57.

Schwartz, M. and Reynolds, R.J. (1983) 'Contestable markets: and uprising in the theory of industry structure: comment' *American Economic Review*, 73: 488–490.

Sharkey, W.W. (1981) 'Existence of sustainable prices for natural monopoly output' *Bell Journal of Economics*, 12: 572–587.

Shepherd, W.G. (1984) '"Contestability" vs. competition' *American Economics Review*, 74: 572–587.

Sinha, D. (1986) 'The theory of contestable markets and US airline deregulation: a survey' *Logistics and Transportation Review* 22: 421–448.

Spence, M. (1983) 'Contestable markets and the theory of industry structure': a review article, *Journal of Economic Literature*, 21: 981–990.

Spulber, D. (1984) 'Scale economies and existence of sustainable monopoly prices' *Journal of Economic Theory*, 34: 149–163.

Stiglitz, J.E. (1981) 'Potential competition may reduce welfare' *American Economic Review*, 71: 184–189.

Strassmann, D.L. (1990) 'Potential competition in the deregulated airlines' *Review of Economics and Statistics*, 72: 696–702.

Weitzman, O.E. (1983) 'Contestable markets: and uprising in the theory of industry structure: comment' *American Economic Review*, 73: 486–487.

2.2 Decoupling transport growth and economic growth in Europe

Dominic Stead and *David Banister***

Abstract

In the past, it has always been assumed that there is a close relationship between the growth in freight and passenger transport, transport energy consumption, and economic growth, at least as measured by Gross Domestic Product (GDP). This raises questions about the underlying rationale for this statistical relationship (if it exists) and, more importantly for sustainable development, whether the relationship will (or should) continue into the future.

The strong premise in this paper is that decoupling economic growth from transport growth is a necessary condition for sustainable development – we need to encourage economic growth (in the widest sense), but with less transport (at least in terms of environmental impacts and the use of resources). This requirement has now been recognised in a series of policy documents. In the UK, for example, the Standing Advisory Committee on Trunk Road Assessment has examined the issue of transport intensity, the prospects for future improvements, and the potential for decoupling transport volumes and economic activity (SACTRA, 1999). At the European level, the 2001 White Paper on Transport states that breaking the link between economic growth and transport growth is central in its proposals (CEC, 2001a), and the EU's sustainable development strategy identifies decoupling transport growth from the growth in GDP as one of its main objectives (CEC, 2001b).

This paper looks at the nature of the relationship between transport growth and economic growth and examines how decoupling might be achieved. Attention is focused on transport energy consumption as an indicator of the resource consumption and the environmental impact of transport. We begin by examining transport and economic trends in Europe and looking at EU policy statements on decoupling. We then discuss the nature of travel and how decoupling can usefully be measured through volumes, distance, and efficiency. Possible approaches and strategies for decoupling are then presented, together with a discussion of how these measures might help to decouple transport growth and economic growth. We conclude that, whilst there are a number of strategies which are likely to help to decouple transport growth and economic growth, there are also a number of factors which are hindering the decoupling process.

Consequently, decoupling transport growth and economic growth is likely to be a difficult goal to achieve.

Keywords: *transport growth, economic growth, decoupling, Europe*

Introduction – trends in transport and economic growth in Europe

A brief overview of trends in transport and economic growth over recent decades is presented below. A more detailed analysis is presented elsewhere (Banister *et al.*, 2000). In terms of passenger transport, the average distance travelled per person per year has doubled in Europe between 1970 and 2000. This was primarily due to people travelling further rather than travelling more frequently. In 1970, the average yearly travel distance was 6271 kilometres per person and by 2000 was 12786 kilometres per person. The use of the car grew rapidly over this period and reliance on it continues to increase (Figure 2.2.1). Travel by car more than doubled between 1970 and 2000 in Europe and, by 2000, more than three-quarters of passenger-kilometres were by car. Air travel, although making up a small proportion of all journeys, is becoming increasingly important in terms of transport energy consumption and emissions. Passenger travel distance by air increased more than sevenfold between 1970 and 2000. In 2000, air transport (international civil aviation and domestic air transport) accounted for 14 per cent of all transport energy consumption in the European Union (OECD, 2002).

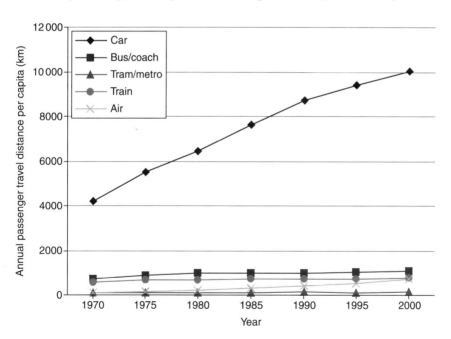

Figure 2.2.1 Trends in passenger transport by mode in Europe, 1970 to 2000 (based on data from European Commission (2003)).

In terms of freight, the number of tonne-kilometres increased by 119 per cent within the European Union between 1970 and 2000, primarily due to goods being moved further rather than more goods being moved (Whitelegg, 1997). In 2000, the average yearly freight transport distance per capita was 3566 tonne-kilometres by road, 3358 tonne-kilometres by sea, 659 tonne-kilometres by rail, 330 tonne-kilometres by inland waterway, and 226 tonne-kilometres by pipeline (Figure 2.2.2). In 2000, more than 43 per cent of freight-kilometres were moved on roads, compared to 35 per cent in 1970. Road freight transport per capita increased by 177 per cent in Europe between 1970 and 2000.

As a result of these trends, transport energy consumption per capita almost doubled between 1970 and 2000 (Table 2.2.1). However, total energy consumption per capita across all sectors increased by just 23 per cent, as a consequence of a reduction in energy consumption by industry and low growth in the domestic sector. Economic activity increased substantially in all European Member States over recent decades. Between 1970 and 2000, the GDP per capita of the European Union (EU15) almost doubled in real terms: an average increase of around 2 per cent per year. The largest increases in GDP per capita were in Luxembourg, Ireland, and Portugal (see also Stead, 2001). Comparing changes in transport energy growth and economic growth between 1970 and 2000, it appears that they are strongly associated and, more importantly from a decoupling point of view, that transport energy consumption is growing at a faster rate than economic growth (Figure 2.2.3).

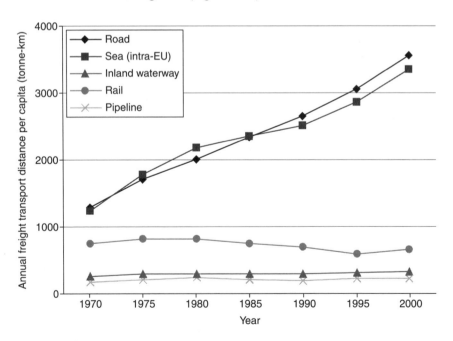

Figure 2.2.2 Trends in freight transport by mode in Europe, 1970 to 2000 (based on data from European Commission (2003)).

Table 2.2.1 Transport and economic trends in Europe (EU15), 1970 to 2000[1]

	1970	*2000*	*% change 1970–2000*
Population (millions)[1]	342	378	11
GDP (billion US$ constant 1995)	3965	8270	109
Energy consumption by sector (Mtoe):[2]			
• Industry	309	325	5
• Transport	145	317	119
• Other[3]	318	410	29
• Total	772	1052	36
Passenger transport (billion passenger-km)	2142	4839	126
Freight transport (billion tonne-km)	1407	3078	119
Per capita:			
GDP per capita (US$ constant 1995)	11 609	21 852	88
Energy consumption per capita by sector (toe):			
• Industry	0.90	0.86	−5
• Transport	0.42	0.84	97
• Other[3]	0.93	1.08	16
• Total	2.26	2.78	23
Travel distance per capita (km per person per year)	6271	12 786	104
Freight transport per capita (tonne-km per person per year)	4119	8133	97
Net mass movement per capita (tonne-km per person per year)[1]	4684	9284	98
Transport intensity ratios:			
GDP per passenger-kilometre	1.85	1.71	−8
GDP per tonne-kilometre	2.82	2.69	−5
GDP per net mass movement	2.48	2.35	−5

Sources: European Commission (2003); OECD (2002).

Various indicators of transport intensity can be used to examine decoupling (see, for example, Stead, 2001). These include the ratios of economic activity with passenger movements, freight movements or a combination of both passenger and freight movements (using the concepts of *net mass movement*[4] and *gross mass movement*,[5] discussed in more detail by Peake, 1994). Between 1970 and 2000, the ratios of GDP per passenger-kilometre, GDP per tonne-kilometre, and GDP per net mass movement all decreased since passenger and freight transport grew faster than GDP (Table 2.2.1). Trends in these three indicators across individual European countries show a substantial amount of variation (see Stead, 2001). Most EU countries experienced quite individual trends and few common patterns are obvious, which corresponds with the observation in the SACTRA report (SACTRA, 1999) that 'traffic intensity, however measured, shows very considerable variation from country to country'. More alarming from a decoupling point of view is the fact that the growth in passenger and freight transport has been higher than economic growth in almost all European countries during

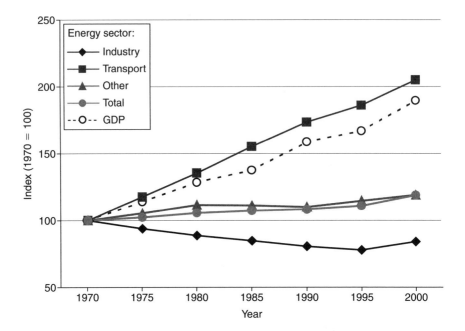

Figure 2.2.3 Trends in energy consumption and economic growth in Europe, 1970 to 2000 (based on data from European Commission (2003)).

the period 1970 to 2000. It seems clear therefore that decoupling transport demand and transport energy from economic growth will not occur by simply allowing the economy to grow, according to the Environmental Kuznets Curve hypothesis,[6] which corresponds with similar observations by authors such as Arrow *et al.* (1995) and Stern *et al.* (1996).

Decoupling – the policy context

The recent European White Paper on Transport Policy identifies decoupling as a *key issue*, arguing that breaking the link between economic growth and transport growth is central in its proposals (CEC, 2001a). This key issue is, however, something of a secondary objective of the document, subservient to the primary objective of shifting the modal split from car and air to rail and water. In contrast, the European Commission's Sustainable Development Strategy top headline objective for transport is decoupling transport growth and economic growth (CEC, 2001b).

The European Transport White Paper contains no formal legislative proposals but indicates areas where the Commission intends to initiate action over the next few years. The document sets out more than 60 transport policy measures to be taken at the Community level over the next ten years (Table 2.2.2). It also con-

Table 2.2.2 Some of the main measures proposed by the European Transport White Paper (2001)

Theme	Examples
Passengers' rights	Changes to air passenger rights including compensation for air travel delays and denied boarding due to overbooking. Extension of passenger protection measures to other modes such as rail and water transport.
Road safety	Proposals concerning the signposting of accident blackspots, combating excessively long driving times, harmonising road transport penalties at the European level, and increasing the use of new technologies in transport.
Congestion	A new programme (the Marco Polo Programme) to support intermodal initiatives and alternatives to road transport in the early stages until they become commercially viable.
Sustainable mobility	Measures to develop fair infrastructure charging, which takes into account external costs and encourages the use of the least polluting modes of transport.
Harmonised taxation	Proposals for harmonising taxes on diesel for commercial use to reduce distortions of competition in the liberalised road transport market.
Transport services	Proposals for harmonising working conditions, especially in road transport, to promote safety and improve transport service quality. Actions to encourage good practice in the provision of high quality urban transport services.
Infrastructure	Completion of 'missing links', particularly the trans-European high-speed passenger rail network and infrastructure with genuine potential for transferring goods from road to rail.
Radionavigation	Proposals for a European radionavigation system with potential applications for transport (location and measurement of vehicle speed) as well as telecommunications, medicine (telemedicine), law enforcement (electronic tagging), and agriculture (geographical information systems).

tains an action programme (as an appendix to the main document), which specifies a timetable for the introduction of various policy measures, and proposes a monitoring system, which will be used to make an overall assessment (including economic, social, and environmental impacts) of the implementation of the measures advocated in the White Paper.

The White Paper reports that 28 per cent of CO_2 emissions are now transport related and transport energy consumption is increasing (CEC, 2001a). In 1990, 739 million tonnes of CO_2 were released from the transport sector, rising to 900 million tonnes in 2000. Further substantial increases are expected in the next decade (1113 million tonnes by 2010). Road transport accounts for 84 per cent of the 2000 figure, and the total will increase substantially with the enlargement of the EU, even though the levels of motorisation in the accession states is lower. Nevertheless, the White Paper is also optimistic about reducing transport emissions and identifies three types of policy options. The three options comprise: (i) pricing (*Option A*); (ii) pricing and efficiency increases (*Option B*); and (iii) pricing, promotion of alternative modes, and targeted investment in the Trans European Networks (*Option C*). The measures in the White Paper build on Option C and aim to return the modal split to 1998 levels in 2010. According to the White Paper:

> by implementing the 60-odd measures set out in the White Paper there will be a marked break in the link between transport growth and economic growth, although without there being any need to restrict the mobility of people and goods.
>
> (CEC, 2001a: 11)

The White Paper also recognises that transport policy alone is not sufficient to tackle current transport problems and advocates an integrated approach with other areas of policy-making, such as economic policy, land-use planning policy, social and education policy, and competition policy.

In their analysis of alternative futures, the EU presents their three options against the trend-based future (1998–2010). As can be seen from Table 2.2.3, the total passenger-kilometres and tonne-kilometres do not change as compared with the trend, but there are reductions in the vehicle-kilometres for both passenger and freight transport as the impact of pricing, greater efficiency, and the other measures take effect. So the transport intensity as conventionally measured is expected to fall over this period. GDP is assumed to increase by 3 per cent per annum (43 per cent over the 12 year period – rather high when compared with performance over recent decades), whilst trends in passenger-kilometres and tonne-kilometres increase by 24 per cent and 38 per cent respectively (Table 2.2.4). Transport intensity reduces by 13 per cent for passenger travel and 3 per cent for freight transport. This is where circularity is introduced as the scale of reduction is based on the assumed increase in GDP, which in turn influences the expected growth in passenger and freight travel. Provided that GDP increases at a higher rate than travel, there will of course be some decoupling of transport growth and economic growth (at least in a relative sense if not in absolute terms). From the perspective of sustainable development, however, this is neither sufficient nor desirable, since transport growth, emissions, and energy consumption will all continue to increase in the absence of other interventions.

The EU policy options forecast a reduction of vehicle-kilometres (both passenger and freight) and the subsequent reductions in CO_2 emissions. The policy instruments proposed in the White Paper are primarily aimed at making more efficient use of the vehicle fleet by raising occupancy levels in all modes, by reducing vehicle-kilometres, and by encouraging modal shift (Option C). The impact is less apparent in the passenger sector (-10 per cent) than in the freight sector (-16 per cent) but this balance is redressed when the changes in CO_2 emissions are viewed, where there are about 10 per cent reductions in both sectors. The improvement in CO_2 emissions relates to expected gains in vehicle efficiency from the voluntary agreements with the car industry. It should also be

Table 2.2.3 Summary of transport policy options for the EU in the 2001 European Transport White Paper

	1998	*Trend 2010*	*Option A 2010*	*Option B 2010*	*Option C 2010*
Passenger					
Passenger-km (billions)	4772	5929	5929	5929	5929
Vehicle-km (billions)	2250	2767	2518	2516	2470
CO_2 (million tonnes)	518.6	593.1	551.9	539.1	523.8
Freight					
Tonne-km (billions)[3]	2870	3971	3971	3971	3971
Vehicle-km (billions)	316	472.8	430	430	397
CO_2 (million tonnes)	300.9	445.4	408.5	405.1	378.6
Total					
Vehicle-km (billions)	2566	3240	2948	2946	2867
CO_2 (million tonnes)	819.5	1038.5	960.4	944.2	902.4

Source: based on CEC (2001a) Table 3 [Annex].

Table 2.2.4 Expected changes in transport intensity in the EU between 1998 and 2010

	1998	*2010*	*Change*
GDP (€ billion)	8000	11400	+43%
Passenger-kilometres	4772	5929	+24%
Tonne-kilometres[3]	2870	3971	+38%
Transport intensity			
Passenger (GDP/pass-km)	1.676	1.923	+15%
Freight (GDP/freight-km)	2.787	2.871	+3%
Passenger and freight (GDP/nmm)	2.425	2.531	+4%

Source: based on CEC (2001a).

noted that all these reductions are taken against the trend, not the 1998 levels. In each option for 2010 there is a substantial increase in travel and CO_2 emissions as compared with 1998 levels.

Underlying this analysis is the strong assumption that decoupling can take place without the need to restrict the mobility of people and goods. We argue that this is a high-risk strategy for the environment and energy use. If absolute levels of decoupling are to be achieved, ways need to be sought to substantially reduce passenger-kilometres and freight-kilometres. In our view, the assumed increases in occupancy levels and load factors, together with voluntary agreements with industry are unlikely to be sufficient to achieve this objective on their own – they might of course help in reducing the relative levels of transport intensity.

From the perspective of decoupling transport growth and economic growth, the picture is bleak. As traffic growth is substantially higher that GDP growth, this means that some 'flip process' is required. Forecasts suggest that this will take place (Table 2.2.3) but there seems to be a technical flaw in the argument. As the SACTRA report points out, there is a clear reasoning why transport intensity should decrease over time as the traffic forecasts are driven by growth in car ownership, not by distance travelled per vehicle (SACTRA, 1999: 295). Car ownership forecasts in turn are determined by income, which itself is assumed to be linked to GDP growth (assumed to rise by 3 per cent per annum). The relationship between car ownership and income is assumed to lead to eventual saturation. These three factors together mean that intensity will decline in the future. The SACTRA report concludes that the difference between 'periods of increasing and reducing intensity will be indications of the maturity of the car ownership growth curve rather than the success or otherwise of policies intended to influence traffic growth' (SACTRA, 1999: 296).

Within European policy documents, however, there are still high expectations that decoupling economic growth and transport growth is possible. Income growth is clearly very important in determining traffic levels as well as transport prices. Both the European Transport White Paper and the SACTRA report are optimistic that decoupling can be achieved, particularly if prices are set at marginal social cost levels, although there have been few recent attempts to shift in transport prices, with the exception of a small number of urban road pricing schemes (e.g. London and Oslo). In general, fuel prices have not increased as much as increases in income in Europe. According to a recent ECMT report, one of the reasons why it has not been possible to introduce a fair system of road pricing in the past is because mobility is seen as a fundamental right and it is therefore extremely difficult for politicians to persuade the populations of democratic countries to accept the idea of fair pricing, particularly with regard to private car use (ECMT, 2001). This suggests that a broader set of options, not just in the transport sector, should be investigated to help achieve decoupling. These are likely to be complementary to pricing policies and more politically acceptable.

Decoupling strategies

Travel can be broken down into three component parts: (i) *volume* (of passengers or goods); (ii) *distance*; and (iii) *efficiency* of transport. The first two components are usually combined to give measures of performance (i.e. passenger-kilometres or tonne-kilometres), but the third element is equally important and it relates to factors such as mode, travel time, resource use, and occupancy or load factor. If we are to achieve absolute reductions in transport intensity, then there are a variety of approaches to achieve this. The three components of travel (distance, volume, and efficiency) are now used to assess the impacts of various decoupling strategies as outlined above. In addition to the conventional transport policies, there are at least four others that need to be considered – information and communications technology (ICT), land use planning, macro-economic approaches, and those relating to dematerialisation and organisational change. Clearly, different policies involve different time horizons and involve different levels of decision-making. In addition, technological developments (e.g. fuel technology or vehicle design) may help to reduce transport energy consumption through efficiency improvements, although there is less evidence that transport has become more efficient through technology over recent decades (see for example van den Brink and van Wee, 2001). Table 2.2.5 presents some examples of different measures that could be used to achieve an absolute reduction in transport intensity and help to decouple transport growth from economic growth. It is structured under the three components of travel, namely volume, distance, and efficiency.

Information, communications and technology (ICT)

The use of the Internet and other communication technologies has made electronic commerce (e-commerce) the fastest growing sector of most Western economies. For many people, the home has become a viable site to conduct certain activities that previously were not possible. In addition, recent developments in ICT have redefined opportunities to conduct business and schedule activities while travelling or at locations away from the home or workplace. The evidence of its impacts on transport has been the subject of much debate, whether it substitutes, stimulates or modifies travel. It is likely to have all three effects, but in different ways according to the particular circumstances (see Banister and Stead, 2004 for a recent review). Examples of ICT strategies are presented in Table 2.2.5 and include navigation systems, tele-services and related activities, and real-time travel information systems. Each of these can potentially reduce transport volume, distance, and/or efficiency, although the overall effects of strategies are often mixed (reducing volumes but increasing distance in the case of tele-services and related activities, for example).

Land use planning

These policies are also reasonably well known and consist of the arguments about density of development, the location of development, mixed use development, and critical thresholds necessary to support the full range of services and facilities, and even employment. Strategies relating to parking policies can be included here or in transport policies. The main aims of these policies are to reduce trip lengths, increase the use of public transport, improve load factors (and occupancy levels), and encourage trip chaining (see Stead and Marshall, 2001 for a review of the literature concerning the impacts of land use patterns on travel). Table 2.2.5 provides some examples of different sorts of land use planning policies. Examples include development density, parking supply, location policy, and control over the local services and facilities. Most of these strategies are perhaps more relevant for passenger transport than for freight transport, and can potentially reduce transport volumes and/or efficiency.

Table 2.2.5 Examples of impacts of decoupling strategies

Strategy	Examples	Impacts on transport volume (journeys)		Impacts on transport distance		Impacts on transport efficiency (mode, occupancy, loading, etc.)	
		Passenger	Freight	Passenger	Freight	Passenger	Freight
Information and Communication Technology (ICT)	Navigation systems			+opportunities for identifying shorter routes –global communication can increase international business travel and therefore distance –new opportunities for longer distance recreation (last-minute) travel	+opportunities for identifying shorter routes –global communication can increase international trade and therefore distance	+could be used for car sharing	+new opportunities for load matching
	Tele-services and activities	+replacement of journeys through ICT applications (video-conferencing, home-banking, tele-medicine, etc.)	+reduction of certain goods normally carried by post through electronic transactions (e.g. documents by email)				
	Real-time travel information (public transport countdown systems, motorway signing)			–less direct routes to avoid congestion/delays	–less direct routes to avoid congestion/delays	+use of less congested routes to improve the vehicle operating efficiency	+use of less congested routes to improve the vehicle operating efficiency
	Other ICT developments	+reduction of work journeys as a result of opportunities for working at home					

Strategy	Examples	Impacts on transport volume (journeys)		Impacts on transport distance		Impacts on transport efficiency (mode, occupancy, loading, etc.)	
		Passenger	Freight	Passenger	Freight	Passenger	Freight
Land use planning	Density			+lowers travel distance		+conducive to green transport modes (walking and cycling)	
	Parking supply			+/− alternative destinations (sign dependent on destination)		+disincentive to car use	
	Location policy				− possibly more points in the distribution chain	+public transport accessible locations may stimulate public transport use	
	Local services and facilities			+lowers travel distance		+conducive to green transport modes (walking and cycling)	
Macro-economic	Energy/carbon tax	+incentive to rationalise journeys (e.g. trip chaining)	+incentive to rationalise distribution	+incentive to minimise travel distance		+incentive to increase occupancy and use less energy intensive modes	+incentive to increase load factors
	Landfill tax		+incentive to reduce waste volumes				
	Vehicle and road tax						+incentive to increase load factors

continued

Table 2.2.5 continued

Strategy	Examples	Impacts on transport volume (journeys)		Impacts on transport distance		Impacts on transport efficiency (mode, occupancy, loading, etc.)	
		Passenger	Freight	Passenger	Freight	Passenger	Freight
Conventional transport measures	Road pricing	+ incentive to rationalise journeys (e.g. trip chaining)	+ incentive to rationalise distribution	− travel to more distant locations to avoid road pricing		+ incentive to use different modes + incentive to share journeys +/− incentive to use public transport (sign dependent on the mode used before)	+ incentive to use different modes
	High occupancy vehicle priority Public transport priority	− may increase travel distance					
	Roadspace capacity			+ shorter (non-motorised) journeys +/− alternative destinations (sign dependent on new destination)	− less direct routes to avoid areas where capacity is lower		+ incentive to improve loading
Dematerialisation and organisational change	Waste/packaging/ recycling regulations		+ less waste transport + more transport of recycled materials				
	Production processes		+ new production processes can reduce the transport of raw materials				

Strategy	Examples	Impacts on transport volume (journeys)		Impacts on transport distance		Impacts on transport efficiency (mode, occupancy, loading, etc.)	
		Passenger	*Freight*	*Passenger*	*Freight*	*Passenger*	*Freight*
	New products		+smaller products can reduce transport volumes +longer-lasting, more durable products can reduce transport volumes				

Notes
+ Indicates a positive (favourable) effect on decoupling.
− Indicates a negative (adverse) effect on decoupling.

Macro-economic

These policies are normally designed to make users aware of the full costs of their transport, principally through raising prices. This can be achieved through marginal cost pricing, but also through energy or carbon taxes, landfill taxes, and vehicle taxes (including fuel taxes), all of which have impacts on transport. Taxes and direct charging mechanisms have some advantages over regulation, such as achieving a certain level of pollution reduction at a lower cost when abatement costs differ across polluters or are costly for authorities to measure. However, a tax base that is well linked to external costs is often hard to find. In these circumstances, regulatory policies such as fitting cars with catalytic converters may be a more effective and less administratively costly tool than taxes. Transport has always been seen by governments to provide a major source of taxation revenues, contributing between 10 and 15 per cent of all exchequer revenues. It is viewed as a sector that is relatively price-inelastic and there are always good reasons for raising transport taxes. Indeed, this has been one of the main arguments used by the motoring lobbies to urge governments to reinvest more of the 'transport' taxes in transport. Governments have strongly resisted the notion of hypothecation and want to maintain maximum flexibility in expenditure patterns. Nevertheless, there is an increasing desire within governments to switch taxation from production (labour taxes) to consumption (environmental taxes) in a revenue neutral manner. Ekins (1999) suggests that such a change might lead to a double dividend by improving both the environment and the efficiency of the tax system. Green or ecological tax reform has thus come to mean a systematic shift of the tax burden away from labour and, perhaps, capital, and onto the use of environmental resources. The case is mainly based on environmental arguments concerning the use of resources and the pollution created. It is essentially a macro-economic means to internalise the externalities caused by transport. However, the levels of taxation on consumption have been established rather arbitrarily and not related directly (or indirectly) to the resources used or the pollution created. Table 2.2.5 provides some examples of macro-economic policies that may affect transport volume, distance, and/or efficiency.

Conventional transport measures

These policies are again well known and relate to road charging, priority to high occupancy vehicles and public transport, and limitations on the use of vehicles in particular locations or at particular times (parking policy, access restrictions, and car free zones for example). A comprehensive discussion of these options is presented elsewhere by Banister and Marshall (2000) under three headings of organisational and operational measures, infrastructure interventions, and financial measures. Table 2.2.5 provides a few examples of these conventional transport measures. Each of these can potentially reduce transport volume, distance, and/or efficiency, although the overall effects of some measures may be mixed (reducing volumes but increasing distance in the case of road pricing, for example), depending on the circumstances.

Dematerialisation and organisational change

Dematerialisation is the achievement of a maintained or improved product or service, whilst also achieving reduced use of material and energy. It concerns production and distribution processes as well as services, both directly and indirectly. Many issues concerning dematerialisation can have repercussions for transport demand. For example, changes in production processes may reduce the use of raw materials and therefore transport volume. New distribution processes could shorten supply chains and transport demand. Changes in product specifications (such as lighter or smaller products) could lower the weight or volume of goods (and raw materials) that need to be transported (see, for example, von Weizsäcker *et al.*, 1997). Although dematerialisation policies and actions are not explicitly being pursued in Europe, there are currently a number of implicit policies and actions in place in some European countries that contribute to dematerialisation. These include policies and actions on packaging reduction, recycling, energy saving, and waste minimisation. Organisational policies relate to the individual firms responding to new production methods and innovation, but also more generally to transport opportunities. The processes of consultation and involvement need to involve all key actors in that debate and discussion. All actors should be seen to 'buy into' the decoupling strategy and see where they can make a contribution. Much recent progress has been made in pushing the issue of transport to the top of the public and political agendas, and in explaining the nature of the problems including the need for various forms of demand management. Decoupling allows further progress to be made if its rationale and outcomes can be successfully communicated to decision-makers at all levels so that barriers to effective action and outcomes can be achieved. Examples of dematerialisation and organisational change strategies are summarised in Table 2.2.5 and include regulations concerning waste, packaging, and recycling as well as new production processes and products. The main impact of these measures is likely to be on transport volumes.

Behavioural change

In addition to the various area policies identified above (information and communications technology, land use planning policies, macro-economic policies, and those relating to dematerialisation and organisational change), behavioural change is another possible mechanism that may have an effect on decoupling transport growth and economic growth. Below, we briefly consider the results of a European opinion survey concerning attitudes towards transport energy consumption. The results suggest that we cannot be overly optimistic about behavioural change bringing about large reductions in transport demand.

In March 2003, Philippe Busquin, European Research Commissioner, presented the findings of the Eurobarometer special survey on 'Energy: Issues, options and technologies' (European Commission, 2003a). The Eurobarometer special survey was based on interviews with 16 000 citizens from the 15 EU

Member States and examined attitudes of the citizens of the European Union to energy and energy technology issues. The results of the survey indicate that most Europeans are aware of the growing energy needs of their countries and recognise that the EU is critically dependent on external energy supply. However, there is little inclination on the part of individuals to change their energy consumption patterns. According to Commissioner Busquin:

> we all know energy consumption is on the rise, and that this increase is not sustainable in the long term but we do not want to change our habits. That is the energy paradox.

(European Commission, 2003b)

The survey shows that most Europeans are essentially unaware of individual behaviour having a potential impact on the overall energy consumption. Most European citizens believe that industry could have the greatest impact on energy saving, and prefer measures which do not impose obligations on individuals. In terms of transport and energy use, many Europeans seem unaware of the impact of their transport habits on energy consumption and few people wish to change their travel behaviour. They see research as the key to reducing pollution and energy consumption, rather than changes in behaviour and lifestyles.

Surprisingly, a number of interviewees already claim to have changed their behaviour in various ways to reduce transport energy use. However, whether energy considerations were the main driving force behind these behavioural changes is debatable. An important finding from the survey of relevance to transport energy use in the future is that few respondents have any intention to take further action to reduce their own use of transport energy in the future.

More than one fifth of interviewees (22 per cent) claim to have already reduced their car *fuel use* and only 11 per cent of interviewees have any intention of taking any more action to reduce their car fuel use. Almost one fifth of interviewees (19 per cent) claim to use *public transport* more to save energy and only 12 per cent of interviewees have any intention of using public transport more than they do at present. Nine per cent of interviewees claim to have reduced *personal travel* to reduce transport energy use and only 6 per cent of interviewees have any intention of reducing their own travel in the future. Thus, many of the ways of reducing individual transport energy use do not appear to be very popular according to this recent study. Even in the case of buying a car, the majority of interviewees (81 per cent) seem unprepared to choose a car that uses less fuel.

Thus, the chances to reduce transport energy use through influencing behaviour appear to be rather low at present. This implies various issues for reducing transport demand and energy consumption. First, more information is needed concerning the impacts of transport habits on energy consumption and the environment in order to convince individuals of the importance of their own behaviour. There also needs to be a willingness to change on the part of the individual or organisation. A second issue concerns information concerning alternative means of transport for journeys (e.g. door-to-door travel information planning using public transport) to try to influence modal shift. Third, attention has to be more closely focused on other means of reducing transport growth and transport energy consumption. Behavioural change is just one way of reducing transport energy use and other ways to influence transport energy use such as economic instruments (e.g. fuel taxes), regulation (e.g. land use planning), and standards (e.g. energy efficiency of vehicles) need to be strengthened.

Conclusions

Increases in transport growth have closely followed increases in economic growth over recent decades but this is no reason for the trend to continue. Decoupling transport growth and economic growth would result in increased economic efficiency, less use of non-renewable resources, and less pollution and waste. In this paper we have sketched out the nature and scale of the problem, together with a list of the individual measures that can be used to reduce transport intensity. We have strongly argued for reductions in the absolute levels of transport intensity and not relative levels, as the expected growth in the economy would mean more transport. We are not looking for economic growth to be higher than transport growth – this has already been achieved in the USA, but not in Europe (see Gilbert and Nadeau, 2002). What we are looking for is economic growth with a *reduction* in transport requirements.

The volume of manufactured goods is clearly falling, which should lower the number of tonne-kilometres. In addition, the share of physical goods in GDP is falling compared with that of services, which should help to reduce the link between economic growth and transport. In practice, however, the volume of just-in-time transport movements has increased in order to offset reduced stock inventories and, at the same time, average trip distances have increased as a result of the specialisation of firms and globalisation of the economy, both of which are liable to increase the volume of transport (ECMT, 2001). In addition, social factors are hindering decoupling. For example, household size is decreasing, with the consequences of increasing the number of dwellings required to accommodate the population and reducing the opportunities for householders to share transport, and this is often matched by increases in the consumption patterns of consumer durables.

Tackling transport demand does not just require transport policies. Decisions in many other sectors affect the demand for transport and these other sectors need to be addressed as well if decoupling is to occur (see also Stead and Banister, 2001). Changes in society and the economy can have some potentially significant effects on decoupling. Shifts in products and production processes, for example, can give rise to opportunities for dematerialisation and consequently for decoupling. Changes in technology may also have some significant effects on travel demand in terms of both passenger and freight transport (see for example Golob and Regan, 2001) and hence on decoupling. There is also the possibility of 'leapfrogging' where countries can jump technologies to take advantage of the newer and cheaper infrastructure. This is particularly true of satellite technology. There are a number of ways in which decoupling may occur but what has not yet been established is the relative potential for each to contribute to decoupling: more research is needed here.

In addition to the issues raised in this paper, there is the question over the limitations of GDP as a measure of economic activity. This relationship should not be limited to a simple ratio of transport growth to GDP growth, as this will inevitably demonstrate a decoupling effect, both in terms of forecasts and assumptions used and in terms of actual change (Stead, 2001; Banister and Stead, 2002).

The main conclusions to this paper are that transport policy and analysis have a major new challenge, namely the means by which transport growth can be decoupled absolutely from economic growth. Some of the options and opportunities have been outlined here, and it is clear that there are no clear directions forward, except to suggest that elements from all decoupling strategies need to be included as the scale and complexity of the issues are vast. It needs the involvement of all actors from all levels of decision-making to accept the challenge so that effective combinations of strategies can be adopted in particular situations to address the key problems identified. Influencing behavioural change might also play an important role in decoupling transport growth and economic growth. In addition, it is essential that actors (including individuals, companies, and governments) accept the need for change and a reorganisation of the way in which business and everyday activities are carried out.

Notes

* OTB Research Institute, Delft University of Technology, PO Box 5030, 2600 GA Delft, The Netherlands, tel: +31 15 2782540, fax: +31 15 2783450, email: d.stead@otb.tudelft.nl, http://www.otb.tudelft.nl.
** The Bartlett School of Planning, University College London, 22 Gordon Street, London WC1H 0QB, United Kingdom, tel: +44 20 76797456, fax: +44 20 76797502, email: d.banister@ucl.ac.uk, http://www.bartlett.ucl.ac.uk.
 1 Only six countries were part of the European Community in 1970 but for comparison purposes, the data for 1970 and 2000 relate to the 15 countries (EU15) that were members of the European Union in 2000.
 2 The energy consumption figures in the first column are for 1971 (not 1970).
 3 This category includes energy use in the agricultural, commercial, public service, and residential sectors.
 4 The net mass movement of people and goods is calculated using a method similar to Peake (1994): by dividing total passenger-kilometres by 11.11 (on the assumption that people with luggage weigh 90 kg on average) and adding this figure to the total volume of freight moved (in tonne-kilometres). Note that the assumption about average weight per passenger here is substantially different to that used by Peake (1994), who assumed an average weight of 50 kg, which seems quite a low estimate.
 5 The calculation of gross mass movement of people and goods is similar to the calculation of net mass movement but also includes the mass of the vehicles used to carry the people and goods and the movements of empty vehicles.
 6 The Environmental Kuznets Curve hypothesis supposes that there is an inverted U-

shaped relationship between economic growth and environmental degradation. Panayotou (1993) is credited as one of the first to use the term 'environmental Kuznets curve', although several studies during the 1990s reported an inverted U-shaped relationship between economic growth and environmental degradation (e.g. Grossman, 1995; Grossman and Krueger, 1995; Selden and Song, 1994; Shafik, 1994).

References

Arrow, K., Bolin, B., Costanza, R., Dasgupta, P., Folke, C., Holling, C.S., Jansson, B.O., Levin, S., Mäler, K.G., Perrings, C., and Pimental, S. (1995) 'Economic growth, carrying capacity, and the environment' *Science*, 268: 520–521.

Banister, D. and Marshall, S. (2000) *Encouraging Transport Alternatives: Good Practice in Reducing Travel*, London: The Stationery Office.

Banister, D. and Stead, D. (2002) 'Reducing transport intensity' *European Journal of Transport and Infrastructure Research*, 2(3/4): 161–178.

Banister, D. and Stead, D. (2004) 'Impact of information and communications technology on transport' *Transport Reviews*, 24(5): 611–632.

Banister, D., Stead, D., Steen, P., Åkerman, J., Dreborg, K., Nijkamp, P., and Schleicher-Tappeser, R. (2000) *European Transport Policy and Sustainable Development*, London: Spon.

Commission of the European Communities (2001a) *European Transport Policy for 2020: Time to Decide [COM(2001)370]*, Luxembourg: Office for Official Publications of the European Communities.

Commission of the European Communities (2001b) *A Sustainable Europe for a Better World: A European Union Strategy for Sustainable Development. Communication of the European Commission [COM(2001)264]*, Luxembourg: Office for Official Publications of the European Communities.

ECMT (2001) *Conclusions of Round Table 119 'Transport and Economic Development'*, Paris: ECMT.

Ekins, P. (1999) 'European environmental taxes and charges: recent experience, issues and trends' *Ecological Economics*, 31(1): 39–62.

European Commission (2002) *European Union Energy and Transport in Figures 2002*, Brussels: European Commission Directorate-General for Energy and Transport.

European Commission (2003a) 'Energy: issues, options and technologies' [Report 20624]. Brussels: European Commission, DG Research.

European Commission (2003b) *Energy: Issues, options and technologies – A survey of public opinion in Europe [Press Release 6 March 2003]*. Brussels: European Commission, DG Research.

Gilbert, R. and Nadeau, K. (2002) *Decoupling Economic Growth and Transport Demand: A Requirement for Sustainability*, paper presented at the Transportation Research Board Conference on Transportation and Economic Development, Portland (Oregon), 5–7 May.

Golob, T.F. and Regan, A.C. (2001) 'Impacts of information technology on personal travel and commercial vehicle operations: research challenges and opportunities' *Transportation Research C*, 9(2): 87–121.

Grossman, G.M. (1995) 'Pollution and growth: what do we know?' in I. Goldin and L.A. Winters (eds) *The economics of sustainable development*, Cambridge: Cambridge University Press, pp. 19–45.

Grossman, G.M. and Krueger, A.B. (1995) 'Economic growth and the environment' *Quarterly Journal of Economics*. 110: 353–377.

OECD (2002) *Energy Balances of OECD Countries, 1999–2000*, Paris: OECD.

Panayotou, T. (1993) *Empirical tests and policy analysis of environmental degradation at different stages of economic development. International Labour Office World Employment Programme Working Paper 238*. Geneva: International Labour Office.

Peake, S. (1994) *Transport in Transition*, London: Earthscan.

Selden, T.M. and Song, D. (1994) 'Environmental quality and development: is there a Kuznets curve for air pollution emissions?' *Journal of Environmental Economics and Management*, 27: 147–162.

Shafik, N. (1994) 'Economic development and environmental quality: an econometric analysis' *Oxford Economic Papers*, 46: 757–773.

Standing Advisory Committee on Trunk Road Assessment – SACTRA (1999) *Transport and the Economy*, London: The Stationery Office.

Stead, D. (2001) 'Transport intensity in Europe – indicators and trends' *Transport Policy*, 8(1): 29–46.

Stead, D. and Banister, D. (2001) 'Influencing mobility outside transport policy' *Innovation*, 14(4): 315–330.

Stead, D. and Marshall, S. (2001) 'The relationships between urban form and travel patterns: an international review and evaluation' *European Journal of Transport and Infrastructure Research*, 1(2): 113–141.

Stern, D.I., Common, M.S., and Barbier, E.B. (1996) 'Economic growth and environmental degradation: the environmental kuznets curve and sustainable development' *World Development*, 24(7): 1151–1160.

Van den Brink, R.M.M. and Van Wee, B. (2001) 'Why has car-fleet specific fuel consumption not shown any decrease since 1990? Quantitative analysis of Dutch passenger car-fleet specific fuel consumption' *Transportation Research D*, 6(2): 75–93.

Von Weizsäcker, E., Lovins, A.B., and Lovins, L.H. (1997) *Factor Four: Doubling Wealth, Halving Resource Use*, London: Earthscan.

Whitelegg, J. (1997) *Critical Mass: Transport, Environment and Society in the Twenty-First Century*, London: Pluto Press.

2.3 Travel plans

Using good practice to inform future policy

Marcus P. Enoch[*] and Tom Rye[**]

Introduction

In Europe, travel plans have been known by many other different names including: 'Site-based Mobility Management', 'Green Transport Plans', 'Green Travel Plans', 'Green Commuting', 'Company Mobility Plans', and 'Employer Transport Plans', while in the USA they are covered by the term TDM (Transportation Demand Management) (Ieromonachou, 2004). UK Government guidance *A Travel Plan Resource Pack for Employers* (Energy Efficiency Best Practice Programme, 2001) defines a travel plan as being:

> a general term for a package of measures tailored to meet the needs of individual sites and aimed at promoting greener, cleaner travel choices and reducing reliance on the car. It involves the development of a set of mechanisms, initiatives and targets that together can enable an organisation to reduce the impact of travel and transport on the environment, whilst also bringing a number of other benefits to the organisation as an employer and to staff.

A second definition is that:

> A formal travel plan is simply a package of measures that aims to reduce an organisation's over dependence on the car.
>
> Howland (2003)

The idea behind travel plans actually started in the USA – particularly on the West Coast – as a quick and easy response to the fuel crises during the 1970s, but was fairly slow to permeate across the Atlantic. Indeed, in the UK the first travel plans only first began to appear during the early 1990s, with the first official policy record being made in the 1998 Transport White Paper – 'A new deal for transport: Better for everyone' (DETR, 1998).

In brief, the attractions of travel plans to governments and local authorities are that they are reasonably quick to introduce, relatively cheap, and importantly are usually politically acceptable. In short, they are an 'easy win'. This is in marked contrast to most other transport improvement schemes which often require high levels of investment over a long period of time and can carry a high political risk – especially in the short term as conditions frequently deteriorate while improvements are being carried out.

Crucially though, travel plans are dependent on other organisations (i.e. traffic generators such as employers, retail parks, hospitals, etc.) being motivated to participate in helping to solve something that 'is not their problem'. Thus, organisations will generally only consider travel plans if they:

- need to solve transport problems – access for employees, shortage of parking, traffic congestion, air pollution (for airports in particular) on-site or off-site;
- need to solve space problems – organisation is expanding and requires more building space, but need to build on parking spaces;
- need planning permission – related to the point above. Organisation is starting up, or moving or expanding and needs planning permission;
- want to save money – parking provision is expensive. Reducing levels of parking can cut company costs. Could be especially powerful where councils introduce workplace parking levies;
- want to enhance their image – locally with neighbours or at a board level – we are an environmentally conscious organisation and so deserve to be invested in by your ethical account holders. Bodyshop is one such example;
- are told to do so – in the UK, the National Health Service now requires its sites to develop plans, as do government departments. And of course schools are now being pushed to adopt travel plans for a number of reasons: reducing congestion, air pollution, and road traffic accidents, and for health reasons too.

As a result, studies have shown at the site level that UK plans combining both incentives to using alternatives to the car, together with disincentives to drive, can achieve a 15–30 per cent reduction in drive-alone commuting (DTLR, 2001), while Knapp and Ing (1996) reported a 20 per cent average reduction at sites in the Netherlands and the USA. Meanwhile Schreffler (1998) noted that some exceptional case studies in the USA reported trip reduction rates of 50 per cent and more. But, at the network level the figures are almost negligible. For instance, Rye (2002) estimates that travel plans have removed just over 150 000 car trips per day from British roads each working day, or 1.14 billion km per year, i.e. around three-quarters of one per cent of the total vehicle-km travelled to work by car overall.[1] In the same paper, the author identifies a number of key barriers to wider travel plan implementation. These are:

- companies' self-interest and internal organisational barriers;
- lack of regulatory requirements for travel plans;
- personal taxation and commuting issues;

- the poor quality of alternatives (particularly public transport); and
- lack of examples due to novelty of the concept.

The purpose of this paper is to use a series of in-depth case studies of cities and regions to consider how these barriers can be addressed in a more systematic way, using *packages* of measures. Thus, the paper will establish a series of models to show how travel plans might be more effectively introduced and supported. These models will then be used to inform how the future of travel plans might develop.

Models to emulate?

The following section looks at four cases where local authorities have taken a comprehensive package approach to delivering travel plans, in order to increase their effectiveness, that illustrate how such packages can work in practice. Nottingham was one of the first local councils in the UK to adopt the idea of travel plans, and has since developed its role as a facilitating body to enable interested organisations to plan, implement, and operate their own travel plans. Meanwhile a different approach has been tried in Birmingham (UK). Here, the local authority has established itself as a central travel plan provider, which other organisations are then invited to buy into. Rotterdam (NL) was moved to look at travel to work as an issue by organisations within the region concerned that business was suffering, and so developed a range of travel plan measures to address this. Finally, Washington State (USA) offers perhaps the most comprehensive range of mechanisms anywhere in the world to encourage organisations to adopt travel plans in order to reduce the impact of the car.

The cases were analysed based on a series of interviews with some of the key players involved in setting up and carrying out the travel plan policies, and on additional existing literature.

Nottingham, UK[2]

Nottingham first adopted mobility management in the early 1990s when Nottinghamshire County Council conducted its first staff travel surveys and employed a travel plan co-ordinator. At almost the same time, the pharmaceutical company, Boots, began modifying its extensive (historic) network of staff buses and implementing other travel plan measures (Rye, 1997).

Work continued during the mid 1990s at the County Council, and at the City Council using money obtained from the European Commission's MOSAIC and then MOST projects. In both organisations, the policy was driven primarily by councillors and key officers who wanted to demonstrate the city's commitment to sustainable development through its economic, land use planning, and transport policies. Other policies aimed at improving social inclusion and cutting air pollution also formed incentives for adopting mobility management. In 1996, Nottinghamshire County Council set up its STEPS (Sensible Travel Equals Perfect Sense) travel plan which was subsequently shown to have reduced the number of County Hall staff travelling to work by car, by 6 per cent over two years (Khan, 1998).

In 2004, a core element of the City Council's travel planning activities is the Commuter Planners Club (CPC) – a network of 50 of the city's largest employers that encompasses around 50 000 employees. Attendees tend to be estates or facilities managers who spend 50 to 100 per cent of their time dealing with transport issues. Meetings are held every three months, and hosted by different member organisations. The CPC is administered by the City Council, which organises and takes minutes of the meetings, and sends out a regular newsletter. It is important to note that the City Council sees itself as a facilitator of the Club, 'not a do-er'. Meetings usually last for half a day including lunch, and generally include presentations on various topics of relevance, e.g. road user charging, electric vehicles, etc. Additional presentations are also made by the City Council, public transport operators, and on local examples of good practice from CPC members, e.g. Queens Medical Centre, Boots, Capital One, City Hospital. The primary aim of the meetings is to enable the city council and public transport operators to inform business about the latest transport situation, while the second is to get views, opinion, and feedback from the companies on the issues. Third, companies can network and share experiences gleaned from seven years of practical implementation.

One relatively recent development has been the setting up of so-called daughter groups – area-based groups – to the CPC. There are currently three such groups – one on the south side of the city centre, one in the Lenton Lane area (west of the city centre) and one to the north of the city centre based around Trent University. There are also discussions about the possibility of establishing another for organisations based around the city's ring road.

In addition to such information initiatives, as with many other UK local authorities the City of Nottingham also uses the regulatory stick of Section 106[3] planning agreements to require organisations wishing to locate, or expand, in the city to set up a travel plan.

One major spin-off of the travel plan process is the value of improved communication between the council and local businesses. This not only pushes the travel plan message but also allows the build up of trust that may well prove critical if more controversial policies such as workplace parking charges are to be successfully implemented in the future.

The City Council acknowledges that the high attendance at the CPC meetings is in part due to its plans to introduce a levy on staff car parking spaces for large employers in Nottingham; but companies also attend because they have parking problems, or because they are required to implement a travel plan as part of a planning obligation related to new development. It should be noted that there is considerable resistance from large companies to the workplace parking levy. Companies such as Boots, IBM, Imperial Tobacco, and Raleigh have backed a campaign called Stop Workplace Parking Tax and claim that a council-funded study, called 'Road User Charging in Nottingham – Feasibility Study', proves that a road charging scheme would be a better option than workplace parking charging to reduce city centre congestion.

Another approach by the City of Nottingham, in conjunction with the Nottinghamshire Chambers of Commerce and Industry and Business Link, is through a subsidy arrangement. The TransACT scheme allocates money from the Department for Transport's congestion charging fund to help companies of between 20 and 50 employees to set up travel plan measures. Eligible companies can claim up to £2000 for expert advice from consultants and a further £18 000 for a grant towards capital costs of implementing a travel plan. One organisation to use this money is the Galleries of Justice tourist attraction, which now encourages bus use by giving a discounted ticket price to visitors presenting a bus ticket.

A further incentive for companies to adopt travel plans in the future is also currently being considered. The proposal is that companies which have adopted an accredited travel plan and spent a set minimum level on developing one would be given a discount on their workplace parking levy charges should it be introduced.

Finally, the city has also offered its time and expertise to help four or five major companies to set up company-specific travel intranets. While these do work, they are also proving to be a significant burden for the City to update and maintain.

Overall the travel plan process has been helped by the stable political regime in Nottingham, which has limited the threat of policies being overturned – as Congestion Metering was in Cambridge in the mid 1990s for example (Ison, 1998). The City Council – a Unitary Authority since 1998 – is also closely supported by the County Council. Indeed, both authorities share a common Local Transport Plan for the Greater Nottingham Area (the City and its commuting hinterland – the boroughs of Broxtowe, Gedling, and the Hucknall part of Ashfield), although both obviously have different strategies for their respective parts of the area. They also jointly run an awareness and information campaign on all transport issues, known as *The Big Wheel*. One of this body's most important functions is to advertise and disburse the travel plan grants described above.

Of crucial importance, is the fact that while encouraging the take up of company travel plans can help improve travel patterns at the margins, it cannot 'solve' the transport problems without parallel improvements to infrastructure and without links to other policy areas, particularly parking and land use planning.

Birmingham, UK[4]

A rather different way of involving companies in demand management activities has been developed in Birmingham. Here, instead of companies developing a travel plan individually, the City Council developed a plan and then invited companies to 'buy into' it.

This model emerged from a process that started in the late 1980s when the City Council began to think of an integrated planning approach. This led to a number of road building schemes being proposed in the early 1990s, but a number of consultations revealed that the public was unhappy about this way forward. As a result, road building plans were dropped and a balanced approach adopted, where bus, rail, and junction improvements, alongside demand management methods were proposed instead.

Consequently, Birmingham Travelwise was set up in 1996. Initially, a small in-house group launched the Travelwise campaign which had four elements – promoting bus showcase, promoting cycling, school run (before safe routes to school), and travel plans. Unfortunately, this did not prove too successful, and so the City looked elsewhere for inspiration, e.g. at Nottingham STEPS (Sensible Travel Equals Perfect Sense), at Lancashire County Council's Travelwise experience, and at several European examples of how to do things better. This led to a document being drawn up and circulated first to the Travelwise group and then to the Chamber of Commerce, City 2000 (Birmingham Business Centre), and the Midland Environmental Business Club (MEBC) of 500 companies interested in green issues for comments. Finally, a modified proposal was sent out to 25 companies of various types, sizes, and locations, most of which were then visited. This proposed that Birmingham Travelwise would set up a travel plan which would offer a range of travel plan services and/or components to its members, thus recognising that transport is not a core concern of the typical employer. All bar one of the employers that were approached by the City Council agreed to join.

At about the same time, in early 1997, bus operator West Midlands Travel (subsequently renamed Travel West Midlands or TWM so as to align itself with the Travelwise initiative) and Passenger Transport Executive Centro were approached and asked to join in. There followed a series of monthly meetings involving chief executives of all parties and more frequent (roughly fortnightly) meetings between the lower more tactical levels (ticketing and policy staff), which resulted in the idea of giving companies 'extras' for joining Travelwise – discounts, services, etc. (see later).

The next decision was whether to ask potential members to pay to join Travelwise or not. In the event, companies were asked to sign a pledge committing their company 'to work towards reducing the environmental and congestion impacts of our organisations' transport activities with particular reference to employee travel'. Once a company decides to join Travelwise it is visited by a team from the City, Centro, and TWM, before being sent an information booklet with an application form to affiliate. The company is also required to appoint/nominate a travel plan co-ordinator. On affiliation, it is sent a folder containing a number of customised sections on topics to do with implementing travel plans, e.g. how to conduct employee surveys, how to monitor the effects of the travel plan, and guidance on what measures might suit their company's needs. This folder is updated on a regular basis, and the company is also visited once again to help conduct a staff information day. One other 'duty' for companies is that they must complete an annual survey form about staff travel behaviour – this is kept as short as possible to improve the response rate. While this was previously sent out in an electronic format, experience suggested that hard copies would actually prove easier to analyse and this has since proved to be true. Once the company data are received by the City Council, they are analysed and turned into a report complete with statistics and recommendations of what the survey reveals for that company. Each report also contains lists of those people interested in more information on alternative modes to the car so that these can be acted on with minimal hassle. A core element of the scheme is that Travelwise companies receive regular travel information packs and specialist advice on how to persuade their employees to use alternative modes in getting to work.

Regulation in the form of withholding planning permission is also used in the Birmingham area to persuade companies to adopt travel plans. Of the 154 members around half joined via the planning condition route. In general, planning condition plans tend to lead to more effective schemes than those of the voluntary members, but need to be monitored. In general, the company must join Travelwise within three months of the site being occupied but this is sometimes difficult to establish. No enforcement actions have yet been required, although one company did come close to not meeting its obligations. Once again this planning condition approach is slightly different from most other authorities. Elsewhere in Britain councils tend to use the Section 106 agreement approach to compel developers to reduce the transport impact generated by their schemes. For a more detailed explanation of how the Birmingham planning conditions approach works see DfT (2002).

Financial incentives in the Birmingham case are almost exclusively provided in the form of discounts. Specifically, before the new arrangement, companies that bought an annual public transport pass from Centro or TWM received a 4 per cent discount, whereby if the pass was £100 the company got it for £96 and could keep the saved £4. Afterwards, this was increased to 5 per cent, but with the proviso that the '£5' must be sent back to TWM. Further, employees of member companies were given monthly instead of four weekly tickets for the same price. TWM also talked with other bus operators and came up with a joint ticket – the bus master. Another promotion saw TWM selling an annual travel pass for half price to staff who either give up a parking space, give up claiming mileage allowance, a company or lease car, or take up a job where one of these perks is offered but refused. Around 600–700 of these have been sold over four years including 100 at the council. Around 65 per cent renew their travel pass at the full rate (some of the rest may move on). Member companies are also entitled to a number of discounts from a range of about 20 supplier members (e.g. of cycle stands, bicycles, etc.) through a discount card scheme. Typically, each company receives a few discount cards that are then made available for temporary use by a staff member wishing to buy a bike with a discount for example. Overall more than 60 companies employing 20 000 staff currently take advantage of the TWM discount scheme.

One other 'company benefits' lever in attracting companies to join, is used when residents complain of companies causing parking or other traffic problems in their local neighbourhood. The Travelwise team is then dispatched with a range of 'solutions' for the company to help improve its local image. Another motivation is that some companies have joined because their competitors have joined.

A key element of the scheme is that the Travelwise team is building bridges between the council and the business community. For example, transport problems are often brought to the attention of the Travelwise team, which then tries to get these solved as quickly as possible, thus further improving rapport. This process has been further enhanced by Travelwise setting up a number of smaller groups. One is the NHS Trust transport group, which includes nine out of ten of the area's hospitals. This has shifted the emphasis from hospital staff and management complaining about parking problems to them encouraging bus companies to alter services to better fit shift changes. There is also a further education sector working group and a number of area based business groups, including one in Five Ways and one based on Brindley Place. These have been quite successful at negotiating for improvements to local transport provision, as well as improving communications more generally between neighbouring businesses.

In total, around one-fifth of Birmingham's employees (135 000) work in member organisations. And, five of the six other West Midlands councils (the exception being Wolverhampton) have adopted the same model. Interestingly the Travelwise concept is not advertised as such – growth is fast enough at present relying on word of mouth and on planning conditions. As of early 2003, there were 154 member companies, of whom 20 were support companies. In a survey of 25 'different' organisations in November 2001, 16 agreed to take part of whom nine had adequate data. The most impressive drop in car use was 17 per cent at the Highways Agency, while two other companies achieved 13 per cent. Two companies in the city centre had no change and one increased car use by 25 per cent (moved from city centre to out of town location). Obviously, the success of a travel plan is heavily dependent on the presence of an enthusiastic co-ordinator.

The chapter now continues to consider two non-UK examples of travel planning activity, in the Netherlands, and the USA. Clearly these are different contexts in terms of a number of factors such as culture, attitudes to different modes, and transport regulatory and financial matters. However, previous international comparative work on travel plans (e.g. Schreffler and Organisational Coaching, 1996) has proved instructive, and it is this chapter's authors' contention that there is sufficient commonality in travel planning experience between countries for such international comparison to be valid.

Rotterdam, NL[5]

The Netherlands is widely regarded as being a leader in the implementation of travel plan or 'mobility management' techniques in Europe, and within the Netherlands, the Province of South Holland (which includes Rotterdam and The Hague) sees itself in the top three provinces (of 12). The South Holland Vervoer

Coordinatie Centrum (VCC) (Transport Coordination Centre) arose from the Stichting Bereikbaarheid Rijnmond (foundation) which was formed in February 1993 by several large companies worried about the deteriorating public transport situation and because there was no longer enough government money to just go on improving infrastructure. Instead, it was decided to try and influence the demand side. The companies did not want to fund the project, so national government through the Ministry of Transport did. VCCs were thus directed from the national government. This changed only in 2000 when the Rotterdam regional government (Rotterdam plus 18 other municipalities) took over. In South Holland, there are four VCCs – with two funded through the Province and two funded through the regional transport authorities of The Hague and Rotterdam – each with around three or four staff, while in North Holland there is a single VCC with around ten staff.

If VCCs do their job properly, they are expected to deliver around a 10 per cent cut in single occupancy car use amongst the employers in their area – although no VCCs to date have information that justifies this claim. The target for VCC Rijnmond in Rotterdam was to inform all 1300 companies with more than 50 employees about mobility management. In South Holland, 60 per cent of companies have been approached and 14 per cent of the total have agreed to take part. Interestingly, the trend is now to talk to groups of companies as opposed to individual companies previously and develop an area travel plan which member companies then join. Typically these area-wide schemes may cover an urban area and consist of 20–50 companies and more than 1000 employees. One other trend is that in the past companies used to be approached and left alone if they were not interested. This has changed and over the last two years or so, more pressure has been applied by attempting to sell the dual themes of 'company responsibility' and 'company benefits' to organisations. This approach is, apparently, proving rather more successful. The idea is therefore, that improving the neighbourhood is not only good for society but improves the value of the company too.

VCCs also regularly organise transport projects. For example, every year the Rijnmond VCC organises a bike project aimed at employees. Usually they get about 100 employers to take part. In 1999 it also managed to do a one-off project to encourage car pooling by lending new cars to car pooling groups so employees could try it out. Around 70 per cent of testers continued car pooling once the cars were returned. The study, which was carried out in partnership with the VCC in The Hague, involved a car leasing company, and a car dealership. One current project is to increase the use of river fast ferries among commuters into Rotterdam – commuters can take their bikes on it. Further, the VCCs approach companies and provide information as to how they can deliver travel plans and make their businesses more efficient, and act as intermediaries between the companies and the province so as to try and deliver improvements to local alternatives to the car. One other service offered by the VCCs is free site-specific advice. Basically, a local VCC will spend two days at a company providing free advice on how to set up a travel plan. Any time spent after that must be paid for.

In terms of regulation, metropolitan areas have regional transport co-ordinating bodies, while in other areas, below national government, there are only two levels of government – provincial and municipal. Provincial government controls spatial planning policy, which effectively decides how many parking spaces a development can have, but the final decision of whether to issue a building permit rests with the municipality. There was new legislation that would enable provinces to better steer municipalities to make the 'right decisions' in a transport sense but this was frozen on the election of a new government late in 2002; the 2003 coalition has yet to reverse this decision.

VCCs are therefore trying to use regulations now at the planning stage using an environmental law passed five or six years ago, but this is proving to be quite difficult. This year the Rotterdam Region is trying to persuade a business park to implement mobility management in order to get an environmental permit. However, what is really needed is a company to challenge the ruling so that a judge can decide what happens next. One problem is that it is a process law not a numbers law – no real targets can be used.

Some local subsidies are offered to companies to pay for car pooling, van pooling or employer buses – the municipality refunds 20 per cent of the company's costs. There are no structural subsidies though, although NOVEM (a public-private national transport body) does provide grants for experimental schemes, e.g. electric bikes.

As of early 2003, the Netherlands has a very progressive tax incentive policy of supporting alternative modes to the car. But, nationally, political instability is having a direct effect on transport policy, and there is a strong possibility that monies used for tax incentives for public transport users will be redirected instead to pay for road improvements.

Washington State, USA[6]

Overall, perhaps the most interesting experience of encouraging employers to adopt travel plans occurs in Washington State on the western seaboard of the USA, where regulation, cash grants, tax breaks, and tax incentives are all used in a bid to reduce traffic problems.

For instance, an example of an effective non planning-based regulatory approach is the Commute Trip Reduction programme, introduced by the State of Washington in 1991 under its Clean Air Act. Subsequently revised in 1997, this law requires employers with more than 100 employees at a work site who begin work between 6 am and 9 am in counties with more than 150 000 population to establish programmes intended to reduce peak-period trips by 20 per cent by 1997 (compared with 1991), 25 per cent by 1999, and 35 per cent by 2005. In Washington State the law requires certain planning and monitoring activities but imposes no punishment if employers fail to meet the planning objectives.

For 2001–2003, the state's Department of Transportation (WSDOT) provided

US$3.9m to counties and cities to carry out the programme, and the jurisdictions contributed US$3m of their own, while a WSDOT budget of US$5.5m has been proposed for the financial years 2003–2005. More than 700 employers at nearly 1100 worksites and over 550 000 employees participate in the programme – accounting for around 25 per cent of employees of the organisations in the nine counties where the CTR operates. WSDOT claims that 20 000 cars are removed from the roads each day, and that the drive alone modal share of CTR-affected work sites is only 65 per cent compared with a state average of 74 per cent. It also reports that each dollar the State invests in CTR levers more than US$15 from public and private partners.

One subsidy for employers is offered by the King County Metro Transit Agency in Seattle, which provides travel passes at a discount to employers to encourage staff to commute by a variety of modes other than the car, as one element of a commute trip reduction programme. Interestingly, employers joining the scheme for the first time may also be eligible for match funding through Federal transport grants.

Another way of directly subsidising employers – this time through tax rebates – occurs more widely in the State of Washington. This applies to employers that pay the business and occupation (B&O) tax (which applies to private and public businesses or agencies that partake in 'enterprising activities') or public utility tax – payable by the public sector water, gas, etc. suppliers – to the Washington State Department of Revenue. Essentially, employers that pay these taxes and provide commute subsidies to employees can apply for tax credits, regardless of the size of the employer. Specifically, credit is allowed for subsidies paid to employees for using public transport, state ferries, car pooling in a vehicle with three or more persons, or cycling or walking to work. The credit is equal to half the amount an employer subsidises for each employee, but may not exceed US$60 per employee per year or a total of US$100 000 in B&O or utility tax credit for an organisation in any calendar year. Subsidies for two-person car-pools are eligible for credit as well but only at 30 per cent up to US$60 a year. In addition, there is a cap on the state-wide allocation of monies for the scheme, and so once this is reached the subsidy ceases. In calculating B&O or public utility tax, the cost of providing employee subsidies is not deducted from income. Instead, a portion of these costs can be deducted from the total tax due. In other words, this is a direct offset of tax. To date it is not known how many employers take part, nor what has been the effect of the subsidy on modal share amongst those employers that did take advantage of the tax credit.

However, this mechanism was subsequently dropped, after a state-wide plebiscite on the issue, which has also threatened the funding of much of the state's public transport. In a further twist though, as of February 2003 it is possible that the tax credit regime could be re-established if the US$5.5m two-year programme is approved.

In addition, businesses in the State are also eligible for a whole range of Federal tax incentives (see The Open University *et al.*, 2001 for more information on these).

It is notable that several other major regions had regulations requiring large employers to implement travel plans. These were the result of Federal Clean Air legislation, and were in force from 1992 to 1996 (with the exception of Southern California, where state legislation required the same from 1988 onwards). The regulations were repealed after lobbying with business, which found them costly and difficult to comply with. Only in Washington has regulation, for congestion management reasons, persisted; it has been suggested that this is because the law is a more local one, implemented in partnership with local municipalities, and because there is a more obvious cause and effect linkage between travel plans and congestion than there is between travel plans and air quality.

Key observations

Table 2.3.1 summarises the case studies.

In terms of motivations/policy goals it is interesting that in both the Birmingham and Rotterdam cases the policy was driven by 'public pressure' in the form of public opposition to road building and companies calling for action to improve the transport situation. By contrast, the motivations were driven by more conventional reasons in Nottingham (where councillors were keen to be seen as supporting the new sustainable development agenda) and in Washington State (where it was required to act by Federal government decree). Despite this though, when actually implemented the structures are fairly similar, in that the local transport authority leads the implementation process, while public transport operators and companies form the other key stakeholder groups.

Regarding the policy delivery mechanism, Nottingham, Rotterdam, and Washington State all rely on the traditional approach (albeit substantially 'beefed up') of relying on the company if not to initiate the process, then at least to devote significant resources to establishing and operating the travel plan. By contrast, the Birmingham solution where the company simply joins a pre-existing plan seems eminently more sensible, and surely must offer a way for travel plans to be developed in the future. Expecting individual companies to devise an individual travel plan seems a backward step when skilled travel planners are such a scarce commodity even in local authorities.

All of the examples have developed local neighbourhood groups too, so as to allow organisations in particular vicinities to contribute towards developing transport solutions that meet their needs. This is important, as neighbourhood-wide improvements potentially allow smaller companies in the area to participate and benefit. However, such arrangements are not yet the norm.

With the key tools, it is instructive that all four cases rely on a combination of information, regulation, and financial incentive arrangements to encourage organisations to participate. Meanwhile, perhaps the most effective route to change company behaviour – the tax regime – plays a vital role in the Washington State case where tax incentives targeted specifically at promoting non-car travel are in place. In the UK, and to a lesser extent in the Netherlands, tax

Table 2.3.1 Summary of the Nottingham, Birmingham, Rotterdam, and Washington State case studies

	Nottingham (UK)	Birmingham (UK)	Rotterdam (NL)	Washington State (USA)
Motivation/ Policy goals	Commitment to sustainable development; enhance social inclusion; improve air quality.	Public opposition to new road schemes so new way needed to meet transport goals.	Concerns over deteriorating transport situation by companies in the region.	Clean Air legislation and congestion management.
Lead organisation	Nottingham City Council	Birmingham City Council	Rotterdam Regional Government	Washington State
Key partners	Local businesses, public transport operators	Public transport operators, local businesses	Province of South Holland, local businesses, public transport operators	Regional and City Governments, public transport operators, local businesses
Method of delivery	Companies develop travel plans with ongoing support from Council.	Companies 'buy in' to area wide travel plan, as if buying any other service.	Transport Co-ordination Centre staff pro-actively seek new companies and offer tailored support and solutions to transport related problems.	Companies required to meet regulations contact State, Region and/or City for support.
Key tools	Appeals to self-interest ('hot line' to council – useful with workplace parking levy threatened – other companies and public transport operators). Section 106 agreements. Financial incentives in form of grants.	Appeals to self-interest (with 'hot line' to council, public transport discounts and information) and planning conditions.	Appeals to self-interest now more aggressively marketed at companies coupled with various projects, site specific advice, tax incentives, grants, etc.	Regulation (Commute Trip Reduction programme), cash grants, tax incentives and breaks.
Performance	50 companies with 50000 employees involved.	Over 150 companies, 135000 employees.	Around 200 companies have agreed to take part.	700 employers and 550000 employees. 20000 cars a day removed from the roads.

barriers to 'greener commuting' have now largely been removed but the step of actively promoting them has not yet been taken.

Benefits of the package approach

Clearly, combining a full raft of complementary policies together has proved remarkably successful in the cases described. In the short term, the UK examples of Nottingham and Birmingham form realistic models to draw inspiration from. In particular, the idea of forming city-wide and neighbourhood travel plan groups offers strong benefits not only to the companies but to local transport operators and the sponsoring local authority as well. Further, the idea of the Birmingham Company Travelwise organisation providing additional benefits to member firms with minimal input required from them would seem to largely overcome the first and largest barrier to companies adopting travel plans – which is that they 'cost' more (in terms of time and hassle as well as money) than they 'pay out' and so do not meet the criterion that they benefit the company's bottom line.

For the longer term, obviously the more mechanisms to deliver fiscal incentives the more likely that firms will take part. Such changes will of course usually require changes in the tax regime, but the signs in recent years in countries including Ireland, the UK, the USA, and the Netherlands, is that finance ministries can be convinced to act if a good case can be made and if money is available. On the issue of new regulations, the major benefit of the Commute Trip Reduction ordinances is that they apply to existing as well as the new businesses presently covered by the planning rules. This would seem to allow the 'burden' of such laws to be spread more widely and hence more effectively and more fairly.

Recommendations for local councils

As stated earlier, travel plans provide a politically acceptable, relatively cheap, and reasonably quick way to reduce local traffic problems. But, travel plans require the cooperation of local businesses, and these will only be interested if it is legally required to implement a travel plan; it would save or make the company money, and/or it would add value to the company's share price or enhance its image. The following recommendations are made bearing these motivations in mind.

Establish a travel plan implementation team

The first stage for a local authority is to establish an implementation team consisting of representatives from the transport and planning sections most involved currently in travel plans.

Develop a travel plan strategy

Second, the local authority should establish how travel plans might fit into its overall transport and land use plans and to what extent travel plans will influence local transport policy in the future.

Develop an authority-wide travel plan for companies to buy into

With the team established, it should then be possible to form a council-wide travel plan, which companies interested in solving some transport problem could buy into with minimal hassle and expense. This should have a dedicated level of staff and financial resources, and seek to offer a range of information, as well as fiscal and other benefits. Such a structure would also allow the creation of Local Travel Plan Groups.

Form Local Travel Plan Groups

Adopting the Nottingham model of setting up one or more Local Travel Plan Groups would enable local employers to meet council officials to air their grievances, share best practice, and become more involved in agreeing transport priorities – a process already underway in the London Borough of Wandsworth. Such an approach is relatively uncontroversial, cheap and quick to introduce, and has been found to pay dividends in terms of improved communication for a wide range of other issues for the council as well as a better transport infrastructure for the businesses involved. One way of giving these bodies 'teeth' might be to use parking revenue money as a way of levering cash out of local employers.

Link planning decisions directly to travel plan effectiveness at reducing traffic levels

Local authorities should look at more closely linking their planning decisions to the predicted level of traffic generated by the proposed development, taking the effectiveness of the travel plan into account. However, this will be difficult to implement where the final occupant of the development is not known, as in most office developments, for example.

Longer term

In the longer term, there may be scope for councils to levy workplace parking charges on companies that were not members of the local authority's travel plan scheme. An alternative might be to look at establishing some kind of Commute Trip Reduction Programme, whereby companies were taxed according to the transport impact they generated (in terms of numbers of trips, etc.). Such a scheme could be seen as an extension to that proposed for new developments above.

Crucially, if companies are to be regulated and taxed into cutting car trips, there is a need for significant (ideally financial) incentives to 'sweeten the pill'. This could come in the form of tax rebates in other areas or from a demonstrably more efficient transport system.

In conclusion, it is suggested that, if the measures above are adopted at the local level, this may make some contribution to overcoming the barrier of company self-interest and, in particular, of a lack of examples of effective travel plans acting as a barrier to their wider adoption.

Recommendations – regional and national government

Education, education, education . . .

Ignorance of what travel plans are and especially what they are for remains the major barrier for their take up. Travel plans as they stand are simply irrelevant to the vast majority of companies. The trick therefore, is to change this perception. Bluntly, expecting companies to engage in travel planning is seen as being unreasonable. Instead, the whole ethos needs to be changed as to what the role of travel plans is, or else the concept will remain a marginal one. Travel plans need to be repackaged as a product that companies buy when required direct from either a local authority or a private travel plan provider, that is designed to lead each company towards greener travel habits through a mix of regulatory and fiscal sticks and carrots.

Look again at giving tax incentives through the personal tax regime to non-car users

In the short term, Finance Ministries should continue to identify tax barriers that put off organisations providing tax incentives to non-car users. The issue of personal tax was researched in a study for the then Department of the Environment, Transport and the Regions by a team led by the Open University (The Open University *et al.*, 2001). In brief, while a general tax concession for all commuting trips creates negative transport and environmental impacts, a capped and targeted commuting concession would address these problems. But beyond the personal tax issue, there are a number of other fiscal mechanisms that could be adopted to further entice companies to persuade motorists from their cars, e.g. company car tax, business taxes, parking levies, etc.

The most effective travel plan measures involve direct financial incentives and disincentives. In general the car use reduction effects of different travel plans are:

- zero for information-only travel plans;
- 5 per cent for schemes consisting mainly of carpooling;
- 8 to 10 per cent for those incorporating financial incentives to use alternative modes; and
- 15 per cent or more for those that included financial disincentives to car use.

Provide incentives to local authorities

It is not only companies and individuals that need incentives though. In general, there are many examples of interaction between government and companies and local authorities and companies. But, there is relatively little interaction between government and local councils. This is surprising in that although responsibility for setting transport policy rests at the national level, it is at the local level that policies are delivered. The problem here is that in the transport sector, as in others, local authorities face a tough political challenge in delivering transport improvements due to a number of reasons. These include the fact that transport policy improvements take far too long to actually address transport problems, and in fact in the short term they usually make things significantly worse. Moreover, transport projects require large amounts of money committed over a long period of time.

In order to overcome this understandable reluctance to act in all but the most desperate circumstances, local authorities need to be in some way convinced that improving transport provision will not be politically suicidal. There are many ways that this could be done. First, empowerment. This process has been started in the Transport Act 2000 with the devolution of revenue raising powers in the form of congestion charging and workplace parking levies. Although this is to be welcomed, there is certainly more that could be done in this area. For instance, possibly allowing local authorities to charge a local income tax or sales tax to pay for transport improvements or (as in France with the *Versement Transport* or in cities across the USA) perhaps with exemptions for companies with accredited travel plans as is suggested in Nottingham when the workplace parking levy is introduced. However, with only two such schemes in place as of September 2004, it could be argued that empowerment alone is not really enough. What is also needed is political support from central government – a currency noticeably lacking before the launch of the London Mayor's congestion charge in February 2003. And, although local authorities interested in adopting such powers have been eligible for cash subsidies to help them develop their schemes further, it does not seem to have been enough to convince any of them to take the plunge.

Another group that needs incentives to become more involved in supporting travel plans is public transport operators. Rye *et al.* (2002) suggests that the reasons for operators not getting involved are that demand is already peaked, and capacity is often already stretched at those times anyway; sites are frequently very congested at peak times; internal layouts are not pedestrian and/or bus friendly; and parking standards are often too generous for bus operators to believe there is a sizeable market to serve.

Conclusions

Travel plans in many countries are currently typically a policy implemented using information and exhortation, which sometimes have been supported by redirecting existing planning gain regulation and/or tinkering with the tax system. Equally when planning consent is needed employers will comply with a travel plan, at least for a year or two. Overall, neither regulation nor tax measures have been used to their full potential. It is all very patchy. The end result is that while travel plans clearly can deliver results, they are not being implemented to their full potential. There is neither sufficiently consistent, targeted regulation nor sufficiently consistent, targeted fiscal measures that will result in anything like the widespread adoption of travel plans.

What is more, this half-hearted approach to travel plans sends contradictory signals. Where it hits, planning consent regulation does get travel plans onto employer agendas, but in these situations it is very much seen as a cost and not as something that employers should do as a normal business practice. Meanwhile information measures are constantly pushing the cost-effectiveness message, but to little effect. At the same time huge subsidies have been used to encourage companies to buy clean vehicles, which are often being promoted alongside travel plans with the implication that if you have a cleaner fleet, there is no real need for modal shift. By contrast no subsidies (besides small amounts for advice) are offered for travel plan development. As a result, the greener vehicle tax incentives and benefits are now becoming part of company culture, whereas as soon as the planning consent pressure is off, travel plans wither away.

Table 2.3.2 shows what has been done so far to address the barriers to wider travel plan implementation, as identified by Rye (2002) and outlined in the intro-

Table 2.3.2 Barriers to wider travel plan implementation

Barrier	Current policy	Recommendations for future
Companies' self-interest and internal organisational barriers	Promotion/exhortation/information	Set up 'VCC' type organisations to market travel plan services to companies; Commuter Planners' Clubs; and tax breaks on travel plans
Lack of regulatory requirements for travel plans	Only for new developments through planning process – varying implementation by area/region	Washington State model of regulation?
Personal taxation and commuting issues	Small changes made to solve most pressing anomalies	Introduce tax-free travel vouchers for green commuting
The poor quality of alternatives (particularly public transport)	Voluntary agreements between local authorities and operators; ring-fenced time-limited grants; improved bus infrastructure	Additional revenue funding for public transport through new funding sources, e.g. versement transport, congestion charging
Lack of examples due to novelty of the concept	Information/exhortation (with a few local exceptions)	Commuter Planners' Clubs or Birmingham Travelwise model

duction; and, based on the discussion in this paper, on what more could be done to overcome the barriers.

The lessons are clear. If the policy is to work, then appropriate instruments are necessary to ensure that the policy objectives are achieved. In the Washington example the travel plan policy was initially regulation-led with tax concessions playing a supporting role, whereas now the balance has been reversed. This has meant that whole private industries are springing up to support and promote tax efficient Travel Plan benefits. The approach in Rotterdam has concentrated on tax incentives at the national level, exhortation and advice at the local and regional levels, and the threat of regulation in the background.

Overall, transport will never be the core concern of the vast majority of employers, and so the current informational instruments-dominated policy is unlikely to be very effective unless it is supported by additional measures. The need to use regulation and fiscal measures seems so obvious but has not as yet been understood. The issue of whether regulation, tax or a subsidy policy works best is a secondary issue to that of needing it in the first place.

The juxtaposition of an ambitious policy for travel plan uptake and the use of insufficiently effective instruments is perhaps a microcosm of transport policy as a whole. The need, in terms of the cost of congestion, transport casualties, climate change emissions, and backlog of under investment is obvious. Yet transport policy is such a politically difficult area that government balks at using the fiscal and regulatory measures that will deliver results and instead talks up minor and ineffective measures as though they will actually deliver significant improvements.

Acknowledgements

Thanks are due to the London Borough of Southwark for funding the research, to the interviewees for their assistance in providing information for this report, and to Dr Stephen Potter of the Open University and Dr Stephen Ison of Loughborough University for their comments.

Notes

* Department of Civil and Building Engineering, Loughborough University, Leicestershire LE11 3TU, UK. Tel: +44 (0)1509 223408. Email: m.p.enoch@lboro.ac.uk.
** Transport Research Institute, School of the Built Environment, Napier University, Merchiston Campus, 10 Colinton Road, Edinburgh, EH10 5DT, Scotland. Tel: +44 (0)131 455 2210. Email: t.rye@napier.ac.uk.
1 There is an argument that any traffic that travel plans remove from the network will simply be replaced by previously suppressed traffic unless some form of congestion charging is in place to prevent this occurring. Nevertheless, travel plans can be a key part of any wider transport strategy to reduce car use and improve travel choices, particularly as they target trips during peak times when the negative impacts of car use (i.e. congestion, noise, emissions, etc.) are at their worst.
2 Based on Batifois and Fleming (2002).
3 Most local authorities tend to require organisations that are wishing to develop a site to look at alternative ways employees or customers may travel through a 'Section 106

agreement'. This is named after the section of the Town and Country Planning Act 1990 that aims to ensure that the additional impacts of the development can be accommodated by the local infrastructure. Specifically it confers legal powers on councils to enable them to require a developer to contribute towards minimising the impacts of the new or expanded development, either financially, by building new infrastructure or by demand management measures, e.g. through a travel plan. In Scotland this is called a 'Section 75 agreement', after the section in Scotland's own Act.

4 Based on Cooper (2002).
5 Based on Van der Hoef (2002) and Beljon and Van der Hoef (2003).
6 Based on King County Metro (1999 and 2000), and WSDOT (1999, 2003 and 2004).

References

Batifois, H. and Fleming, C. (2002) Interview with Transport Strategy Team, Nottingham City Council, Nottingham, 18 November.
Beljon, R. and Van der Hoef, H. (2003) Interview with officials of the Province of South Holland, The Hague, 12 February.
Bunting, P. (2003) Interview, Director of Business Development, Stagecoach plc, London, 6 August.
Cooper, M. (2002) Interview with Project Leader, Birmingham Travelwise, Birmingham City Council, Birmingham, 20 November.
Department of the Environment, Transport and the Regions (1998) *A new deal for transport: Better for everyone*, DETR, The Stationery Office, London, July.
Department for Transport, Local Government and the Regions (2001) 'Evaluation of Government Departments' Travel Plans' Report for the DTLR, London, April. Online. Available at http://www.dft.gov.uk (accessed 31 May 2004).
Department for Transport (2002) *Making Travel Plans Work*, Department for Transport, London, July.
Department for Transport (2002) 'Using the planning system to secure travel plans: best practice guidance for local authorities, developers and occupiers' Department for Transport, The Stationery Office, London.
Energy Efficiency Best Practice Programme (2001) *A Travel Plan Resource Pack for Employers*, Energy Efficiency Best Practice Programme, Crown Copyright, The Stationery Office, London, June.
Enoch, M.P. and Potter, S. (2003) 'Encouraging the commercial sector to help employees to change their travel behaviour' *Transport Policy* 10(1): 51–58.
Howland, J. (2003) 'Planning ahead' *Going Green*, Environmental Planning Association, Autumn, 30.
Ieromonachou, P. (2004) 'Managing regime change in urban mobility management' PhD thesis, Centre for Technology Strategy, The Open University, Milton Keynes (to be submitted).
Ison, S.G. (1998) 'A concept in the right place at the wrong time: congestion metering in the city of Cambridge' *Transport Policy*, 5(3): 139–146.
Khan, S. (1998) 'STEPS – second year evaluation' Paper to 2nd European Conference on Mobility Management, Nottingham.
King County Metro (1999) *Flexpass*, King County Metro, 12 April. Online. Available at http://transit.metrokc.gov (accessed 15 August 2001).
King County Metro (2000) *Pass Subsidy Programs*, King County Metro, 10 January. Online. Available at http://transit.metrokc.gov (accessed 15 August 2001).

Knapp, R.J.J. van der and Ign, A.G. (1996) 'Effective TDM at worksites in the Netherlands and the US' Organisational Coaching in association with Eric N. Shreffler.

Litman, T. (2001) *Commute Trip Reduction (CTR): Programs That Encourage Employees to Use Efficient Commute Options*, TDM Encyclopedia, Victoria Transport Policy Institute, March. Online. Available at http://www.vtpi.org (accessed 15 August 2001).

The Open University, WS Atkins and Napier University (2001) *The impact of the personal tax regime on modal choice.* Prepared for the DETR and Inland Revenue, Final Report, London. Online. Available at http://www.dtlr.gov.uk/itwp/modalshift/index.htm (accessed 13 December 2002).

Rye, T. (2002) 'Travel plans: do they work?' *Transport Policy*, 9(4): October, 287–298.

Rye, T., Black, C., and MacGuigan, D. (2002) 'Effects of travel plans on public transport users and revenues' *Traffic Engineering and Control*, 43(2): February, 71–75.

Rye, T. (1997) 'The implementation of transport demand management in large organisations' unpublished PhD thesis, Nottingham Trent University.

Schreffler, E.N. and Organisational Coaching (1996) 'The effectiveness of travel plans in the USA and the Netherlands' report to Netherlands Ministry of Transport.

Schreffler, E.N. (1998) 'Travel demand management evaluation: current practice and emergent issues, TDM Innovation and Research Symposium – Setting a Strategic Agenda for the Future' *Transportation Research Circular*, 433: 87–96.

Van der Hoef, H.A. (2002) Interview with Mobility Manager, Province of South Holland, Amsterdam, 29 November.

Washington State Department of Transportation (1999) *Employee Transportation Coordinator Handbook*, Washington State CTR Program, Olympia, Washington. Online. Available at www.wsdot.wa.gov/pubtran/ctr (accessed 13 December 2002).

Washington State Department of Transportation (2003) *The Commute Trip Reduction Program Saves Space on our Roads and Improves Air Quality*, WSDOT Public Transportation and Commute Options Office, Olympia, Washington, February.

Washington State Department of Transportation (2004) *Commute Trip Reduction Task Force 2003 Report to the Washington State Legislature*, WSDOT Public Transportation and Commute Options Office, Olympia, Washington, February. Online. Available at www.wsdot.wa.gov/tdm/tripreduction/download (accessed 28 May 2004).

2.4 Economies of scale, efficiency, and government intervention in public transport

*Arnoud Mouwen and Piet Rietveld**

Abstract

In the bus sector public transport firms on average produce under constant or increasing returns to scale. Government should keep this in mind when developing a policy for non-interference in mergers and acquisitions. In this chapter we assess five regulatory regimes on efficiency and equity objectives of regional and local public transport authorities. For that purpose data on 21 European cities and regions are used. We find that a strong regulatory national climate coincides with priority to equity objectives at the regional level. Also, a laissez faire regime tends to go together with priority on efficiency objectives. Furthermore gross costs contracts (cost risks borne by the operator, revenue risks borne by the responsible authority) are the most popular in Europe.

1 Introduction

The policy trend in the public transport sector in the last three decades has been one of deregulation and privatisation in most countries. This applies for almost all transport sectors: urban transit, rail and bus, road haulage, shipping, and aviation. The underpinning of this policy change rests on three main arguments:

1   price setting for public services is not based on the market principles of supply and demand, but based on planning and budgeting. This has led to inefficiencies and a low pace of technical progress. Privately owned companies in general operate more efficiently and effectively than public companies (see for instance Cowie and Asenova, 1999);
2   the rising deficits of the public sector in the mid 1970s gave rise to a different view on public expenditures and on the role of government production and subsidising;
3   possible regulatory failures such as lack of information, wrong decisions, non-consumer orientation led to reassessment of the role of the state in the organisation of the transport sector (for reviews see Berechman, 1993).

Recently however we see a Europe-wide trend towards a more intervening role of government in public transport. It seems as if the pendulum is starting to swing back again. Authorities who ran on to negative effects of deregulation, are considering regulative measures again, for instance by means of setting up public agencies responsible for the definition of public transport service levels. So the appropriate role and function of government in the regulation of the public transport sector is an interesting topic to study. Should government intervene in the market forces on the public transport market? And where the answer is positive, what is the best regime for intervention? These questions will be addressed in this chapter. The objective of the chapter is therefore to study the relationship between regulatory regimes and the expected outcomes of applying these regimes. The results or outcomes are marked out against the goals or objectives of government.

For assessing the economic effects, insight into the behaviour of both customers and firms is necessary. In this chapter we focus our attention on the behaviour of firms operating in the public transport market. Therefore knowledge of the cost and production structure of the transport sector is of utmost importance for the government to determine how to intervene in the market organisation.

In the theoretical part of this chapter we address public transport in general but in the empirical part we will mainly address urban public transport (transit) in order to achieve sufficient focus. Further, it should be noted that there are several interrelated markets in public transport. Quinet (2000) for instance defines a series of vertical integrated markets: infrastructure management, the rolling stock market, the operators market, the transport auxiliaries market (mainly applicable on freight transport), and the market for transport services. The focus of the paper is on the market for transport services. In addition it is clear that naturally, subsidisation is also an import means for government to influence market outcomes.

In this chapter we first describe the main characteristics of the public transport sector. Important from an economic perspective is that public transport markets are network markets with accompanying specific economies and efficiencies. Many public transport markets have features of monopolies. The nature of monopolies is also the topic of Section 2. In Section 2 we explain a few costs concepts so as to better understand firm behaviour. Then we proceed with a discussion of the (regulating) role of government (Section 3). There we first describe the objectives of government and the instruments government has at hand to regulate. In Section 3 we also distinguish five so called 'regulatory regimes'. Based on a data set of 21 European cities and regions, in Section 4 we assess the regimes. First we describe their characteristics, then investigate interrelationships between these features.

2 Network characteristics of public transport

We focus in this chapter on urban transit as an exponent of underlying processes in the whole transport sector. What many transport sectors have in common is that services are provided via a physical network. For the cost structure this means a relatively high portion of fixed costs in total operating costs, especially in the short run. Of course this applies more for rail companies, but also urban transit bus companies are confronted with fixed costs due to the need for terminals, depots, traffic information systems, etc. Production under fixed costs may lead to monopolies (see also Pels and Rietveld, 2000). This is the reason that we elaborate in Section 2.3 on monopolies. Another feature of producing under network conditions are economies of scale and density.

2.1 Cost concepts

Infrastructure is an essential input factor, necessary for production of transport services. The services and the infrastructure are interrelated. Two concepts are relevant here: sunk costs and cost complementarity.

Sunk costs

Transport infrastructure has the nature of unrecoverable outlay. Sunk costs are related to specific capital assets. These assets have very few alternative uses or have lower revenue when sold. These assets often occur in network sectors. For example investments in cable networks, rail track, gas pipes, etc. are very specific. But also in public transport, investments in rolling stock can be specific to a certain sector.

Costs complementarity

Joint production in transport occurs when a firm uses a common or shared major input factor such as rail track, depot, terminal, etc. This means that companies can use the same factor for production of several products and services, e.g. passenger and freight transport, peak and off-peak transit, etc. Once these facilities are produced by the firm for the production of a single service, they can be used at no further cost for the production of other services. Joint production implies that the total cost of producing a set of outputs by a single firm is less than the sum of the cost of producing each separated output by a specialised firm (Baumol *et al.*, 1982). So the use of a shared input factor means that the costs of producing several commodities or services are complementary. Cost complementarity implies that the marginal costs of producing output type i decline when the level of output type j increases. The cost function is said to be subadditive. Subadditivity means that it costs less to produce the various outputs together (in one firm) than to produce them separately (in several firms).

2.2 Economies

Producing under network conditions implies relatively high fixed costs and enhances the chance for economies of scale and density. More insight into the appearance of economies of density and of scale is of importance for (de)regulation policy and helps governments by defining the optimal size of the network. If economies of density prevail under conditions of subadditivity (everywhere decreasing marginal, and thus, average costs), Tirole (1988) concludes that it is not wise for government to allow direct competition over the same track (competition on the road). Competition via tendering of concessions (competition for the road) is then more appropriate.

There are three types of relevant economies: economies of scale, scope, and network density.

Economies of scale

The question for public transport firms and authorities is, what is the optimal size of the network and what is the optimal size of the firm, for instance expressed in fleet size. Most recent studies provide evidence for the classical U-shaped ('bath tube') cost function (see Figure 2.4.1 where MC stands for marginal costs and AC for average costs). This implies decreasing returns to scale for the big companies.

There is an optimal scale level for bus transit companies. Berechman (1993) for instance summarises the results of a number of studies and reports for western bus companies an optimal fleet size of 300 to 500 buses. The results of Cowie and Asenova (1999) confirm these findings. They report an optimal size of 200 to 400 buses. As aforementioned most recent empirical studies in public transport find results in favour of the U-shaped cost curve with a very broad range of constant returns to scale (Viton, 1997; Kerstens, 1999).

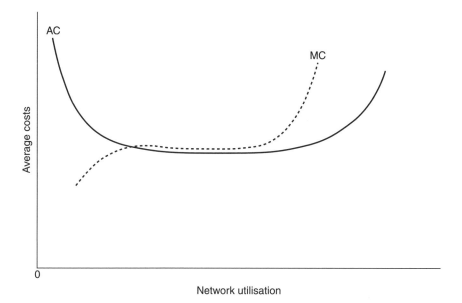

Figure 2.4.1 Typical cost function in public transport.

Consider an elementary costs function where total costs C depend on total output y and other factors X. Thus, $C = C(y, X)$. Then the elasticity of costs with respect to output ϵ is defined as $\partial \ln C / \partial \ln y$. Returns to scale (RTS) are then defined as the reciprocal of the elasticity of costs with respect to (total) output.

$$RTS = \frac{1}{\partial \ln C / \partial \ln y} = \frac{1}{\epsilon}$$

In the case of multiple outputs this generalises to:

$$RTS = \frac{1}{\sum_j \partial \ln C / \partial \ln y_j} = \frac{1}{\sum_j \epsilon_j}$$

where ϵ_j is the elasticity of costs with respect to output j. If network effects are included in the formula, RTS are defined as the proportional increase in outputs and points served (P) due to a proportional increase in all inputs:

$$RTS = \frac{1}{\Sigma \epsilon_j + \epsilon_p}$$

where ϵ_p is the elasticity of costs with respect to the number of points served (Pels and Rietveld, 2000).

Economies of scope

Economies of scope are defined as the reduction in unit costs in a multiple output product setting, caused by changes in the product mix. It is efficient to produce multiple outputs, for instance because the production processes of each of these products are very similar. So it is obvious that a railroad company produces both passenger and freight services on the same track. Economies of scope imply that the average production costs of joint production are lower than the production cost when each of the products is produced separately. There are diseconomies of scope when the average production costs rise when both services are combined. This is for instance the case when there are differences in speed and weight of passenger and freight trains, which means different demands on the flexibility of the schedule.

There is little empirical work done on economies of scope in public transport. An exemption is Vitton (1992, 1993) who reports on economies of scope for the transit companies in the San Francisco Bay area.

Economies of density

Economies of traffic density are an important concept in transport industries. It is defined as the decline in unit cost resulting from the carrying of more traffic on a given network, e.g. total cost decline as the occupancy rate of the network (vehicles per hour) increases.

The question is what is the optimal interval supplied on a given infrastructure network. Economies of density apply to the utilisation of a given network. For instance increasing returns to density in rail services means that an increase in the utilisation of the rail track network (more train-kilometres per track-kilometre) can be attained with lower unit costs. In Figure 2.4.1 this is seen in the decreasing part of the curve. Purely seen in the light of production efficiency, it is wise to increase output. Whether this is also a commercially viable strategy of course depends on market demand. When the network is already used at full capacity, increasing output is only possible at high costs. Congestion then leads to decreasing returns to density (the rising part of the AC-curve of Figure 2.4.1). Many empirical studies find that public transport, and especially bus transit, is characterised by economies of density (see for instance Oum and Zhang, 1997; De Borger *et al.*, 2002).

We have seen that the existence of economies of scale and density can lead to a monopoly. Whether this is favourable or not is the topic of the next section.

2.3 Natural monopoly

Economic theory states that under conditions of perfect competition firms set their prices to a level were $P = $ marginal cost, which is, in the situation of economies of scale, lower than average costs. So perfect competition under economies of scale (high amount of fixed costs) does not work. A monopolistic market outcome is more probable.

In some cases a monopoly is the best form of market organisation. Due to economies of scale and density in this situation, it is for society as a whole more efficient to produce a product or service through one firm rather than through several firms. This situation is called a natural monopoly. So for society as a whole it is favourable that one company produces for the whole market. Baumol *et al.* (1982) define an industry as a natural monopoly if, over the relevant range of outputs, the cost function is subadditive.[1] This means everywhere declining average costs. To prevent market failure, the authorities can use instruments such as price caps to avoid abuse of market power by the monopolist.

In a non-natural or artificial monopolistic situation, there is no subadditivity. The monopolist in this case does not sustain the monopoly because of cost advantages, but because it succeeds in creating barriers to entry. Natural monopolies can easily shift to artificial monopolies. Therefore artificial monopolies that do not have a subadditive cost structure can only prevail when barriers to entry exist and government is unable or unwilling to remove these.

Regulation of a monopoly

Government control and marginal price setting under monopolistic conditions are necessary to ensure a fair market outcome, skimming off monopolistic rents, and to force firms to behave competitively. Several public transport sectors are often claimed to be a natural monopoly (for urban transit see Mills, 1980 and De Borger *et al.*, 2002; for rail see Nyfer, 2002; Savage, 1997; and van Ooststroom,

1999). The crucial factor is whether economies of scale or density are present in the production of these transport services. This issue was dealt with in the previous section.

A monopolist can influence market prices. Therefore some kind of regulation by the government is necessary. In case of a natural monopoly (subadditivity on the relevant part of the demand function) this regulation often takes the form of tariff regulation (price cap regulation or rate-of-return regulation – see Ministerie van Economische Zaken, 2002 and Berechman, 1993). It is essential to investigate whether entry barriers prevail, since the monopoly may be artificial and regulation should encourage more competition. So different regulatory measures apply in different situations. Of importance for this paper is a form of regulation that is called 'public service obligation'. The authorities impose on the monopolist the obligation to supply a certain service that in itself makes a loss for the firm. For instance supply of off-peak services in public transport. In this way government assures that certain products or services are supplied. The consequence of this kind of regulation is that firms are obliged to cross subsidise the loss-making services through their profit-making services. In public transport cross-subsidisation has several dimensions:

- in space: between profitable lines and money losing lines, or between profitable inner city transit services and money losing rural services;
- in time: the fact there is in many cases a flat fare implies that the difference between peak hour and off-peak hour fares, which stems from the cost differences between peak and off-peak, is not charged to the customers.

By definition, a monopoly where there is cross-subsidisation is not sustainable (Quinet, 2000). Oum *et al.* (1992) stipulate that cross-subsidisation leads to allocative inefficiencies. Following Berechman (1993) a prerequisite for a proper deregulation policy in transit is the absence of cross-subsidisation. If authorities regulate in a way that the firm is obliged to cross-subsidise, they actually weaken the monopoly. If authorities do not protect that weakened firm, it is exposed to creaming off the profits by smart competitive firms. Despite these drawbacks, authorities are eager to use this instrument of public service obligation, because in this way a service that is non-profitable but nevertheless considered useful can be sustained and the prices of this service can be held the same as for the profitable services.

3 Regulating transport activities

3.1 Introduction

What happens if the government does not regulate the public transport market? We have seen in the previous sections that the most likely market outcome in that case is a monopoly. Because government is the safeguard of social welfare, potential market failure makes it necessary for government to regulate. In this section we discuss the regulatory instruments at hand for governments. In this we distinguish the national from the regional or local level. Before doing so, we pay attention to government objectives.

3.2 Government objectives

There is a broad literature on the role of the public sector in transport. The key question is what is the fundamental reason for the public sector to intervene in the market forces on the mobility market and what are the effects? (see for instance van Delden en Veraart, 2001; Berechman, 1993; Ministerie van Economische Zaken, 2002). The main economic arguments underlying (de)regulation in public transport are market failure and income distribution (Berechman, 1993).[2] These arguments run parallel with the policy goals of efficiency and equity.

Market failure and efficiency objectives

Under certain conditions markets may fail to allocate resources effectively. The main reason for this is that under these conditions the marginal costs faced by individuals in consuming the goods and services are not equal to the marginal cost to society as a whole or not equal to market prices. This leads to inefficiencies such as over or underproduction or consumption of these goods and services. The main reasons for market failure are externalities, public goods, imperfect information, and (natural) monopolies. This paper is not the place to elaborate further on these issues (we refer to Hillier, 1997 and Button, 1993 for more literature on this theme). Market failure is often associated with efficiency goals. Government often wants companies to improve the way they allocate scarce resources (static efficiency).

Fair distribution of incomes and equity objectives

The equity principle is often another important argument for government intervention in the public transport market. Government considers public transport as essential for welfare of the individual citizens and therefore a reason for regulation (sustaining a socially minimum level of public transport for specific target groups (elderly, handicapped) and in low density rural areas for those who don't have a car). When government pursues equity objectives, we see government in her role as the 'patras familia', the guardian of public interest. Non-discriminating service supply, guarantee of deliverance, protecting the weak and the poor in society, prevention of negative effects on the environment, safety and public health – all of these objectives stem from fairness and equity as driving forces for governments.

3.3 Regulation at the national level

At the national level there are several instruments government may use to regulate public transport:

*   control of market structure (for instance by means of ownership (private versus public production));
*   control of market prices (price cap regulation or rate-of-return regulation);
*   control of the external organisation (splitting up or vertical integration of firms);
*   influencing the way firms compete with each other (for instance competition on or for the market);
*   additional regulation (quality demands, implementation of public service obligation, etc.).

When we take a closer look at these tools for national government we find that they are not all of the same order. Three main dimensions can be distinguished: (a) changing the market dimension by liberalisation (monopoly versus pure market competition); (b) changing the organisational and legal dimension by privatisation (public or private ownership); (3) influencing the steering dimensions of individual firms, either private or public, by (de)regulation (autonomous behaviour versus regulated behaviour).

In this paper we use the word 'regulation' in a broad sense that is meant to cover all three above mentioned dimensions.

3.4 Regulation at the regional and local level

As mentioned above the national regulatory environment for public transport consists of three dimensions. Together with a given historic situation the specific interpretation of these dimensions leads to a certain regulatory context or climate at national level. However the focus of this paper is on the regional and local level. At that level local or regional authorities take the national regulatory climate and legislation as conditional. As the research topic of this paper is public transport, we focus on the objectives of local/regional authorities with respect to public transport in general and buses in particular. A main tool or instrument for the responsible authorities (RA) is the way in which they design the contractual relationships with the operator (OP). We address this topic later on.

Regulatory regimes

For the regional and local level we distinguish five so called regulatory regimes (see Table 2.4.1). These regimes apply to the public transport sector and are of course closely related to the national regulatory climate.

We follow Berechman 1993, Isotope 1997, and Maretope 2002 by classifying the regimes according to managerial freedom. For the market outcome there is

Table 2.4.1 Description of regulatory regimes

Organisational form or regulatory regime	Production by publicly owned company	Concession via operational franchise	Concession exclusive	Rules of the game	Free market
Strategic level freedom of designing the network	RA	RA	RA	OP	OP
Tactical level freedom of designing the services	RA	RA	RA or OP*	OP or RA	OP
Operational level freedom of operations	RA	OP	OP	OP	OP

Note
RA = responsible authority, OP = operator.
* given the objectives of regional authorities, in exclusive concession regimes in Europe the competence for designing the services mostly rests with the RA, although there are cases where the OP performs these tasks, such as for instance is the case in the city of Amersfoort, the Netherlands. In 'rules of the game' regimes the situation is just the opposite. Managerial freedom on the tactical level mostly rests with the OP.

no difference whether a company is privately or publicly owned, but it does matter whether the management of the company has freedom to decide itself what is best for the company. It appears that it is not ownership that determines the efficiency of a firm, but managerial freedom. The order of the regimes is hierarchical in a way that when moving from left to right freedom for the OP increases and the influence of the RA diminishes.

The regimes we distinguish are:

- production of the services by government itself. Service by a publicly controlled or publicly owned company. Public agency;
- tendering, granting a concession. The government has to define the terms of requirements for a service. There are three types of tendering:

  a   operational franchise: government owns both infrastructure and rolling stock and gives these assets in loan to the operator who only has operational risks. In this regime government has the initiative. It makes it possible for government to level market barriers by preventing sunk cost becoming a barrier for entrance to the market;

  b   exclusive concessions: potential public transport operators have to compete for the exclusive right to operate that service for a given period of time. After the tendering a temporary monopoly exists. Companies that subscribe for the concession can be either private or public;

  c   granting non-exclusive concessions. In that case more than one (but a limited number) operator acquires the right to operate a certain service for a given period. Customers have freedom to choose between either operators;[3]

- 'setting the rules of the game'. Government sets rules that limit operational freedom of the companies only a little. This regime is competition on the road or on the track with a few operational limits such as for instance a minimum frequency per route per operator and a minimum age of the rolling stock. A special case here is the situation in the UK outside of London, where as a result of the Transport Act of 1985 competition on the road was permitted. New entrants only have the obligation to give 42 days' notice in advance of starting operations, to the government of their intentions. Besides rules on bus safety and licensing no other rules apply. In this regime government hardly interferes in operational, financial or investment decisions of the companies;
- free competitive markets. No rules that restrict operational freedom whatsoever.[4] This means that government has no say in decisions on fare level and fare structure, use of input factors, quality of service, route network, design and size of rolling stock, vehicle type, freedom of entry and exit, investment policy, legal ownership of firms, and fixed facilities such as terminals, depots, and central bus stations.

To give more substance to the regimes, in Table 2.4.1 they are specified in three layers. These are the layers where managerial freedom exposes itself:

1 Strategic level: the topics in this level concern policy definition and decision-making. At this level the objectives of public transport and global definition of the network are defined.

2 Tactical level: based on the objectives where the level of service (operations) is defined, including the accompanying assets such as vehicles, personnel, etc.

3 Operational level: operation itself, tariff collection and sales, etc.

Table 2.4.2 shows the regimes with respect to the aspects of competition and legal ownership.

3.5 Effects of regulation

We argued above that regulatory regimes and the need to regulate are interconnected, but what are in the real world the effects of (highly) regulated environments? Several authors have reported on this relation. For instance Oum *et al.* (1992) state that over-capitalisation of highly regulated companies is a well-known example of allocative inefficiency. They state that deregulation can be the means to correct allocative and technical inefficiency. Gillen, Oum, and Tretheway (1987) identified allocative inefficiencies for outputs in the Canadian air sector. Canadian regulatory policy induced the carriers to expand their fleet size beyond the economic optimal level. Berechman (1993) and Levaggi (1994) find a similar result for urban bus transit in a highly regulated and subsidised environment. Cowie (2002) reports a declining X-inefficiency (management slack) in the UK bus sector when companies entered a more competitive regime. Johansen, Larsen, and Norheim (2001) come to the same conclusion for the bus sector in Norway. Apparently management of public transport companies is more stimulated to act efficiently under competitive pressure in a deregulated environment.

It is also interesting to consider the relation between ownership of the operating company and efficiency of that company. Oum, Waters, and Yu (1999) report as a result of their empirical work that efficiency is positively influenced by managerial freedom, apart from public or private ownership. Also Pina and Torres (2001) conclude in their survey on efficiency in public transport in a number of Spanish cities, that private management is not necessarily more efficient than public management. So the regulatory and competitive surrounding is of greater importance for efficiency than ownership.

After the wave of mergers and acquisitions in the private UK bus sector, Cowie and Asenova (1999) report a high degree of technical inefficiency due to lack of competition. An oligopoly situation resulted as a consequence of non-interference of government in this merger process. According to Cowie and Asenova (1999) re-regulation should be considered again. Oum and Zhang (1997) report that also in the US in, among others, the railroad sector government did not interfere in the process of mergers and acquisitions. In that case the argument used was that increasing the scale of production should lead to

Table 2.4.2 Competition, ownership and regulatory regimes

Organisational form or regulatory regime	Production by publicly owned company	Concession via operational franchise	Concession exclusive	Rules of the game	Free market
Number of competitors	non (monopoly)	During tendering phase temporally many	During tendering phase temporally many	many	many
Fierceness of competition	non	modest	modest	strong	strong
Ownership of the company	public	public or private	public or private	public or private	private

efficiency gains. And also in the railway sector the evidence is strong that increasing competitiveness due to liberalisation and deregulation leads to more efficient companies (for a comprehensive review see Oum, Waters, and Yu (1999).

4 Assessment of regulatory regimes

In this section we first give examples of the regulatory regimes in a cross-national setting. Second, we give an assessment of some of these examples by investigating their structure. The authors used, for the empirical part of the paper, a sample that is indicated in Table 2.4.3. The data set for this sample is based on a study by AGV (VGG, 2002) and an UITP/EMTA report on contractual relations between authorities and operators (UITP, 2003). The authors enriched the data set by sending a questionnaire to the cities. This questionnaire was focused on the public transport objectives of the authorities. Some limitations of the data set are that there are no indicators available on efficiency and equity and that it is probably not entirely random. Therefore it is not necessarily representative for the whole of Europe, and it is not possible to determine what type of regime is performing best. It is the aim of this section to relate the type of regime to the type of objective of government and to analyse similarities and correlations between the regimes

4.1 Examples of regulatory regimes in public transport

In Table 2.4.3 we give some examples of regulatory regimes in various countries. Per country it is indicated which municipality or region is an exponent of that regime. Note that it is possible for countries to appear in more than one regime. The numbers between brackets refer to the cases that are used by the authors in the case study.

4.2 Features of regulatory schemes in European public transport

Allocation of risks

We analysed the allocation of risks between the operator (OP) and the responsible authority (RA). The RA has to decide on how to allocate the division of the risks associated with public transport between the OP and the RA itself. There are two main risks associated with public transport, i.e. risks concerning operating costs and risks concerning revenues. The allocation of risks is formalised in a contract between the OP and the RA. We distinguish in this respect three types of contracts (see Table 2.4.4).

In our sample of 21 cases gross costs contracts are by far the most frequently used (N = 14). Management contracts and net costs contracts are more rare (N respectively 3 and 4).

Table 2.4.3 Examples of regulatory regimes in public transport

Right to initiate public transport	Authority				Market	
Management of public transport	Authority itself	Delegated by the authority			Market	
Organisational form or regulatory regime	Production by publicly owned company	Concession via operational franchise	Concession exclusive	Concession non-exclusive	Rules of the game	Free market
Examples	**France:** • Strasbourg • Paris (18) **Belgium:** • Brussels (1) • Flanders (5) **Germany:** • commercial services: • Frankfurt (6) • Leipzig (12) • Munich (15) **The Netherlands:** • Amsterdam • Rotterdam **Austria:** • Vienna (21)	**France:** • Lille • Clermont Ferrand (2)	**The Netherlands:** • Almere (13) • Amersfoort • Gelderland-Oost (7) **Germany:** • non-commercial services e.g. Hamburg (9) Hannover (10) **Finland:** • Helsinki (11) **Sweden:** • Gotenburg (8) • Sundsvall (19) **Italy:** • Torino (20) **Norway:** • Oslo (16 + 17)	**Chile:** • Santiago **Canada:** • long distance buses on two corridors	**UK:** • Outside London, commercial	**Developing Countries**

Table 2.4.3 Continued

Organisational form or regulatory regime	Production by publicly owned company	Concession via operational franchise	Concession exclusive	Concession non-exclusive	Rules of the game	Free market
			UK: • London and outside London non-commercial e.g. Manchester (14) **Denmark** • Copenhagen (3 + 4)			

Notes
* This is a specific case of concessions. In practice it is not very widespread. The examples given are exceptions. Both Chile and Canada are more characterised by the rules of the game and the exclusive concessions regimes. In the rest of the paper this regime is neglected.

Table 2.4.4 Types of contracts and allocation of risks

Contract type	Management contract		Gross cost contract		Net cost contract	
Risks:	RA	OP	RA	OP	RA	OP
Costs	X			X		X
Revenues	X		X			X

Tendering

Approximately in half of the cases the contract is tendered. That applies mostly to the concessional regimes. There are hardly any cases where the contract is privately allocated.

Division of responsibilities between OP and RA

It is obvious that authorities want to have a firm say in those aspects that directly influence the quality of supply and the fare level. It appears that in only one out of the 21 valid cases the RA decides to leave the responsibility of setting the fare level to the OP. In all the other cases it is the government itself that sets the fare level. The same holds for the service level: although the outcomes are more dispersed, in the majority of the cases (14 out of 21) this responsibility also rests with the RA.

Incentive schemes

In order to ensure that the operator contributes to the fulfilment of the objectives of the RA incentives may be used. Necessarily to have an impact on the operator's performance, bonus/penalty amounts need to be sufficient with respect to the total amount that is allocated in the contract. In the studied cases incentives are indeed commonly used. There is a relation between the contract type/allocation of contract risks and incentive schemes. For instance in the region of Clermont-Ferrand the contract between the RA and the OP can be considered as a classic management contract: the RA bears both costs and revenue risks. In this case incentives have been formulated with regard to the number of passengers, the quality, and the cost efficiency of the services. If we consider the total sample we see that, in only four out of 21 cases, the RA don't use bonuses or penalties. When we have a closer look at the basis of the incentive schemes it shows that in general incentives based on quality of supply are favoured (seven out of 17), followed by incentives based on patronage (four out of 17).

Contract duration

The duration of the contract between RA and OP is determined by the RA. The authority has to take into account that a short duration of the contract will imply that the operator has only little time to earn back his investments for instance in new rolling stock and hence will charge a relatively high price per unit. In the studied sample authorities seem to be aware of this mechanism. The average duration of the contracts, all bus contracts, is five years. Since the economic life-cycle of buses is approximately ten years, a duration of five years may be considered reasonable with respect to the pay back period of the operator.

Ownership infrastructure and rolling stock

In all of our relevant cases infrastructure is owned by the RA. In 15 out of the 20 valid cases legal ownership rests with the RA. In the other five cases ownership of infrastructure rests with the OP, but in all these five cases this is a public operator (regime one). This is consistent with theories of for instance Berechman (1993) who considers the ownership of infrastructure as an important asset for OP in exercising market power. Ownership of infrastructure in private hands would therefore form a bottleneck for competition.

The above described findings are presented in Table 2.4.5.

4.3 Variability within regulatory regimes

In this section we take a closer look at the regimes from two perspectives. The first perspective concerns the confrontation of the regimes with the objectives with respect to public transport. We investigate to what extent the priority given to efficiency or equity by public authorities has an impact on the choice of regulatory regime. The second perspective concerns the steering mechanisms available to the RA, i.e. the way they design the contractual relation with the OP. We investigate among others what steering mechanisms are often found to be combined in regulatory regimes, and which are not.

Because the variables are ranked we chose Spearman's rank correlation to quantify the dependence between the variables. The encoding of the variables is reported in Appendix 2.4.1. The correlation coefficients are numbers between -1 and $+1$. The outcome 0 implies no correlation. We tested the significance of the correlation at the 0.01 level (two tailed).

Regimes, objectives, and national regulatory climate

First we give a short description of the meaning and the expected correlation between the variables.

Concerning the national regulatory climate we cluster the case studies into four broad categories that represent the way national authorities act with respect to questions of introducing more competition in formerly publicly owned or steered sectors. This climate applies not only to the transport sector but also to many public sectors in these countries, such as telecom, water supply, energy supply, airports, etc. A central issue here is whether the market should be freed completely, or whether the industry may gain from keeping some responsibilities or

Table 2.4.5 Description of variety of regulatory tools in European public transport

	Type of contract			Contracts tendered	Contracts not tendered	Responsibility service level		Responsibility fare level	
	Management	Gross cost	Net cost			RA	OP	RA	OP
No. of cases (%)	14%	66%	20%	52%	48%	66%	34%	95%	5%
Total no. valid cases		21		21			21		21

Basis for incentives

	Cost reduction	Combination of supply, efficiency, and quality	Quality of supply	Patronage	Combination of patronage and environment
N~o. of cases (%)	0	29%	41%	24%	6%
Total no. valid cases			17		

	Duration of contract (years)					Ownership infrastructure		Ownership rolling stock	
	2	3	4	5	6	RA	OP	RA	OP
No. of cases (%)	5%	16%	5%	53%	21%	75%	25%	95%	5%
Total no. valid cases			19				20		21

ownership of assets in the hand of the public sector. The four types of climates we distinguish are ranked according to an increasing appreciation of market forces in network markets.

- A first group of countries has a low appreciation of market forces and emphasises the role of the public sector. Liberalisation and deregulation is hardly noticeable. Examples in Europe are Belgium, France, and Finland.
- The second group consists of countries that have started the process of deregulation. Examples are Germany and Austria.
- The third group consists of countries that tend to more market and less government but still want to influence market outcome in a certain way. The Nordic countries are front runners in deregulation of some public sectors. The Netherlands and Italy follow their leads. These countries are characterised by moderate reforms in public transport.
- The final type of climate we define is characterised by deregulation and privatisation of network sectors on a large scale, i.e. postal services, water supply, transport. The main trigger is a right wing political climate. A good example in Europe is the UK.

Transport plans comprise for public transport a great number of objectives. Examples are growth in patronage, enhancing the quality of public transport, maximising the number of vehicle-kilometres supplied, improving the accessibility of public transport, improving the cost/benefit ratio, etc. We have summarised the prevailing objectives of our cases in three categories: (1) mainly aimed at efficiency; (2) aimed at both efficiency and equity; and (3) mainly aimed at equity.

We expect that the public transport objectives that a RA strives for (in terms of efficiency and equity) have implications for the regulatory regimes described in Section 3.4. In addition, we expect that the national regulatory climate also gives direction to the regional regimes: regions are not entirely free to choose their own way.

For the used data set the correlation between these three variables is expressed in Table 2.4.6. We refer to Appendix 2.4.1 for the underlying definition of the variables. The table shows that all correlations are significant at the 0.01 level (two tailed) and we may conclude that in the data set indeed a strong

Table 2.4.6 Correlation between objectives, regimes, and national climate

	National regulatory climate	*Regional objectives (efficiency versus equity)*
Objectives	$R = -0.844$ $p = 0.0000$	
Regulatory regime	$R = 0.692$ $p = 0.0005$	$R = -0.788$ $p = 0.0000$

regulatory national climate coincides with priority to equity objectives at the regional level. Also, a laissez faire regime tends to go together with priority on efficiency objectives. Moreover as may be expected the national climate and the regimes are positively correlated. This means that in this sample, countries where free markets in public transport are distributed at the national level tend to have regional public transport authorities that operate public transport on their own behalf by means of a public company. As indicated earlier these regimes mainly focus on equity objectives.

Ownership and efficiency objectives

If we take a closer look at the ownership data in the sample, it is noticeable that legal ownership (either public or private) of the OP is significantly related to the question of whether public transport is tendered or not, to ownership of the infrastructure, to the objectives of the authorities, and to the prevailing regulatory regime (see Appendix 2.4.2). The signs of the correlations are in all cases as expected and we can interpret these findings as follows: when the RA exercises a liberal or deregulated policy with regard to public transport it is probable that the company that has a contract for public transport services with the RA is in private hands. In those cases the RA owns the infrastructure so as to exercise power over the OP. This is consistent with the policy of the EU that aims at a separation of ownership of infrastructure and the right to operate services on that infrastructure. Furthermore when efficiency objectives prevail in the policy of the authority the operator is a private firm. If on the other hand the authority focuses on equity objectives, the operator is publicly owned.

Regimes and regulatory tools

The research topic we study here is the possible relation between the regulatory regimes and the tools used by the RA.

The tools available to the RA are:

- the type of contract between RA and OP which represents the division of risks between the OP and the RA;
- division of responsibilities between RA and OP concerning the tactical level of operations (see Table 2.4.1);
- the ownership of infrastructure and rolling stock.

TYPE OF CONTRACT

We expect a relation between the regimes and the contract types in a way that management contracts (both cost and revenue risks carried by RA) are most commonly used in regimes where the public transport production is done by a publicly owned company and granting an exclusive concession is accompanied by a net cost contract (both risks borne by the OP). In our sample however this

Table 2.4.7 Regulatory regimes and type of contract in the sample

| | Regulatory regime | | | | |
Contract type:	Production by publicly owned company	Concession via operational franchise	Concession exclusive	Rules of the game	Free market
Management contract	Flanders	Clermont-Ferrand	Torino		
Gross costs contract	Brussels bus Frankfurt Hamburg bus Hannover Leipzig Munich bus Paris Vienna		Copenhagen bus Copenhagen metro/Gothenburg Helsinki Oslo city Oslo region		
Net costs contract			Gelderland-Oost Almere Manchester nc. Sundsvall		

is not the case as is shown in Table 2.4.7. The correlation between the regimes and the type of contract is not significant (R = 0.33).

Eight of the nine self-production regimes have a gross costs contract (cost risks borne by the OP, revenue risks by the RA). The only exception is Flanders that combines a self-production regime with a management contract. An overall observation is therefore that, independent of the type of regime, gross costs contracts are the most popular in Europe. Probably this has something to do with the new view on public transport of the recent decades. The new era marks the shift in objectives from deficit suppletion (loss equalisation) through to sound contracting and funding of transport services (efficiency objectives). In this respect the RA introduced a more business like relation to the OP and in such a relation the company is the only actor who knows the operating costs and is able to influence them. So it is natural that the OP bears the costs or industrial risk. The responsibilities for the fare level setting on the other hand still rests with the RA. Fares are seen by the RA as the main instrument to steer demand for public transport services (equity objectives). So if operators cannot influence fares it is not reasonable that they have to bear the revenue risks.

DIVISION OF RESPONSIBILITIES BETWEEN OP AND RA AND INCENTIVES

Independent of regulatory regimes, authorities consider fare level setting and service level setting as important tools as is shown in Table 2.4.5. It is therefore not surprising that there is not a significant correlation between these tools and the regimes (see Table 2.4.8, R = -0.25 and -0.17 respectively).

The fact that authorities consider definition of the services as their territory coincides with the fact that they are also responsible for the co-ordination of the services between the different operators and modes. Nevertheless, if the decision of defining the services comes under the responsibility of the RA, the operator still plays a role by making use of his practical expertise in bringing solutions to local mobility problems. A good example is Flanders, where the Flemish government has entrusted 'de Lijn' (OP) with the entire responsibility for organising, promoting, and co-ordinating all local and regional public bus transport activities on its territory. In the case of Flanders it is interesting to note that, though the contract can be considered a management contract (see Table 2.4.7) the responsibility for service planning is in the hands of 'de Lijn' and does not belong to the agenda of the RA. All issues related to the structure, level, and reduction of fares and ticketing are, in all types of contracts, under the competence of the RA.

The region of Hannover, Germany is a striking exception to the observation that in general authorities are responsible for fare matters. In Hannover the two joint operators (Ustra and RegioBus Hannover) are responsible for developing a common fare structure, for distribution of the fare income between the two of them and for ticketing. This is extraordinary because the OPs and the Region Hannover agreed upon a gross costs contract in which the risk of the fare revenues is allocated to the Region. So the steering instruments for fare revenues are in the hands of the OP notwithstanding that the RA bears the financial risk

Table 2.4.8 Regulatory regimes and division of responsibilities

		Regulatory regime				
		Production by publicly owned company	Concession via operational franchise	Concession exclusive	Rules of the game	Free market
Responsibility for service level	RA	Frankfurt Hamburg Munich Paris Vienna	Clermont-Ferrand	Copenhagen metro & bus Gothenburg Manchester Oslo c + r Sundsvall Torino		
	OP	Brussels bus Flanders Hannover Leipzig		Gelderland Helsinki Almere		
Responsibility for fare level	RA	Frankfurt Hamburg Munich Paris Vienna Brussels bus Flanders Leipzig	Clermont-Ferrand	Copenhagen metro & bus Gothenburg Manchester Oslo c + r Sundsvall Torino Gelderland Helsinki Almere		
	OP	Hannover				

for the revenues. Maybe this has something to do with the strong accent on quality of supply of public transport in the Hannover Region. A quality management agreement is the core of the contracts of carriage between the Region and the OP. These contracts have the purpose of guaranteeing high quality public transport. Poor fulfilment of agreed-upon quality standards leads to application of penalties. It seems that in the Hannover Region quality of supply is of larger importance than the financial performance of the system.

OWNERSHIP OF INFRASTRUCTURE AND ROLLING STOCK

In our sample ownership of infrastructure is negatively correlated to the regulatory regimes ($R = -0.69$, $p = 0.0008$). In a majority of cases ownership of the infrastructure rests with the RA, and it is no coincidence that in the cases where the OP owns the infrastructure the regime is characterised by a public company. So in these cases the RA exercises its power through its own company. That ownership of rolling stock is not significantly correlated to the regimes ($R = -0.21$) is not surprising since we only studied bus cases and in these situations there is no need for government to own the buses because there is a vivid second-hand market for buses and when an OP loses a contract he doesn't have to depreciate his assets that much.

4.4 Subsidy and incentives

It is interesting to take a closer look at the relationship between the variable that represents the base for subsidy and the variable that expresses the basis for the incentives. Subsidies themselves work as an incentive: subsidy is only paid if the OP performs as agreed upon in the contract. So we can argue that incentives on top of formal subsidy arrangements are not necessary. When a RA uses a form of subsidy that is independent of both supply and demand (lump sum subsidy) it seems obvious that the RA enforce on the OP a form of incentive, i.e. a bonus/penalty scheme. So we expect a negative correlation between the two: when the basis of the subsidy is fixed or nearly fixed, we expect incentive schemes based on variable elements such as quality of supply, patronage, and environmental issues. If on the other hand the subsidy is already variable (dependent on supply or demand) there is less need for additional incentives. These expectations coincide with Principal-Agent theories (see for instance Walker, 1998).

However this conjecture is not supported by empirical reality ($R = 0.174$). When we look at the cases more closely it is striking that among the sample of 21 cities/regions, there are four who subsidise their OP a lump sum budget and don't have incentive schemes as outlined above. For most of the other cases the practice is just the other way around as one might expect: a variable subsidy is in many cases accompanied by a variable incentive. We conclude that there is a wide variety in subsidy and incentive schemes. It is clear that there is scope for a more intensive use of these instruments by RAs to ensure that public interests are well served by public transport operations.

5 Concluding remarks

For government policies in public transport (railroads and bus transit) insight into economies of scale and density is of importance. Due to the relatively high proportion of fixed costs in total costs, on the public transport market a monopolistic market organisation is probable. If economies prevail under conditions of subadditivity, a natural monopoly will emerge. This calls for regulatory measures by the public sector. In a study of 21 European public transport cases, it was shown that competition is positively related to efficiency objectives of authorities. In regulatory regimes that are characterised by deregulation and liberalisation efficiency objectives prevail. On the other hand highly regulated regimes opt for equity objectives. Increasing deficits in the public sector result in the prevalence of efficiency goals nowadays. Introducing forms of (regulated) competition can help to bring these goals nearer. Conditionally it is here that operators get sufficient freedom to organise their production in harmony with network characteristics that exist. A well defined contract between authority and operator can in this respect act as a solid and effective steering mechanism. However, experience in European cities and regions shows that there is still a wide variety of practices and that some of these practices most probably are not efficient.

Notes

* Faculty of Economics, Free University Amsterdam, amouwen@feweb.vu.nl; prietveld@ feweb.vu.nl.
1 Subadditivity in transport has been explained above.
2 A third objective is stimulating innovation. This topic is not dealt with in this paper.
3 In real world public transport this regime does not exist very often, so in the empirical section this regime is omitted.
4 Note that even under complete deregulation government will enforce rules of a more institutional nature, such as rules on safety, emission of pollutants, and administrative rules (licensing).

References.

Baumol, W.J., Panzar, J.C., and Willig, R.D. (1982) *Contestable markets and the theory of industry structure*, Harcourt Brace Jovanovich, New York.
Berechman, J. (1993) 'Public Transit Economics and Deregulation Policy' *Studies in regional science and urban economics*, Vol. 23: Elsevier Science Publishers.
Button, K.J. (1993) *Transport Economics*, 2nd edn, Edward Elgar, University Press, Cambridge.
Cantos, P. and Maudos, J. (2001) 'Regulation and efficiency: the case of European railways' *Transportation Research, part A*, 459–472.
Cowie, J. and Darinka Asenova, 'Organisation form, scale effects and efficiency in the British bus industry' *Transportation 1999*, Vol. 26, 231–248.
Cowie, J. (2002) 'Acquisition, efficiency and scale economics: an analysis of the British bus industry' *Transport Reviews*, Vol. 22, No. 2, 147–157.
De Borger, B., Kerstens, Kristiaan, and Costa, Alvaro (2002) 'Public transport performance: what does one learn from frontier studies?' *Transport Reviews*, Vol. 22, No. 1, 1–38.

Delden, P. van and Veraart, M. (2001) 'Publieke dienstverlening in de markt' *Business Contact*, Amsterdam/Antwerpen.

Gillen, D.W., Oum, T.H., and Tretheway, M.W. (1985) *Airline cost and performance: implications for public industry policies*, University of British Columbia Press, Vancouver, B.C.

Hillier, B. (1997) *The Economics of Asymmetric Information*, MacMillan Press Ltd., London.

ISOTOPE, 'Improved structure and organisation for urban transport operations of passengers in Europe', EC-DGVII, 1997.

Johansen, K.W., Larsen, O.I., and Nordheim, B. (2001) 'Towards achievement of both allocative efficiency and X-efficiency in public transport' *Journal of transport economics and policy*, Vol. 35, part 3, 491–511.

Kerstens, K. (1999) 'Decomposing technical efficiency and effectiveness of French urban transport' *Annales d'economie et de Statistique*, 54: 129–155, in De Borger, B., Kristiaan Kerstens and Alvaro Costa (2002) 'Public transport performance: what does one learn from frontier studies?' *Transport Reviews*, Vol. 22, No. 1, 1–38.

Levaggi, R. (1994) 'Parametric and non-parametric approach to efficiency, the case of public transport in Italy' *Studi Economici*, 49: 67–88, in De Borger, B., Kristiaan Kerstens, and Alvaro Costa (2002) 'Public transport performance: what does one learn from frontier studies?' *Transport Reviews*, Vol. 22, No. 1, 1–38.

Maretope, European conference on public transport regulatory change, Brussels, 25 October 2002.

Mills, E. (1980) *Urban Economics*, 2nd edn, Scott, Foresman and Company, Glenview Ill.

Ministerie van Economische Zaken (2003) *Vragenderwijs*, vraagsturing in de praktijk, Den Haag.

Ministerie van Economische Zaken (2002) *Welvaart en de regulering van netwerksectoren*, Den Haag.

Nyfer (2002) *Grenzen aan Benutting*, Joost P. Poort.

Ooststroom, H.P.C. (1999) *Marktwerking en regulering bij de spoorwegen*.

Oum, T.H., Trethaway, M.W., and Waters II, W.G. (1992) *Transportation Research, Part A*, Vol. 26a, No. 6, 493–505.

Oum, T.H., Waters II, W.G., and Yu, C. (1999) 'A survey of productivity and efficiency measurements in rail transport' *Journal of transport economics and policy*, Vol. 33, part 1, 9–42.

Oum, T.H. and Zhang, Y. (1997) 'A note on scale economies in transport' *Journal of transport economics and policy*, Vol. 31, No. 3, 309–316.

Pels, E. and Rietveld, P. (2000) 'Cost functions in transport' in D.A. Hensher and K.J. Button (eds) *Handbook of Transport Modeling*.

Pina, V. and Torres, L. (2001) 'Analysis of the efficiency of local government services delivery. An application to urban public transport' *Transportation Research, Part A*, 35: 929–944.

Quinet, E. (2000) 'Imperfect competition in transport markets' in B. Polak and A. Heertje (eds) *Analytical Transport Economics, an international perspective*.

Rijkswaterstaat, Adviesdienst verkeer en vervoer, Tweede en derde tussenrapportage VGG, Rotterdam, April 2002.

Savage, I. (1997) 'Scale economies in United States rail transit systems' *Transportation Research, Part A*, Vol. 31, No. 6, 459–473.

Tirole, J. (1988) *The theory of industrial organisation*, MIT Press, Cambridge, Massachusetts.

UITP, Contractual relationships between authorities and operators, Vienna, February 2003.

Viton, P. (1997) 'Technical efficiency in multimode bus transit: a production frontier analysis' *Transportation Research*, 31B: 23–39, in De Borger, B., Kristiaan Kerstens and Alvaro Costa (2002) 'Public transport performance: what does one learn from frontier studies?' *Transport Reviews*, Vol. 22, No. 1, 1–38.

Viton, P. (1992) 'Consolidations of scale and scope in urban transit', *Regional Science and urban economics*, Vol. 22: 25–49, in De Borger B., Kristiaan Kerstens and Alvaro Costa (2002) 'Public transport performance: what does one learn from frontier studies?' *Transport Reviews*, Vol. 22, No. 1, 1–38.

Viton, P. (1993) 'How big should transit be? Evidence from the San Francisco bay area' *Transportation*, 20: 35–57, in De Borger B., Kristiaan Kerstens and Alvaro Costa (2002) 'Public transport performance: what does one learn from frontier studies?' *Transport Reviews*, Vol. 22, No. 1, 1–38.

Walker, M. (1998) 'Information economics and agency theory: elements for a theory of corporate reporting' in T.A. Lee, *Making Corporate Reports Valuable – The Literature Surveys*, Institute of Chartered Accountants of Scotland, Edinburgh.

Appendix 2.4.1

Code table, meaning of the variables

	Variable name	Code	Meaning of code
1	National regulatory climate	1	liberalisation and deregulation hardly noticeable
		2	process of deregulation has only just started
		3	policy of more market less government is implemented
		4	deregulation and privatisation on large scale
2	Risk of the RA/type of contract	1	management contract
		2	gross costs contract
		3	net costs contract
3	Is contract tendered	1	yes
		2	no
4	Basis for subsidy	1	fixed, production independent, lump sum
		2	mainly fixed, production dependent
		3	partly fixed, partly variable
		4	variable based on PAX or revenues
5	Responsibility service level	1	Responsible Authority
		2	Operator
6	Responsibility fare level	1	Responsible Authority
		2	Operator
7	Basis of incentive	1	reduce costs (efficiency)
		2	combination of supply, quality of supply, and efficiency
		3	quality of supply
		4	combination of supply and quality of supply
		5	combination quality of supply and patronage
		6	patronage
		7	combination of patronage and environment
8	Duration of contract	3	3 years
		4	4 years
		5	5 years
		6	6 years
9	Ownership infrastructure	1	Responsible Authority
		2	Operator
10	Ownership rolling stock	1	Responsible Authority
		2	Operator
11	Objectives	1	efficiency
		2	efficiency and equity
		3	equity
12	Regulatory regime	1	production by publicly owned company
		2	concession via operational franchise
		3	concession exclusive
		4	rules of the game
		5	free market
13	Legal ownership	1	publicly
		2	privately

Appendix 2.4.2

Correlation and significance of public transport characteristics of 21 European cities and regions

R	1. National regulatory climate	2. Type of contract	3. Tendered	4. Basis for subsidy	5. Responsibility service level	6. Responsibility fare level	7. Type of incentives	8. Duration of contract	9. Ownership infrastructure	10. Ownership rolling stock	11. Objectives	12. Regulatory regime	13. Legal ownership
1. National regulatory climate		0.537	−0.526	−0.039	−0.344	−0.073	0.260	−0.013	−0.372	−0.181	−0.844 *	0.692*	0.526
2. Type of contract			−0.245	0.335	0.117	−0.019	0.129	0.099	−0.107	0.019	−0.293	0.333	0.245
3. Tendered				0.141	0.135	0.235	−0.070	−0.077	0.638*	−0.235	0.598*	−0.879*	−0.809*
4. Basis for subsidy					0.337	0.011	0.174	−0.080	0.000	−0.011	0.222	−0.093	−0.045
5. Responsibility service level						0.316	−0.034	−0.072	0.378	0.158	0.455	−0.173	−0.135
6. Responsibility fare level							0.129	−0.286	0.397	0.050	0.216	−0.252	−0.235
7. Type of incentives								0.182	−0.088	−0.129	−0.265	0.229	−0.009
8. Duration of contract									−0.214	−0.083	−0.005	0.098	−0.004
9. Ownership infrastructure										0.132	0.585*	−0.689*	−0.638*
10. Ownership rolling stock											0.288	−0.208	−0.213
11. Objectives												−0.788*	−0.598*
12. Regulatory regime													0.879*
13. Legal ownership													

Note

* = significant at the 0.01 level

Part III

Methods and models related to valuation and efficiency analysis

3.1 Dynamics of global supply chain supernetworks in a new era of risk and uncertainty

Anna Nagurney and Dmytro Matsypura[*]

Abstract

In this paper, we consider the *dynamics* of a global supply chain network economy in the presence of risk and uncertainty. In particular, we assume three tiers of decision-makers: manufacturers, distributors, and retailers, who acquire the product in order to satisfy the demand at the demand markets. The manufacturers, distributors, and retailers may be based in the same or in different countries and may transact in different currencies. We allow for electronic transactions in the form of electronic commerce between the manufacturers and the retailers as well as between the distributors and the retailers since the retailers may be physical or virtual. In addition, supply-side risk and demand-side risk are handled in our formulation with the former being expressed as a multicriteria decision-making problem for each manufacturer and distributor (with distinct weights associated with the criteria) and the latter being handled with the use of uncertain demands. The proposed framework allows for the modelling and theoretical analysis of such global supply chain supernetworks, which involve competition within a tier of decision-makers but cooperation between tiers, as well as the dynamic tracking of the evolution of the associated prices and product transactions to the equilibrium state. Numerical examples are provided for illustrative purposes.

1 Introduction

Fewer than ten years ago, the purchase of a product, typically, involved getting dressed, using some mode of transport to reach the shopping destination, selecting the product physically, and then paying for the purchase. Today, many consumers, be they at home, at work, or at some other location, can go online 24 hours a day, seven days a week, and select and purchase a great assortment of products over the Internet while doing their 'shopping'. Indeed, it is now possible, in many instances, to buy books, videos, and CDs online as well as to order food from a supermarket or restaurant in an electronic manner, and have the items delivered afterwards to the desired destination.

The revolution in electronic commerce has affected not only consumers and their decision-making but has also influenced the producers/manufacturers, the distributors, as well as the retailers (be they physical or virtual), and, in effect, the entire product *supply chain*. According to Salkever (2003), Intel, one of the world's largest computer chip manufacturers, last year generated 85 per cent of its orders – some $22.8 billion worth – online. Moreover, 26 per cent of the sales occurred after the company's physical offices had closed for the day. Furthermore, Intel estimates that it saved $500 million in the year 2002 due to greater control over the supplies that it requires for chip manufacture. Indeed, both business-to-consumer (B2C) commerce and business-to-business (B2B) commerce via the Internet are thriving. For example, in Europe alone, the amount of goods and services purchased online by companies in 2002 surpassed $200 billion (cf. Reinhardt and Majidi, 2003), resulting in a 100 per cent growth in the number of transactions, with B2C commerce in Europe growing at an annual rate of 75 per cent.

The advent of electronic commerce is enabling the world to move closer to the realisation of a single, borderless market and driving the increasing globalisation of not only businesses but also supply chains. At the same time, increasing globalisation exposes supply chains to new risks and uncertainties. For example, recently, the threat of illness in the form of SARS (see Engardio *et al.*, 2003) disrupted supply chains as have terrorist threats and wars (see Sheffi, 2001). Although the importance of global issues in supply chain management and analysis has been emphasised in several papers (cf. Kogut and Kulatilaka, 1994; Cohen and Mallik, 1997; Nagurney, Cruz, and Matsypura, 2003), the topic of supply chain risk modelling is fairly new and requires novel methodological approaches that are able to capture the operational as well as the financial aspects of such decision-making. In addition, it is imperative to be able to address *dynamic* issues since the speed of the Internet allows for not only an increasing volume of transactions across the globe but such transactions can occur very rapidly.

Frameworks for risk management in a global supply chain context with a focus on centralised decision-making and optimisation have been proposed by Huchzermeier and Cohen (1996), Cohen and Mallik (1997), and Cohen and Huchzermeier (1998) (see also the references therein). Nagurney, Cruz, and Dong (2003), in turn, proposed a global supply chain model with both supply-side risk (handled as multicriteria decision-making problems) and demand-side risk (formulated through the use of random demands). Moreover, they allowed for competition across a tier of decision-makers but cooperation between tiers in the supply chain network. In this paper, motivated by the need to include dynamics into the modelling, analysis, and solution of global supply chains in the presence of electronic commerce and in the new era of risk and uncertainty, we build upon the contributions of Nagurney, Cruz, and Dong (2003) and that of Nagurney, Cruz, and Matsypura (2003) to propose a *dynamic* global supply chain supernetwork model which captures decision-making under risk and uncertainty associated with both the supply-side as well as the demand-side.

In particular, in this paper, we focus on the development of a dynamic global supply chain supernetwork model with supply-side and demand-side risk that considers the interactions among three distinct tiers of decision-makers, notably, the manufacturers, the distributors, as well as the retailers, who must respond to the consumers as represented by the associated demand functions for the product. The idea of supernetworks, as utilised in this paper, was introduced by Nagurney and Dong (2002) in their book to capture the trade-offs associated with decision-making on transportation versus telecommunication networks in the Information Age.

This paper is organised as follows. In Section 2, we develop the global supply chain supernetwork model and derive its projected dynamical system formulation (see Nagurney and Zhang, 1996 and Nagurney and Dong, 2002). The projected dynamical system describes how the product transactions evolve through time between the tiers of the supernetwork as well as how the prices associated with the retailers and the distributors evolve. We establish that the set of stationary points of the projected dynamical system coincides with the set of equilibrium points (formulated as a variational inequality problem) of the global supply chain network model of Nagurney, Cruz, and Dong (2003). We also discuss some theoretical properties of the projected dynamical system. In Section 3, we apply the Euler method to numerical global supply chain supernetwork examples. We conclude the paper with a summary and discussion in Section 4.

2 The dynamic global supply chain supernetwork model with risk and uncertainty

In this section, we develop the dynamic global supply chain supernetwork model in which physical and electronic transactions are allowed and in which both supply-side and demand-side risks are included. In particular, we consider (cf. Figure 3.1.1) a three tiered supply chain network consisting of: *manufacturers*, *distributors*, and *retailers*, and these are associated, respectively, with the top tier, the middle tier, and the bottom tier of nodes of the network. Both the manufacturers and the distributors are assumed to be multicriteria decision-makers and concerned not only with profit maximisation but also with risk minimisation. The risks that manufacturers and distributors face may include, for example, the political risk, the currency risk, or a combination thereof, etc. The bottom tier of decision-makers, namely, the retailers, in turn, are faced with the risk associated with the uncertainty in demands.

We consider a global setting, in which there are L countries, with a typical country denoted by l, $\hat{l}$ or $\bar{l}$ (since we need to distinguish a given country by tier). There are I manufacturers in each country with a typical manufacturer i in country l denoted by il and associated with node il in the top tier of nodes in the global supply chain supernetwork (cf. Figure 3.1.1). There are, hence, a total of IL manufacturers in the global economy. Also, we consider J distributors in each country with a typical distributor j in country $\hat{l}$ being denoted by $j\hat{l}$ and associated with the second tier node $j\hat{l}$ in the network. There are, thus, a total of JL distributors in the global supply chain network. A typical retailer k in country $\bar{l}$

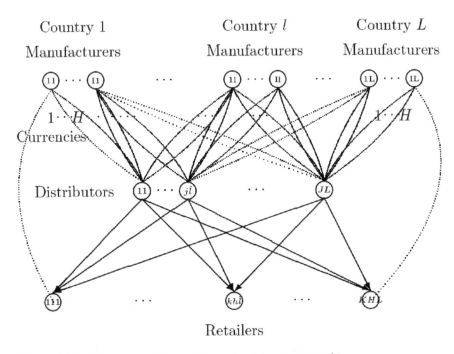

Figure 3.1.1 The structure of the global supply chain supernetwork.

dealing in currency h is denoted by $kh\bar{l}$ and is associated with the corresponding node in the bottom tier of the network and is, referred to, henceforth, as retailer $kh\bar{l}$, with the understanding that the retailer is associated with a country and transactions in a currency. There are a total of KHL bottom tiered nodes in the global supply chain with K denoting the number of retailers and H the number of currencies.

In order to more clearly understand the processes that drive the dynamics of the proposed system, we assume a homogeneous product economy meaning that the same product is being produced by all manufacturers, shipped to the distributors, who, in turn, distribute the product to the retailers. We allow the manufacturers to transact either physically with the distributors, or directly, in an electronic manner, with the retailers, which reflects the development and popularisation of the electronic mode of doing business in today's economy. Therefore, the links connecting the top and the bottom tiers of nodes in Figure 3.1.1 represent electronic links. The retailers associated with the bottom tier of nodes of the global supply chain supernetwork may not necessarily be physical. They may represent online stores or other kinds of virtual retailers. The framework can also handle multiple products, but with a concomitant increase in notation.

Note that in Figure 3.1.1, there are H distinct links between a manufacturer and a distributor pair. For example, the *h-th* link connecting manufacturer il with distributor $j\hat{l}$ denotes the possibility of a transaction between this pair of decision-makers in currency h. The flow on such a link, hence, is the volume of product transacted between this pair in currency h with the flow denoted by $q_{jh\hat{i}}^{il}$. We group all such flows for all the manufacturers (in all the countries) and transacting with all the distributors (in all the countries) via the currencies into the column vector $Q^1 \epsilon R_+^{ILJHL}$. In addition, we note that there is a single link connecting each manufacturer il with each bottom tiered node in the network in Figure 3.1.1 and denote the volume of product transacted between il and retailer $kh\bar{l}$ by $q_{kh\bar{l}}^{il}$. Such links denote transactions conducted electronically. We group all the product flows between the manufacturers and the retailers into the column vector $Q^2 \epsilon R_+^{ILKHL}$.

Finally, note that the links connecting the distributors with the retailers reflect transactions conducted in a specific currency since the bottom tiered nodes denote retailer/currency/country combinations, and the flow on such an abstract link denotes the volume of product transacted in such a fashion between the distributor and retailer pair. Since we allow retailers to be either physical or virtual the link between a distributor and retailer pair may correspond to a physical transaction or to an electronic transaction. We let $q_{kh\bar{l}}^{jl}$ denote the volume of product transacted between distributor $j\hat{l}$ in currency h with retailer k in country $\bar{l}$ and group all such flows into the column vector $Q^3 \epsilon R_+^{JLKHL}$.

We now turn to the description of the dynamic adjustment processes which govern the disequilibrium dynamics as the various global supply chain decision-makers adjust their product transactions between the tiers and the prices associated with the different tiers adjust as well. We begin with a discussion of the price dynamics and then describe the dynamics of the product transactions.

The retail price dynamics

We begin by describing the dynamics underlying the prices of the product associated with the retailers since the demand for the product drives both the manufacture and the distribution of the product. Let $\rho_{3kh\bar{l}}$ denote the price of the product associated with retailer $kh\bar{l}$. We assume that $\hat{d}_{kh\bar{l}}(\rho_{3kh\bar{l}})$ is the demand for the product at the price $\rho_{3kh\bar{l}}$ at retailer $kh\bar{l}$, where $\hat{d}_{kh\bar{l}}(\rho_{3kh\bar{l}})$ is a *random* variable with density function $F_{kh\bar{l}}(x, \rho_{3kh\bar{l}})$, with $\rho_{3kh\bar{l}}$ serving as a parameter. Hence, we assume that the density function may vary with the retailer price. Let $P_{3kh\bar{l}}$ be the probability distribution function of $\hat{d}_{kh\bar{l}}(\rho_{3kh\bar{l}})$, that is,

$$P_{kh\bar{l}}(x, \rho_{3kh\bar{l}}) = P_{kh\bar{l}}(\hat{d}_{kh\bar{l}} < x) = \int_0^1 F_{kh\bar{l}}(x, \rho_{3kh\bar{l}})dx.$$

See also the discussion in Nagurney, Cruz, and Dong (2003).

We assume that the rate of change of the price $\rho_{3kh\bar{l}}$, denoted by $\dot{\rho}_{3kh\bar{l}}$, is equal to the difference between the *expected* demand, where the expected demand is $d_{kh\bar{l}}(\rho_{3kh\bar{l}}) \equiv E(\hat{d}_{kh\bar{l}}(\rho_{3kh\bar{l}}))$, and the total amount transacted with the retailer. Hence we have that for each $k, h, \bar{l}$ that:

$$
\dot{\rho}_{3khl} = \begin{cases} d_{khl}(\rho_{3khl}) - \sum_{i=1}^{I} \sum_{l=1}^{L} q_{khl}^{il} - \sum_{j=1}^{J} \sum_{l=1}^{L} q_{khl}^{jl}, & \text{if} \quad \rho_{3khl} > 0 \\[2em] \max\{0, d_{khl}(\rho_{3khl}) - \sum_{i=1}^{I} \sum_{l=1}^{L} q_{khl}^{il} - \sum_{j=1}^{J} \sum_{l=1}^{L} q_{khl}^{jl}\}, & \text{if} \quad \rho_{3khl} = 0. \end{cases}
$$

$$(1)$$

Moreover, we assume that the price dynamics according to (1) occur for all retailers k, all countries $\bar{l}$, and transacting in any currency h. Hence, if the demand for the product at the retailer (at an instant in time) exceeds the amount available, the price of the product at that retailer will increase; if the amount available exceeds the demand at the price, then the price at the retailer will decrease. Furthermore, we guarantee that the prices do not become negative.

The dynamics of the prices at the distributors

The prices charged for the product by various distributors must reflect supply and demand conditions, similar to the case of the retailers. We let $\dot{\gamma}_{ji}$ denote the rate of change of the price of the product at distributor $j\hat{l}$. Thus, we assume that the price for the product charged by distributor $j\hat{l}$, associated with the node $j\hat{l}$ in the middle tier of the supply chain network, evolves over time according to:

$$
\dot{\gamma}_{ji} = \begin{cases} \sum_{k=1}^{K} \sum_{l=1}^{L} q_{khl}^{jl} - \sum_{i=1}^{I} \sum_{l=1}^{L} q_{jhl}^{il}, & \text{if} \quad \gamma_{ji} > 0 \\[2em] \max\{0, \sum_{k=1}^{K} \sum_{l=1}^{L} q_{lkhl}^{j} - \sum_{i=1}^{I} \sum_{l=1}^{L} q_{jhl}^{il}\}, & \text{if} \quad \gamma_{ji} = 0. \end{cases}
$$

$$(2)$$

and that such dynamics hold for all the distributors j, $\hat{l}$.

In other words, if the amount of the product desired to be transacted by the retailers (at an instant in time) exceeds that available at the distributor, then the price charged at the distributor will increase; if the amount available is greater than that desired by the retailer, then the price charged at the distributor will decrease. As in the case of the retail prices, we guarantee that the prices charged by the distributors remain non-negative.

Precursors to the dynamics of the product transactions

Before we describe the dynamics of the product transactions, it is necessary to describe the behaviour of the first tier of decision-makers, that is, the manufacturers, and also to introduce some additional notation. Let q^{il} denote the production output of manufacturer il, which is a non-negative quantity. We group the production outputs of all manufacturers into the column vector $q \in R_+^{IL}$ and assume that each manufacturer il has a production cost function f^{il}, which can depend, in general, on the entire vector of production outputs, that is,

$$
f^{il} = f^{il}(q), \quad \forall i, l.
$$

$$(3)$$

Therefore, the production cost of a particular manufacturer can depend not only on his production output but also on the production outputs of the other manufacturers. This allows one to model competition.

Let c_{jhl}^{il} denote the transaction cost (which we assume includes the cost of transportation and other expenses) that manufacturer il is faced with in transacting with distributor $j\hat{l}$ in currency h. Let $c_{kh\bar{l}}^{il}$, in turn, denote the transaction cost (which also includes the cost of transportation and other expenses) that manufacturer il is faced with transacting directly with retailer k in currency h and country $\bar{l}$. These transaction costs may depend upon the volume of transactions between each such pair in a particular currency, and their form depends on the type of transaction. They are given, respectively, by:

$$c_{jhl}^{il} = c_{jhl}^{il}(q_{jhl}^{il}), \ \forall i, l, j, h, \hat{l} \tag{4a}$$

and

$$c_{kh\bar{l}}^{il} = c_{kh\bar{l}}^{il}(q_{kh\bar{l}}^{il}), \ \forall i, l, k, h, \bar{l}. \tag{4b}$$

The following conservation of flow equation must hold:

$$q^{il} = \sum_{j=1}^{J}\sum_{h=1}^{H}\sum_{\bar{l}=1}^{L} q_{jhl}^{il} + \sum_{k=1}^{K}\sum_{h=1}^{H}\sum_{\bar{l}=1}^{L} q_{kh\bar{l}}^{il}, \ \forall i, l. \tag{5}$$

Thus, according to (5) the amount of the product produced by a manufacturer is equal to the amount transacted with the distributors and with the retailers in the various currencies.

Note that one can express the production cost function of manufacturer il (cf. (3)) as a function of the vectors Q^1 and Q^2: $f^{il}(Q^1, Q^2)$ and we use this notation, henceforth.

It is assumed that each manufacturer seeks to maximise his profits which is the difference between his revenue and the total costs incurred. The revenue is equal to the product of the price and the total quantity transacted with all the distributors and with all the retailers. Since we allow the transactions to take place in different currencies, the prices of the product in different currencies associated with transactions with different tiers of decision-makers may be distinct. Let ρ_{ijhl}^{il} denote the price associated with the product transacted between manufacturer il and distributor $j\hat{l}$ in currency h, and let $\rho_{1kh\bar{l}}^{il}$ denote the price of the product associated with a transaction between manufacturer il and retailer k in currency h and country $\bar{l}$.

Another assumption to be noted is that all the cost functions are given in the base currency. Considering the fact that the prices are in different currencies and costs are all in the base currency, we need to introduce a device that will bring all the measures to one common denomination. Hence, we introduce the currency appreciation rate e_h, which is the exchange rate of currency h relative to the base currency (see, e.g. Nagurney and Matsypura, 2005 for further details). Given the above, the total revenue of manufacturer il can be expressed as:

$$\sum_{j=1}^{J}\sum_{h=1}^{H}\sum_{\bar{l}=1}^{L} (\rho_{1jh\bar{l}}^{il} \times e_h)q_{jh\bar{l}}^{il} + \sum_{k=1}^{K}\sum_{h=1}^{H}\sum_{\bar{l}=1}^{L} (\rho_{1kh\bar{l}}^{il} \times e_h)q_{kh\bar{l}}^{il}.$$

Consequently, using the conservation of flow equation (5), the production cost functions (3), and the transaction cost functions (4a) and (4b), one can express the profit maximisation criterion for manufacturer *il* as:

$$\text{Maximise} \sum_{j=1}^{J}\sum_{h=1}^{H}\sum_{\bar{l}=1}^{L} (\rho_{1jh\bar{l}}^{il} \times e_h)q_{jh\bar{l}}^{il} + \sum_{k=1}^{K}\sum_{h=1}^{H}\sum_{\bar{l}=1}^{L} (\rho_{1kh\bar{l}}^{il} \times e_h)q_{kh\bar{l}}^{il} -$$

$$f^{il}(Q^1, Q^2) - \sum_{j=1}^{J}\sum_{h=}^{H}\sum_{\bar{l}=1}^{L} c_{jh\bar{l}}^{il}(q_{jh\bar{l}}^{il}) - \sum_{k=1}^{K}\sum_{h=1}^{H}\sum_{\bar{l}=1}^{L} c_{kh\bar{l}}^{il}(q_{kh\bar{l}}^{il}), \tag{6}$$

subject to: $q_{jh\bar{l}}^{il} \geq 0$ for all $j, h, \hat{l}$ and $q_{kh\bar{l}}^{il} \geq 0$, for all $k, h, \bar{l}$.

In addition to the criterion of profit maximisation, we also assume that each manufacturer is concerned with risk minimisation. Here, for the sake of generality, we assume, as given, a risk function r^{il}, for manufacturer i in country l, which is assumed to be continuous and convex and a function of not only the product transactions associated with the particular manufacturer but also of those of other manufacturers. Hence, we assume that

$$r^{il} = r^{il}(Q^1, Q^2), \text{ for all } i, l. \tag{7}$$

Note that according to (7), the risk as perceived by a manufacturer is dependent not only upon his product transactions but also on those of other manufacturers. Hence, the second criterion of manufacturer *il* can be expressed as:

$$\text{Minimise } r^{il}(Q^1, Q^2) \tag{8}$$

subject to: $q_{jh\bar{l}}^{il} \geq 0$, for all $j, h, \hat{l}$ and $q_{kh\bar{l}}^{il} \geq 0$, for all $k, h, \bar{l}$. The risk function may be distinct for each manufacturer/country combination and can assume whatever form is necessary.

Multicriteria decision-making behaviour of the manufacturers

Each manufacturer *il* considers the risk minimisation criterion to be of a certain level of importance, but this level is not necessarily the same for all manufacturers. In order to emphasise this fact, we associate a non-negative weight α^{il} with the risk minimisation criterion (8), with the weight associated with the profit maximisation criterion (6) serving as the numeraire and being set equal to one. Thus, we can construct a *value function* for each manufacturer (cf. Keeney and Raiffa, 1993 and the references therein) using a constant additive weight value function. Consequently, letting U^{il} denote the multicriteria objective function faced by manufacturer *il*, the decision-making problem for manufacturer *il*, for $i = 1,\ldots, I; l = 1,\ldots, L$, can be transformed into:

$$\text{Maximise } U^{il} = \sum_{j=1}^{J}\sum_{h=1}^{H}\sum_{\hat{l}=1}^{L}(\rho_{1jh\hat{l}}^{il}\times e_h)q_{jh\hat{l}}^{il} + \sum_{k=1}^{K}\sum_{h=1}^{H}\sum_{\bar{l}=1}^{L}(\rho_{1kh\bar{l}}^{il}\times e_h)q_{kh\bar{l}}^{il} -$$

$$f^{il}(Q^1,Q^2) - \sum_{j=1}^{J}\sum_{h=1}^{H}\sum_{\hat{l}=1}^{L}c_{jh\hat{l}}^{il}(q_{jh\hat{l}}^{il}) - \sum_{k=1}^{K}\sum_{h=1}^{H}\sum_{\bar{l}=1}^{L}c_{kh\bar{l}}^{il}(q_{kh\bar{l}}^{il}) - \alpha^{il}r^{il}(Q^1,Q^2), \qquad (9)$$

subject to: $q_{jh\hat{l}}^{il} \geq 0$ for all j, h, $\hat{l}$ and $q_{kh\bar{l}}^{il} \geq 0$, for all k, h, $\bar{l}$.

It is assumed that the production cost functions and the transaction cost functions for each manufacturer are continuous and convex. It is also assumed that the manufacturers compete according to Nash's concept of non-cooperative behaviour (cf. Nash, 1950, 1951), which states, in this context, that each manufacturer will determine his optimal production quantity and transactions, given the optimal ones of his competitors. We ignore, for the time being, the non-negativity constraints on the transaction variables. Let the gradient of manufacturer il's multicriteria objective function U^{il} with respect to the $\hat{q}c^{il}$ variables be denoted by:

$$\nabla_{\hat{q}^{il}}U^{il} = \left(\frac{\partial U^{il}}{\partial q_{111}^{il}}, \dots, \frac{\partial U^{il}}{\partial q_{JHL}^{il}}\right)$$

We note that this gradient represents manufacturer il's *idealised direction* with respect to $\hat{q}^{il}$, with the $jh\hat{l} - component$ of $\nabla_{\hat{q}^{il}}U^{il}$ being given by:

$$\left(\rho_{1jh\hat{l}}^{il}\times e_h - \frac{\partial f^{il}(Q^1,Q^2)}{\partial q_{jh\hat{l}}^{il}} - \frac{\partial c_{jh\hat{l}}^{il}(q_{jh\hat{l}}^{il})}{\partial q_{jh\hat{l}}^{il}} - \alpha^{il}\frac{\partial r^{il}(Q^1,Q^2)}{\partial q_{jh\hat{l}}^{il}}\right) \qquad (10)$$

Similarly,

$$\nabla_{\bar{q}^{il}}U^{il} = \left(\frac{\partial U^{il}}{\partial q_{111}^{il}}, \dots, \frac{\partial U^{il}}{\partial q_{KHL}^{il}}\right)$$

represents manufacturer il's *idealised direction* with respect to $\bar{q}^{il}$, with the $kh\bar{l}$ component of $\nabla_{\bar{q}^{il}}U^{il}$ being given by:

$$\left(\rho_{1kh\bar{l}}^{il}\times e_h - \frac{\partial f^{il}(Q^1,Q^2)}{\partial q_{kh\bar{l}}^{il}} - \frac{\partial c_{kh\bar{l}}^{il}(q_{kh\bar{l}}^{il})}{\partial q_{kh\bar{l}}^{il}} - \alpha^{il}\frac{\partial r^{il}(Q^1,Q^2)}{\partial q_{kh\bar{l}}^{il}}\right) \qquad (11)$$

where

$$\hat{q}^{il} \equiv (q_{111}^{il}, \dots, q_{jh\hat{l}}^{il}, \dots, q_{JHL}^{il})$$

and

$$\bar{q}^{il} \equiv (q_{111}^{il}, \dots, q_{kh\bar{l}}^{il}, \dots, q_{KHL}^{il})$$

Later, we include the non-negativity assumption on the product transactions, when we construct the projected dynamical system that captures the dynamics of all the product transactions and prices.

Multicriteria decision-making behaviour of the distributors

The distributors are involved in transactions with both the manufacturers (since they need to obtain the product for distribution) and with the retailers, who sell the product to the consumers. As was mentioned earlier, since we are dealing with a global supply chain, the distributors, similar to the manufacturers, are allowed to transact in any of the H available currencies.

A distributor $j\hat{l}$ is faced with certain expenses, which may include, for example, the loading/unloading costs, the storage costs, etc. associated with handling the product. We refer collectively to such costs as a *handling* cost and denote it by c_{ji}. In a simple situation, one might have that

$$c_{ji} = c_{ji} \left(\sum_{i=1}^{I} \sum_{l=1}^{L} \sum_{h=1}^{H} q_{jhi}^{il}, \sum_{k=1}^{K} \sum_{h=1}^{H} \sum_{\bar{l}=1}^{L} q_{kh\bar{l}}^{ji} \right), \tag{12a}$$

that is, the *handling* cost of a distributor is a function of how much of the product he has obtained and how much of the product he has transacted with the various retailers. However, for the sake of generality, and to enhance the modelling of competition, we allow the function to depend also on the amount of the product acquired and transacted by other distributors. Hence, we assume that, for all $j\hat{l}$:

$$c_{ji} = c_{ji}(Q^1, Q^3). \tag{12b}$$

Let $\rho_{2kh\bar{l}}^{ji}$ denote the price in currency h associated with the transaction between distributor $j\hat{l}$ and retailer $kh\bar{l}$. The total amount of revenue the distributor obtains from his transactions is equal to the sum of the price (transformed into the base currency) and the amount of the product transacted with the various retailers in the distinct countries and currencies. Indeed, since transactions can be made in distinct currencies and with different retailers, who, in fact, may even be virtual, the total revenue of distributor $j\hat{l}$ can be expressed in the base currency as follows:

$$\sum_{k=1}^{K} \sum_{h=1}^{H} \sum_{\bar{l}=1}^{L} (\rho_{2kh\bar{l}}^{ji} + e_h) q_{kh\bar{l}}^{ji}. \tag{13}$$

The profit maximisation problem for distributor $j\hat{l}$ can be expressed as:

$$\text{Maximise} \sum_{k=1}^{K} \sum_{h=1}^{H} \sum_{\bar{l}=1}^{L} (\rho_{2kh\bar{l}}^{ji} \times e_h) q_{kh\bar{l}}^{ji} - c_{ji}(Q^1, Q^3) - \sum_{i=1}^{I} \sum_{l=1}^{L} \sum_{h=1}^{H} (\rho_{1jhi}^{il} \times e_h) q_{jhi}^{il}$$

$$\tag{14}$$

subject to:

$$\sum_{k=1}^{K} \sum_{h=1}^{H} \sum_{\bar{l}=1}^{L} q_{kh\bar{l}}^{ji} \leq \sum_{i=1}^{I} \sum_{l=1}^{L} \sum_{h=1}^{H} q_{jhi}^{il}, \tag{15}$$

and the non-negativity assumptions: $q_{jh\hat{l}}^{il} \geq 0$ for all i, l and $q_{kh\hat{l}}^{jl} \geq 0$, for all k, h, $\bar{l}$.

Constraint (15) states that a distributor in a country cannot transact more of the product than he has obtained from the various manufacturers.

In addition, distributor $j\hat{l}$ is faced with his own perception of risk associated with obtaining and shipping the product, which we assume is incorporated into a continuous risk function of a general form given by:

$$r^{j\hat{l}} = r^{j\hat{l}}(Q^1, Q^3), \quad \forall j, \hat{l}. \tag{16}$$

Note that we allow the risk function of a particular distributor to depend on the transactions to and from all the distributors in the supply chain network economy.

We assume also that each distributor associates a weight of 1 with the profit criterion (14) and a weight of $\beta^{j\hat{l}}$ with his risk level. Therefore, the multicriteria decision-making problem for distributor $j\hat{l}$; $j = 1,\ldots, J$; $\hat{l} = 1,\ldots, L$, faced now with a multicriteria objective function denoted by $U^{j\hat{l}}$ can be transformed directly into the optimisation problem:

$$\text{Maximise } U^{j\hat{l}} = \sum_{k=1}^{K}\sum_{h=1}^{H}\sum_{\bar{l}=1}^{L} (\rho_{2kh\bar{l}}^{j\hat{l}} \times e_h)q_{kh\bar{l}}^{j\hat{l}} - c_{jl}(Q^1, Q^3) - \sum_{i=1}^{I}\sum_{l=1}^{L}\sum_{h=1}^{H} (\rho_{ljh\hat{l}}^{il} \times e_h)q_{jh\hat{l}}^{il}$$

$$- \beta^{j\hat{l}}r^{j\hat{l}}(Q^1, Q^3) \tag{17}$$

subject to:

$$\sum_{k=1}^{K}\sum_{h=1}^{H}\sum_{\bar{l}=1}^{L} q_{kh\bar{l}}^{j\hat{l}} \leq \sum_{i=1}^{I}\sum_{l=1}^{L}\sum_{h=1}^{H} q_{jh\hat{l}}^{il}, \tag{18}$$

and the non-negativity assumptions: $q_{jh\hat{l}}^{il} \geq 0$ for all i, l and $q^{j\hat{l}}_{kh\bar{l}} \geq 0$, for all k, h, $\bar{l}$.

Objective function (17) represents a value function for distributor $j\hat{l}$ with $\beta^{j\hat{l}}$ having the interpretation as a conversion rate in dollar value.

For simplicity of notation we let:

$$q_{j\hat{l}} = (q^{11}_{j1\hat{l}},\ldots, q^{il}_{jh\hat{l}},\ldots, q^{IL}_{jH\hat{l}})$$

and

$$q^{j\hat{l}} = (q^{j\hat{l}}_{111},\ldots, q^{j\hat{l}}_{kh\bar{l}},\ldots, q^{j\hat{l}}_{KHL}).$$

Ignoring, for the time being, the non-negativity constraints (as was done above for the manufacturers), and constraint (18),

$$\nabla_{q_{j\hat{l}}}U^{j\hat{l}} = \left(\frac{\partial U^{j\hat{l}}}{q^{11}_{j1\hat{l}}},\ldots, \frac{\partial U^{j\hat{l}}}{q^{IL}_{jK\hat{l}}} \right)$$

represents distributor $j\hat{l}$'s *idealised direction* in terms of $q_{j\hat{l}}$, where component ilh is given by:

$$\left(\gamma_{ji} - \frac{\partial c_{ji}(Q^1, Q^3)}{\partial q_{jhi}^{il}} - \beta^{ji} \frac{\partial r^{ji}(Q^1, Q^3)}{\partial q_{jhi}^{il}} - \rho_{1jhi}^{il} \times e_h\right),\tag{19}$$

whereas

$$\nabla_{\hat{q}^{il}} U^{j\hat{l}} = \left(\frac{\partial U^{j\hat{l}}}{q_{111}^{j\hat{l}}}, \ldots, \frac{\partial U^{j\hat{l}}}{q_{KHL}^{j\hat{l}}}\right)$$

represents distributor $j\hat{l}$'s *idealised direction* in terms of the $q^{j\hat{l}}$ variables, with component $kh\hat{l}$ given by:

$$\left(\rho_{2kh\hat{l}}^{j\hat{l}} \times e_h - \frac{\partial c_{ji}(Q^1, Q^3)}{\partial q_{kh\hat{l}}^{j\hat{l}}} - \beta^{ji} \frac{\partial r^{ji}(Q^1, Q^3)}{\partial q_{kh\hat{l}}^{j\hat{l}}} - \gamma_{ji}\right).\tag{20}$$

However, manufacturer il and distributor $j\hat{l}$ must agree on the volume of q^{il}_{jhi} in order for the transaction to actually take place in currency h. Therefore, direction (10) of manufacturer il must coincide with direction (19) of distributor $j\hat{l}$ transacting in currency h, yielding, after algebraic simplification, a *combined direction*, which signifies cooperation, given by:

$$\left(\gamma_{ji} - \frac{\partial f^{il}(Q^1, Q^2)}{\partial q_{jhi}^{il}} - \frac{\partial c_{jhi}^{il}(q_{jhi}^{il})}{\partial q_{jhi}^{il}} - \frac{\partial c_{ji}(Q^1, Q^3)}{\partial q_{jhi}^{il}} - \alpha^{il} \frac{\partial r^{il}(Q^1, Q^2)}{\partial q_{jhi}^{il}}\right.$$

$$\left. - \beta^{ji} \frac{\partial r^{ji}(Q^1, Q^3)}{\partial q_{jhi}^{il}}\right).\tag{21}$$

Moreover, (21) must hold for all i, l and j, $\hat{l}, h$ for the supply chain to allow for links between the top two tiers of nodes.

Optimising behaviour of the retailers with uncertain demands

The retailers, in turn, are faced with the decision of how much product to acquire from the distributors and from the manufacturers (via the Internet) in order to satisfy the random demand while still seeking to maximise profits. A retailer $kh\hat{l}$ has his own handling cost, which may include, for example, various expenses related to the display and storage of the product. We denote this cost by $c_{kh\hat{l}}$ and, in the simplest case, we would have that $c_{kh\hat{l}}(s_{kh\hat{l}})$, where

$$s_{kh\hat{l}} = \sum_{i=1}^{I} \sum_{l=1}^{L} q_{kh\hat{l}}^{il} + \sum_{j=1}^{J} \sum_{\hat{l}=1}^{L} q_{kh\hat{l}}^{j\hat{l}}$$

that is, the holding cost of a retailer is a function of how much of the product he has obtained from transactions with the various manufacturers and the various distributors. However, in general, this cost may be affected by the amounts of the product held by other retailers. Therefore, we write:

$$c_{kh\hat{l}} = c_{kh\hat{l}}(Q^2, Q^3), \quad \forall k, h, \hat{l}.\tag{22}$$

Recall that $\rho_{3kh\bar{l}}$ denotes the price of the product associated with retailer $kh\bar{l}$. Also recall that $\hat{d}_{kh\bar{l}}(\rho_{3kh\bar{l}})$ is the demand for the product at the price $\rho_{3kh\bar{l}}$ at retailer $kh\bar{l}$, where $\hat{d}_{kh\bar{l}}(\rho_{3kh\bar{l}})$ is a random variable with a density function $F_{kh\bar{l}}(x, \rho_{3kh\bar{l}})$.

Since the demand is random and a retailer does not know how much he will sell beforehand, the actual sale of the product at retailer $kh\bar{l}$ cannot exceed $\min\{s_{kh\bar{l}}, \hat{d}_{kh\bar{l}}\}$. Let

$$\Delta_{kh\bar{l}}^+ \equiv \max \{0, s_{kh\bar{l}} - \hat{d}_{kh\bar{l}}\} \tag{23}$$

and max

$$\Delta_{kh\bar{l}}^- \equiv \max \{0, \hat{d}_{kh\bar{l}} - s_{kh\bar{l}}\}, \tag{24}$$

where $\Delta_{kh\bar{l}}^+$ is a random variable representing the excess supply (inventory), whereas $\Delta_{kh\bar{l}}^-$ is a random variable representing the excess demand (shortage).

Note that, as discussed in Nagurney, Cruz, and Dong (2003), the expected values of excess supply and excess demand of retailer $kh\hat{l}$ are scalar functions of $s_{kh\bar{l}}$ and $\rho_{3kh\bar{l}}$. In particular, let

$$\pi_{kh\bar{l}}^+(s_{kh\bar{l}}, \rho_{3kh\bar{l}}) \equiv E(\Delta_{kh\bar{l}}^+) = \int_0^{s_{kh\bar{l}}} (s_{kh\bar{l}} - x) F_{kh\bar{l}}(x, \rho_{3kh\bar{l}}) dx, \tag{25}$$

and

$$\pi_{kh\bar{l}}^-(s_{kh\bar{l}}, \rho_{3kh\bar{l}}) \equiv E(\Delta_{kh\bar{l}}^+) = \int_{s_{kh\bar{l}}}^{\infty} (x - s_{kh\bar{l}}) F_{kh\bar{l}}(x, \rho_{3kh\bar{l}}) dx. \tag{26}$$

Assume now that retailer $kh\bar{l}$ is faced with certain penalties for having an excess or shortage in regards to the supply. Let $\lambda_{kh\bar{l}}^+ \geq 0$ denote the unit penalty of having excess supply at retail outlet $kh\bar{l}$, and let $\lambda_{kh\bar{l}}^- \geq 0$ denote the unit penalty of having excess demand at outlet $kh\bar{l}$. Then the expected total penalty of retailer $kh\bar{l}$ can be expressed as:

$$E(\lambda_{kh\bar{l}}^+ \Delta_{kh\bar{l}}^+ + \lambda_{kh\bar{l}}^- \Delta_{kh\bar{l}}^-) = \lambda_{kh\bar{l}}^+ \pi_{kh\bar{l}}^+(s_{kh\bar{l}}, \rho_{3kh\bar{l}}) + \lambda_{kh\bar{l}}^- \pi_{kh\bar{l}}^-(s_{kh\bar{l}}, \rho_{3kh\bar{l}}).$$

Assuming also profit-maximising behaviour of the retailers, one can state the following optimisation problem for retailer $kh\bar{l}$:

$$\text{Maximise } E((\rho_{3kh\bar{l}}^\times \times e_h^\times) \cdot \min\{s_{kh\bar{l}}, \hat{d}_{kh\bar{l}}\}) - E(\lambda_{kh\bar{l}}^+ \Delta_{kh\bar{l}}^+ + \lambda_{kh\bar{l}}^- \Delta_{kh\bar{l}}^-) + c_{kh\bar{l}}(Q^2, Q^3)$$

$$- \sum_{i=1}^{I} \sum_{l=1}^{L} (\rho_{1kh\bar{l}}^{il} \times e_h) q_{kh\bar{l}}^{il} - \sum_{j=1}^{J} \sum_{l=1}^{L} (\rho_{2kh\bar{l}}^{jl} \times e_h) q_{kh\bar{l}}^{jl}, \tag{27}$$

subject to: $q_{kh\bar{l}}^{il} \geq 0$, $q_{kh\bar{l}}^{jl} \geq 0$, for all $i, l, j, \bar{l}$.

Applying now the definitions of $\Delta_{kh\bar{l}}^+$, and $\Delta_{kh\bar{l}}^-$, we can express the objective function (27) (and denoted by $U^{kh\bar{l}}$) as:

$$\text{Maximise } U^{kh\bar{l}} = (\rho_{3kh\bar{l}} \times e_h)d_{kh\bar{l}}(\rho_{3kh\bar{l}}) - (\rho^{\times}_{3kh\bar{l}} \times e_h + \lambda^{-}_{kh\bar{l}})\pi^{-}_{kh\bar{l}}(s_{kh\bar{l}}, \rho_{3kh\bar{l}})$$

$$- \lambda^{+}_{kh\bar{l}}\pi^{+}_{kh\bar{l}}(s_{kh\bar{l}}, \rho_{3kh\bar{l}}) - c_{kh\bar{l}}(Q^2, Q^3) - \sum_{i-1}^{I}\sum_{l-1}^{L}(\rho^{il}_{1kh\bar{l}} \times e_h)q^{il}_{kh\bar{l}}$$

$$- \sum_{j-1}^{J}\sum_{l-1}^{L}(\rho^{jl}_{2kh\bar{l}} \times e_h)q^{jl}_{kh\bar{l}}, \tag{28}$$

where $d_{kh\bar{l}}(\rho_{3kh\bar{l}}) \equiv E(\hat{d}_{kh\bar{l}})$ is a scalar function of $\rho_{3kh\bar{l}}$.

At this point it is necessary to note the following relationships, which were derived in Nagurney, Cruz, and Dong (2003):

$$\frac{\partial \pi^{+}_{kh\bar{l}}(s_{kh\bar{l}}, \rho_{3kh\bar{l}})}{\partial q^{il}_{kh\bar{l}}} = \frac{\partial \pi^{+}_{kh\bar{l}}(s_{kh\bar{l}}, \rho_{3kh\bar{l}})}{\partial q^{jl}_{kh\bar{l}}} = P_{kh\bar{l}}(s_{kh\bar{l}}, \rho_{3kh\bar{l}}) =$$

$$P_{kh\bar{l}}\left(\sum_{i-1}^{I}\sum_{l-1}^{L}q^{il}_{kh\bar{l}} + \sum_{j-1}^{J}\sum_{l-1}^{L}q^{jl}_{kh\bar{l}}, \rho_{3kh\bar{l}}\right), \tag{29}$$

and

$$\frac{\partial \pi^{-}_{kh\bar{l}}(s_{kh\bar{l}}, \rho_{3kh\bar{l}})}{\partial q^{il}_{kh\bar{l}}} = \frac{\partial \pi^{-}_{kh\bar{l}}(s_{kh\bar{l}}, \rho_{3kh\bar{l}})}{\partial q^{jl}_{kh\bar{l}}} = P_{kh\bar{l}}(s_{kh\bar{l}}, \rho_{3kh\bar{l}}) - 1$$

$$= P_{kh\bar{l}}\left(\sum_{i-1}^{I}\sum_{l-1}^{L}q^{il}_{kh\bar{l}} + \sum_{j-1}^{J}\sum_{l-1}^{L}q^{jl}_{kh\bar{l}}, \rho_{3kh\bar{l}}\right) - 1. \tag{30}$$

Similar to the case of the manufacturers, it is assumed that all the functions in (28) are continuous. It is also assumed that the retailers compete according to Nash's concept of non-cooperative behaviour, which states, in this context, that each retailer will determine his optimal transactions, given the optimal ones of his competitors. Moreover (as we have done previously for the manufacturers and the distributors) if we ignore, for the time being, that the product transactions must be non-negative, then retailer $kh\bar{l}$ is faced with an *unconstrained* utility maximisation problem, where:

$$\nabla_{\hat{q}kh\bar{l}}U^{kh\bar{l}} = \left(\frac{\partial U^{kh\bar{l}}}{\partial q^{11}_{kh\bar{l}}}, \ldots, \frac{\partial U^{kh\bar{l}}}{\partial q^{JL}_{kh\bar{l}}}\right)$$

represents retailer $kh\bar{l}$'s idealised direction with respect to the $\hat{q}_{kh\bar{l}}$ variables, with the $j\bar{l}$-component being given by:

$$\left((\lambda^{-}_{kh\bar{l}} + \rho_{3kh\bar{l}} \times e_h)(1 - P_{kh\bar{l}}(s_{kh\bar{l}}, \rho_{3kh\bar{l}})) - \lambda^{+}_{kh\bar{l}}P_{kh\bar{l}}(s_{kh\bar{l}}, \rho_{3kh\bar{l}})\right.$$

$$\left. - \frac{\partial c_{kh\bar{l}}(Q^2, Q^3)}{\partial q^{jl}_{kh\bar{l}}} - \rho^{jl}_{2kh\bar{l}} \times e_h\right) \tag{31}$$

whereas

$$\nabla_{\hat{q}kh\bar{l}}U^{kh\bar{l}} = \left(\frac{\partial U^{kh\bar{l}}}{\partial q^{11}_{kh\bar{l}}}, \ldots, \frac{\partial U^{kh\bar{l}}}{\partial q^{IL}_{kh\bar{l}}}\right)$$

represents retailer $khl\bar{}$'s idealised direction with respect to the $\bar{q}_{khl\bar{}}$ variables, with the il-component being given by:

$$\left((\lambda_{khl\bar{}}^- + \rho_{3khl\bar{}} \times e_h)(1 - P_{khl\bar{}}(s_{khl\bar{}}, \rho_{3khl\bar{}})) - \lambda_{khl\bar{}}^+ P_{khl\bar{}}(s_{khl\bar{}}, \rho_{3khl\bar{}})\right.$$

$$\left. - \frac{\partial c_{khl\bar{}}(Q^2, Q^3)}{\partial q_{khl\bar{}}^{il}} - \rho_{1khl\bar{}}^{il} \times e_h\right) \tag{32}$$

Note that in order for the transaction between distributor $jl\hat{}$ and retailer $khl\bar{}$ to take place, they must agree in terms of the $q_{khl\bar{}}^{jl\hat{}}$. Therefore, directions (20) and (31) must coincide, with the summation of the two yielding a *combined* direction given by, after algebraic simplification:

$$\left((\lambda_{khl\bar{}}^- + \rho_{3khl\bar{}} \times e_h)(1 - P_{khl\bar{}}(s_{khl\bar{}}, \rho_{3khl\bar{}})) - \lambda_{khl\bar{}}^+ P_{khl\bar{}}(s_{khl\bar{}}, \rho_{3khl\bar{}})\right.$$

$$\left. - \frac{\partial c_{ji}(Q^1, Q^3)}{\partial q_{khl\bar{}}^{jl\hat{}}} - \frac{\partial c_{khl\bar{}}(Q^2, Q^3)}{\partial q_{khl\bar{}}^{jl\hat{}}} - \beta^{ji} \frac{\partial r^{jl\hat{}}(Q^1, Q^3)}{\partial q_{khl\bar{}}^{jl\hat{}}} - \gamma_{ji}\right). \tag{33}$$

Similarly, for the transaction between a retailer $khl\bar{}$ and a manufacturer il to take place, both must agree on the $q_{khl\bar{}}^{il}$. Therefore, directions (32) and (11) must coincide as well, with the summation of the two yielding also a combined direction, which, after algebraic simplifications, reduces to:

$$\left((\lambda_{khl\bar{}}^- + \rho_{3khl\bar{}} \times e_h)(1 - P_{khl\bar{}}(s_{khl\bar{}}, \rho_{3khl\bar{}}))\right.$$

$$- \frac{\partial f^{il}(Q^1, Q^2)}{\partial q_{khl\bar{}}^{il}} - \frac{\partial c_{khl\bar{}}^{il}(q_{khl\bar{}}^{il})}{\partial q_{khl\bar{}}^{il}} - \frac{\partial c_{khl\bar{}}(Q^2, Q^3)}{\partial q_{khl\bar{}}^{il}} - \alpha^{il} \frac{\partial r^{il}(Q^1, Q^2)}{\partial q_{khl\bar{}}^{il}}$$

$$\left. - \lambda_{khl\bar{}}^+ P_{khl\bar{}}(s_{khl\bar{}}, \rho_{3khl\bar{}})\right). \tag{34}$$

We are now ready to express the dynamics of the transactions between the tiers of decision-makers in the supply chain supernetwork. Moreover, we now explicitly include the non-negativity constraints associated with the product transactions and note that (18) has actually been subsumed within the distributor price dynamics given by (2). We then provide a unified expression in the form of a projected dynamical system for the dynamic evolution of all the product transactions and the product prices simultaneously.

The dynamics of the product transactions between manufacturers and distributors

We are now ready to express the dynamics of the product flows between the manufacturers and the distributors. The rate of change in the amount of product q_{khi}^{il}, transacted between manufacturer il and distributor $jl\hat{}$, and denoted by $\dot{q}_{khi}^{il}$, is equal to the combined direction (21) which states that the price γ_{ji} the distributor is willing to pay for the product minus the various transaction costs that are faced by both manufacturer and distributor while transacting via this particular link minus the weighted marginal risk of the transaction associated with the manufacturer and distributor pair. Guaranteeing now that the product transactions do not assume negative quantities, we get the following dynamics for the transactions between each manufacturer il and every distributor $j\hat{l}$ transacting in currency h, for all h:

$$
\dot{q}_{jh\hat{l}}^{il} =
\begin{cases}
\begin{aligned}
&\{\gamma_{ji} - \frac{\partial f^{il}(Q^1, Q^2)}{\partial q_{jh\hat{i}}^{il}} - \frac{\partial c_{jh\hat{i}}^{il}(q_{jh\hat{i}}^{il})}{\partial q_{jh\hat{i}}^{il}} - \frac{\partial c_{ji}(Q^1, Q^3)}{\partial q_{jh\hat{i}}^{il}} \\
&\quad - \alpha^{il} \frac{\partial r^{il}(Q^1, Q^2)}{\partial q_{jh\hat{i}}^{il}} - \beta^{ji} \frac{\partial r^{ji}(Q^1, Q^3)}{\partial q_{jh\hat{i}}^{il}}, & \text{if } q_{jh\hat{i}}^{il} > 0
\end{aligned} \\[2em]
\begin{aligned}
&\max\{0, \gamma_{ji} - \frac{\partial f^{il}(Q^1, Q^2)}{\partial q_{jh\hat{i}}^{il}} - \frac{\partial c_{jh\hat{i}}^{il}(q_{jh\hat{i}}^{il})}{\partial q_{jh\hat{i}}^{il})} - \frac{\partial c_{ji}(Q^1, Q^3)}{\partial q_{jh\hat{i}}^{il}} \\
&\quad - \alpha^{il} \frac{\partial r^{il}(Q^1, Q^2)}{\partial q_{jh\hat{i}}^{il}} - \beta^{ji} \frac{\partial r^{ji}(Q^1, Q^3)}{\partial q_{jh\hat{i}}^{il}}\}, & \text{if } q_{jh\hat{i}}^{il} = 0.
\end{aligned}
\end{cases}
\tag{35}
$$

Another way of looking at the expression above is the following. Whenever there is a positive difference between the shadow price of the distributor and the aggregated marginal costs and risks associated with a transaction, the amount of flow on that particular link will increase. Otherwise, the amount of flow will either decrease or remain the same.

The dynamics of the product transactions between manufacturers and retailers

In a similar manner, we can derive the dynamics associated with the transactions between the manufacturers and the retailers. Recall that such transactions take place on the Internet, and that the combined direction of a transaction between manufacturer il and retailer $kh\bar{l}$ is given by expression (34). Indeed, we may immediately write, requiring now that these transactions must also yield non-negative values, that for all manufacturers il and all retailers $kh\bar{l}$, with $\dot{q}_{kh\bar{l}}^{il}$ denoting the rate of change of the transactions between manufacturer il and retailer $kh\bar{l}$:

$$
\dot{q}_{kh\bar{l}}^{il} =
\begin{cases}
\begin{aligned}
&(\lambda_{kh\bar{l}}^- + \rho_{3kh\bar{l}} \times e_h)(1 - P_{kh\bar{l}}(s_{kh\bar{l}}, \rho_{3kh\bar{l}})) - \frac{\partial f^{il}(Q^1, Q^2)}{\partial q_{kh\bar{l}}^{il}} \\
&\quad - \frac{\partial c_{kh\bar{l}}^{il}(q_{kh\bar{l}}^{il})}{\partial q_{kh\bar{l}}^{il}} - \frac{\partial c_{kh\bar{l}}(Q^2, Q^3)}{\partial q_{kh\bar{l}}^{il}} - \alpha^{il} \frac{\partial r^{il}(Q^1, Q^2)}{\partial q_{kh\bar{l}}^{il}} - \lambda_{kh\bar{l}}^+ P_{kh\bar{l}}(s_{kh\bar{l}}, \rho_{3kh\bar{l}}), \\
&\hspace{8cm} \text{if } q_{kh\bar{l}}^{il} > 0
\end{aligned} \\[2em]
\max\{0, (\lambda_{kh\bar{l}}^- + \rho_{3kh\bar{l}} \times e_h)(1 - P_{kh\bar{l}}(s_{kh\bar{l}}, \rho_{3kh\bar{l}})) - \frac{\partial f^{il}(Q^1, Q^2)}{\partial q_{kh\bar{l}}^{il}}
\end{cases}
$$

$$\left. -\frac{\partial c_{kh\bar{l}}^{il}(q_{kh\bar{l}}^{il})}{\partial q_{kh\bar{l}}^{il}} - \frac{\partial c_{kh\bar{l}}(Q^2, Q^3)}{\partial q_{kh\bar{l}}^{il}} - \alpha^{il}\frac{\partial r^{il}(Q^1, Q^2)}{\partial q_{kh\bar{l}}^{il}} - \lambda_{kh\bar{l}}^{+}P_{kh\bar{l}}(s_{kh\bar{l}}, \rho_{3kh\bar{l}}) \right\},$$

$$\text{if } q_{kh\bar{l}}^{il} = 0.$$

$$(36)$$

Hence, (36) expresses that the volume of transactions between a manufacturer and retailer pair will increase if the, what may be termed, *generalised* price associated with the product in that currency at the retailer exceeds the various marginal costs and risks (with the probabilities associated with excess supply and demand incorporated into the computations).

The dynamics of the product transactions between distributors and retailers

The combined direction associated with a transaction between a distributor and retailer pair, in turn, is given by expression (33) but now we guarantee that the evolution of the product transactions cannot yield negative values. Hence, letting $\dot{q}_{kh\bar{l}}^{il}$ denote the rate of change of the transaction between distributor $j\hat{l}$ and retailer $kh\bar{l}$, we obtain the following dynamics, which hold for all distributors and all retailers:

$$\dot{q}_{kh\bar{l}}^{il} = \begin{cases} (\lambda_{kh\bar{l}}^{-} + \rho_{3kh\bar{l}} \times e_h)(1 - P_{kh\bar{l}}(s_{kh\bar{l}}, \rho_{3kh\bar{l}})) - \lambda_{kh\bar{l}}^{+}P_{kh\bar{l}}(s_{kh\bar{l}}, \rho_{3kh\bar{l}}) \\ \\ -\dfrac{\partial c_{ji}(Q^1, Q^3)}{\partial q_{kh\bar{l}}^{il}} - \dfrac{\partial c_{kh\bar{l}}(Q^2, Q^3)}{\partial q_{kh\bar{l}}^{il}} - \beta^{il}\dfrac{\partial r^{il}(Q^1, Q^3)}{\partial q_{jh\bar{l}}^{il}} - \lambda_{ji}, \quad \text{if } q_{kh\bar{l}}^{il} > 0 \\ \\ \max\{0, (\lambda_{kh\bar{l}}^{-} + \rho_{3kh\bar{l}} \times e_h)(1 - P_{kh\bar{l}}(s_{kh\bar{l}}, \rho_{3kh\bar{l}})) - \lambda_{kh\bar{l}}^{+}P_{kh\bar{l}}(s_{kh\bar{l}}, \rho_{3kh\bar{l}}) \\ \\ -\dfrac{\partial c_{ji}(Q^1, Q^3)}{\partial q_{kh\bar{l}}^{il}} - \dfrac{\partial c_{kh\bar{l}}(Q^2, Q^3)}{\partial q_{kh\bar{l}}^{il}} - \beta^{il}\dfrac{\partial r^{il}(Q^1, Q^3)}{\partial q_{jh\bar{l}}^{il}} - \gamma_{ji}\}. \text{ if } q_{kh\bar{l}}^{il} = 0. \end{cases}$$

$$(37)$$

The volume of the product transacted between a distributor/retailer pair increases if the sum of the *price* that the consumers, in effect, are willing to pay at the retailer exceeds the various marginal costs, marginal risk associated with the distributor and the price charged at the distributor. If the latter sum exceeds the former price, then the volume of transaction will decrease.

The projected dynamical system

Consider now a dynamical system in which the retailer prices evolve according to (1) for all retailers $kh\bar{l}$; the prices at the distributors evolve according to (2) for all distributors $j\hat{l}$; the product transactions between the distributors and the retailers evolve according to (37); the product transactions between manufacturers and distributors evolve according to (35); and the product transactions between manufacturers and retailers evolve according to (36).

Let now X denote the aggregate column vector $(Q^1, Q^2, Q^3, \gamma, \rho_3)$ in the feasible set $K \equiv R_+^{ILJHL+ILKHL+JLKHL+JL+KHL}$. Define the column vector

$$F \equiv (F_{jh\bar{i}}^{il}, F_{kh\bar{i}}^{il}, F_{kh\bar{i}}^{j\hat{i}}, F_{j\hat{i}}, F_{kh\bar{i}})_{i=1,...I;l=\hat{i}=\bar{l}=1,...L;j=1,...J;k=1,...K;h=1,...H}$$

with components: $-F_{jh\bar{i}}^{il}$ given by (21) $\forall i, l. j, h, \hat{l}$; $-F_{kh\bar{i}}^{il}$ given by (35) $\forall i, l, k,$

$h, \hat{l}$; $-F_{kh\bar{i}}^{j\hat{i}}$ given by (33) $\forall j, \hat{l}, k, h, \bar{l}$; $-F_{j\hat{i}} \equiv \sum_{k=1}^{K} \sum_{l=1}^{L} q_{kh\bar{l}}^{j\hat{l}} - \sum_{i=1}^{I} \sum_{l=1}^{L} q_{jh\hat{i}}^{il} \forall j, \hat{l}; -$

$$F_{kh\bar{l}} \equiv d_{kh\bar{l}}(\rho_{3kh\bar{l}}) - \sum_{j=1}^{J} \sum_{l=1}^{L} q_{kh\bar{l}}^{j\hat{l}} - \sum_{i=1}^{I} \sum_{l=1}^{L} q_{kh\bar{l}}^{il} \forall k, h, \bar{l}.$$

Then the dynamic model described by (35), (36), (37), and (2), (1), for all $i, l,$ $j, \hat{l}, k, h, \bar{l}$, can be rewritten as a *projected dynamical system* (PDS) (see Nagurney and Zhang, 1996) defined by the following initial value problem:

$$\dot{X} = \Pi_K(X, -F(X)), X(0) = X_0, \tag{38}$$

where Π_K is the projection operator of $-F(X)$ onto K at X and $X_0 = (Q^{10}, Q^{20}, Q^{30}, \gamma^0, \rho_3^0)$ is the initial point corresponding to the initial product transaction and price pattern. Note that since the feasible set K is simply the non-negative orthant the projection operation takes on a very simple form as revealed through (35), (36), (37), and (2), (1).

The trajectory of (38) describes the dynamic evolution of the product transactions between tiers of decision-makers in the supply chain supernetwork as well as the prices associated with the bottom two tiers of the network. The dynamical system (38) is non-classical since it has a discontinuous right-hand side due to the projection operation. Such dynamical systems were introduced by Dupuis and Nagurney (1993) and have been used to study a plethora of dynamic models in economics, finance, and transportation (see Nagurney and Zhang, 1996). In addition, the projected dynamical systems methodology has been used to date to formulate dynamical supply chain network models, with and without electronic commerce, respectively, by Nagurney *et al.* (2002b, a).

A stationary/equilibrium point

We now discuss the stationary point of the projected dynamical system (38). Recall that a stationary point of a dynamical system is that point where $\dot{X} = 0$

and, hence, in the context of our model, when there is no change in the product transactions in the supply chain supernetwork and no change in the prices.

The following result is immediate from the results in Dupuis and Nagurney (1993).

Theorem 1: set of stationary points coincides with the set of solutions of a variational inequality problem

Since the feasible set K *is a convex polyhedron, the set of stationary points of the projected dynamical system given by (38), that is,* X^* *such that* $0 = \Pi_k(X^*, -F(X^*))$ *coincides with the set of solutions to the variational inequality problem given by: Determine* $X^* \in K$, *such that*

$$<F(X^*), X - X^*> \geq 0, \quad \forall X \in K, \tag{39}$$

where $F(X)$ *and* X *are as defined above and* $<.,.>$ *denotes the inner product in N-dimensional Euclidian space where here* $N = ILJHL + ILKHL + JLKHL + JL + KHL$.

Variational inequality (39) is precisely the variational inequality (cf. Nagurney, 1999) derived in Nagurney, Cruz, and Dong (2003) in which it was also established that the solutions of the variational inequality coincide with the equilibrium solutions of a global supply chain network model with risk management. The variational inequality therein, however, was derived from the optimality conditions of the various network decision-makers as well as the equilibrium conditions concerning the prices. Moreover, that model was static and focused on the equilibrium state. Here, in contrast, the above derived projected dynamical system now provides the disequilibrium dynamics as well as the dynamic evolution of the product transactions and prices which converge to a stationary point; equivalently, to an equilibrium point. Thus, with this paper, we now have described the dynamics of the global supply chain supernetwork and not only the statics and have made the crucial connection between the stationary point of the projected dynamical system (38) and the variational inequality formulation (39) in which the solutions of the former coincide with the solutions of the latter.

We now provide some qualitative properties of the dynamical global supply chain supernetwork model with risk and uncertainty. In particular, we state the conditions for establishing the existence of a unique trajectory to the initial value problem (38) and a global stability analysis result.

Theorem 2: existence and uniqueness

Assume that the function F *is Lipschitz continuous. Then, for any* $X_0 \in K$, *there exists a unique solution* $X_0(t)$ *to the initial value problem (38).*
Proof: Follows from Theorem 2.5 in Nagurney and Zhang (1996).

Another very important issue to address is the stability of the proposed system. We first recall the following definition (cf. Zhang and Nagurney, 1995).

Definition 2: stability of the system

The system defined by (38) is stable if, for every X_0 and every equilibrium point X^*, the Euclidean distance $\|X^* - X_0(t)\|$ is a monotone non-increasing function of time t.

Using Definition 2, a global stability result for the dynamical system (38) can be stated as follows.

Theorem 3: stability of the global supply chain supernetwork

Assume that the function F is monotone. Then the dynamical system (38) underlying the global supply chain supernetwork with risk management is stable.

Proof: The conclusion follows directly from Theorem 4.1 of Zhang and Nagurney (1995).

From the above results, we see that the dynamic global supply chain supernetwork with demand-side and supply-side risks as given by (38) is well-defined and, moreover, the supernetwork system is stable. In Nagurney, Cruz, and Dong (2003) conditions that guarantee Lipschitz continuity of the function F (cf. (38)) as well as monotonicity of F are given. In the next section, we apply a discrete-time algorithm, the Euler method, which will track the dynamic trajectories until a stationary state is attained.

3 Numerical examples

In this section, we apply the Euler method (cf. Dupuis and Nagurney, 1993; Nagurney and Zhang, 1996; and Nagurney, Cruz, and Matsypura, 2003, and the references therein) to two numerical examples, the first of which had been solved using the modified projection method in Nagurney, Cruz, and Dong

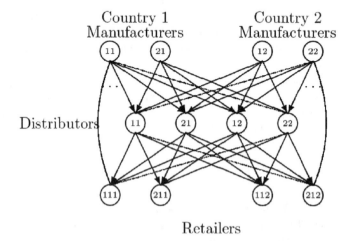

Figure 3.1.2 Global supply chain supernetwork for the numerical examples.

(2003). Due to the fact that the feasible set underlying the supply chain supernetwork model is that of the non-negative orthant, the solution of the induced variational inequality subproblems at each iteration of the Euler method can be solved explicitly and in closed form. Hence, the algorithm is simple to implement in practice.

The Euler method was coded in FORTRAN and the computer used was a SUN system at the University of Massachusetts at Amherst. The convergence criterion utilised was that the absolute value of the product transactions and prices between two successive iterations differed by no more than 10^{-5}. The parameter α_τ in the Euler method (cf. Dupuis and Nagurney, 1993) was set to $\{1, 1/2, 1/2, 1/3, 1/3, 1/3, \ldots\}$ for all the examples.

The structure of the global supply chain supernetwork for the examples is given in Figure 3.1.2. Specifically, we assumed that there were two countries, with two manufacturers in each country, and two distributors in each country. In addition, we assumed a single currency (for example, the euro) and two retailers in each country. Note that electronic transactions were permitted between the manufacturers and the retailers. Hence, we had that $I = 2$, $L = 2$, $J = 2$, $K = 2$, and $H = 1$.

In the examples, we assumed that the demands associated with the retail outlets followed a uniform distribution. In particular, we assumed that the random demand $\hat{d}_{kh\bar{l}}(\rho_{3kh\bar{l}})$, of retailer $kh\bar{l}$, is uniformly distributed in

$\left[\dfrac{b_{kh\bar{l}}}{\rho_{3kh\bar{l}}} \right]$, with $b_{kh\bar{l}} > 0$; $k = 1, 2$; $h = 1$, and $\bar{l} = 1, 2$. Therefore, we have that:

$$P_{kh\bar{l}}(x, \rho_{3kh\bar{l}}) = \frac{x\rho_{3kh\bar{l}}}{b_{kh\bar{l}}}; \quad k = 1, 2; h = 1; \bar{l} = 1, 2, \tag{40}$$

$$F_{kh\bar{l}}(x, \rho_{3kh\bar{l}}) = \frac{\rho_{3kh\bar{l}}}{b_{kh\bar{l}}}; \quad k = 1, 2; h = 1; \bar{l} = 1, 2, \tag{41}$$

$$d_{kh\bar{l}}(\rho_{3kh\bar{l}}) = E(\hat{d}_{kh\bar{l}}) = \frac{b_{kh\bar{l}}}{2\rho_{3kh\bar{l}}}; \quad k = 1, 2; h = 1; \bar{l} = 1, 2, \tag{42}$$

It is straightforward to verify that the expected demand function $d_{kh\bar{l}}(\rho_{3kh\bar{l}})$ associated with retailer $kh\bar{l}$ is a decreasing function of the price at the demand market in the particular country.

The Euler method was initialised as follows: all variables were set equal to zero, except for the initial retail prices ρ_{3khl}, which were set to 1 for all $k, h, \bar{l}$.

Example 1

The data for this example were constructed for easy interpretation purposes. The production cost functions of the manufacturers in the two countries (cf. (3)) were given, respectively, by:

$$f^{11}(q) = 2.5(q^{11})^2 + q^{11}q^{21} + 2q^{11}; \quad f^{21}(q) = 2.5(q^{21})^2 + q^{11}q^{21} + 2q^{21}$$

$$f^{12}(q) = 2.5(q^{12})^2 + q^{12}q^{22} + 2q^{12}; \quad f^{22}(q) = 2.5(q^{22})^2 + q^{12}q^{22} + 2q^{22}.$$

The transaction costs faced by the manufacturers and associated with transacting with the distributors (cf. (4a)) were given by:

$$c_{jhi}^{il} = 0.5(q_{jhi}^{il})^2 + 3.5q_{jhi}^{il} \quad \text{for } i = 1, 2; l = 1, 2; j = 1, 2; h = 1; \hat{l} = 1, 2.$$

The transaction costs faced by the manufacturers but associated with transacting with the retailers electronically (cf. (4b)) were given by:

$$c_{khi}^{il} = 0.5(q_{khi}^{il})^2 + 5q_{khi}^{il} \quad \text{for } i = 1, 2; l = 1, 2; j = 1, 2; h = 1; \hat{l} = 1, 2.$$

The handling costs of the distributors in the two countries, in turn, (cf.(12b)), were given by:

$$c_{ji} = 0.5\left(\sum_{i=1}^{I} \sum_{l=1}^{L} q_{khi}^{il}\right)^2 \quad \text{for } j = 1, 2; \hat{l} = 1, 2.$$

The handling costs of the retailers (cf. (22)) were:

$$c_{khi} = 0.5\left(\sum_{j=1}^{J} \sum_{l=1}^{L} q_{khi}^{jl}\right)^2 \quad \text{for } k = 1, 2; h = 1; \hat{l} = 1, 2.$$

The b_{khi}'s (cf. (40)–(42)) were set to 100 for all $k, h, \hat{l}$. The weights associated with excess supply and with excess demand at the retailers were (see following (26)): $\lambda_{khi}^+ = \lambda_{khi}^+ = 1$ for $k = 1, 2; h = 1; \bar{l} = 1, 2$. Thus, we assigned equal weights for each retailer in each country for excess supply and excess demand.

In Example 1, we set all the weights associated with risk minimisation to zero, that is, we had that $\alpha^{il} = 0$ for $i = 1, 2$ and $l = 1, 2$ and $\beta^{jl} = 0$ for $j = 1, 2$ and $\hat{l} = 1, 2$. This means that in the first example all the manufacturers and all the distributors were concerned with profit maximisation exclusively.

The Euler converged and yielded the following equilibrium pattern. All physical transactions were equal to 0.186, that is, we had that $q_{jhi}^{il*} = q_{khi}^{il*} = 0.186$ for all $i, l, j, h, \hat{l}, k,$ and $\bar{l}$. All product transactions conducted electronically via the Internet, in turn, were equal to 0.175, that is, we had that $q_{jki}^{il*} = 0.175$ for all $i, l, k, h, \bar{l}$. Note that there was a larger volume of product transacted physically than electronically in this example.

The computed equilibrium prices, in turn, were as follows. The equilibrium prices at the distributors were: $\gamma_{ji}^* = 15.09$ for $j = 1, 2$ and $\hat{l} = 1, 2$, whereas the demand market equilibrium prices were: $\rho_{3khi}^* = 32.88$ for $k = 1, 2, h = 1,$ and $\bar{l} = 1, 2$. Note that, as expected, the demand market prices exceed the prices for the product at the distributor level. This is due to the fact that the prices increase as the product propagates down through the supply chain since costs accumulate.

Example 2

Example 2 was constructed from Example 1 as follows. All the data were as in Example 1 except that now we set the $b_{khi} = 1000$. This means (cf. (40)–(42)) that, in effect, the demand has increased for the product at all retailers in all countries.

Also, we assumed now that the first manufacturer in the first country was a multicriteria decision-maker and concerned with risk minimisation with his risk function being given by:

$$r^{11} = \left(\sum_{kh\bar{l}} q_{kh\bar{l}}^{11} - 2 \right)^2,$$

that is, the manufacturer sought to achieve, in a sense, a certain goal target associated with his electronic transactions. The weight associated with his risk measure was $a^{11} = 1$.

The Euler method yielded the following new equilibrium pattern. The computed equilibrium product transactions between the first manufacturer in the first country and the distributors were now: $q_{jh\bar{l}}^{11*} = 0.700$, for $j = 1, 2, h = 1$, and $\bar{l} = 1$, 2. The analogous transactions, but from the second manufacturer in the first country were; $q_{jh\bar{l}}^{21*} = 0.185$. All other product transactions between the manufacturers and the distributors were equal to 0.182.

The equilibrium product transactions associated with electronic transactions were as follows. For the first manufacturer in the first country (who is now concerned with risk associated with electronic transactions) the product transactions were: $q_{kh\bar{l}}^{11*} = 0.633$, for $k = 1, 2, h = 1, \bar{l} = 1$, 2. The analogous transactions but from the second manufacturer in the first country, were all 1.18, with the remainder of the electronic transactions at equilibrium also equal to 1.18.

The product transactions at equilibrium between the distributors and the retailers, in turn, were: $q_{kh\bar{l}}^{jl*} = 0.312$, for $j = 1, 2, k = 1, 2, h = 1$, and $\bar{l} = 1$, 2. The equilibrium prices were now: $\gamma_{ji}^* = 39.54$ for $j = 1, 2, \hat{l} = 1$, 2 whereas $\rho_{3kh\bar{l}}^* = 92.32$ for $k = 1, 2, h = 1$, and $\bar{l} = 1$, 2.

Clearly, the above examples are stylised but they, nevertheless, demonstrate the efficacy of the model and the computational procedure. One may now conduct numerous simulations by modifying the data as well as adding decision-makers with their associated functions and weights and investigating the effects on the equilibrium product transactions and product prices.

4 Summary and conclusions

In this paper, we have developed a dynamic, multi-tiered global supply chain supernetwork model consisting of manufacturers, distributors, and retailers and analysed it both from theoretical and computational perspectives. The model allows for electronic commerce and handles decision-making under risk and uncertainty. Specifically, the manufacturers as well as the distributors are assumed to be multicriteria decision-makers and concerned not only with profit maximisation but also with risk minimisation. The demands for the product, in turn, are random.

The framework permits for the handling of as many countries, as many manufacturers in each country, as many currencies in which the product can be obtained, and as many retailers, as required by the specific application. Moreover, the generality of the framework allows for the demand to have almost any distribution as long as it satisfies certain technical conditions. In addition, the retailers need not be country-specific and can transact either virtually or physically with both the manufacturers and the consumers.

The dynamic model, which is formulated as a projected dynamical system, provides the evolution of the product transactions between tiers of the global supply chain supernetwork as well as the prices associated with the product at the retailer and at the distributor levels. The model generalises the recent work of Nagurney, Cruz, and Matsypura (2003) to include supply-side risk and demand-side risk. Moreover, it provides a natural dynamics to the static global supply chain network model with risk management introduced by Nagurney, Cruz, and Dong (2003), on which many of the developments in this paper are based.

Future research will include the addition of risk associated with transportation between the different tiers of decision-makers in the supply chain supernetwork, the exploration of insurance policies in this framework, as well as empirical work.

Notes

* Department of Finance and Operations Management, Isenberg School of Management, University of Massachusetts, Amherst, Massachusetts 01003. October, 2003; revised March, 2004.

This research was supported in part by NSF Grant No.: IIS-0002647 and by an AT&T Industrial Ecology Fellowship. This support is gratefully acknowledged. The authors are grateful to the editor and the anonymous reviewer for helpful comments on an earlier version of this paper and for future research suggestions.

An expanded version of this chapter appears in *Transportation Research E*, Nagurney and Matsypura (2005).

References

Cohen, M.A. and Mallik, S. (1997) 'Global Supply Chains: Research and Applications' *Production and Operations Management*, 6: 193–210.

Cohen, M.A. and Huchzermeier, A. (1998) 'Global Supply Chain Management: A Survey of Research and Applications' in S. Tayur, M. Magazine, and R. Ganeshan (eds) *Quantitative Models for Supply Chain Management*, New York: Kluwer Academic Publishers.

Dong, J., Zhang, D., and Nagurney, A. (2002) 'A Supply Chain Network Equilibrium Model with Random Demands' to appear in *European Journal of Operational Research*.

Dupuis, P. and Nagurney, A. (1993) 'Dynamical Systems and Variational Inequalities' *Annals of Operations Research*, 44: 9–42.

Engardio, P., Shari, M., Weintraub, A., and Arnst, C. (2003) 'Deadly Virus' *Business-Week Online;* see: http://www.businessweek.com.

Huchzermeier, A. and Cohen, M.A. (1996) 'Valuing Operational Flexibility Under Exchange Rate Uncertainty' *Operations Research*, 44: 100–113.

Keeney, R.L. and Raiffa ,H. (1993) *Decisions with Multiple Objectives: Preferences and Value Tradeoffs*, Cambridge: Cambridge University Press.

Kogut, B. and Kulatilaka, N. (1994) 'Options Thinking and Platform Investments: Investing in Opportunity' *California Management Review*, 36, No. 4.

Nagurney, A. (1999) *Network Economics: A Variational Inequality Approach*, 2nd and revised edn, Dordrecht: Kluwer Academic Publishers.

Nagurney, A., Cruz, J., and Dong, J. (2003) 'Global Supply Chain Networks and Risk Management' see http://supernet.som.umass.edu/dart.html.

Nagurney, A., Cruz, J., and Matsypura, D. (2003) 'Dynamics of Global Supply Chain Supernet-works' *Mathematical and Computer Modelling*, 37: 963–983.

Nagurney, A. and Dong, J. (2002) *Supernetworks: Decision-Making for the Information Age*, Cheltenham: Edward Elgar Publishers.

Nagurney, A., Dong, J., and Zhang, D. (2002) 'A Supply Chain Network Equilibrium Model' *Transportation Research E*, 38: 281–303.

Nagurney, A., Ke, K., Cruz, J., Hancock, K., and Southworth, F. (2002a) 'Dynamics of Supply Chains: A Multilevel (Logistical/Informational/Financial) Network Perspective' *Environment & Planning B*, 29: 795–818.

Nagurney, A., Loo, J., Dong, J., and Zhang, D. (2002b) 'Supply Chain Networks and Electronic Commerce: A Theoretical Perspective' *Netnomics*, 4: 187–220.

Nagurney, A. and Matsypura, D. (2005) 'Global Supply Chain Network Dynamics with Multicriteria Decision-Making under Risk and Uncertainty' *Transportation Research E*, 41: 585–612.

Nagurney, A. and Siokos, S. (1997) *Financial Networks: Statics and Dynamics*, Heidelberg: Springer-Verlag.

Nagurney, A. and Zhang, D. (1996) *Projected Dynamical Systems and Variational Inequalities with Applications*, Boston: Kluwer Academic Publishers.

Nash, J.F. (1950) 'Equilibrium Points in N-Person Games' in *Proceedings of the National Academy of Sciences, USA*, 36: 48–49.

Nash, J.F. (1951) 'Noncooperative Games' *Annals of Mathematics*, 54: 286–298.

Reinhardt, A. and Majidi, N. (2003) 'Europe's Borderless Market: The Net' *Business Week Online*, May 12.

Salkever, A. (2003) 'Up and Comer: Intel's Sandra Morris' *Business Week Online*, May 29.

Sheffi, Y. (2001) 'Supply Chain Management under the Threat of International Terrorism' *The International Journal of Logistics Management*, 12: 1–11.

Zhang, D. and Nagurney, A. (1995) 'On the Stability of Projected Dynamical Systems' *Journal of Optimization Theory and Applications*, 85: 97–124.

3.2 Evaluating accessibility gains produced by new high-speed train services

Juan Carlos Martín, *Javier Gutiérrez,* ** *and Concepción Román* ***

Abstract

In this paper, we apply Data Envelopment Analysis (DEA) methodology to analyse the accessibility impact of the new high-speed train (HST) between Madrid and Barcelona. Accessibility is not usually defined; however, a great variety of indicators with different theoretical backgrounds and complexities has been proposed and implemented in empirical investigations. Here, we develop some synthetic indices to measure the accessibility impact of the new line using four complementary indicators: an index of location; economic potential; relative efficiency of the network; and daily accessibility. A geographic information system (GIS) was used to calculate these indices. The relative performance of each individual economic centre is discussed according to the results of these partial accessibility indicators, and DEA is used to obtain a better understanding of the overall performance of the new infrastructure. Thus, we propose two different synthetic indices to evaluate the accessibility overall performance. The results of the model will be used to extract some policy considerations with respect to the (polarising/balancing) effects of the line within the Spanish territory.

Keywords: *Data envelopment analysis (DEA), Geographic Information System (GIS), accessibility; high-speed train*

1 Introduction

During recent years, after the completion of the Madrid–Seville high-speed line, other lines have been considered in Spain. One of the principal lines that is nowadays under construction is the object of study in this paper: the connection between Madrid and Barcelona. This project is being built up in standard gauge and will be completed by the year 2005. In Spain, this line will be connected with the HST Madrid–Seville that was inaugurated in the year 1992, when universal exposition was held in Seville (see Figure 3.2.1).

New transport infrastructures cause a progressive contraction of space, in the sense that travel times are shortened and generalised costs reduced if prices do

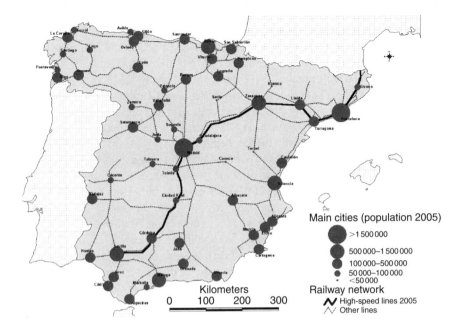

Figure 3.2.1 Spanish railways network.

not change substantially. Forslund and Johansson (1995) demonstrated that improvements of transportation networks reduce interaction costs, increase the overall competitiveness of the system, and allow the use of economies of scale and specialisation in order to obtain more benefits. Hence, we can observe that the quality and capacity of a region's transportation network is a necessary condition to achieve efficiency in production and economic development. Vickerman *et al.* (1999) are not so optimistic and declared that the precise role of transport infrastructure in the process of regional development and the direction of causality are still open to much debate.

High-speed trains shorten the surface trip times between cities to limits that we could not have imagined some years ago and are considered the best alternative for medium distance trips (1–3 hours or 400–1200 km). Their comparative advantages over the competing modes are based on quality of service, reduction of access times to the principal economic centres, the possibility of handling large volumes of passengers, and a better adjustment to shocks or peaks in demand. These characteristics are really important in the European transport markets, where large conurbations are separated by distances of several hundred kilometres (Campenon, 1995). These new infrastructures change the accessibility conditions and the relative location of cities, affecting the attractiveness and the potential economic development of the regions (Lutter *et al.*, 1992). Besides these facts, Bruinsma and Rietveld (1993) argued that good connections in international networks are critical issues to obtain an adequate distribution of economic activity inside Europe.

The HST Madrid–Barcelona will circulate at up to 350 km/h, so travelling times between the main cities on the corridor will be drastically reduced. These reductions are above 50 per cent in all city-pairs in the corridor (e.g. Madrid–Barcelona will obtain a 51.2 per cent reduction, reaching a maximum figure of 74.7 per cent between the cities of Lleida and Tarragona). The new line will improve the accessibility by rail in several cities and regions and it will play an important role for the Spanish eastern corridor linking the most important economic activity centres of the Iberian Peninsula.

The study of the impact of transport infrastructure on accessibility has been traditionally based on the analysis of some partial indicators frequently used in the literature (see e.g. Gutierrez, 2001). Selection of indicators as well as geographical dimension are determinant variables in measuring accessibility changes produced by the construction of a new project. Bruinsma and Rietveld (1988) made a comparison of different accessibility indicators at European level, and they sustained the idea that accessibility depends strongly on the indicators selected and the geographical area under study. In this paper, we apply the DEA methodology to develop a synthetic accessibility index to evaluate the impact of the new HST Madrid–Barcelona. The proposed index combines the complementary information provided by the distinct accessibility indicators. In order to study and isolate the effects of the new line, two scenarios are considered: the year 2005 'with' and 'without' project. We distinguish the cities along the corridor, inside the neighbour provinces, and the rest of the cities to analyse accessibility patterns taking into consideration a geographical dimension. We also try to analyse whether this project will reduce or increase accessibility disparities between the cities in each of these groups using inequality measures and one-way analysis of variance.

The rest of the paper is divided into six sections. Section 2 describes the selection of the four partial accessibility indicators. Section 3 introduces the new approach based on the DEA accessibility index, as a way to synthesise the

Table 3.2.1 Travel times by train between some Spanish cities in the corridor

City-Pair	Travel times		Travel time savings	
	Without project	With project	Difference	%
Madrid–French border	7h.36	3h.40	3h.56	51.7
Madrid–Barcelona	5h.28	2h.40	2h.48	51.2
Madrid–Zaragoza	3h.03	1h.25	1h.38	53.5
Zaragoza–Barcelona	3h.27	1h.15	2h.12	68.6
Zaragoza–Lleida	1h.34	35	59	62.8
Leida–Tarragona	1h.19	20	59	74.7
Tarragona–Barcelona	52	20	32	61.5
Barcelona–Girona	1h.18	37	41	52.5

complementary information provided by partial accessibility indicators. Section 4 explains the different multimodal network configuration introduced in the GIS, that was employed in order to calculate the partial accessibility indicators, and the impact of the new line is analysed with respect to accessibility patterns observed in the different cities. The impacts of the new line in terms of whether the new project will increase or reduce accessibility disparities across different geographic locations are discussed in Section 5. Section 6 summarises and concludes.

2 Accessibility indicators

Accessibility can be defined as the ease with which activities can be reached from a certain place and with a certain system of transport (Morris *et al.*, 1978). This concept is also related to the set of opportunities that is available to people and firms located in a determined area (Linneker and Spence, 1992) and its technical measurement is based on the combination of nodes and networks (Vickerman, 1974). Activities are usually concentrated in some urban agglomerations (Fujita and Mori, 1997) and the comparative advantages of high-speed trains versus other modes of transport are basically oriented to a better performance with respect to the quality of service and access times to the principal centres of economic activity.

Accessibility has been traditionally measured by a large variety of indicators (see e.g. Vickerman, 1974; Pirie, 1979; Jones, 1981; Bruinsma and Rietveld, 1993; and Reggiani, 1998). These measures usually combine the concept of transportation costs and the attraction to a group of cities that are considered centres of economic activity. Travel cost is a measure of the difficulties or resistance to movement between two nodes. It is usually expressed in different units, such as, distance, travel time, or generalised cost of transport. Attraction or attractiveness of urban agglomerations depends on their population or other variables, such as, employment or gross domestic product (see Table 3.2.2 for a classification of the main accessibility indicators studies).

In this study we selected four indicators that respond to different conceptualisations of accessibility: location; relative network efficiency; economic or potential market; and daily accessibility. Table 3.2.3 shows the mathematical expressions of these indicators.

The location indicator represents the average weighted travel time between each node and all the cities in the set of urban agglomerations. The gross domestic product of the urban agglomeration is used to weight the minimal-time routes (Gutiérrez and Urbano, 1996; Gutiérrez *et al.*, 1996). This indicator reflects quite well central and peripheral locations of a nation with respect to the cities that are considered centres of economic activity. A new infrastructure will modify this location indicator by reducing the travel time to the urban agglomerations if the minimum-time route includes some link of the new infrastructure.

The relative network efficiency indicator measures the accessibility in terms of the relative ease of access and it is based on a measure known as the route or

Table 3.2.2 Classification of accessibility indicators studies

Transportation costs		
Distance	*Travel time*	*Generalised cost*
Keeble *et al.* (1988)	Lutter *et al.* (1992) Bruinsma and Rietveld (1993) Dundon-Smith and Gibb (1994) Geertman and Ritsema van Eck (1995) Gutiérrez and Urbano (1996)	Linneker and Spence (1992) Spence and Linneker (1994)
	Attraction	
Population	*Employment*	*GDP*
Lutter *et al.* (1992) Bruinsma and Rietveld (1993)	Linneker and Spence (1992) Spence and Linneker (1994)	Keeble *et al.* (1988) Gutiérrez and Urbano (1996) Gutiérrez *et al.* (1996)

circuitry factor, which is usually used to calculate the extra distance incurred by some individual link with respect to a hypothetical straight line link (Chapman, 1979; Chorley and Haggett, 1969).

This index neutralises the effect of geographical location, and the ordinary notion of costs is replaced by the ease of access in relative terms. Thus, a weighted average of the ratio $\frac{t_{ij}}{t_{ij}^*}$ is calculated considering the gross domestic product of the economic centres in the destination city *j*. It does not take into account real transport demand in each city-pair, but the network efficiency for the multiple connections. However, depending on the object of the study other different weights can be used. The relative network efficiency indicator is a unit-less figure that represents the distance between the real accessibility against the best accessibility that can be obtained (Euclidean impedance), if the node *i* is connected with all the economic centres with the best possible infrastructure (in our case a high-speed train link of 350 km/h) in a straight line connection. This index can only be calculated in compact spaces, because geographical conditions can impede the construction of a hypothetical high-speed train link in straight line (for example, it is not possible to construct a high-speed train link in straight line between Barcelona and Naples over the Mediterranean). However, in these cases it will be possible to calculate the shortest surface path between this city-pair with a high-speed train connection as the best hypothetical connection with the capabilities of a raster GIS.

The economic or potential market indicator is a gravity-based measure that has been extensively used in accessibility studies (see, e.g. Harris, 1954; Keeble *et al.*, 1988; Linneker and Spence, 1992; Smith and Gibb, 1993; Spence and Linneker, 1994). It measures the closeness of potential economic activity to a particular node. This index uses a distance decay function to take into consideration the possible interaction level between the different city-pairs.

In this paper (as in the majority of accessibility studies), the value of the parameter x (see Table 3.2.3) representing the grade of friction of the distance decay function is one. This parameter can also have a big influence on the problem known as self-potential (see Frost and Spence, 1995; Bruinsma and Rietveld, 1993). This indicator gives more importance, *ceteris paribus*, to short distances because short trips are more frequent than long distance trips, and for this reason it seems reasonable to introduce this type of gravitational-based indicator.

The daily accessibility indicator calculates the amount of population or economic activity that can be reached from each node within a travel time limit. The threshold figure is usually three or four hours, so that it is possible to go and return in the same day and carry out some activity at the destination city (Lutter *et al.*, 1992). In our case, we considered the number of inhabitants that can be reached in less than four hours of travel time. This measure is very sensitive to the time threshold considered because some big economic centres can or cannot enter in the calculation of the index depending on this figure. This indicator calculates the potential accessibility for business and tourist trips since the need to stay overnight at the destination city imposes important extra expenses for firms or individuals. Bonnafous (1987) studied the high-speed train between Paris and Lyon, and found empirical evidence of the increase of return trips in the same day on this link.

Table 3.2.3 Accessibility indicators

Location	Relative network efficiency	Potential market	Daily accessibility
$L_i = \dfrac{\sum\limits_{j=1}^{n} t_{ij}\, gdp_j}{\sum\limits_{j=1}^{n} gdp_j}$	$A_i = \dfrac{\sum\limits_{j=1}^{n} \dfrac{t_{ij}}{\hat{t}_{ij}}\, gdp_j}{\sum\limits_{j=1}^{n} gdp_j}$	$P_i = \sum\limits_{j=1}^{n} \dfrac{gdp_j}{d_{ij}^{x}}$	$DA_i = \sum\limits_{j=1}^{n} p_j \delta_{ij}$

Where:
- L_i is the accessibility location indicator of node i
- t_{ij} is the travel time by the minimum-time route through the network between node i and urban agglomeration j (in minutes).
- gdp_j is the gross domestic product of the urban agglomeration j.
- A_i is the accessibility of node i according to this network efficiency indicator
- $\hat{t}_{ij}$ is the ideal time inverted between the nodes (i, j) assuming the hypothetical existence of a high-speed train link of 350 km/h in straight line (Euclidean impedance).
- P_i is the accessibility potential market indicator of node i
- d_{ij} is a the distance between the cities i and j
- x is a parameter that reflects the grade of friction of the distance decay function.
- DA_i is the daily accessibility indicator of node i
- p_j is the number of inhabitants of the economic centre j
- δ_{ij} is 1 if t_{ij} is less than 4 hours and 0 otherwise.

The four indicators selected present complementary information and emphasise some cost or attraction attributes in a different way. Although they analyse the impact of the new infrastructure under a different perspective, they are not exempt from possible drawbacks. Bruinsma and Rietveld (1998) showed that the internal accessibility of a city has not had a significant influence on the calculation of indicators with no distance decay function, but may have a substantial impact on the final outcome in the case of gravity type models. This problem is known as 'self-potential' bias in gravity models, i.e. the contribution of the potential of an individual city itself to the total potential market of that city in accessing the rest of the economic centres. Thus, if we analyse the effects of a new high-speed train, potential market indicators may depend to a great extent on local accessibility, for example the relationship Paris–Paris distorts this indicator but the demand is not important in this context (Gutiérrez *et al.*, 1996).

If accessibility indicators do not employ a distance decay function, the calculations depend extremely on the geographical area under study. For this reason, Bruinsma and Rietveld (1993) argue that this area needs to be chosen carefully, and suggest that the area has to be in concordance with the distance in which the new transport infrastructure presents some comparative advantage over the rest of the transport modes. In this sense, it is necessary to balance adequately the geographical area in order to include the appropriate centres of economic activity.

3 Data envelopment analysis: a way to synthesise partial accessibility indicators

Accessibility is a complex concept that involves more than one single criterion. The interpretation of partial accessibility indicators is clear, but it does not provide an overall performance of accessibility of cities and regions. Policymakers may obtain different conclusions when they use each partial accessibility indicator on their own. However, they find it imperative to evaluate accessibility changes as a direct consequence of the construction of a new project according to these multiple criteria, and to synthesise all the information provided by partial indicators. Another issue that is not well resolved with the aforementioned analysis is whether the new line will increase or reduce accessibility inequalities of Spanish cities.

In this paper, we will fully rank the Spanish cities according to the degree of accessibility provided by the railways system taking into account two scenarios: 'with' and 'without' the project. We use data envelopment analysis (DEA) to obtain a synthetic accessibility index to evaluate what changes the project procures. DEA methodology provides a single unit-less overall index of accessibility efficiency that summarises the multifaceted partial accessibility indicators in a single synthetic measure for comparison and ranking purposes. Besides the application of this multi-criteria approach, this problem may be solved by applying different methods such as analytical hierarchical process (AHP), cluster methods, and principal component analysis (PCA).

Charnes *et al.* (1978) developed DEA to assess the relative efficiency of organisational units using multiple inputs to produce multiple outputs. The efficiency of a unit was calculated as the ratio of its virtual output to its virtual input.

DEA has progressed throughout a variety of formulations and uses different kinds of industries and applications. This methodology has been applied to scenarios where the data cannot be strictly interpreted as inputs or outputs or there is no direct functional relationship between the variables. A general guideline to the classification of the variables is that inputs/outputs are those variables for which lower/greater levels are better. Readers can see more details of the DEA methodology in Charnes *et al.* (1994), Ali and Seiford (1993), and Coelli *et al.* (1998). Nowadays, DEA has become one of the most popular fields in operations research with applications involving a wide range of contexts.

Macmillan (1986) was one of the pioneers applying DEA to regional economics to assess the efficiency of cities in China. Hashimoto and Ishikawa (1993) use DEA with multiple social indicators to measure the desirability of living in some prefectures of Japan. They replaced inputs and outputs in DEA with negative and positive social indicators, respectively. Similarly, Athanassopoulos and Karkazis (1997) use DEA to assess the social and economic efficiency of 20 regions in Greece, and Karkazis and Thanassoulis (1998) studied the causality of public infrastructure investments and investment incentive policies on private investments in Greece using DEA. They succeeded identifying regions where the incentives and infrastructure expenditures effectively attract private investment.

In this paper, we use the location and the relative network efficiency indicators provided by a GIS model as two inputs; and the economic potential and the daily accessibility indicators as outputs. Then, we estimate how accessible Spanish cities are for both scenarios, 'with' and 'without' the project. For that purpose, we calculated an output-oriented variable returns to scale (VRS) DEA model for each economic centre. This model provides a ranking of inefficient accessible cities, but does not allow for the ranking of efficient accessible ones. We also propose a procedure for ranking efficient accessible cities using a virtual accessible city that dominates all the economic centres included in the study.

4 The model and data

A geographic information system (ARC/INFO) is used to calculate the partial accessibility indicators. The railways network is logically the main focus of interest, however a multimodal network (road and railways) has been modelled in order to obtain a denser area of nodes and to calculate the accessibility indicator in nodes that do not have railway stations.

In order to study the impact of the HST line Madrid–Barcelona–French border, we obtained network information for the scenarios mentioned above. The chosen nodes provide enough coverage of the Spanish territory, and 58 destination economic activity centres with more than 75 000 inhabitants were considered. Although the aim of the study is to calculate the accessibility changes by rail, it is also necessary to take into account road transport as a complementary mode.

Concerning railway networks, we have considered all the interurban lines with their respective train stations. For each ARC, we recorded different information in the GIS, such as, type of line, distance, speed, and travel times. We have also recorded for each ARC on the road network the length, the estimated speed according to the different type of Spanish roads and travel times. We have assumed that there is no congestion on the roads, thus travel times were obtained according to the following hypothesis about the estimated speeds: 120 km/h for motorways, 110 km/h for expressways, 90 km/h for interregional roads, and 70 km/h for the rest of the roads. The simulation of the modal change was penalised with 60 minutes' time.

The population and GDP data have been obtained from the official data published by Spanish Statistical Office, and predictions of these variables for the year 2005 have been estimated according to former growth tendencies.

There exist some uncertainties in the predictions of population and GDP, but these estimations do not influence largely on the results obtained, since these estimations are used in the two scenarios considered. When we compare the accessibility indicators in these two scenarios, we are assessing the impact of this new line in the global picture of the railways network in the Spanish regions.

For each scenario, we calculated the travel time between each node and all the possible destinations included in the set of economic activity centres. Access times were calculated for each relationship, and the partial accessibility indicators were obtained applying the appropriate formula. Figure 3.2.2 shows the accessibility maps of the location and economic potential for the scenario in which the line has been constructed.

Average travel times between the centres of economic activity will be reduced approximately 90 minutes (−10 per cent). Logically, the biggest reductions are observed along the corridor, because the new line will offer these cities a better access with each other and with the rest of the cities of Spain. Gerona, Lleida, Zaragoza, Barcelona, Tarragona, Guadalajara, and Madrid are the cities of Spain where the partial indicator of location accessibility presents the higher improvements. However, the cities located near the Mediterranean axis that use the HST-line for a small number of relationships obtain insignificant improvements. Other important benefits appear in some neighbour provinces, such as Segovia, Avila, and Valladolid. These cities will benefit from the construction of this line, because important 'spill over effects' exist due to their proximity to Madrid.

The average variation in the economic potential of the selected economic activity centres is 8.81 per cent. This figure in absolute value is smaller that the one obtained for the partial index of location (average reduction of 10 per cent). This result is consistent with the fact that the distance decay function used in gravity models penalises largely peripheral locations. Lleida, Gerona,

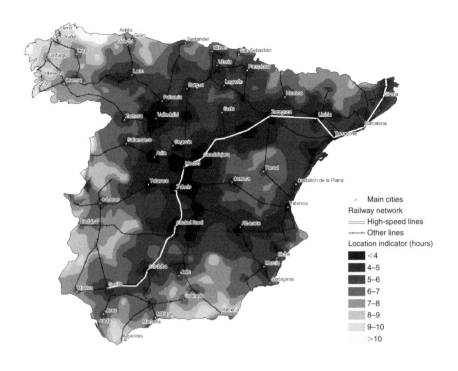

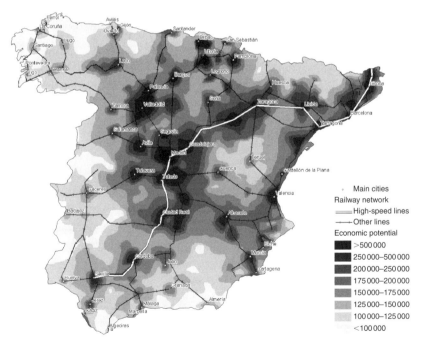

Figure 3.2.2 Maps of location and economic potential indicators.

Tarragona, Zaragoza, and Guadalajara are characterised by being nodes of the new line and they are located between the cities of Madrid and Barcelona, the most important poles of economic activity of Spain. For this reason, it is not a surprise that these cities obtain the highest relative improvements. Madrid is an exceptional case because it only obtains a small gain of 4.5 per cent of economic potential due to its high auto-potential and a prior good connection with the rest of Spanish cities.

The accessible population within four hours will be increased from 5 987 000 to 7 272 000 inhabitants by the construction of the new line. The partial index of daily accessibility is not continuous and presents important jumps depending on how important the inclusion of big cities is within the travel time considered. In this sense, the benefits of the new line are again concentrated along its corridor; however there exist important 'spill over effects' beyond the line due to the proximity to Zaragoza. Pamplona and Huesca are two cities that do not lie in the line but obtain important relative gains in terms of daily accessibility. It is clear that for these cities, the changes are the consequence of being connected to Madrid and Barcelona in less than four hours. On the other hand, the new line will not provide any gain with respect to daily accessibility to many cities in Spain. Gijón, La Coruña, Vigo, Granada, and Almería are examples of this situation, where the new line will not produce any change regarding the accessible population within four hours that can be reached from the respective locations.

In summary, it seems that accessibility changes are more pronounced along the corridor, but if we compare the accessibility performance of Spanish cities according to the only assessment of each partial accessibility indicator, the conclusions obtained may be misleading in many cases. Table 3.2.4 presents the Spearman rank correlation coefficients of accessibility indicators. Results show that the different accessibility partial indicators can be considered complements instead of substitutes, because they present a different perspective of accessibility. In the trivial case, we would have obtained a matrix of 1 or -1, depending on the type of the objective function employed. For this reason, it is necessary to synthesise the partial information provided by the different accessibility indicators. The ideal way to synthesise this partial information would be to find a general agreement about a protocol to evaluate a policy-maker's utility function U that depends on these partial indicators.

Table 3.2.4 Spearman rank correlation coefficients of accessibility indicators

Partial indicators	With project			Without project		
	Location	Network efficiency	Potential market	Location	Network efficiency	Potential market
Network efficiency	0.779			0.640		
Potential market	−0.942	−0.828		−0.911	−0.739	
Daily accessibility	−0.952	−0.810	0.930	−0.928	−0.716	0.878

In this section, we use DEA as an adequate technique to synthesise the partial information provided by the four accessibility indicators. The nature of our problem has determined the selection of a VRS model because there exists a great heterogeneity among the different cities of Spain; and an output orientation because some priority has been given to location and relative network efficiency.

The model for the different scenarios is used to seek which of the 58 cities determine the frontier of the envelopment surface, and are deemed efficient from an accessibility perspective. Thus, in our analysis, we evaluate the grade of accessibility of each of the 58 economic activity centres considered in the study, using location and relative network efficiency indicators as inputs, and economic potential and daily accessibility as outputs.

Formally, the accessibility-DEA efficiency index for each city o is calculated through the following linear programming problem:

$$
\begin{aligned}
\max_{\phi,\lambda,s+,s-} \ & z_0 = \phi + \epsilon \cdot \vec{1}s^+ + \epsilon \cdot \vec{1}s^- \\
s.t. \quad & \\
& Y\lambda - s^+ = \phi Y_o \\
& X\lambda + s^- = X_o \\
& \vec{1}\lambda = 1 \\
& \lambda, s+, s^- \geq 0
\end{aligned}
\tag{1}
$$

where, X and Y are the input and output partial accessibility matrixes, respectively. X_o and Y_o are the input and output accessibility vectors of the city o, respectively. ϕ and λ are parameters calculated in the model, and represent the maximum proportional output accessibility (economic potential and daily accessibility) that can be attained and the linear convex combination that dominates the $o'th$ city, respectively. ϵ and s are the Archimedian constants and the slack variables, respectively. The model compares the city o with all the convex linear combinations of the rest of the cities. Due to the existence of different size of Spanish cities, a VRS approach is used.

The linear programming problem is solved for every city considered as an economic activity centre in order to obtain the accessibility-DEA index that embraces all the partial accessibility indicators. As we obtained some cities that can be considered accessible efficient, and we could not fully rank the Spanish cities, a virtual super efficient city was introduced for each scenario with the existing cities. Then the accessibility DEA index was obtained trough a CRS (constant returns to scale) model. This model ensures that there is only one accessible efficient city with others being inefficient. The input and output for this virtual super accessible city are:

$$
X_v = \min_{j} \{X_j\},
$$

$$
Y_v = \max_{j} \{Y_j\},
$$

where X_v and Y_v are the input and output vectors of the virtual super accessible city and X_j and Y_j are the input-output vectors of the jth city. In other words, the

248   *Martín* et al.

Table 3.2.5 Accessibility-DEA indicators of Spanish cities

Cities	VRS indicator		CRS indicator	
	Without line	With Mad–Bcn line	Without line	With Mad–Bcn line
Madrid	1.000	1.000	1.000	1.000
Guadalajara	1.270	1.041	1.578	1.162
Ciudad Real	1.065	1.000	1.073	1.205
Segovia	1.073	1.023	1.191	1.213
Zaragoza	1.112	1.067	1.562	1.258
Valladolid	1.000	1.061	1.004	1.259
Barcelona	1.424	1.000	1.625	1.292
Tarragona	1.724	1.095	2.310	1.314
Lleida	1.977	1.188	2.973	1.353
Girona	2.333	1.470	3.473	1.680
Albacete	1.016	1.216	1.175	1.794
Valencia	1.059	1.268	1.279	1.922
Alicante	1.074	1.343	1.266	2.025
Castellón	1.092	1.311	1.430	2.109
Córdoba	1.414	1.630	1.581	2.164
Murcia	1.571	1.400	2.019	2.303
Sevilla	1.504	1.755	1.661	2.335
Teruel	4.023	4.820	8.213	11.186
Santiago de Compostela	5.677	5.828	8.775	11.452
Avilés	5.138	5.271	9.276	12.072
Badajoz	5.773	5.792	10.400	13.002
Pontevedra	6.070	6.231	10.147	13.303
Algeciras	6.393	6.420	11.395	14.284
Vigo	5.720	5.897	10.916	14.389
Almería	5.841	6.024	11.436	15.151
Marbella	6.395	6.427	12.595	15.809
Ferrol	6.777	6.964	12.390	16.261

virtual city has the lowest location and relative network indicators and the highest economic potential and daily accessibility indicators.

Table 3.2.5 shows the accessibility-DEA indicators of Spanish cities for both scenarios 'with' and 'without' the project.

Madrid, Valladolid, Albacete, Valencia, and Ciudad Real are the more accessible cities of Spain in the scenario without the project. These cities are characterised by their proximity to Madrid or because they stretch throughout the Spanish Mediterranean ARC. All these cities are important railway nodes in the Iberian Peninsula, and it can be seen that only Madrid and Valladolid, two central locations and important railway nodes, can be considered accessible efficient.

If we summarise the accessibility performance of the cities of Spain, when we consider the scenario in which the new high-speed line Madrid–Barcelona–French border is built, we see that Madrid, Ciudad Real, Barcelona, Segovia,

Guadalajara, and Valladolid are the more accessible cities of Spain. We can observe a big change with respect to the situation that was explained before. First, all the Catalonian province capital cities change their relative position in the ranking and now they all present a good accessibility performance. Second, the rest of the important stations of the line Zaragoza and Guadalajara also obtain an important relative change, improving their global accessibility. And finally, only Madrid, Barcelona, and Ciudad Real can be considered accessible efficient.

Results of the CRS indicator are quite similar, but they show that Madrid is the city of Spain that can be exclusively deemed as accessible efficient for both scenarios. In the scenario without the project Valladolid is the city that loses its privileged position. Meanwhile, Barcelona and Ciudad Real lose their position in the scenario with the project.

5 Accessibility regional cohesion

The question of whether this new line will contribute to increasing or decreasing accessibility inequalities among the cities and regions of Spain needs to be addressed. Increase or reduction of disparities among the Spanish cities has been measured by some of the more important inequality indices employed in economic literature (Cowell, 1995): Gini, Atkinson (0.5), Theil (0) and the coefficient of variation of both DEA accessibility indicators that have been calculated in the previous section.

Table 3.2.6 presents the inequality indices and, looking at the evolution of all the inequality measures, it seems that the project will increase regional

Table 3.2.6 Inequality indices of different accessibility indicators

Gini	Without project	With project
Global accessibility-DEA indicator (VRS)	0.344	0.346
Global accessibility-DEA indicator (virtual CRS)	0.407	0.429

Atkinson (0.5)	Without project	With project
Global accessibility-DEA indicator (VRS)	0.094	0.095
Global accessibility-DEA indicator (virtual CRS)	0.133	0.149

Theil (0)	Without project	With project
Global accessibility-DEA indicator (VRS)	0.191	0.193
Global accessibility-DEA indicator (virtual CRS)	0.268	0.299

Variation Coefficient	Without project	With project
Global accessibility-DEA indicator (VRS)	0.632	0.635
Global accessibility-DEA indicator (virtual CRS)	0.750	0.791

Table 3.2.7 One-way analysis of variance. Accessibility patterns

Variable	F(2.55)	Prob.	Average values			(1)
			Corridor	Neighbour	Rest	
Accessibility DEA VRS without project	7.73	0.002	1.54	1.84	3.50	***
Accessibility DEA CRS without project	7.06	0.002	2.07	2.82	5.82	***
Accessibility DEA VRS with project	12.44	0	1.12	1.82	3.72	***
Accessibility DEA CRS with project	11.79	0	1.29	3.18	7.69	***

Notes
(1) *Significant at 90%, **significant at 95%, ***significant at 99%.

accessibility disparities. We could have predicted this conclusion, because we have seen that some of the cities that present the more important benefits lie in the corridor that is being analysed. Especially, all the Catalonian capital cities are largely favoured by the construction of this line. This result is opposite to the analysis of the spatial distribution of the effects of the same line when the study is done taking into account other spatial context such as Europe. In this case, the transport infrastructure mainly favours a peripheral territory (the Iberian Peninsula), contracting the centre–periphery disparities (Gutiérrez, 2001).

We use one-way analysis of variance to test if the accessibility pattern under different scenarios, 'with' and 'without' project, differs significantly across three distinct spatial contexts: cities along the high-speed-train corridor, neighbouring cities, and rest of the territory.

Table 3.2.7 shows the results of this analysis for both DEA accessibility indicators and scenarios. We have also studied the relative gains of each accessibility indicator in order to evaluate different behaviour with respect to each geographic area. It can be observed that accessibility patterns differ by geographic area (corridor, neighbour, and the rest), so null hypothesis $H_0(\mu_c = \mu_n = \mu_r)$ can be rejected for all DEA accessibility indicators at 99 per cent level of significance.

So, it appears unlikely that accessibility patterns are equal across different geographic areas. However, the null hypothesis can be rejected in a variety of situations. For example, it may be that patterns differ for all of the three different geographic groups, or it may be that only one group differs from the other two groups. Since we have rejected the null hypothesis for almost all the accessibility indicators and scenarios, we would like to pinpoint where the sources of these differences come from.

For this reason, we have also studied pair wise mean differences to assess what geographic areas are more or less accessible. To do this, we need to employ some multiple comparison procedures. In our case, we need to determine if mean accessibility or relative gains differences between distinct geographic areas are statistically different from zero. Thus, we assess three mean

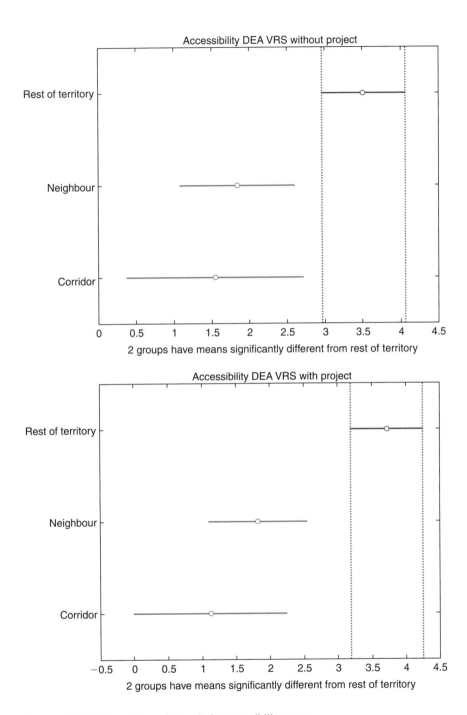

Figure 3.2.3 95% confidence intervals for accessibility means.

differences (corridor-neighbour, corridor-rest, and neighbour-rest). Figure 3.2.3 shows that cities along the corridor are more accessible than cities in the rest of Spanish territory; and that cities in the neighbour provinces are significantly more accessible than cities in the rest of the territory if we compare accessibility using the DEA accessibility index VRS for both scenarios: 'with' and 'without' the project. However, cities along the corridor do not behave significantly different from neighbour cities. In summary, we highlight how the construction of the project will increase accessibility inequalities between different geographic areas of Spain.

6 Conclusions

In this paper, we evaluated accessibility gains due to the construction of the HST line Madrid–Barcelona–French border. Madrid and Barcelona, the two most important economic poles of Spanish economy will be connected by HST services in the near future. In our analysis we introduced different partial indicators to analyse a complex phenomenon such as accessibility. We proposed the study of location, relative network efficiency, economic potential, and daily accessibility indicators.

These partial indicators respond to different conceptualisations of this complex entity, and offer a complementary vision that needs to be embraced. We studied and isolated the effects of the new line, studying two different scenarios in the horizon 2005: 'with' and 'without' the project. Logically, the impacts on accessibility of the new infrastructure are quite different regarding individually each of the accessibility indices. For this reason, we have introduced a DEA accessibility indicator as a methodological approach to synthesise all the complementary information provided by partial indicators. Inequality measures and one-way analysis of variance have been used in order to analyse whether the new infrastructure reduces or increases existing accessibility disparities among cities separating the effects regarding different geographical areas.

The new line will bring about a reduction of almost 90 minutes (-10 per cent) in the average travel times between the selected cities. The biggest reductions are observed along the corridor, because the new line will link these cities with each other and with the rest of the cities of Spain. Spanish peripheral cities obtain the smaller gains in terms of the relative efficiency of the network. The average variation in the economic potential of the selected economic activity centres is 8.81 per cent. The construction of the new line will increase the average accessible population within four hours for the selected urban agglomerations from 5 987 000 to 7 272 000 inhabitants, which means a relative increase of 24 per cent.

The proposed accessibility-DEA indices synthesise the partial information provided by the individual indicators. These indices are based on output information provided by economic potential and daily accessibility indicators, and input information measured by location and relative network efficiency indicators.

Under the scenario in which the new high-speed line Madrid–Barcelona–French border is built, we see that Madrid, Ciudad Real, Barcelona, Segovia, Guadalajara, Valladolid, Zaragoza, Tarragona, and Lleida are the more accessible cities of Spain. All the Catalonian province capital cities belong to this new privileged set of cities, and the rest of the important stations of the line Zaragoza and Guadalajara belong to this set. Madrid, Barcelona, and Ciudad Real can be considered accessible efficient, i.e. they are not dominated for some convex combination of the cities of Spain. When we fully rank the accessible cities of Spain with the virtual CRS approach, Madrid is the only city that may be considered accessible efficient.

The evolution of all the inequality measures point to the same conclusion: the project will increase regional accessibility disparities. However, it appears unlikely that accessibility patterns are equal across different geographic areas.

In summary, accessibility is a multi-faceted concept that is difficult to analyse. Different patterns can be obtained depending on what partial accessibility indicator is being analysed and conclusions may be misleading. In order to obtain a synthetic accessibility index that embraces all the information provided by the multiple partial accessibility indicators, it would be ideal to have some multiple objective programme according to some policy-maker's utility function that depends on partial accessibility indices. However, we do not have explicit knowledge of this function, and we really need to find out the space of tradeoffs among the different partial accessibility measures. This is not an easy task because the space of tradeoffs is not small. DEA methodology can help as an interesting and powerful tool in searching these tradeoffs. In this fashion, we have found the cities that can be considered DEA-accessibility efficient, where the vector of partial accessibility indicators is not dominated, i.e. it is not possible to improve some partial accessibility indicator without worsening at least one of the others.

Notes

* Departamento de Análisis Económico Aplicado. Universidad de Las Palmas de Gran Canaria, 35017 Las Palmas G.C., Spain. Author for correspondence. e-mail: jcmartin@daea.ulpgc.es. Financial support of Spanish Ministry of Public Works is also acknowledged.

** Departamento de Geografía Humana. Universidad Complutense de Madrid, 28040 Madrid, Spain.

*** Departamento de Análisis Económico Aplicado. Universidad de Las Palmas de Gran Canaria, 35017 Las Palmas G.C., Spain.

References

Ali, A. and Seiford, L.M. (1993) 'The mathematical programming approach to efficiency analysis' in Fried, H.O., Lovell, C.A.K., and Schmidt, S.S. (eds) *The Measurement of Productive Efficiency: Techniques and Applications*, New York: Oxford University Press.

Athanassopoulos, A. and Karkazis, J. (1997) 'The efficiency of social and economic image projection in spatial configuration' *Journal of Regional Science*, 37: 75–97.

Bonnafous, A. (1987) 'The regional impact of the TGV' *Transportation*, 14: 127–137.

Bruinsma, F.R. and Rietveld, P. (1996) 'Urban agglomeration in European infrastructure networks' *Urban Studies*, 30: 919–934.

Bruinsma, F.R. and Rietveld, P. (1998) 'The accessibility of European cities: theoretical framework and comparison approaches' *Environment and Planning A*, 30: 449–521.

Campenon, G. (1995) *2nd report of the working group of the European Commission High-Speed Europe*, Warwick: PTRC Proceedings.

Chapman, K. (1979) *People, patterns and process*, London: Edward Arnold.

Charnes, A., Cooper, W.W., and Rhodes, E. (1978) 'Measuring the efficiency of decision making units' *European Journal of Operational Research*, 2: 429–444.

Charnes, A., Cooper, W., Lewin, A.Y., and Seiford, L.M. (1994) *Data Envelopment Analysis. Theory, Methodology and Applications*, Boston: Kluwer Academic.

Chorley, R.J. and Haggett P. (1969) *Network Analysis in Geography*, London: Edward Arnold.

Coelli, T., Rao, D.S.P., and Battese, G.E. (1998) *An Introduction to Efficiency and Productivity Analysis*, Boston: Kluwer Academic.

Cowell, F. (1995) *Measuring Inequality*, 2nd edn, London: LSE Handbooks in Economics, Prentice Hall.

Dundon-Smith, D.M. and Gibb, R.A. (1994) 'The Channel Tunnel and regional economic development' *Journal of Transport Geography*, 2: 178–189.

Forslund, U.M. and Johansson, B. (1995) 'Assessing road investments: accessibility changes, cost benefits and production effects' *The Annals of Regional Science*, 29: 155–174.

Frost, M.E. and Spence, N.A. (1995) 'The rediscovery of accessibility and economic potential: the critical issue of self-potential' *Environment and Planning A*, 27: 1833–1848.

Fujita, M. and Mori, T. (1997) 'Structural stability and evolution of urban systems' *Regional Science and Urban Economics*, 27: 399–442.

Geertman, S.C.M. and Ritsema Van Eck, J.R. (1995) 'GIS and models of accessibility potential: an application in planning' *International Journal of Geographical Information Systems*, 9: 67–80.

Gutiérrez, J. (2001) 'Location, economic potential and daily accessibility: an analysis of the accessibility impact of the high-speed line Madrid–Barcelona–French border' *Journal of Transport Geography*, 9: 229–242.

Gutiérrez, J. and Urbano, P. (1996) 'Accessibility in the European Union: the impact of the trans-European road network' *Journal of Transport Geography*, 4: 15–25.

Gutiérrez, J., González, R., and Gómez G. (1996) 'The European high-speed train network: predicted effects on accessibility patterns' *Journal of Transport Geography*, 4: 227–238.

Harris, C.D. (1954) 'The market as a factor in the localisation of industry in the United States' *Annals of the Association of American Geographers*, 44: 315–348.

Hashimoto, A. and Ishikawa, H. (1993) 'Using DEA to evaluate the state of society as measured by multiple social indicators' *Socio-Economic Planning Sciences*, 27: 257–268.

Jones, P.C. (1981) 'A network model of economic growth: a regional analysis' *Regional Science and Urban Economics*, 11: 231–237.

Karkazis, J. and Thanassoulis, E. (1998) 'Assessing the effectiveness of regional development policies in Northern Greece using data envelopment analysis' *Socio-Economic Planning Sciences*, 32: 123–137.

Keeble, D., Offord, J., and Walker S. (1988) *Peripheral Regions in a Community of Twelve Member States*, Luxembourg: Office for Official Publications of the EC.

Linneker, B. and Spence, N.A. (1992) 'Accessibility measures compared in an analysis of the impact of the M25 London Orbital Motorway on Britain' *Environment and Planning A*, 24: 1137–1154.

Lutter, H., Pütz, T., and Spangenberg, M. (1992) *Accessibility and peripherality of Community regions: the role of road, long-distance railways and airport networks*, Brussels: Commission of the European Communities.

Macmillan, W.D. (1986) 'The estimation and applications of multi-regional economic planning models using data environment analysis' *Papers of the Regional Science Association*, 60: 41–57.

Morris, J.M., Dumble, P.L., and Wigan, M.R. (1978) 'Accessibility indicators for transport planning' *Transportation Research*, 13A: 91–109.

Pirie, G.H. (1979) 'Measuring accessibility: a review and proposal' *Environment and Planning A*, 11: 299–312.

Reggiani, A. (1998) 'Accessibility trade and locational behaviour: an introduction' in A. Reggiani (ed.) *Accessibility Trade and locational behaviour*, Aldershot: Ashgate.

Smith, D.M. and Gibb, R.A. (1993) 'The regional impact of the Channel Tunnel. A return to potential analysis' *Geoforum*, 24: 183–192.

Spence, N. and Linneker, B. (1994) 'Evolution of the motorway network and changing levels of accessibility in Great Britain' *Journal of Transport Geography*, 2: 247–264.

Vickerman, R.W. (1974) 'Accessibility, attraction and potential: a review of some concepts and their use in determining mobility' *Environment and Planning*, 6: 675–691.

Vickerman, R.W., Spiekermann, K., and Wegener M. (1999) 'Accessibility and economic development in Europe' *Regional Studies*, 33: 1–15.

3.3 Evaluation of the cost performance of pre- and post-haulage in intermodal freight networks

Analysis of the interaction of production models and demand characteristics

Ekki Kreutzberger,[*] Rob Konings,[**] and Leon Aronson[***]

Abstract

Pre- or post-haulage (PPH) is an important part of intermodal freight chains and networks, as it substantially contributes to the door-do-door performance and costs. PPH easily stands for 50 per cent of the chain costs (both sides of the network). The new wave of transport sustainability research has clarified that PPH is also a crucial part of the environmental performance and external costs of chains and networks. The relevance of PPH stands in contrast to the limited amount of research devoted to this transport area. Central publications are Spasovic (1991), Transcare (1996), Nierat (1996), and the European research project Imprend (Buck *et al.*, 1999). Finally there is a large range of affiliated operations research, which deals with strategies to collect and distribute freight in general.

Each of the sources is specific, and not sufficient to answer the central question of this chapter, namely: what are the cost quality ranges of PPH for the distance classes 5 km, 25 km, 50 km, and 100 km, taking account of alternative types of typical European operations? This question is important for the design of intermodal rail or barge networks.

With this background research in PPH was started at the Delft University of Technology. It consists of the working lines 'overview model' (spreadsheet), 'development of (heuristic) planners' (micro-simulation) (Aronson, Konings, and Kreutzberger, 2003), and 'provision of field data'. The overview model distinguishes operational strategies, but is deterministic. Stochastic influences can be incorporated by implementing the results of simulations, such as from the heuristic planner. The latter is more sophisticated, but quite labour intensive, if it is to establish an overview of strategy results. The complexity of the planner also requires means to test its plausibility. The spreadsheet calculations are easy to understand, as the output can be directly traced to the initial and intermediate input. They can serve as plausibility instrument for the planner.

This chapter describes the three working lines, presents intermediate and final results of the overview model, amongst which answers to the central question, and shows how the heuristic planner tool can be used to validate assumptions about network unreliability.

Keywords: *intermodal pre- and post-haulage, cost and performance models*

1 Introduction

A typical intermodal transport service consists of a long haul rail or barge service between terminals and a short haul truck service between these terminals and shippers or receivers. This pick-up or delivery portion of an intermodal trip is known as pre- or post-haulage (PPH[1]).

PPH is an important part of intermodal freight chains and networks, as it substantially contributes to the door-to-door performance in terms of service quality and costs. Service quality features such as door-to-door transit time, reliability (variability in transit time), and flexibility are determined by the performances on the different chain links, including the PPH part. Since PPH is the linking part between shippers and intermodal transport providers it has to take into account the requirements of both actors. In general the greatest challenge in offering a high service level is to meet the pick-up and delivery times set by shippers and intermodal transport providers. As regards costs, PPH usually implies relatively short distance transport, but the costs of these services are relatively high. Dependent of the intermodal transport distance the costs of PPH can rise to 50 per cent of the total chain costs. The service and cost performance of PPH therefore have a great influence on the competitiveness of intermodal transport.

In addition, the new wave of transport sustainability research has clarified that PPH is also a crucial part of the environmental performance and external costs of chains and networks (see for instance the overview work of Kreutzberger, Macharis, Vereecken, and Woxenius, 2003).

The relevance of PPH stands in contrast to the rather limited amount of research devoted to this transport area. Major work in this field has been carried out by Spasovic (1990), Walker (1992), Morlok and Spasovic (1994), Transcare (1996), Niérat (1997), in the European research project Imprend (Buck *et al.*, 1999), Wang and Regan (2002), and Taylor *et al.* (2002). In addition, there is abundant affiliated literature in the field of operations research, which deals with strategies to collect and distribute freight in general (e.g. Daganzo and Newell, 1986; Golden and Assad, 1988; Hall, 1993; Savelsbergh and Sol, 1995; Hall and Sabnani, 2002). In these papers transport operations are usually identified and modelled as vehicle routing problems. Although these models do not incorporate the typical characteristics of PPH transport they could have methodological relevance for PPH issues.

The studies which explicitly addressed the PPH issue have identified different opportunities for improvement of PPH services, including changes in legal, logistical, organisational, communicational, and technological conditions. A major conclusion of all these studies is that, among many other determinants, the organisation of PPH strongly influences its cost performance. For example, Walker (1992) and Morlok and Spasovic (1994) found empirical evidence for a possible 30 per cent reduction in PPH costs by either concentrating all traffic in one carrier or centralising the planning of PPH operations. These studies also illustrate that organisation comprises the way transport trips are planned and executed and that it is generally steered by driving forces to maximise the productivity of transport equipment and to minimise the number of empty vehicle-kilometres. The first goal is related to, in literature well-known, 'stay-with' or 'drop-and-pick' procedures. The second goal refers to opportunities to combine trips.

Transcare (1996) also emphasises the effectiveness of central planning to reduce costs. Empirical evidence for this is found in Italy (Sicily), where PPH operations are organised by a corporate body. In addition, Transcare points at opportunities to reduce the duration time at terminals and shippers and to increase the average transport speed, which also contribute to cost reductions.

In testing the existence of network economies of scale in PPH Walker (1992) focused on market characteristics in terms of different PPH company sizes. As regards the spatial characteristics of the terminal service area and their impact on PPH performance the study was limited to variation in average length of PPH trips. In the work of Nierat (1997) the spatial characteristics have been more explicitly incorporated by the examination of terminal area shape and size relative to freight characteristics. Nierat indicates that the service area tends to be cone-shaped with the apex in the direction of the long intermodal haul. This shape reflects the border lines where intermodal transport can be competitive to unimodal road transport. In his model Nierat demonstrates the effects on size and shape of the terminal service area through variations in several parameters: the rate of empty hauls, the number of operations per driver day, good weights, traffic imbalance, discounts for shippers using intermodal transport, and the length of the intermodal haul. However, due to using a generic cost model, in which time and distance costs are not distinguished on a trip-based level, the effects of different kind of PPH operations are not clear and may perhaps even contaminate the results.

Reviewing the previous research on PPH we may conclude that most of these studies did consider organisational alternatives for PPH, but the relationship between PPH operations and different transport landscape characteristics has not been systematically covered.

In this chapter we will elaborate the relation between the cost performance of different kinds of PPH operations and transport landscape characteristics, i.e. the spatial and temporal pattern of transport volumes in a terminal service area. The aim of this analysis is to gain insights into the performance of PPH under different operational conditions (business and market conditions) and to explore the 'best match' between type of PPH operation and type of terminal service area. In addition, knowledge on the relation between terminal service area and the cost performance of PPH is important for the design of intermodal rail or barge networks.

Against this background a research project on PPH was formulated at the Delft University of Technology. It consists of the working lines 'overview model' (spreadsheet calculations), '(heuristic) planner' (micro-simulation; see Aronson, Konings, and Kreutzberger, 2003), and 'provision of field data'. The overview model distinguishes operational strategies, but is deterministic. Stochastic influences can be incorporated by implementing the results of simulations, such as from the heuristic planner. The latter is more sophisticated, but quite labour intensive, if it is to establish an overview of strategy results. The complexity of the planner also requires means to test its plausibility. The spreadsheet calculations are easy to understand, as the output can directly be traced to the input. They can serve as plausibility instrument for the planner. Figure 3.3.1 visualises the relation between the three working lines.

This chapter has the following structure. Section 2 gives a brief overview of performances and costs of PPH in Europe. Section 3 describes the overview model and presents the results. In Section 4 the heuristic planner approach is described and applied as a tool to elaborate and evaluate the assumptions of 'PPH inefficiency' in the overview model. The conclusions are formulated in Section 5.

2 Costs and performances of PPH: some facts and practices

2.1 PPH at inland terminals

In Europe most PPH operations around inland terminals have a distance of 0–25 km (one direction). Only few trips exceed a distance of 100 km. Longer trips are common in special situations, for instance around terminals located near the Alps. The number of terminal visits per day is 1.4–2.1. The annual performance of a truck is about 60 000 km or more.

The combination of these characteristics implies that a PPH truck serving an

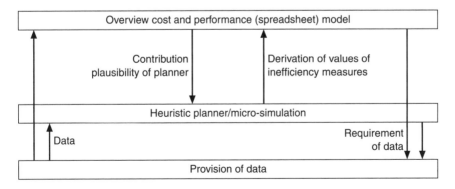

Figure 3.3.1 Relationship between overview model, heuristic planner and data layer.

inland terminal visits four to five shippers per roundtrip. Apparently the size of many consignments is rather small (less than a full container load = LCL), which makes it interesting to consolidate consignments of different shippers and to deliver/collect them in one trip. This leads to relative small costs and volumes per shipper, but does not significantly affect the costs per load unit. In other words, the costs per load unit stay on an acceptable level despite the small volumes per shipper/location.

Such facts can be used for a first rough estimation of costs. As a truck including a driver costs about 350 euro per day (Transcare, 1996), one can divide this amount by the number of roundtrips and involved load units (LU). With only one roundtrip a day and one load unit per roundtrip the costs have that level. With either two load units per roundtrip or two roundtrips per day the costs are 175 euro/LU. Independently of such estimation Transcare reports PPH bottom prices in Europe, which adjusted for inflation, are now 165–230 euro/LU. These prices include two hours of (un)loading.

2.2 PPH at maritime terminals

At maritime terminals we must distinguish road transport:

- from and to ocean vessels. This will – in statistics – often be qualified as unimodal road transport;
- from and to barges or trains, which are always considered as PPH.

A PPH truck roundtrip from maritime terminals will usually cover a smaller number of shippers than from inland terminals, generally only one. This can be explained by a strong dominance of full container loads (FCL) at maritime terminals.[2] In addition, at maritime terminals only containers are handled, which are less convenient for sequential loading and unloading of consignments at different shipper locations compared to swap bodies, which are predominantly found at inland terminals. Since only one shipper is visited, the total duration time at shippers per roundtrip is smaller than at inland terminals. So the average number of roundtrips per day will be larger and hence the PPH costs per load unit will be lower than at inland terminals.

A special feature of intermodal transport services which start or end at ocean terminals is the possibility that PPH costs are absent at the ocean side. This situation can occur when the rail or barge terminal is located at the site of the maritime terminal, because then exchange between ocean vessels and trains or barges is possible by terminal internal transport. This absence of PPH at one side of the intermodal chain supports the competitiveness of intermodal transport.

2.3 PPH in general

CEMT (1998) enlists the following characteristics of PPH: truck and driver costs per day are approximately 300 euro, the number of roundtrips a day range from one to two. Assuming two roundtrips per day and two load units per roundtrip the PPH costs per load unit would be 75 euro, in case of only one unit 150 euro. This is likely to be the case for longer distances. CEMT mentions a PPH distance limit of 150 km.

RECORDIT (2002), acronym for 'real cost reduction of door-to-door intermodal transport', an ambitious project to investigate internal and external transport costs, has calculated the costs of three chains: Greece–Italy–Sweden, Italy–Netherlands–UK, and Spain–Poland. In the chains from Greece to Sweden and Spain to Poland there is pre- and post-haulage, while the chain from Italy to UK has only a post-haulage operation (because the chain starts in the seaport of Genua). In all these chains the PPH distance is 50 km, except for the pre-haulage in Greece (210 km). The weight of PPH costs in the total chain costs appears to be significantly smaller than normally assumed, namely 5–10 per cent. However, one should be aware that these chains are rather long and complicated, e.g. due to cross-bordering, causing relatively high costs for the intermodal part of the chain.

The variety of cost and cost improvements and the incomparability of studies underline the necessity to present a systematic overview of PPH cost levels and ranges.

3 Overview model (spreadsheet)

3.1 General

The overview model investigates the costs and performances, i.e. lead time, of single PPH operations or sequences of such operations. It does not directly take into account the interactions between parallel operations. However, the impacts of such interactions can be incorporated by variables, which represent network inefficiency. The values of inefficiency variables may be derived from field observations, literature reviews, or stochastic modelling. This chapter discusses network inefficiency assumptions in the overview model (Section 3.3) and their validation by comparing the assumptions with the results of the heuristic planner (Section 4).

3.2 Calculation steps

The calculations of PPH costs and performances is structured by the following steps:

a   Define PPH operations for which cost calculations are to be carried out (operations 1–10; see below). These differ by number of shippers per roundtrip, the availability of retour freight, the production model, the amount of co-ordination between sub-operations.

b   Define the values of input variables, which are crucial for PPH costs and performances. Generally, three groups of input variables can be distinguished:

i   transport landscape variables, such as the location of shippers around a terminal (hence distances) and freight volumes per shipper or area;

ii PPH-specific km- and hour-coefficients, which express the resource productivity, in other words the effect of for instance labour or fuel cost levels, or of depreciation and maintenance patterns;

iii operational variables which influence the proportion of waiting or empty riding and therefore represent the network productivity. Most important are the design of roundtrips (one or more shippers, number of roundtrips per load unit), speeds, loading/unloading times, the choice of production models (stay with, drop and pick the semi-trailer, or drop and pick the load unit; see below), the co-ordination of sequences of (sub)operations.

c   Obtain clarity about the required number of vehicles for these operations.

d   Calculate the costs and performances per load unit. Notify for which transport landscape the operations 1–10 are suitable.

e   Interpret (a)–(c) and define a cost range.

In general costs per load unit are obtained by adding the products 'km-coefficient * number of km per roundtrip/number of load units per roundtrip' and 'hour-coefficient * number of hours per roundtrip/number of load units per roundtrip'.

3.3 Operations

The operations 1–10 are based on the operations A–G, which are shown in Figures 3.3.2 to 3.3.8. The operations A–G are suitable to explain the principles. The operations 1–10 are relevant for the cost calculations.

The *production models* describe which vehicle types are involved and how the operations at the shippers' premises are carried out. Three production models can be distinguished. These are:

a   the *stay-with production model*: the tractor and semi-trailer of a truck stay together. Also the load unit remains on the semi-trailer;

b   the *pick-up-and-drop-semi-trailer production model*: the tractor and semi-trailer of a truck are split at the shippers location. During (un)loading of the load unit, the tractor returns to the terminal, with or without a new semi-trailer and load unit. It can also first move on to a second shipper to fetch a new semi-trailer with load unit;

c   the *pick-up-and-drop-load-unit production model*: the load unit is (un)loaded from/to the truck at the shippers location. As normally a shipper has no own crane, this operation can traditionally only be applied for continental load units, i.e. swapbodies, which have foldable legs and therefore can stand independently from any semi-trailer.

Generally speaking, (almost) any PPH network, whether a truck serves one shipper or several shippers in one roundtrip, can be carried out in the stay-with, drop-and-pick-semi-trailer or drop-and-pick-load-unit mode. Figures 3.3.7 and 3.3.8 show exceptions. In roundtrips in which several shippers are served obviously semi-trailers cannot be dropped and picked up at the shippers' location.

The set of PPH-operations A–G (Figures 3.3.2–3.3.8) gives an overview of typical operations. The operations A–E are applied for all flows but are most typical for flows with containers, i.e. maritime flows. The operations F and G are more likely in case of swapbodies, that is to say continental flows.

Most operations A–G are alternatives. Some can also be combined, for instance operation B and D. The operations have in common that there is no freight transported between only shippers, but only between a terminal and shippers.

Which is the best operation? Stay-with operations have the advantage that a tractor and a semi-trailer never need more than one roundtrip per load unit, also if the flows are rather small. This advantage is visible in Figures 3.3.3 and 3.3.4 (operation B and C). The disadvantage of operations with a stay-with configuration is, that the tractor and semi-trailer have to wait at shippers for (un)loading, 'doing nothing' and nevertheless generate time costs. The time costs of the tractor are rather high.[3] Drop-and-pick operations are of advantage if an order can be carried out with only one roundtrip. However, if the transport volumes are rather small, which means that a shipper is not visited frequently, a semi-trailer or load unit needs to be picked up after (un)loading at the shipper. This implies a second roundtrip by the tractor (drop-and-pick semi-trailer) or truck (drop-and-pick load unit), generating additional time and distance costs. All of this implies that the transport volume per shipper or spatial cluster of shippers is an important factor for the choice of operation, and hence for the achievable cost levels. This issue will be further discussed later on.

Stay with	**Drop and pick semi-trailer (with load unit)**	**Drop and pick load unit**
1 truck with 1 ROT, to be paid by 2 payloads	*1 tractor with 1 ROT, 2 STs with 1/2 ROT each, all to be paid by 2 payloads*	*1 truck with 1 ROT, to be paid by 2 payloads*
LEGEND: ST = semi-trailer, T = terminal, S = shipper, ROT = roundtrip ■ = loaded load unit ▨ = load unit being (un)loaded ▭[] = truck		

Figure 3.3.2 Operation A: very large flows per shipper, two payloads at one shipper (i.e. perfect match of inbound and outbound freights). Continuous follow-up of cycles.

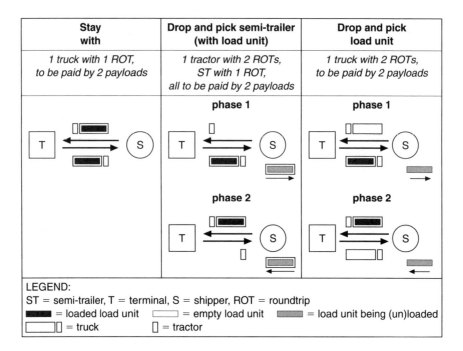

Stay with	Drop and pick semi-trailer (with load unit)	Drop and pick load unit
1 truck with 1 ROT, to be paid by 2 payloads	1 tractor with 2 ROTs, ST with 1 ROT, all to be paid by 2 payloads	1 truck with 2 ROTs, to be paid by 2 payloads

LEGEND:
ST = semi-trailer, T = terminal, S = shipper, ROT = roundtrip
▰▰▰ = loaded load unit ▭ = empty load unit ▱▱ = load unit being (un)loaded
▭▯ = truck ▯ = tractor

Figure 3.3.3 Operation B: large flows per shipper, two payloads at one shipper with different times of arrival and departure of payload (i.e. imperfect match of inbound and outbound freight).

Stay with	Drop and pick semi-trailer (with load unit)	Drop and pick load unit
1 truck with 1 ROT, to be paid by 1 payload	1 tractor with 2 ROTs, 1 ST with 1 ROT, all to be paid by 1 payload	1 truck with 2 ROTs, to be paid by 2 payloads

LEGEND:
ST = semi-trailer, T = terminal, S = shipper, ROT = roundtrip
▰▰▰ = loaded load unit ▭ = empty load unit ▱▱ = load unit being (un)loaded
▭▯ = truck ▯ = tractor

Figure 3.3.4 Operation C: medium flows per shipper, one payload at one shipper (only inbound or outbound freight).

Stay with	Drop and pick semi-trailer (with load unit)	Drop and pick load unit
1 truck with 1 ROT*, to be paid by 2 payloads	*1 tractor with 1 triangle ROT*, 2 STs with 1/2 direct ROT each, all to be paid by 2 payloads*	*1 truck with 1 ROT*, to be paid by 2 payloads*

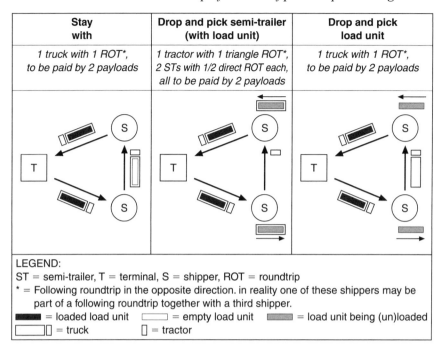

LEGEND:
ST = semi-trailer, T = terminal, S = shipper, ROT = roundtrip
* = Following roundtrip in the opposite direction. in reality one of these shippers may be
    part of a following roundtrip together with a third shipper.
■■■■ = loaded load unit   ▭ = empty load unit   ▨▨▨ = load unit being (un)loaded
▭〕 = truck   〔〕 = tractor

Figure 3.3.5 Operation D: large flows per shipper, two payloads at two shippers in a triangle (perfect match of inbound and outbound freight). Continuous follow-
up of cycles.

The major differences of the operations in a brief overview are as follows.
Operation A in general is the most efficient one, if the required transport
volumes are present. It allows transport of two payloads[4] with only one truck
roundtrip, regardless of the applied configuration (stay with, drop and pick),
since, due to the very large transport volumes, inbound and outbound freight can
be matched. As the shipper is served frequently, it is not required to separately
fetch the semi-trailer in the drop-and-pick operation after unloading. With only
one roundtrip for all configurations, the drop-and-pick load unit operation
implies lowest costs (assuming insignificant cost for dropping or picking up the
load unit), as both the tractor and the semi-trailer lose no time at the shipper
during the (un)loading of the load units.

Operation B can be a suitable operation for flow sizes that are still large, but
insufficiently large to have a perfect match of inbound and outbound freight as
regards its arrival and departure time. Therefore a continuous follow-up of transport cycles is not possible. The involved shipper is served less frequently. To
avoid that in the drop-and-pick operations the semi-trailer or load unit stands at
the shipper inactively, a second roundtrip must be undertaken. The stay-with
operation only has one roundtrip, making this likely to be the cheapest one.
However, it depends on the involved loading/unloading times, the time interval

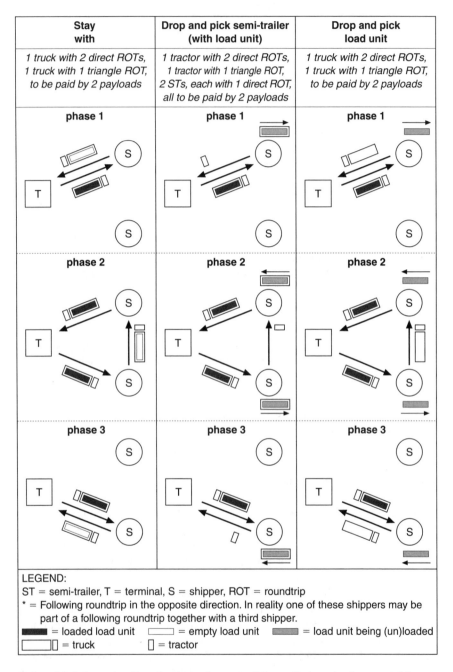

Stay with	Drop and pick semi-trailer (with load unit)	Drop and pick load unit
1 truck with 2 direct ROTs, 1 truck with 1 triangle ROT, to be paid by 2 payloads	*1 tractor with 2 direct ROTs, 1 tractor with 1 triangle ROT, 2 STs, each with 1 direct ROT, all to be paid by 2 payloads*	*1 truck with 2 direct ROTs, 1 truck with 1 triangle ROT, to be paid by 2 payloads*

LEGEND:
ST = semi-trailer, T = terminal, S = shipper, ROT = roundtrip
* = Following roundtrip in the opposite direction. In reality one of these shippers may be
     part of a following roundtrip together with a third shipper.
▬▬▬ = loaded load unit   ▭▭ = empty load unit   ▬▬▬ = load unit being (un)loaded
▭▭◫ = truck   ▯ = tractor

Figure 3.3.6 Operation E: rather large flows per shipper, four payloads at two shippers, triangle roundtrips for tractors and trucks, direct roundtrips for semi-trailers in drop-and-pick semi-trailer operations.

of inbound and outbound freight, link distances (between terminal and shipper) and speeds. In particular the time interval between inbound and outbound freight will be most decisive, because time costs are relatively high compared to distance costs (see footnote 3).

Operation C is nearly the same as B, but the difference is that the costs are only covered by one payload. The drop-and-pick operations of C are less favourable than of B, but unavoidable because the flows of a shipper are more restrictive. In this situation, just as in B, the stay-with procedure is likely to be most efficient, but it depends on the loading or unloading time, the link distances, and speeds.

Operation D has a triangle roundtrip for trucks or tractors. The semi-trailers in the drop-and-pick semi-trailer operation have a direct roundtrip (i.e. only

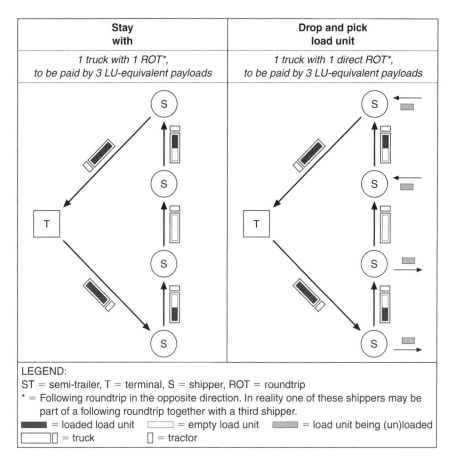

Stay with	Drop and pick load unit
1 truck with 1 ROT,* *to be paid by 3 LU-equivalent payloads*	*1 truck with 1 direct ROT*,* *to be paid by 3 LU-equivalent payloads*

LEGEND:
ST = semi-trailer, T = terminal, S = shipper, ROT = roundtrip
* = Following roundtrip in the opposite direction. In reality one of these shippers may be part of a following roundtrip together with a third shipper.
■■■ = loaded load unit   ▭ = empty load unit   ▨ = load unit being (un)loaded
▭]] = truck   [] = tractor

Figure 3.3.7 Operation F: rather small flows per shipper. 'Continental' roundtrip: four LCL-loads (stay-with) or four 7m-swapbodies/20′ containers (drop-and-pick load unit) in a triangle serving four shippers (perfect match of inbound and outbound freight). Continuous follow-up of cycles.

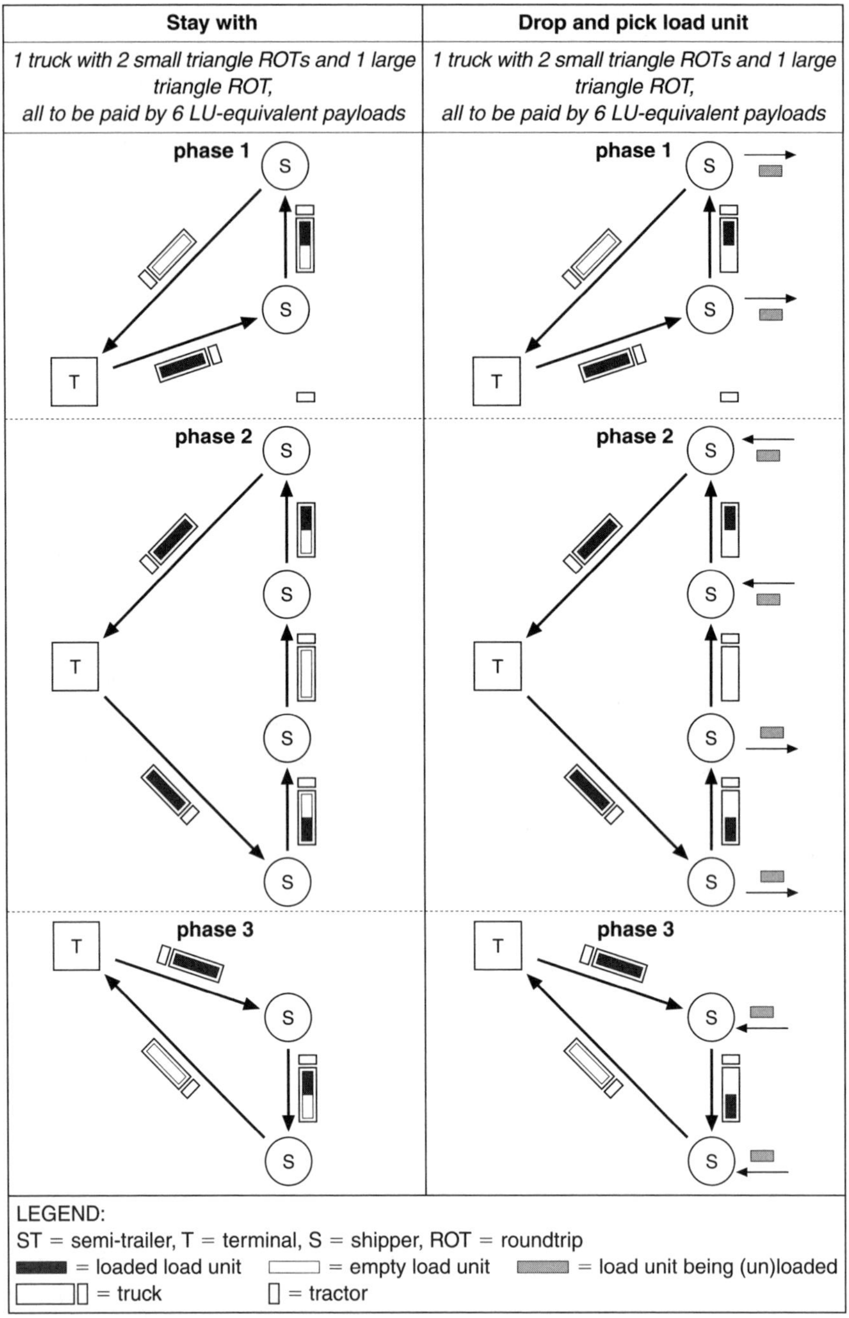

Stay with
Drop and pick load unit
1 truck with 2 small triangle ROTs and 1 large triangle ROT, all to be paid by 6 LU-equivalent payloads
1 truck with 2 small triangle ROTs and 1 large triangle ROT, all to be paid by 6 LU-equivalent payloads
phase 1
phase 2
phase 3
S
T
LEGEND:
ST = semi-trailer, T = terminal, S = shipper, ROT = roundtrip
= loaded load unit
= empty load unit
= load unit being (un)loaded
= truck
= tractor

Figure 3.3.8 Operation G: small flows per shipper. 'Continental' roundtrip: eight LCL-loads (stay-with) or eight 7 m-swap bodies/20′ containers (drop-and-pick load unit) in a multiple triangle serving four shippers (imperfect match of inbounds and outbound freight).

moving between terminal and shipper). The operation has large similarity to A, but the retour-freight is not available at the shipper, which has received a delivery. It therefore has to be picked up at a second shipper. Nevertheless, the two shippers commonly have sufficient freight to be served frequently. If the following cycle can be carried out in the opposite direction, dropped semi-trailers or load units can be picked up in the following cycle.

Operation E is in fact not a basic type of operation, but rather a combination of operation C and D. As such, operation E would be suitable for transport volumes in between those of operation C and D, that is to say for rather large flows. Two shippers generate a transport demand of four payloads, but not in a way that it is perfectly matched on the level of an individual shipper (otherwise this would be operation A).

As the operations A to D show, transport volumes and their time pattern are important determinants for the most suitable type of operation, but also other market features may restrict the possibilities to carry out operations. The best example is operation D in the stay-with mode. It is for instance not possible to move freight for different ocean carriers in the same load unit which only has the label of one carrier. Unless the retour freight of the second shipper is for the same ocean carrier, this network-production combination must be excluded for maritime flows. Such a restriction remains valid as long as carrier-neutral (= grey) load units are not operated in practice.

The operations F and G represent a PPH-haulage line network, which serves four shippers. The operations are typical for continental flows and suitable for rather small flow sizes per shipper.[5] To enable stay-with in these operations, the freight should be LCL-cargo, while for the drop and pick load unit configuration a truck must be able to carry two load units, two 20′ containers or two (7.15 m) swapbodies. Both operations cannot be based on the drop-and-pick semi-trailer configuration, given the current vehicle designs.

Operation F requires a continuous follow-up of cycles, opposite to operation G. This can take place with larger intervals between cycle(-cluster)s, making it suitable for even very small flows per shipper. Opposite to maritime flows the grey box principle is well known in the market of continental flows, allowing it to carry out the networks F and G in the stay-with mode.

The costs per load unit and pre-and end-haulage performances have been calculated for ten operations (1–10), which are not exactly the same ones as shown in the previous figures (A–G). The introduction of this difference has two reasons.

- Not all operations A–G are equally relevant to establish a cost range. Operation B represents a middle position between A and C as regards costs. To discover the bounds of reasonable ranges, calculations of B are not required.
- It is necessary to introduce operational inefficiency. If only operational optimality is assumed, the calculation results represent lower bound costs. Optimality in the operations A–G is present if:
    - a truck or a tractor is available, whenever a load unit or semi-trailer respectively needs one. So load units or semi-trailers never have to wait.

–   trucks and tractors have a high utilisation rate. The equipment reserves are near to zero after trucks or tractors respond to transport requests of shippers.

In reality, sub-optimality is common: there will be waiting times for semi-trailers and load units, and utilisation reserves of trucks and tractors. The size of such inefficiencies is not well known. Spasovic (1991) gives indications of utilisation reserves,[6] but they refer to American circumstances. Also, his work does not include drop-and-pick load-unit operations. Transcare (1996) discusses utilisation reserves, but not systematically, which therefore does not enable to derive useful parameters for this.

Given this background, network inefficiency has to be introduced by calculating models D, E, F, and G with an additional time of 30 per cent for (un)loading transport units (semi-trailers or trucks) at shippers. The 30 per cent inefficiency calculations (model 5, 6, 9 and 10) effect the truck in stay-with operations and the semi-trailer in drop-and-pick semi-trailer operations. In case of drop-and-pick semi-trailer operations the additional time may reflect the non-availability of tractors at the required moment. This choice of 30 per cent is an intuitive value. Its validity is discussed in Section 4. Given this uncertainty, the option to introduce waiting time distributions has been rejected as an inappropriate research approach.

In the pursuit of this chapter the operations 1–6 are called *maritime triangles*, those in the operations 7–10 *continental triangles*. These names indicate what types of load units are involved (maritime containers or swapbodies).

3.4 Performance input

The height of PPH-costs depends on the resource productivity and network characteristics. The resource productivity is expressed as kilometre- and hour-costs of a truck. Calculation of these costs coefficients is based on cost data for short distance road transport and empirical data about the number of kilometres and business hours per year for a PPH-truck. This calculation is shown in Table 3.3.1.

The PPH-costs per load unit are calculated by:

a   selecting the relevant kilometre and hour-coefficients (tractor, semi-trailer or truck);
b   multiplying these with the number of kilometres and hours of an operation;
c   dividing the product by the number of payloads. A *payload* is the paying freight of a load unit. This has to cover its transport costs including empty transport, if there is no other freight to avoid empty transport. In the operations F and G the LCL-shipments are converted to LU-equivalent payloads.

Table 3.3.2 summarises the calculation input for each operation, which includes, as regards the resource productivity a high and a low value for the hour- and

Table 3.3.1 Calculation of kilometre- and hour-coefficients (minimum value*)

Code	Cost type	Calculations	Amounts in euro (2001)		
			Tractor	Semi-trailer	Both
a	Purchase money		81 841	24 958	
b	Rest value (in %)		15	15	
c	Life time in years		8	10	
d	Life time in km		500 000	–	
e	Number of tyres (incl. spare tyre)		7	6	
f	Value of tyre		400	400	
g	Life time tyre in km		200 000	200 000	
h	Repair and maintenance/km		0.07	0.01	
i	Fuel consumption (in litres)/100 km		40	–	
m	Wages and expenses truck driver/year	Northern Europe 56 882	Southern Europe	51 194	
n	Interest rate (in %)		6	6	
o	Fuel price		0.76		
p	Productive (business) hours/year		2500		
q	Number of kilometres/year		62 500		
qa	Number of business days/year		250	250	
qb	Number of business hours day		10	10	
	Distance costs				
r	km-costs tyre	=f/g	0.002	0.002	
s	km-costs all tyres	=s*e	0.014	0.012	0.026
t	Repair and maintenance/km	=h	0.070	0.010	0.080
u	Fuel/km	=o*i/100	0.304		0.304
v1	**Total distance costs/km**	=r + s + t + u	**0.39**	**0.02**	**0.41**
v2	**Total distance costs/km, incl. 5% overhead**	=v1*1.05	**0.41**	**0.02**	**0.43**
	Time costs				
w	Depreciation truck and trailer/year	=a(100 − b)/c	8696	2121	10 817
x	Interest truck and trailer/year	=a(n/100))/2	2455	749	3204
y	Insurance/year	**	3562	499	4061
z	Motor vehicle tax/year	***	953		953
aa	Eurovignet/year		1256		1256
ab	Wages and expenses truck driver/year	=m	51 194		51 194
ac	Total time costs/year	=w + x + y + z + aa + ab	**68 116**	**3369**	**71 485**
ad	Total time costs/business day	=ac/qa	**272**	**13**	**286**
ae1	**Total time costs/business hour**	=ad/qb	**27.2**	**1.3**	**28.6**
ae2	**Total time costs/business hour, incl. 5% overhead**	=ae1*1.05	**28.6**	**1.4**	**30.0**

Source: OTB-road resource cost model, adjusted to the price level of the beginning of 2002.

Notes
In bold-lined cells the values which are different form unimodal road transport.
*   Maximum value is based on northern European wage level and 10 per cent overhead.
**   Insurance in some European countries is much lower. For instance in Greece: 1500 euro/year for a whole truck (RECORDIT; O'Bacelli *et al.*, 2002). Such low values are not considered in the cost calculations of this report.
*** Motor and vehicle taxes are much lower in some European countries. For instance in Greece: 390 euro/year for a whole truck (RECORDIT; O'Bacelli *et al.*, 2002). Such low values are not considered in the cost calculations of this report.

Table 3.3.2 Input parameters for resource and network productivity

Resource productivity	
Km-coefficient truck minimum (euro/km)*	0.43
Km-coefficient truck maximum (euro/km)*	0.45
Km-coefficient tractor minimum (euro/km)*	0.41
Km-coefficient tractor maximum (euro/km)*	0.43
Km-coefficient semi-trailer minimum (euro/km)*	0.02
Km-coefficient semi-trailer maximum (euro/km)*	0.02
Hour-coefficient truck minimum (euro/hour)**	30.0
Hour-coefficient truck maximum (euro/hour)**	34.0
Hour-coefficient tractor minimum (euro/hour)**	28.6
Hour-coefficient tractor maximum (euro/hour)**	32.5
Hour-coefficient semi-trailer minimum (euro/hour)*	1.4
Hour-coefficient semi-trailer maximum (euro/hour)*	1.4
Network productivity	
Average speed links (km/h) for distance class 5 km	25
Average speed links (km/h) for distance class 25 km	35
Average speed links (km/h) for distance class 50 km	35
Average speed links (km/h) for distance class 100 km	50
Terminal time per terminal visit (hours)	1
Unload or load at shipper, minimum (hours)	1.2
Unload or load at shipper, maximum (hours)	2.0
Unload and load at shipper minimum (hours)	2.3
Unload and load at shipper maximum (hours)	4.0
Unload or load at shipper, minimum (hours), 30% inefficiency	1.6
Unload or load at shipper, maximum (hours), 30% inefficiency	2.6
Unload and load at shipper minimum (hours), 30% inefficiency	3
Unload and load at shipper maximum (hours), 30% inefficiency	5.2
Exchange time at shipper: (un)coupling semi-trailer or on-/offloading load unit	0.5
Factor overhead costs minimum	1.05
Factor overhead costs maximum	1.1

Notes
* = Difference between minimum and maximum caused by overhead.
** = Difference between minimum and maximum caused by wage level and overhead.

km-coefficients, and variations in speed links and loading/unloading times to represent different network productivity. Table 3.3.3 shows the distances and times of all different operations for the distance class of 25 km. The same kind of tables can be drawn for the other PPH distance classes. Table 3.3.4 is a generalised presentation of the distances in Table 3.3.3. Also all distances are divided by the number of load units. The table shows that the costly tractor must cover long distances in operation 2, unless the stay-with procedure is carried out. Maritime triangles (operations 3–6) in general have larger tractor distances, whereas the distance per load unit of tractors in continental triangles (operations 7–10) is rather more favourable. These tables help to understand and interpret the calculation results (Figure 3.3.9).

Table 3.3.3 Number of hours and kilometres resulting from different operations for the PPH-haulage distance of 25 km

Calculated models	Stay with		Drop and pick semi-trailer				Drop and pick load unit models	
	Truck		Tractor		Semi-trailer		Truck	
	min	max	min	max	min	max	min	max
Distance roundtrip(s) (km)								
1 = A	50	50	50	50	50	50	50	50
2 = C	50	50	100	100	50	50	100	100
3 = D	75	75	75	75	50	50	75	75
4 = E	175	175	175	175	100	100	175	175
5 = D 30%*	75	75	75	75	150	150	75	75
6 = E 30%*	175	175	175	175	100	100	175	175
7 = F	75	75	–	–	–	–	75	75
8 = G	75	75	–	–	–	–	200	200
9 = F 30%*	75	75	–	–	–	–	75	75
10 = G 30%*	75	75	–	–	–	–	200	200
Time roundtrip(s) (hours)								
1 = A	4.7	6.4	2.9	2.9	5.2	6.9	2.9	2.9
2 = C	3.6	4.4	5.9	5.9	4.1	4.9	5.9	5.9
3 = D	5.4	7.1	4.1	4.1	5.2	6.9	4.1	4.1
4 = E	11.6	15.0	9.0	9.0	8.2	9.9	9.0	9.0
5 = D 30%*	6.3	8.3	4.1	4.1	5.9	8.1	4.1	4.1
6 = E 30%*	13.4	17.4	9.0	9.0	9.1	11.1	9.0	9.0
7 = F	4.6	5.7	–	–	–	–	5.1	5.1
8 = G	13.7	18.1	–	–	–	–	9.7	9.7
9 = F 30%*	5.1	6.5	–	–	–	–	5.1	5.1
10 = G 30%*	15.7	21.3	–	–	–	–	9.7	9.7

Note

* The input time for loading/unloading has been increased by 30 per cent. The additional time represents waiting time for a tractor or a truck.

3.5 Calculation output

Figure 3.3.9 visualises the final results of the cost calculations. The figure has comprised the two drop-and-pick operations to one set of values, in favour of a comprehensive overview.

The figure allows us to derive a cost range per distance class. But the results must be seen in relation to the involved transport volumes. Generally speaking, operation 1 generally requires large (stay with) to very large volumes (drop and pick)[7] *per shipper*. Otherwise the low costs are not obtainable. Operation 2 needs medium sized volumes per shipper.[8] In the maritime triangles (operations 3–6) stay-with operations can have small flows per shipper. Drop-and-pick operations require medium to large flows. The continental triangles (operations 7–10) are all suitable for small flows.

Table 3.3.4 Distance (in number of trip distances) of tractor or semi-trailer per LU-equivalent payload * in each operation 1–10

	Number of involved LU-equivalent payloads	SW Tractor	D+P ST Tractor	D+P LU Tractor	SW ST	D+P ST ST	D+P LU ST
1 = A = direct	2	1	1	1	1	1	1
B = direct	2	1	2	2	1	1	2
2 = C = direct	1	2	4	4	2	2	4
3 = D = simple triangle**	2	1.5	1.5	1.5	1.5	1	1.5
4 = E = triangle/direct**	4	1.8	1.8	1.8	1.8	1	1.8
5 = D with 30% additional (un)load time at shippers	2	1.5	1.5	1.5	1.5	1	1.5
6 = E with 30% additional (un)load time at shippers	4	1.8	1.8	1.8	1.8	1	1.8
7 = F = continental LU simple triangle tractor**	2.7****	1.1	1.1	1.1	1.1	0.8	1.1
8 = G = continental LU multiple triangle tractor***	5.4******	1.3	1.3	1.3	1.3	0.8	1.3
9 = F with 30% additional (un)load time at shippers	2.7****	1.1	1.1	1.1	1.1	0.8	1.1
10 = G with 30% additional (un)load time at shippers	5.4******	1.3	1.3	1.3	1.3	0.8	1.3

Notes

* = 1 for a load unit and 0.67 for a TEU.

** = assuming all edges of the triangle to be equally long = input distance.

*** = assuming all edges of the large triangle to be equally long = input distance, and the third edge of the small triangle to be half this length.

**** = 4 TEU = 2.7 load units.

****** = 8 TEU = 5.4 load units.

SW = Stay With, D + P = Drop and Pick, ST = Semi-Trailer, LU = load unit.

The flow size differences between minimum and maximum costs are much larger than those between maximum cost operations.

The flow size per operation can be obtained by:

- taking the number of load units moved per operation A, B, ... G;
- correcting this for the difference in required time per operation. The result is a number of load units moved per operation during one hour. The *required network volumes* of operation A are about a four-fold increase of operation G (max variant).

If the latter result is also divided by the number of shippers visited per operation, the required volume (in number of load units) per shipper is known. The *required volumes per shipper* of operation A are about a 15-fold increase of operation G (max variant).

The cost range derived from Figure 3.3.9 takes volumes into consideration.

- Operation 1 should be used carefully to fix minimum costs. Because the expectable volumes are restricted, it is reasonable to make use of minimum stay-with or maximum drop-and-pick values for the lower bound of the maritime cost range. These values also lie on the same level as the minimum values of inefficient maritime triangles (operations 5 and 6).
- Operation 2 indicates where the upper bound of the range lies. Because of required volumes and generated costs only stay-with operations are reasonable in this operation. The upper stay-with value then is suitable for determining the upper bound of the maritime costs range.
- The operations 3–10 excluding the upper values of stay-with operations are used to determine the lower and upper bound of the continental cost range.
- The cost range for 'all flows' is derived from the two other ranges by slightly reducing the common range.

The 'regression' line of all distance classes for 'all flows' is:

- (maximum line) $y = 2.2x + 90$;   (1)
- (average line) $y = 1.55x + 70$;   (2)
- (minimum line) $y = 0.9x + 50$,   (3)

in which x is the distance of the PPH (5 km, 25 km, 50 km, or 100 km), and y is the PPH cost per load unit at one side of the door-to-door network.

The cost range per distance class is larger than the cost differences between distance classes on the average line.

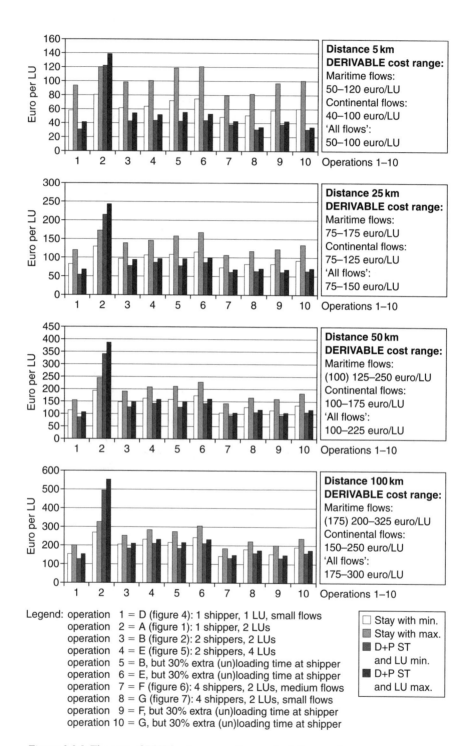

Legend: operation 1 = D (figure 4): 1 shipper, 1 LU, small flows
operation 2 = A (figure 1): 1 shipper, 2 LUs
operation 3 = B (figure 2): 2 shippers, 2 LUs
operation 4 = E (figure 5): 2 shippers, 4 LUs
operation 5 = B, but 30% extra (un)loading time at shipper
operation 6 = E, but 30% extra (un)loading time at shipper
operation 7 = F (figure 6): 4 shippers, 2 LUs, medium flows
operation 8 = G (figure 7): 4 shippers, 2 LUs, small flows
operation 9 = F, but 30% extra (un)loading time at shipper
operation 10 = G, but 30% extra (un)loading time at shipper

☐ Stay with min.
▨ Stay with max.
▧ D+P ST and LU min.
■ D+P ST and LU max.

Figure 3.3.9 The cost of PPH-haulage operations: calculation results.

4 Heuristic planner (micro-simulation)

4.1 Intention

The ranges of costs per distance class are derived from the calculating results for the lowest cost operations without inefficiencies and the highest cost operations with inefficiencies. Inefficiencies were hereby assumed to be time (and money) losses, which have the global size of 30 per cent of (un)loading times at shippers locations. The realism of this assumption can be evaluated by means of micro-simulation.

4.2 Type of model

The heuristic planner is the result of a micro-simulation. This assigns trucks (agents) to orders in a structured way, given the inputs distance and time between locations, and a cost function. The model documents the performance results. When these are satisfactory, the model can (almost) be used as a planner in reality.

More concretely, the model is to solve a so-called Transport Agent Planning Problem (TAPP). Ingredients of the challenge are a network of locations and roads, vehicles capable of transporting freight, and a set of orders saying which freight must be moved where and when. The orders may not all be known in advance, but will partly be inserted dynamically. The cost function on the actions of vehicles is based on time and distance, and it includes penalties for delays. The vehicles are capable of moving one unit of freight at a time (e.g. containers or semi-trailers). The challenge now is to assign orders to the vehicles such that all orders are executed with relative low costs.

The model, which solves the TAPP, is a so-called strategic planner. It communicates with so-called tactical planners, the truck drivers and/or software which supports truck drivers or guides robotised vehicles.

4.3 Model approach

This chapter describes and discusses the results of a first phase of simulations. This focuses on stay-with operations with:

- direct routes and freight in two directions (inbound and outbound);
- direct routes and freight in one direction (inbound or outbound);
- triangle routes and freight in two directions (inbound and outbound);
- triangle routes and freight in one direction (inbound or outbound),

all in accordance to roundtrip characteristics in the overview model. Opposite to the overview model the simulation is not restricted to a single roundtrip or a sequence of those, but covers all (parallel and sequential) operations of a certain period. The sequence of truck operations is determined by the coincidence of

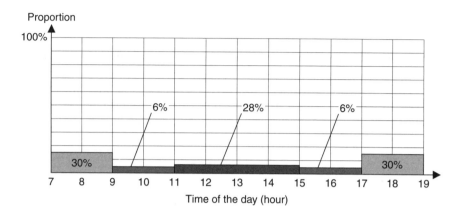

Figure 3.3.10 Global distribution of orders in time (from and to terminal).

being available at certain moments in the sequence of shippers orders, which are distributed in time and space. The global time distribution of orders (Figure 3.3.10) in the sense of average number of orders per hour is derived from field observations at terminals and literature statements on the one side and conceptual argumentation on the other side. The conceptual logic incorporates the idea of a 'balance in directions per day' and 'part of the trucks has two terminal visits per day'. The specific time distribution of orders per hour is obtained by randomisation of hour averages. Orders refer to shippers to be visited. The time distribution has its origin at the terminal and is translated to shippers times. The (un)loading of orders takes place in time windows.

The planner assigns trucks to orders for the whole service area. From the trucks' point of view a typical question after unloading at a shipper is, whether to return directly to the terminal or to move to a following shipper in order to fetch a new load unit to the terminal. The last option implies waiting costs and additional distance costs in turn for letting the roundtrip be paid by two payloads.

From the planners' point of view the truck with the shortest distance to the location of an order is assigned to the order. Other available trucks have to wait or are assigned to other orders. The amount of waiting in the whole service area depends on the number of trucks in operation. If too many trucks are in operation, the waiting times of trucks will increase. If the number of trucks in operation is too small, the number of orders carried out 'too late' will increase. So will the penalty costs for serving too late. Also, the distance covered by trucks is likely to increase, due to the fact that there is less freedom to wait for shorter distances. The planner searches for best solutions, anticipating on possible future assignments.[9]

The distribution of orders in time and space and the number of required trucks depend on the envisaged distance class and the assumed network volume. Both are likely to be related. The following model run input was used:

- service area with distance class 5 km has a transport volume of 25 000 LUs/year;
- service area with distance class 25 km has a transport volume of 25 000 LUs/year;
- service area with distance class 50 km has a transport volume of 25 000 or 50 000 LUs/year;
- service area with distance class 100 km has a transport volume of 25 000, 50 000 or 100 000 LUs/year.

Table 3.3.5 shows the distribution of load units amongst shippers and the number of shippers. In this model run there is no mix of distance classes (as in the overview model), no mix of production models (e.g. stay-with; as in the overview model), but there is a mix of roundtrip types (e.g. triangle roundtrip; unlike the overview model).

4.4 Results

The simulation results describe the types of realised operations, their time and cost performances at links, terminals and shippers' locations, and the required means. Some of the results are summarised in Table 3.3.6. The table shows that direct routes dominate. Possibly an improved planner would increase the proportion of triangle routes. The simulation suggests that the value of the unreliability measure (column h) lies higher than assumed in Section 3, namely at 50–60 per cent rather than at 30 per cent. A reduction of the number of trucks will reduce the waiting time of trucks, but only at the cost of unacceptable increases of the 'time too late' at the shipper.

5 Conclusions and future research

The TU Delft research on PPH, reported here, has led to an answer to the central question of the chapter, namely a range of costs per distance class. These results are related to a large range of types of operations and service area characteristics. As the overview model does not model the mutual influences of parallel operations ('network unreliability'), such influences need to be estimated. Network unreliability hereby is a summarising indicator which incorporates logistic and route unreliability. The realism of initial estimations on network unreliability in the framework of the overview model has been evaluated by means of a micro-simulation. The simulation results suggest that the initial estimations are on the low side. This means that the upper bound of the cost ranges which are the result of the overview model, would slightly shift upwards.

However, before adjusting the cost ranges, it seems reasonable to improve the models and data provision first. Of special interest are:

- (micro-simulation) simulate the other production models (drop and pick) and improve the simulation algorithms which optimise waiting times, route lengths and penalty costs;

Table 3.3.5 Combination of input values in the model run: network volumes, distance class, and number of shippers

Annual volume (payloads or LUS per shipper) →	250 LUs	500 LUs	1000 LUs	2500 LUs	5000 LUs
Annual volume = 25 000 LUs. Number of shippers = 38	of which 5000 for 20 very small	of which 5000 for 10 small shippers	of which 5000 for 5 medium shippers	of which 5000 for 2 large shippers	of which 5000 for 1 very large shipper
Annual volume = 50 000 LUs. Number of shippers = 76	of which 10 000 for 40 very small shippers	of which 10 000 for 20 small shippers	of which 10 000 for 10 medium shippers	of which 10 000 for 4 large shippers	of which 10 000 for 2 very large shippers
Annual volume = 100 000 LUs. Number of shippers = 152	of which 20 000 for 80 very small shippers	of which 20 000 for 40 small shippers	of which 20 000 for 20 medium shippers	of which 20 000 for 8 large shippers	of which 20 000 for 4 very large shippers

Table 3.3.6 Results of simulation (stay-with)

a	b	c	d	e	f	g	h	i	j
Distance class	Annual volume (LUs)	Direct, laden, unladen %	Direct, laden, laden %	Triangle, laden, laden %	Time at shipper	...of which waiting time	d in % of c	'Time too late' at shipper per order	Number of trucks
5	25 000	60	28	12	512	296	**58**	2.0	32
5	50 000	59	33	8	530	261	**49**	0.2	75
5	100 000	63	32	5	527	256	**49**	0	132
25	25 000	56	33	11	439	206	**47**	0.7	44
25	50 000	53	40	7	459	238	**52**	0.2	90
25	100 000	58	38	4	456	234	**51**	0.2	90
50	25 000	48	40	12	374	182	**49**	1.7	52
50	50 000	43	50	8	395	208	**53**	0.9	108
50	100 000	44	51	6	404	224	**55**	0.7	197
100	25 000	46	44	10	329	173	**53**	1.1	64
100	50 000	42	50	8	342	185	**54**	1.5	129
100	100 000	44	52	5	347	193	**56**	1.7	231

Note
c + d + e = 100%.

- (overview model) assign route lengths per distance class which reflect service area road networks more realistically. Holroyd (1969) gives an overview of average length of journeys in a circular town dependent on the type of network structure. Alternatively, concrete networks could be implemented in the overview model. The latter has the advantage that also other area types (e.g. industrial areas, regional networks) can be considered. Also, route unreliability for network types could be introduced. Figure 3.3.11 gives an impression of such options, which then should also be incorporated in the micro-simulations;
- (data provision) achieve more robust and representative information about shipment sizes, time rhythms and volumes.

On the basis of the improved data and models the assumptions about network unreliability and cost ranges can be validated.

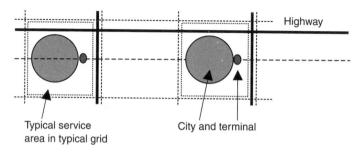

Figure 3.3.11 Examples of network concretisation for future modelling.

Notes

  * Delft University of Technology, OTB Research Institute for Housing, Urban and Mobility Studies, Jaffalaan 9, 2628 BX Delft, The Netherlands, E.Kreutzberger@otb.tudelft.nl or Sokreue@dso.denhaag.nl
 ** Delft University of Technology, Research Institute for Housing, Urban and Mobility Studies, Jaffalaan 9, 2628 BX Delft, The Netherlands, R.Konings@otb.tudelft.nl
*** Delft University of Technology, Faculty of Electrical Engineering, Mathematics and Computer Science, Mekelweg 4, 2628 CD Delft, The Netherlands, L.D.Aronson@ewi.tudelft.nl

1 In literature also referred to as *pre- and end-haulage, collection and delivery*, or *drayage*.
2 In case of LCL-cargo, these containers usually have their origin/destination in a consolidation company, where consignments are reloaded to non-intermodal trucks. So these LCL-containers will still have their origin/destination at one shipper.
3 As shown below, a tractor costs about 30 euro per hour, a semi-trailer about 1.5. The distance costs of a tractor are about 21 euro, if the roundtrip consists of 2×25 km. The distance costs of a semi-trailer are about one euro.
4 A payload is the paying freight of a load unit.
5 In model F 4 TEU (=2.7 LUs) are moved from and to the terminal, in model G these are 8 TEU (=5.4 LUs).

6 In the analysed frameworks 'one of the ten tractor-driver units is utilised only 12.5 per cent of time for which it is actually paid' (Spasovic, 1990: 25). Tractor-driver unit is in terms of the thesis a tractor. This implies an average sub-utilisation rate of at least – rounded off – 8 per cent, dependent on what the utilisation characteristics of the other nine tractor-driver units are.

Such values refer to American PPH-haulage distances: '...typical drayage distances of less than 100 miles'. In Europe, distances beneath 25 km are most typical. Distances up 100 km or more can be observed. They have restricted proportions (less than 10 per cent of all orders), with few exceptions, like Alpine corridors (Transcare, 1996). The utilisation rates therefore are likely to be higher in Europe.

7 The reason is that drop-and-pick operations are calculated in a way that (un)loading at a shipper can more or less take place continuously. This makes drop-and-pick in operation 1 cheaper than a stay-with operation, but only if they are kept busy by the shipper continuously.

8 Drop-and pick allows smaller flows.

9 The time distribution is considered to be known at the beginning of the day.

References

Aronson, L.D., Konings, R., and Kreutzberger, E.D. (2003) 'Heuristic planning in intermodal drayage', NECTAR website conference proceedings 2003.

Baccelli, O., Black, I.G., Búhler, G., Capka, M., Cini, T., Droste-Franke, B., Enei, R., Engelund, P., Handanos, Y., Henriques, M., Kunth, A., Kubásek, M., Maas, N., Seaton, R., Tamás, A., Vaghi, C., Vannoni, C., Weibel, T.G., and Weinreich, S. (2001) *External Cost calculation for selected corridors (deliverable 4)*, European research project RECORDIT, Brussels.

Buck, NEA, Institut National de Recherche sur les transports et leur sécurité, Stichting intermodaal transport, European intermodal association, Informore, Gemeentelijk havenbedrijf Amsterdam, 5MDN, Telecotrans, Port authority of Barcelona (1999) *Validation of the Formulas: Demonstration projects (deliverable 3)*, European research project IMPREND, Brussels and Nijmegen.

CEMT (1998) *Report on the Current State of Combined Transport in Europe*, Paris.

Daganzo, C.F. and Newell, G.F. (1986) 'Configuration of physical distribution networks' *Networks*, 16: 113–132.

Golden, B.L. and Assad, A.A. (eds) (1988) *Vehicle routing: methods and studies*, Amsterdam.

Hagget, P. and Chorley, R.J. (1969) *Network Analysis in Geography*, Edward Arnold, London.

Hall, R.W. (1993) 'Design for local area freight networks' *Transportation Research B*, 27B, 2: 79–95.

Hall, R.W. and Sabnani, V.C. (2002) 'Control of vehicle dispatching on a cyclic route serving trucking terminals' *Transportation Research Part A: Policy and Practice*, 36(3): 257–276.

Holroyd, E.M. (1966) *Theoretical average journey lengths in circular towns with various routing systems*, Ministry of Transport, Road Research Laboratory, Reports, 43, London. Presented in: Hagget and Chorley (1969).

Kreutzberger, E., Macharis, C., Vereecken, L., and Woxenius, J. (2003) 'Is Intermodal freight transport more environmental friendly than all-road freight transport?', a review, NECTAR website conference proceedings 2003.

Nierat, P. (1997) (INRETS) 'Market area of rail-truck terminals: pertinence of the spatial theory' *Transport Research, A*, 31(2): 19–127.

Savelsbergh, M.W.P. and Sol, M. (1995) 'The general pickup and delivery problem' *Transportation Science*, 29(1): 17–29.

Spasovic, L.N. (1990) *Planning intermodal drayage network operations*, UMI dissertation services, Ann Arbor.

Taylor, G.D., Broadstreet, F., Meinert, T.S., and Usher, J.S. (2002) 'An analysis of intermodal ramp selection methods' *Transportation Research Part E*, 38: 117–134.

Transcare (1997) *Rationalisierungspotentiale im Vor- un Nachlauf zum Kombinierten Verkehr,* Kurzfassung, Wiesbaden.

Walker, W.T. (1992) 'Network economies of scale in short haul truckload operations' *Journal of Transport Economics and Policy*, XXVI(1): 3–17.

3.4 A methodological framework to analyse the market opportunities of short sea shipping:

The Adaptive Stated Preference approach

Angela Bergantino, * *Simona Bolis,* ** *and Carla Canali* ***

Abstract

Although in the last few years at both national and European level a number of documents have been put forward on the great opportunities offered by the development of the 'Motorways of the sea' in re-directing freight flows, there is a lack of any empirical analysis on the determinants of such choice by operators. In other words, a lot has been done in analysing supply and very little in analysing demand. Identifying the value that users assign to the specific transport alternative would strongly contribute to evaluating the possibility of a trade-off between the maritime short sea shipping (SSS) mode and the other modes. Furthermore, the identification of the factors related to both the mode and the specific organisation of the companies that exert a significant influence on the choice of operators and the magnitude of their impact would represent, in such instances, a necessary prerequisite for any forecasts. In the last decade significant improvements have been made in the definition of a methodology capable of realistically interpreting the decision-making process of operators with respect to transport service choice, especially when facing only potential alternatives. Using a methodology falling within the broad definition of conjoint analysis – the adaptive stated preferences approach – we measure the trade-offs among service characteristics that shippers make when evaluating the Ro-Ro option (already present on the market or still hypothetical) against surface alternative services. The paper is based on data collected through questionnaires and direct interviews carried out on a sample of operators located in the north-western regions of Italy. Given the characteristics of the data-base, the estimation has been carried out using a tobit model.

Keywords: *Ro-Ro services, short sea shipping, Adaptive Stated Preferences, discrete choice model, tobit*

1 Introduction

In the last few years the re-balancing of freight traffic over the different modes is increasingly capturing the interest of policy-makers. In many European countries, ecological concerns and, more practically, the congestion of most of the surface infrastructure networks and the state of the public finance have redirected attention towards the sea alternative. At EU level, first through the 2001 White Paper 'European transport policy for 2010: time to decide' which introduced in the European language the use of the term 'Motorways of the sea', then with the Marco Polo project which grants 120 million euro to the development of sea transport and, very recently, through the inclusion in the 'quick start' list of projects (EU, 2003) of both the Adriatic and the Tyrrenian Sea Corridors, the attention towards the potential for re-directing freight traffic towards Ro-Ro maritime services is gaining concrete support. The capacity of the political and financial support of transforming itself into a significant reallocation of traffic flows and in the consolidation and emergence of new Ro-Ro services depends, however, on the response of the shippers. In order to evaluate the real potential of the maritime alternative it would be necessary, thus, for an indepth analysis of the behaviour of traffic operators which would yield insights on their choice when faced with new alternative routes and/or services: a sort of market analysis of the new 'Ro-Ro product'. The new Ro-Ro services aiming at becoming real alternatives to surface transport, should, in fact, be evaluated in the light of the level of competitiveness required nowadays by the freight operators. They need, in fact, a flexible transport system, capable of adapting to the modern structure of production and completely integrated within the logistics networks (both existing and under construction). In this paper we present the preliminary results of a pilot study aimed at identifying the value that the user assigns to the specific transport alternative and the factors – related to both the mode and the specific organisation of the companies – that exert a significant influence on the choice of the shipper in relation to the transport service. These elements represent a necessary prerequisite for traffic flow predictions and investment decisions. Using a methodology falling within the broad definition of conjoint analysis – the Adaptive Stated Preferences (ASP) approach – we have been able to measure the trade-offs among service characteristics that shippers make when evaluating alternative services already present on the market or still hypothetical. We have demonstrated how this methodology, which has already gained overwhelming success in surface transport studies, can be successfully applied, making the appropriate variations, in the analysis of maritime services and in particular, in verifying the potential success of initiatives directed at enhancing the use of the maritime Ro-Ro services. To our knowledge, this is the first ASP experiment performed with the scope of determining the preferences of operators in terms of service attributes of sea transport and of studying the potential reallocation of traffic from surface transport services to short sea shipping services.[1]

In Section 2 we describe the methodology used to carry out the analysis and the criteria adopted to assemble the dataset. Section 3 illustrates the steps followed in the data-gathering exercise and briefly describes the design and the outcome of the ASP experiment. The estimating procedure is illustrated in Section 4 while the main findings, with some comparisons with other similar studies, are commented on in Section 5. In Section 6 a brief summary of the main conclusions is provided.

2 Overview of the methodology

2.1 The choice of Adaptive Stated Preference

Nowadays, the superiority of Stated Preference techniques (SP) versus Revealed Preference techniques (RP) in the study of the behaviour towards transport mode decisions is generally accepted, due, mainly, to the characteristics of the data needed for the experiment. In particular, in the context of freight transport, since the late 1970s, following the pioneering work by Fowkes and Tweddle (1979), SP techniques have been used, among others, by Bates (1988), Fowkes and Tweddle (1996 and 1997), Bolis and Maggi (1999), Fowkes and Shinghal (2002), Danielis and Rotaris (2002), and Maier and Bergman (2002).[2]

In this work, we assume that the transport service can be 'broken down' into its component attributes and that each component generates a specific level of utility for the user. In particular, we attempt to measure the trade-offs users make in choosing between alternative modes with a specific focus on maritime Ro-Ro services. The methodology used falls within the broad family of conjoint analysis experiments, as we attempt to determine the value that individuals place on any product as equivalent to the sum of the utility they derive from all the attributes making up a specific 'transport product'. However, given the need to adapt the choice set to the real context of the decision-maker interviewed in order to avoid offering the respondent choices/options which are irrelevant for him/her, we discard traditional stated preference techniques in favour of the 'Adaptive Stated Preference' (ASP) techniques.[3] The existence of an alternative which is not sufficiently used, in fact, is analogous to analysing the choice of a new alternative (Tweddle *et al.*, 1996).

The ASP technique is an interactive data collection method which allows amending attribute levels offered to the respondent during the experiment on the basis of the responses he/she gives. One significant advantage of this method in studying freight transport decisions is that it makes it possible to cope with a wide range of 'situations' which are comparable with the real world known by the respondent, and that the experiment is trying to recover (type of commodity, time variance of attribute valuation, etc.). The ASP starts from an existing freight transport option chosen by the respondent and implies asking the respondent to rate various hypothetical alternatives, expressed in terms of the relevant attributes, for performing the same transport task.

2.2 Identification of the sample: category and geographical coverage

Different from many previous studies, instead of considering as the subjects of our experiments producers or suppliers, we have decided to run our experiment on a sample of freight-forwarding agencies. Freight forwarders have been assimilated to actual shippers on several accounts. First, it is increasingly common, especially for medium-long distance transfers, to delegate the decision on the mode to be used outside the firm to third parties: choosing freight-forwarding agencies makes it possible to intercept information from a sector of the industry which accounts, on average, for more than half of the transport decisions, as outsourcing of transport operations is spreading rapidly.[4] Freight forwarders represent, in fact, a large and growing share of the consumers of transport services. Second, the focus on freight forwarders has allowed us to obtain a sample which, although small, is homogeneous as to the type of activity carried out by the respondents. Given the limited resources available, selecting producers would have limited the scope of the analysis to a specific productive sector or excessively constrained the dimension of the dataset for each industrial sector. Finally, recent studies have demonstrated that the definition of the freight forwarder is changing from 'that of an agent who arranges transport and prepares shipping documentation' to that of a 'provider of a whole range of additional value-added services to shippers' which range from 'the organisation of the shipment to the setting up of the whole logistic process': freight forwarders are becoming 'one-stop shop' specialist companies (KNP, 2002). According to the results of the market review carried out by the Unescap in 2001, this is part of a process that has led to the blurring of boundaries between what were formerly distinct activities. There is a growing body of evidence showing that 'freight forwarders, from the perspective of the shipper, assume the role of the carrier, from the point of view of the actual carrier, they assumes the role of the shipper' (Unescap, 2001: 1).

All in all, selecting freight-forwarding agents instead of producers, allows, on the one hand, gaining insights from a wider spectrum of possible uses; on the other hand, to gathering a set of information on the subject who is really behind the decision-making process in transport attribute choices. Although we recognise that the objective function of the freight forwarder would necessarily differ from that of the producer, it could reasonably be argued that, given the recent evolution of the market and of the contractual agreements tying the two, once the organisation of the transport service has been outsourced the real (final) decision-maker, the shipper, would be the freight forwarder himself. He would be the residual claimant to any cost-quality advantages obtained.

Given that the purpose of this study is that of focusing on the factors influencing the choice of the maritime mode against available alternatives, we have concentrated the empirical application on a specific geographical context. In particular, we have analysed the preferences of operators localised in the northwest regions of Italy with regard to the possibility of accessing a maritime Ro-Ro service from the ports of Genoa or La Spezia. In particular, in order to present the participating operators with comparable alternatives, we have considered traffic-flows between origin-destination areas which are reachable from the area of the study both by sea and by land. Also, in line with the scope of our investigation we have restricted the interviewed sample to those freight forwarders who have a certain familiarity with the maritime mode.

This approach has enabled us to analyse consumers' preferences for the maritime alternative and to identify the service attributes which most influence operators' attitudes towards short sea shipping Ro-Ro services. The analysis has been carried out through a postal survey and direct interviews with freight forwarders.

3   Data gathering

3.1 Preliminary survey

Once the type of companies to consider in the experiment and the area to be covered by the study was identified, the data were collected in two steps. First a sufficient number of companies suitable for the investigation and interested in collaborating were identified, mainly through direct telephone contact with the managers. Forty-six freight-forwarding companies localised in the area between Genoa, La Spezia, and Parma were identified and were asked to respond to a series of questions concerning firm characteristics, geographical coverage, reference markets, most common type of shipments, type of activity carried out for clients, modes of transport mainly used, and so on. Ample space was left to describe a typical shipment currently carried out by the company by land transport which could be carried out, instead, by using Ro-Ro transport. Questions were directed at acquiring sufficient information to define a stated preference experiment suitable in the context of maritime transport involving the respondent.

The overall response rate was relatively good (about 40 per cent) and resulted in the collection of information on the activities of the companies and in the identification of the ones suitable for the study.[5] Of the 18 companies which replied, however, four returned incomplete questionnaires and three did not seem suitable to continue the experiment due to the characteristics of their activity. Inclusion, in fact, depended not only on the willingness of the company to be included but also on its geographical coverage and on the type of traffic it served. In order to compare surface and sea transport it was necessary to identify companies which could consider the hypothetical alternative feasible, given the characteristics of their traffic. For instance, including companies serving the route from northern Italy to Sardinia would not be appropriate (no surface alternatives could be considered viable); similarly, it would not be appropriate to include in the analysis companies serving the routes Turin to Trieste (no sea alternative would be considered viable). On the basis of the responses and of the information gathered during the first part of the survey, thus, it was possible to select only 11 potential participants to the second stage of the experiment; four of them, however, refused to proceed with the experiment due to lack of time/interest or the inability to disclose reserved data. The final sample was thus composed of seven companies, four located in Liguria and three in Emilia-Romagna.[6]

Following a thorough pre-test of all instruments, appointments were set with the managers responsible for the mode choice and the interactive experiment took place.

3.2 The ASP experiment

The second phase of the study consisted if an interactive conjoint analysis interview defined as the 'ASP experiment'. It consisted of a repeated set of choices recorded directly onto the interviewer's portable computer, whose software presented a consistent, on-screen series of price-attribute scenarios as alternatives to the baseline shipment facts provided by the respondent: on the first screen the respondent is asked to provide information to describe a 'typical transport' operation performed by the company with respect to the set of attributes previously identified, plus some additional information which is used to differentiate observation later in the analysis. The information on typical transport is used, instead, to 'customise' the 'current choice' (A) of the respondent which becomes the 'reference option' and does not change for the whole experiment. This option is reported, at each iteration, on the left-hand side of the screen – column A – and it is automatically assigned a rating of 100: it is assumed that, among the existing alternatives, this is the preferred one, and it thus represents the operator current utility level. The other columns, which appear from the second screen onwards, report hypothetical options (B and C) for which the attribute values are generated by the program on the basis of the known characteristics of the firms' original transport service (data inputted in screen 1 and the choices reported in each iteration). In every repetition of the conjoint experiment, the hypothetical alternatives presented in column B and C change – new computer generated alternatives are presented – and the respondent is asked to rank the two alternatives against option A on the basis of the value he/she assigns to the service. In choosing the rating, the respondent has to use the value scale carefully illustrated by the interviewer, which ranges between 0 and 200.

The task to perform during the experiment is to assign ratings to hypothetical options presented on the screen, hence the respondent is asked to rate an option B with respect to A on a scale such that option A (current option) is 100 and option B can either be considered worse (rating below 100) or better (rating above 100). The important point is that respondents should rank options in their desired order, and use the rating scale to roughly indicate their strength of preference where the analogy is an index with 100 equals present value (see Tweddle *et al.*, 1995).

Once the rating on screen one (iteration one) is performed, the following screens propose new alternatives but always with respect to the actually chosen alternative A. During the iterations, the respondent is confronted with a choice among A and alternatives that are, e.g. cheaper but slower or cheaper but less reliable. Iterations will continue between cost and the same attribute until the rating is in the 95 to 105 range. At this point the screen that follows will present options where the remaining attributes change following the same procedures.[7] The experiment terminates either at the 20th iteration or when, for all attributes, convergence is found. It is extremely important that the respondent rank options in the desired order, having a clear understanding of the scaling, so to indicate as accurately as possible his/her strength of preference (Tweedle *et al.*, 1995). The variables included in the experiment are:

- cost (c);
- time (t);
- reliability (r); and
- frequency (f).

The choice to include these variables stems from the results of the questionnaire; this is in line with the other ASP experiments conducted in Europe.[8] Column B always refers to the same mode as that of the typical transport defined by the respondent, while column C refers to a different mode of transport which, in the current experiment was always Ro-Ro maritime service. Each response given during the experiment is taken as a separate observation at the analytic phase. The respondent's selections have been automatically coded into the analytic categories subsequently used in a series of maximum likelihood estimation, one for each respondent.

4 Estimation methodology

In order to estimate the *n* respondents' probability of opting for Ro-Ro services the recorded ratings (R_n) collected through the ASP experiment are assimilated to utilities (U_n). We are implicitly assuming, thus, that what has been recorded during the experiment is an implicit estimation of the utility the respondent places on the hypothetical offers:

$$R_{nA} \cong U_{nA}; R_{nB} \cong U_{nB}; R_{nC} \cong U_{nC} \tag{1}$$

where R_{nA} is the rating of the current transport (actual choice) performed by the company and R_{nB} and R_{nC} are, instead, the rating of the two alternative services. U_{nA} is the level of the utility of the respondent when choosing alternative A, while U_{nB} and U_{nC} are the levels of the respondent's utility generated by alternatives B and C, respectively.

From [1] we have that:

$$R_{nA} \geq R_{nB} \Leftrightarrow U_{nA} \geq U_{nB}$$

and, equally, that:

$$R_{nA} \geq R_{nC} \Leftrightarrow U_{nA} \geq U_{nC}$$

Let $i = B, C$; the probability of the respondent to choose alternative A can be written as:

$$P_{nA} = Pr (U_{nA} \geq U_{ni}) \tag{2}$$

The ratings are, thus, transformed into binary choices: A *vs.* B, A *vs.* C. The process is repeated for each iteration in each case study (maximum 20 times per respondent). A dataset is constructed where every difference in rating between an alternative offered, i (B or C), and the current alternative A, is transformed into a choice probability for the typical service A. For each case study, there are, thus, about 40 degrees of freedom available for the calibration of the model.[9]

Assuming that the utilities can be divided into two parts, one which is the systematic component of utility (V_n) and the other which represents the random component (ϵ) and simplifying notation, equation [1] can be rewritten as:

$$R_{nA} \cong U_{nA} = V_{nA} + \epsilon_{nA}$$

$$R_{ni} \cong U_{ni} = V_{ni} + \epsilon_{ni}$$

where and V_{nA} and V_{ni} represent the part of the utility that the decision-maker (respondent) derives from alternative A or from alternative i (B or C), respectively, explained by the selected variables. Assuming, thus, that the latter are functions of the various attributes of the transport service alternative observed through the experiment – the vector z_n – we have:

$$V_{nA} = V(z_{nA}) \tag{3a}$$

$$V_{ni} = V(z_{ni}) \tag{3b}$$

Adopting, as it is done typically, a functional form for V which is linear in the parameters, we have:

$$V_{nA} = \alpha_{nA} + \beta' z_{nA}$$

$$V_{ni} = \alpha_{ni} + \beta' z_{ni}$$

where $\beta' = [\beta_1, \beta_2, \ldots, \beta_k]'$ is a vector of k unknown parameters. Now equation [2] can be rewritten as:

$$P_{nA} = Pr(V_{nA} + \epsilon_{nA} \geq V_{ni} + \epsilon_{ni}) = Pr(\alpha_{nA} + \beta' z_{nA} + \epsilon_{nA} \geq \alpha_{ni} + \beta' z_{ni} + \epsilon_{ni}) \tag{4}$$

Turning to the standard approach of choice theory applied to mode choice and assuming that the unobserved errors (ϵ_n) are independent and identically logistically distributed,[10] considering only two alternatives (A and i, the 'other') we can formulate the decision taken by the company as a binary logit model. The probability of respondent n choosing alternative A rather than i is:

$$P_{nA} = \frac{e^{(R_A)}}{e^{(R_A)} + e^{(R_i)}} = \frac{e^{(V(z_{nA}))}}{e^{(V(z_{nA}))} + e^{(V(z_{ni}))}} = \frac{1}{1 + e^{V(z_{nA}) - V(z_{ni})}} \qquad [5]$$

With the assumption of linearity of the parameters, equation [5] can be rewritten as:

$$P_{nA} = \frac{1}{1 + e^{\beta'(z_{nA} - z_{ni})}} \qquad [6]$$

Through the assumption stated in equation [1], it is as if, by recording the ratings assigned by the respondent to each alternative as the service attributes were varied, we have observed the probability of alternative A to be chosen (or discarded) over (in favour of) alternative B or C as a function of the transport service characteristics. With the dataset available, we can thus estimate the probability of choosing A over the other alternatives as a function of the differences in the service attributes (e.g. $c_A - c_B$, $c_A - c_C$, $t_A - t_B$, $t_A - t_C$, and so on).

Taking logs and maintaining the assumption of linearity of the parameters we can estimate a model relating the log-odds of choosing A over i ($Log(P_A/P_i)$) – i.e. the frequency of the choice – to the difference in the attributes between each proposed alternative (i) and the reference alternative A and, consequently, the impact and the relative importance of each attribute in determining the probability of the change. Transforming equation [6] we have:

$$Log(P_{nA}/P_{ni}) = Log(P_{nA}/1 - P_{nA}) = V(z_{nA}) - V(z_{ni}) + \epsilon_{nA} - \epsilon_{ni} = (\alpha_{nA} - \alpha_{nA}) + \beta'(z_{nA} - z_{ni}) + (\epsilon_{nA} - \epsilon_{ni})$$

which, expanding, becomes:

$$Log(P_A/1 - P_A) = \alpha + \beta_1(c_A - c_i) + \beta_2(t_A - t_i) + \beta_3(r_A - r_i) + \beta_4(f_A - f_i) + \beta_5 Ro\text{-}Ro + \epsilon_n \qquad [3]$$

where:

$\epsilon_n = \epsilon_{nA} - \epsilon_{ni}$

c = transport cost (expressed in euro) for a door-to-door service (including transhipment);

t = scheduled journey time (expressed in hours) between origin and destination (including transhipment);

r = expected number of shipments per year arriving on time (expressed in percentage of the total number of shipments);

f = number of shipments per month;

Ro-Ro = dummy variable which takes the value of 1 when Ro-Ro transport is used and 0 otherwise.

The α and the βs are the estimated coefficients. In particular, β_1 to β_4 represent the value, for the respondent, of the differences in the attributes of the alternatives faced with respect to the current service (variation in cost, frequency, reliability, and in journey time). β_5 measures the respondent's attitude towards the maritime mode. An estimated positive value of the latter implies that, *ceteris paribus*, the respondent would be more likely to opt for Ro-Ro services. In other words, respondents who have recurred to maritime transport services will be more inclined to choose one of the services alternative to the one currently used.

The estimated values of the constant and of the dummy variables identify shifts on the log-odds ratio – i.e. on the probability that option A is preferred to option *i*. The estimated coefficients of continuous variables can be interpreted by analogy, indicating marginal effects rather than shifts. Elevating the estimated coefficients to the power of 'e', yields how many times more likely it is to observe A rather than *i* by changing the values of the specific variable, all else being equal.

5 Main findings

5.1 Estimation results

The procedure chosen to estimate the empirical model is the tobit ML estimator. The dataset, in fact, contains a number of zero values corresponding to those alternatives which, given the value of their attributes, have received a rating of zero. Since we can assume that those zero values correspond, in principle, to cases in which the latent variable – the indirect utility – might take negative values (i.e. unacceptable levels of reliability or frequency which would compromise the respondent activity), we can treat the zeros as a result of censoring and nonobservability.

The results of the estimation are shown in Table 3.4.1.

The coefficients reproduced in Table 3.4.1 refer to the effect of a change in the respective variable on the respondent's utility (rating). For the coefficients of cost, time, and frequency it is possible, in most cases, to reject the null hypothesis that the true value is zero at both the 10 per cent and the 5 per cent significance level. In particular, the coefficient of the variable cost is always significant at least at the 10 per cent level with an expected negative sign while the coefficients of the variable indicating frequency of service have the expected positive sign, except for Case 2, in which, however, the coefficient is not significant. In addition, the variable time is generally significantly different from zero (except for Case 1), and it has, in general, the expected sign: an increase in the difference in journey time between the current option (A) and the alternative (i = B, C) is likely to have a negative impact on the probability of maintaining the current service.

Specific to our study is the valuation of the willingness to use the maritime mode, which is picked up by the Ro-Ro dummy. The estimation has yielded interesting results: although the valuation differs widely among the respondents,

Table 3.4.1 Estimation results on ASP data

	Case 1	Case 2	Case 3	Case 4	Case 5	Case 6	Case 7	Exp. sign
Intercept	1.29	−15.61**	−7.67	−4.68	−9.15	12.58	−9.79*	+
Cost	−0.48**	−1.13**	−0.74**	−1.35**	−1.11**	−1.57**	−0.99**	−
Time	0.70	−0.13**	−1.18*	−1.56*	0.81*	−1.14**	−0.97*	−
Reliability	1.41	5.42*	1.99*	1.64*	−0.18	6.11*	1.57	+
Frequency	1.18**	−0.71	7.13**	10.13**	9.90**	6.29**	12.99**	+
Use of Ro-Ro	−9.11	15.61	−22.64*	8.05	−12.40	10.57*	14.59*	
Adj. ρ^2	15%	49%	28%	59%	54%	48%	39%	
N. obs.	41	27	33	31	35	29	28	167

Note
* = 5%; ** = 10%.

it is possible to infer that, there is no strong 'a priori' reluctance from those operators interviewed to using Ro-Ro services. Only Case 3 has a negative parameter which is significantly different from zero; it implies that Respondent 3 has an attitude of diffidence towards the maritime alternative. Respondents 6 and 7 have instead a significant positive attitude towards Ro-Ro services. The remaining operators do not seem to have strong preferences either way.[11]

From Table 3.4.1 it can be noted that, in general, the estimated coefficients are quite small:[12] the marginal impact of a change in a variable on the propensity to switch from the current service to an hypothetical one would, thus, be quite minor. Consequently, also the estimated elasticities would be of limited magnitude (see Bolis and Maggi, 1999).

In Table 3.4.2 we report the monetary valuations of trade-offs between attributes given by the ratio of the parameter estimates to the cost parameter estimate; the values referring to parameters which are not significantly different from zero at least at the 10 per cent confidence level are reported in parenthesis.

Each cell of Table 3.4.2 shows the amount of money that the respondent would be willing to pay (in case of a positive value) or to receive as compensation (in case of a negative value) for a one-unit variation in each variable. The ratio of the service attributes to the cost coefficient yields, in fact, the monetary values of an attribute at the margin; hence, it gives an idea of how changes in attributes are traded off against a monetary change in transport costs. In the case of time this is the Value of Time (VOT), in case of reliability and frequency this is VOR and VOF, respectively. As it can be seen, on average, an hour reduction of journey time is valued 0.64 euro per ton, while a 1 per cent reduction in reliability would require a compensation of 3.15 euro per ton. Finally, a one step reduction in the frequency supplied (one time per month) would require almost 8 euro per ton (7.61) compensation.[13] In general, it seems that, for the sample analysed, frequency is the most precious service attribute: this is true, in particular for Cases 3, 4, 5, and 7 which assign to frequency a value significantly higher that the remaining respondents. These operators are very conscious of changes in the frequency of service. Even though the sample considered is extremely small and not representative of the category, it is interesting to note that, as expected, freight forwarders tend to value more factors which widen their freedom of choice and the regularity of service than those elements, like time of journey, which, although important, are more easily taken account of in the planning of their activity. Since there is a substantial, although not univocal, body of evidence signalling the potential impact of the 'ordering effect' in SP experiments, in order to substantiate the outcome of the estimation, we present, in the following section, a brief summary of the main findings obtained via the questionnaires returned and the short interviews carried out with the participants. As we shall see, these seem to give confirmation to the relative ranking of the various service characteristics and of the preference scale emerging from the estimation.[14]

Table 3.4.2 ASP attribute service to cost trade-off ratio (absolute values – euro per ton)

Value	Case 1	Case 2	Case 3	Case 4	Case 5	Case 6	Case 7	Corrected average**
VOT	(−1.46)	0.12	1.59	1.16	−0.73	0.73	0.98	0.64
VOR	(−2.94)	−4.80	−2.69	−1.21	(0.16)	−3.89	(−1.59)	−3.15
VOF	−2.46	(−0.63)	−9.64	−7.50	−8.92	−4.01	−13.12	−7.61

Notes
* the values in parenthesis are not significantly different from zero at the 5% confidence level.
** the corrected average includes only the values of the trade-off relative to coefficients which are significantly different from zero, at least at the 5% confidence level.

5.2 Brief description of the case studies

Given the limited amount of data collected in this first pilot study, in order to gain a deeper understanding of the results that are presented in the next section and to place the main findings into the appropriate context, in this section we discuss the outcome of the seven experiments in the light of the general characteristics of the forwarding companies obtained through both the questionnaire and the direct interviews.

Case 1

Typical transport: *From*: Parma (I) *To* Badaioz (F); *Via*: Moncenisio; *Distance*: 1500 km; *Volume*: 60 m³; *Mode*: road; *Transport performed by*: road haulier; *Shipments per year*: 20 (every two weeks); *Product transported*: machinery; *Product value/consignment*: 100 000 euro; *Transport cost/consignment*: 1125 euro.

Forwarding agent 1 operates mainly for firms producing machinery and its main markets are France and Spain. It does not perform the transport itself but contracts it out to well-known road hauliers or shipping companies; the concern for granting his direct customers the quality of service required induces the respondent to work with a level of reliability of 100 per cent and thus different levels of reliability become not relevant. Apart from cost, the only service attribute which appears significant for Case 1 is frequency (VOT and VOR – not significant; VOF 2.5 euro for one additional shipment/months).

Case 2

Typical transport: *From*: Guastalla (I) *To* Barcelona (E); *Via*: sea; *Distance*: 900 km; *Volume*: 25/26 tons; *Mode*: Ro-Ro; *Transport performed by*: the firm; *Shipments per year*: 500 (two each day); *Product transported*: steel tube; *Product value/consignment*: 75 000 euro; *Transport cost/consignment*: 1175 euro.

This is a very important Italian carrier, leader in the national and international markets. Along this route the company operates by sea, and the transport manager evaluates this mode of transport as very uncertain by definition: the company, when choosing to use maritime services, seems to take into account the fact that a one-day delay in consignment has to be expected and places high value on reliability (VOR takes, in fact, the highest value of the sample). VOF is not significantly different from zero while VOT, although significant, has an extremely low value (12 cents per ton per hour); the lowest of our sample. The latter is a clear indication of the way Ro-Ro transport is perceived. Operators are quite willing to adopt it for shipments which do not require high frequency of service nor low travel time: both characteristics which can be taken account of while planning the operation. They, however, are less likely to accept failures in reliability levels. Respondent 2 is willing to pay almost five euros for improvements in 1 per cent reliability per ton shipped.

Case 3

Typical transport: *From*: Udine (I) *To* Tallin (FIN); *Via*: Germany; *Distance*: 2000 km; *Volume*: 45 m³; *Mode*: road; *Transport performed by*: road haulier; *Shipments per year*: 100; *Product transported*: machinery; *Product value/consignment*: 50 000 euro; *Transport cost/consignment*: 1750 euro.

As for Case 1, this forwarding agent does not perform the services in-house. It operates mainly with shipping companies; in fact, about 95 per cent of his shipments are performed by sea (equivalent to 1500 shipments per year) and only 5 per cent by road. It is specialised in the transport of machinery. As in Case 1, for the company it is very important to work with 'well-known' shipping companies or road hauliers. It is mainly for this reason that we have noted credibility problems when performing the experiment: 'we can't evaluate a service if we don't really know who is going to carry it out!'. The estimation outcomes, are, however, quite interesting: Respondent 3 shows the highest willingness to pay for a variation improving travel time, the second highest for the possibility to be granted the availability of an additional shipment per month. Also the value of reliability is relatively high (VOT 1.6 euro; VOR 2.7; and VOF 9.6 euros). All the estimated coefficients are significant.

Case 4

Typical transport: *From*: Goole (GB) *To* Brescia (I); *Via*: France; *Distance*: 1000 km; *Volume*: 24 tons; *Mode*: road; *Transport performed by*: road haulier; *Shipments per year*: 100; *Product transported*: Refractory materials; *Product value/consignment*: 25 000 euro; *Transport cost/consignment*: 700 euro.

This shipping company operates only on international markets, mainly Great Britain/England and the U.S. The availability of the services along these routes, where little or no alternatives exist, is very important. From the estimation it appears, in fact, that the respondent places a high value on frequency (VOF 7.5 euro per ton), while it is less concerned with journey time and reliability (VOT 1.16 and VOR 1.2).

Case 5

Typical transport: *From*: Milan (I) *To* Barcelona (E); *Distance*: 900 km; *Volume*: 8 tons; *Mode*: road; *Transport performed by*: road haulier; *Shipments per year*: 100; *Product transported*: furniture; *Product value/consignment*: 50 000 euro; *Transport cost/consignment*: 1500 euro.

This company operates mainly on the Spanish market; there is no evidence of a modal preference and during the interview the respondent stated that when using maritime transport services, time is not very important: 'one additional day of travel time is not so influential in the modal choice process of the firm'. On the contrary, frequency is very relevant, as the company serves with regularity one main market. The estimated coefficients confirm the statements of the director of the company: the respondent's VOF is the most relevant service attribute (VOF – 8.92 euro per ton for one more shipment per month), while VOR is not significantly different from zero. The valuation of journey time seems to be negative for respondent 5: the magnitude of the coefficient is, however, relatively small.

Case 6

Typical transport: *From*: Bari (I) *To* Parma (IT); *Via*: Adriatica; *Distance*: 800 km; *Volume*: 30 m³; *Mode*: road; *Transport performed by*: road haulier; *Shipments per year*: 40 (every week). *Product transported*: food; *Product value/consignment*: 10 000 euro; *Transport cost/consignment*: 750 euro.

This forwarding agent operates mainly for firms producing food products and its main markets are south of Italy. It does not perform the transport itself but contracts it out to small road hauliers; the concern for granting his direct customers the quality of service required induces the respondent to work with a high level of reliability (100 per cent) and frequency. The respondent has stated that he would not be interested in any level of reliability different than 100 per cent. Reliability and frequency are thus the most relevant attribute of the transport service. His willingness to pay/accept is, however, generally more limited than the other respondents.

Case 7

Typical transport: *From*: Foggia (I) *To* Milan (IT); *Via*: Adriatica; *Distance*: 900 km; *Volume*: 50 m³; *Mode*: road; *Transport performed by*: road haulier; *Shipments per year*: 20 (every two weeks); *Product transported*: machinery; *Product value/consignment*: 100 000 euro; *Transport cost/consignment*: 2000 euro.

This forwarding agent operates mainly for firms producing machinery and its main Italian markets are in the north of Italy. It does not perform the transport itself but contracts it out to either road hauliers, train operating companies, shipping companies. His main concern seems to rest with reliability; he cannot take into consideration any variation of the current level of reliability as he generally forwards component parts of mechanical systems. The respondent valuation comes out explicitly from the estimation: the concern with time is very limited (VOT 0.98), frequency of service is, instead, extremely highly valued, while reliability appears not too significant. The respondent has not accepted any variation of reliability levels during the interview.

5.3 A short comment on comparison with other European studies

The findings on the trade-off ratios confirm the results of similar research carried out in a European context, although the calculated values are generally lower: for instance, in Maier and Bergman (2002) the values for time, reliability, and frequency are 9.7, 46.5, and 16.1 euro, respectively; in Danielis and Rotaris (2002) the values for time and reliability are 7.3 and 10.7 respectively, and in Bolis and Maggi (1999) the values for time, reliability, and frequency are 11.8, 24.9, and 11.3 euros respectively.[15]

The results vary significantly among the different experiments both in absolute and in relative value. Anyway, it is important to underline that the monetary values per ton relate to specific transports (of a given distance, with specific network, etc.) and cannot be compared directly with results from other studies. This highlights how differences in geographical contexts, estimation techniques, respondent characteristics, type of freight, and so on might influence the outcome of the analysis. However, in general there are some common traits: among the three attributes, time seems to be the one which is valued the least, while reliability is definitely the service characteristic which is most highly valued when considering combined transport. This outcome is confirmed by our analysis: in fact it shows that operators, when considering whether to use the maritime alternative, do not seem to have a preclusion towards the specific mode but evaluate it on even terms with other services.

6 Concluding remarks

In this paper we have presented preliminary evidence obtained by estimating a model of forwarding agents' behaviour with respect to the maritime alternative, using adaptive conjoint data collecting methods. The application has been done on a small sample of operators – which are considered as case studies – localised in the north-western region of Italy. The final objective of the research, once completed, is to produce realistic estimates of the determinants of service choice in relation to Ro-Ro transport service. The analysis carried out so far has allowed us to test our methodology and the strategies adopted for carrying out the experiment. A specificity of the ASP design chosen here is, in fact, that the transport modes alternative is always Ro-Ro (combined transport by sea). The analysis illustrated in this paper shows that the valuations placed on alternative attributes of the transport services by the seven freight-forwarding companies interviewed are generally consistent. Despite certain important critical variations, in fact, the outcome of the estimation shows a strong and reliable influence of certain characteristics on the decision process. Most notably, and in line with the results of other studies, reliability and frequency seem to be the key factors in the choice of the transport service alternative. Even more so when the choice set includes maritime Ro-Ro transport. The empirical evidence has shown that no substantial 'a priori' preclusion for Ro-Ro services emerges from the sample of operators interviewed.

According to our estimation, although referred only to a very limited database and thus to be taken with due scepticism, freight forwarders seem to value, on average, a 1 per cent improvement in reliability at 3.15 euro per ton and a variation in frequency at 7.61 euro per ton. Apart from the estimated values, what emerges from the study is the fact that operators are more interested in the last two attributes of transport than in the actual time of journey. In line with other studies, journey time does not seem to be more valuable than the time lost for low levels of reliability and frequency. In order to improve the use of the maritime Ro-Ro alternative, the maritime transport should, thus, focus on these two factors.

Although the outcome of this research has to be taken with extreme caution due, principally to the limitedness of the sample, the study can be used to confirm that the use of SP could be a valid option in order to estimate the attitude of operators towards the attributes of the Ro-Ro freight transport market. Overall, initial evidence is, in fact, encouraging and offers some understanding of the determinants of the maritime transport choice. With the availability of a more extensive sample the impact of frequency and reliability of services could be included in a model of general freight transport cost referred to Ro-Ro services.

Contribution and acknowledgements

Although this research is the outcome of joint work, sections 2.1, 3.2 and 5.1 can be attributed to A.S. Bergantino, 2.2, 3.1, 5.2, 5.3 to S. Bolis, and section 1 to C. Canali. Sections 4 and 6 are attributable to both A.S. Bergantino and S. Bolis.

The authors are indebted to Prof. Rico Maggi of the Institute of Economic Research (IRE) of Lugano and to Michel Beuthe, Groupe for Transports et Mobilitè – Facultés Universitaires Catholique de Mons, for his helpful comments on an earlier version of this paper. Any remaining error is ours. Financial support from MIUR – Cofin 2003 grant no. 2003134052, 'Prospectives of short sea shipping in the Mediterranean area' is gratefully acknowledged.

Notes

* Department of Economics, University of Bari, Via C. Rosalba, 53, 70124 Bari (Italy), abergan@tin.it.
** IRE – Department of Economics, University of Lugano, Via G. Buffi, 13, 6900 Lugano (Switzerland), simona.bolis@lu.unisi.ch.
*** Department of Economics, University of Parma, Via Kennedy, 6, 43100 Parma (Italy), carla.canali@unipr.it.
1 A previous study carried out on the routes between Sicily and the Continent by Gattuso and Pastorino (1996) adopted standard SP methodology.
2 Among these applications, the latter introduces some interesting differences with respect to the original approach: Maier and Bergman (2002), in fact, implement a fractional factorial design instead of a standard adaptive SP experiment, estimate a discrete choice model without weighting the elicited ratings, and tackle the problem of repeated observations in the database.
3 As Fowkes and Shinghal (2002) remind us, initially SP experiments in transport were conducted through 'pen and paper' direct interviews or through self-compilation questionnaires, with both methods sometimes involving cards showing one or more alternatives; the data collected was then elaborated with the support of statistical analysis. The development of *ad hoc* computer program, has allowed the experiment to be 'customised' or 'adapted' to the profile and the choices of the interviewee. For a detailed review of the evolution of SP techniques, the reader is referred to the work of Fowkes and Shinghal (2002).

4 A recent survey on the evolution of the freight-forwarders business and type of services offered is contained in KNP (2002) and Unescap (2002). At European level interesting insights are given by Logiq (1999).

5 For the detailed illustration of the outcome of the analysis of the data retrieved through the questionnaires see Bergantino *et al.* (2003).

6 The direct interviews took place between September 2002 and September 2003. Although a larger sample would have been desirable, even for the pilot study, sampling costs are considerable and organising the meetings quite burdensome and time consuming. Interviews with relevant decision-makers have to be agreed upon, set up, and often postponed due to impediments of the respondent. Nevertheless, we are currently organising additional interviews.

7 The authors are aware of the risk that in Stated Preference experiments the ordering with which attributes are presented for valuation might influence the final ranking by the respondent (Boyle *et al.*, 1993; Halvorsen, 1996). Recent studies, however, have reported encouraging results (Sjostrand, 2001; Farrar and Ryan, 1999) in terms of the actual impact of the ordering effect. Nevertheless, in the follow-up work, differing ordering will be adopted to test the robustness of our current findings.

8 Fowkes and Tweddle (1996 and 1997), Bolis and Maggi (1999), Fowkes and Shinghal (2002), Danielis and Rotaris (2002), and Maier and Bergman (2002).

9 Since the rating exercise generally involved 20 iterations per firm there are about 40 such differences in each case. In some instances, however, the experiment was interrupted before the 20th iteration was reached either because convergence had been obtained or because the level of concentration of the respondent had reduced.

10 The assumption that the error term – or, more correctly, the difference between the error terms – is logistically distributed is equivalent to assuming normal or Gumbel distribution (Ben Akiva and Lerman, 1994: 71).

11 We are aware that the results obtained might be somehow affected by the fact that the companies interviewed were not randomly chosen but, on the contrary, were selected on the basis of a certain degree of familiarity with the maritime mode.

12 In particular, the extremely low value of the parameter of the cost variable might be due to the fact that, in order to generate a very extreme situation from which rapidly reach convergence towards an alternative that would be indifferent to the A alternative, has yielded relatively large average adjustment of transport cost (price) in the experiment. It might be that, starting the experiment with another attribute or with a price increase, a change in the respondent behaviour might be induced. These possibilities will be carefully evaluated and accounted for in the next set of interviews.

13 The reduction in frequency of services varies between twice daily (upper value) and once every two weeks (lower value).

14 Furthermore, the findings on the trade-off ratios confirm the results of similar research carried out in a European context (Maier and Bergman, 2002; Danielis and Rotaris, 2002; Bolis and Maggi, 1999). In particular, although the absolute values present some variance among the different studies, a consistent trend emerges as to the relative ranking of the value assigned to the three attributes.

15 The definition of reliability for Danielis and Rotaris (2002) varies from the one adopted in the present paper in that they define it as value of risk of an hour late arrival. The definition adopted by Bolis and Maggi (2002) is also different. The calculated value is referred to an additional shipment per month.

References

Ben Akiva, M. and Lerman, S.T. (1994) *Discrete Choice Analysis*, 6th edn, MIT, Boston, USA.

Bergantino, A.S. and Bolis, S. (2003) 'An Adaptive Conjoint Analysis of Freight Service

Alternatives: Evaluating the Maritime Option' in A. Reggiani and L. Schintler (eds) forthcoming.

Bolis, S. and Maggi, R. (2002) 'Stated Preference – Evidence on Shippers' Transport and Logistics Choice' in R. Danielis (ed.) *Domanda di trasporto merci e preferenze dichiarate – Freight Transport Demand and Stated Preference Experiments*, F. Angeli, Milan.

Boyle, K.J., Welsh, M.P., and Bishop, R.C. (1993) 'The role of question order and respondent experience in contingent valuation studies' *Journal of Environmental Economics and Management*, 25(1): 80–99.

Danielis, R. (ed.) (2002) *Domanda di trasporto merci e preferenze dichiarate – Freight Transport Demand and Stated Preference Experiments*, Franco Angeli, Milan.

Danielis, R. and Rotaris, L. (2002) 'Characteristics of Freight Transport Demand in the Friuli Venezia Giulia Region: a Summary' in R. Danielis (ed.) *Domanda di trasporto merci e preferenze dichiarate – Freight Transport Demand and Stated Preference Experiments*, F. Angeli, Milan.

Farrar, S. and Ryan, M. (1999) 'Response-ordering effect: a methodological issue in conjoint analysis' *Health Economics*, 8: 75–79.

Fowkes, A.S. and Tweedle, G. (1996) *Modelling and forecasting freight transport demand*, Mimeo, Leeds.

Fowkes, A.S. and Tweddle, G. (1997) 'Validation of Stated Preference Forecasting: A case study involving Anglo-Continental Freight, European Transport Forum – 25th Annual Meeting' *Proceedings of Seminar F*, PTRC, London,

Fowkes, T. and Shinghal, N. (2002) 'The Leeds Adaptive Stated Preference Methodology' in R. Danielis (ed.) *Domanda di trasporto merci e preferenze dichiarate – Freight Transport Demand and Stated Preference Experiments*, Franco Angeli, Milan.

Gattuso, D. and Postorino, M.N. (1996) *L'applicazione del metodo SP per l'analisi di scenari di mobilità delle merci fra Sicilia e Continente*, Serie Rapporti Scientifici, CISUT, Università degli studi di Reggio Calabria, Reggio Calabria.

Halvorsen, B. (1996) 'Ordering effects in contingent valuation surveys' *Environment and resources economics*, 8(4): 485–499.

KNP (2002) *Freight Forwarding Market Report 2002*, Key Note Publications Ltd, London.

Logiq (1999) *The decision-making process in intermodal transportation*. Deliverable 1 and 2nd–4th Framework Programme on RTD. European Commission DG Ten, Brussels.

Maier, G. and Bergman, E.M. (2002) 'Conjoint Analysis of Transport Options in Austrian Regions and Industrial Clusters' in R. Danielis (ed.) *Freight Transport Demand and Stated Preference Experiments*, F. Angeli, Milan.

Sjostrand, H. (2001) 'The ordering effect in stated Preference – a study of public transport passengers' valuation of standards' paper presented at the 9th World Transport Research Conference, Soul, Korea.

Tsamboulas, D. and Kapros, S. (2000) 'The Decision making Process in Intermodal Transport' *Transportation Research Record*, n. 1707, Washington D.C.

Tweddle, G., Fowkes, A.S., and Nash, C.A. (1995) *Impact of the Channel Tunnel: A Survey of Anglo-European Unitised Freight. Results of Phase I Interviews*, Working Paper 443, Institute for Transport Studies, University of Leeds.

Unescap (2002) 'Major Issues in Transport, Communications, Tourism and Infrastructure Development: Developments in Multimodal Transport and Logistics', Bangkok.

3.5 An improved framework for large-scale multi-agent simulations of travel behaviour

Bryan Raney and *Kai Nagel***

Abstract

We describe a framework for running large-scale multi-agent simulations of travel behaviour. The framework represents each traveller as an individual 'agent' that makes independent decisions about its desired use of the transportation system during a typical day. An agent keeps a record of its decisions in a 'plan'. A plan contains the agent's schedule of activities it wants to perform during the day, including times and locations, along with the travel modes and routes it intends to utilise to travel between activities.

An agent database gives every agent a memory where it can store several possible plans, as well as performance information it uses to compare how well different plans meet its needs. Agents score a plan's performance based on the output of the micro-simulator. The agent database also allows agents to periodically generate new plans by connecting them to behavioural modules that model the different kinds of decisions that affect an agent's plan. For example, one module chooses routes, while another chooses activity durations. This paper describes the design and our current implementation of this framework, plus the results of some verification scenarios.

1 Introduction

The established model for transportation planning is the four-step process, consisting of the four modules: trip generation, trip distribution, modal split, and route assignment. It is well known that the traditional (static) four-step process falls short of many requirements that are desirable for modern transportation planning, for example:

1   There is no time-of-day in the static modelling approach.
2   Because there is no time-of-day, it is difficult or impossible to model any kind of time-dependent effect, such as emissions (which depend on engine temperature, which in turn depends on how long the car has been running), or peak traffic spreading.
3   Decisions are decoupled from persons and therefore from demographic attributes.

Item (3) is, at least conceptually, easy to fix by making the first three steps of the four-step process explicitly person-dependent. The most common solution to this is *activity-based demand generation (ADG)*, which is discussed in many places (e.g. Hensher and King, 2001), and implemented in some (e.g. Bowman *et al.*, 1999; Vovsha *et al.*, 2002; Jonnalagadda *et al.*, 2001). ADG typically consists of the following steps:

i   Generation of a *synthetic population* by disaggregating census data into individual people. The synthetic population is a random realisation of the census, that is, a census taken from the synthetic population would return, within statistical limits, the original census. The typical data content of a synthetic population is households, which are located spatially, and which possess some attributes, such as household income, or car ownership. These households are populated with individuals, who possess additional attributes, such as gender and age.

ii   For each individual of the synthetic population, a complete *daily activity plan* is then generated. The word 'activity' refers to actions such as 'being at home', 'shopping', 'working', 'being at school', etc. Besides the activity pattern, the activity plan also contains the location of each activity, and some timing information, such as when activities are started and ended.

iii   Each individual selects a *mode* of transportation.

It is more difficult to solve items (i) and (ii), i.e. the lack of time-dependence of static assignment. The advantage of static assignment over other methods is that it has a range of mathematically proven properties, in particular the uniqueness of the solution in terms of the link volumes. Clearly, this simplifies the comparison of implementations and the interpretation of different scenarios enormously.

When making the assignment formulation dynamic (*dynamic traffic assignment, DTA*; e.g. Kaufman *et al.*, 1991; Astarita *et al.*, 2001; Friedrich *et al.*, 2000), the extent of mathematically proven properties becomes much smaller. In particular, when the dynamic formulation includes spillback (also called physical queues), then one can construct examples of non-uniqueness, i.e. there are multiple user equilibrium solutions to the same origin-destination matrix and the same network (Daganzo, 1998). In consequence, one may have to accept that DTA with spillback is in general mathematically less well behaved than static assignment.

Conceptually, DTA can be decomposed into two components (Bottom, 2000): route generation, and *network loading*.[1] In static assignment, the network loading is done via the volume-cost function, which returns the cost of a link as a function of the trips using that link. In a dynamic context, the relationship is much more complicated, and it makes sense to look at simulation as a solution to the network loading. Simulation, as is well known, is a technique where a dynamic model is implemented on a computer, and run forward in time. Its conceptually simplest incarnation with respect to transportation planning is a representation of roads, and a way to move traffic forward along the links. Network loading models are classified according to the following criteria:

1 Resolution: Traffic can be represented by individual vehicles, but vehicles can also be aggregated into packets or cells.
2 Fidelity: The behaviour of each individual entity can be more or less realistically represented.
3 Modes: The simulation can concentrate on one mode only, or can combine several modes including their interaction.
4 Time resolution/time step.

Note that at one end of this classification, one finds the traditional assignment model (resolution aggregated on link level; fidelity reduced to volume-cost-functions; car mode only; no time-dependency). Examples for more realistic, simulation-based network loading models are DYNAMIT (MIT ITS Program, 2004), DYNASMART (University of Maryland at College Park, 2002), METROPOLIS (de Palma and Marchal, 2002), TRANSIMS (The Regents of the University of California, 2003), or the queue model (Gawron, 1998a, b).

So far, this introduction discusses that demand generation can be made more realistic by moving to activities, and traffic assignment can be made more realistic by making it time-dependent and then using simulation for the network loading. Since these were discussed as separate changes, it is natural to assume that they are designed so that they are backwards compatible to the four-step process, which means that the ADG produces origin-destination (OD) matrices as output, and the DTA takes them as input. This also means that ADG can be fed into a traditional static assignment, and DTA can take its input from the traditional demand generation.

However, the OD matrices generated by ADG are usually time-dependent, while traditional static assignment works with a single, time-independent OD matrix. Conversely, traditional demand generation produces a single, time-independent OD matrix, but DTA needs time-dependent OD matrices to make sense. Therefore, although the use of OD matrices superficially maintains backward compatibility, this backward compatibility cannot be used for any meaningful study. In order to obtain meaningful results, *static* demand generation needs to be fed into a *static* assignment, or *dynamic* demand generation needs to be fed into a *dynamic* assignment.

METROPOLIS (de Palma and Marchal, 2002) approaches this problem by accepting a static OD matrix, but generating a time-dependent solution internally. In consequence, this allows one to feed a *static* OD matrix into a *dynamic* assignment. It does not, however, offer a better solution if the demand generation is already dynamic.

An additional disadvantage of using OD matrices to couple ADG to DTA is that it gives up the connection to the individual persons – the same connection that was just gained in steps one to three of the four-step process by moving to ADG. However, routing decisions can depend on individual attributes. The decision to use a toll road can depend on income; a person needing to catch an airplane may prefer a road with lower variability; etc. In addition, activity chains have dependencies in the time direction – a delay in the morning may trigger changes in the afternoon – and the OD matrix severs this connection. It makes sense, therefore, to bypass OD matrices completely and to feed the complete information from the activity-based demand generation into the DTA. This means that throughout the whole process, including the DTA, the travellers are maintained as individual entities with individual attributes, and make individual decisions based on these attributes. This is what is meant by an *agent-based* or *multi-agent* approach (e.g. Ferber, 1999). And indeed, there are numerous papers related to transport that mention 'agent' in their title (e.g. Arentze *et al.*, 2000; Wahle *et al.*, 2002).

This paper concentrates on the multi-agent approach as an improvement of the complete four-step process. The main differences against coupling ADG to DTA via OD matrices are:

- The DTA is completely agent-based, as discussed above. In particular, it is capable of feeding back agent-based information, not just link-based information.
- The ADG is included into the feedback process. Historically, systematic feedback is mostly between the route generation and the network loading; feedback to the demand generation was often done manually by the analysts. However, it has been said for a long time (e.g. Loudon *et al.*, 1997) that this process should be automated.

It is useful to conceptually differentiate between a mental and a physical layer (Figure 3.5.1):

- The *mental layer* represents the processes that are internal to the travellers. It is sometimes also called the *strategic layer*.

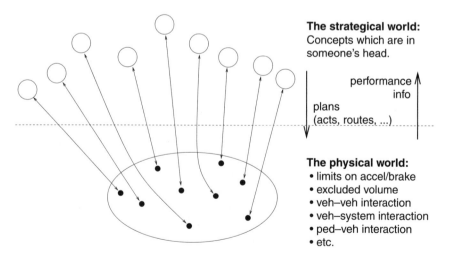

The strategical world:
Concepts which are in someone's head.

performance info

plans (acts, routes, ...)

The physical world:
- limits on accel/brake
- excluded volume
- veh–veh interaction
- veh–system interaction
- ped–veh interaction
- etc.

Figure 3.5.1 Physical and strategic layers of the framework.

- The *physical layer* represents what the travellers actually do in the physical world. In traffic, this is normally called the network loading, or the traffic (micro-)simulation. In this paper, it will be called the *mobility simulation*, to stress its total independence from the mental/strategic layer.
- There are mechanisms that couple the two layers. The attempt to execute a plan causes changes in the physical layer; inability to execute the plan as intended, for example because of congestion, feeds back into the strategic layer.

There is, to our knowledge, no simulation package that executes this approach in its entirety. Part of the challenge is that this necessitates a large number of modules and module interfaces, which in itself is quite a challenge, in particular in view of the fact that there are few programming and/or data exchange standards in the community. Another part of the challenge is that one needs parallel computing techniques for metropolitan-size scenarios, and no established technology is available to even define a viable standard for module interaction once the simulation becomes parallel (Nagel and Marchal, 2003). Some partial packages are discussed in the following.

Dynamic traffic assignment (DTA)

There are a large number of packages that do dynamic traffic assignment (e.g. MIT ITS Program, 2004; University of Maryland at College Park, 2002; de Palma and Marchal, 2002; Gawron, 1998b). As discussed above, these packages typically take time-dependent OD matrices as input, assign routes according to user equilibrium, and return time-dependent link travel times and other link-based information as output. Although most of these packages have individual travellers inside their model, often these are not fully developed. For example, routes are calculated by the network rather than by the agent, and agent-based output is often not available. While the latter is conceptually easy to fix, the former means that making route choice dependent on agent attributes is close to impossible. This is related to the fact that those models take OD matrices as inputs, which contain no demographic attributes. A direct consequence is that it will not be possible to connect an agent's performance in the DTA to the demand generation, since the OD matrices sever the connection to the individual agents; it is only possible to feed aggregated information, such as link travel times, back to the demand generation modules. In summary, although the DTA models have a large number of agent-based elements, they are not fully agent-based.

TRANSIMS

TRANSIMS (The Regents of the University of California, 2003) indeed replaces the complete four-step process by an agent-based approach that as its first step disaggregates census data and then works with individual travellers in all modules. In addition, TRANSIMS uses parallel computing to tackle large-scale problems. The main shortcomings of TRANSIMS, in our view, are as follows:

- Although travellers are individually identifiable throughout all modules, agent information is spread throughout the simulation system. For example, the activity file does not contain demographic information, and the route file contains neither demographic nor activity information. This makes it rather difficult to use such 'higher level' information in the 'lower level' modules. It also makes it possible, for example, that an agent leaves a location before it has arrived – this is possible since the agent is not a singular entity in the simulation.
- The file formats are rather inflexible. This makes it difficult to add/modify information, for example when adding new modules to the system.
- The feedback mechanism 'forgets' old plans and their performance. Although it is a bit difficult to see at first glance, this means that TRANSIMS plans generation modules need to fulfil rather strong requirements. For example, the routing module ('router') does not only have to generate plausible routes, but also correct probabilities to choose between different alternatives.
- Finally, it was impossible to obtain an academic license, including source code, outside the United States. This made it impossible to improve the above aspects inside TRANSIMS.

Land use simulations

There are land use simulations, such as URBANSIM (University of Washington, 2004), ILUTE (Salvini and Miller, 2003), or that of Hunt *et al.* (2001), which are more or less agent-based, and which have the conceptual intention to couple to the transportation system. However, in practice this connection is not well established in those models at this point in time.

This paper will present an approach that is based on TRANSIMS but solves the above TRANSIMS shortcomings. The conceptual idea behind our approach is that we keep the agent concept consistent everywhere. The main technical improvements are in the following areas:

- The different TRANSIMS files are replaced by a single XML file format. That file contains, agent by agent, all information related to the agents, from demographic information via activities to routes.
- An agent cannot be 'divided'. This means in particular that the traffic simulation (network loading) executes daily plans, rather than just trips.
- An agent database keeps track of agents' past plans and performance of those plans.

In the next section (Section 2), we describe the basic design of the framework, including the agent and plan entities, the agent database, plan scoring, and iterations between the parts of the framework. Section 3 goes on to describe our current implementation of this framework, in particular introducing the XML data format that is one of the cornerstones of this framework. This is followed by a description, in Section 4, of the set-up of our case study for verifying the operation of this framework, including the specific behaviour of our mobility simulator, and route and time choice modules. This section also describes the utility function used by the modules to score plans, and the transportation scenario we have executed. Section 5 then explains the results obtained by our framework for this case study. Finally, we end with a discussion (Section 6) and summary (Section 7).

2 Framework design

2.1 The core: agents and plans

The framework models the travel behaviour of a population of people living in a given geographical region (e.g. town or metropolitan area) as they go about their lives during a certain, often repeated period. The arguably most typical example is a 24-hour weekday, but also other days (such as Sundays) or longer periods (such as complete weeks) can be modelled as long as there is some repetition from one period to the next, i.e. as long as there is something 'typical' about the period.

During that period, the people carry out *activities*, such as sleeping, working, shopping, eating, etc., at various locations in the region, and utilise the transportation system of that region to travel between activities at different locations. Thus, their activities motivate their travel choices. In addition, the limitations caused by the transportation system, such as limited accessibility or congestion, affect their activity choices.

The framework represents each person as an individual entity, called an *agent*. Each agent makes independent decisions about which activities to perform during the day, where and when to perform them, and what travel modes and routes to take to travel between activities. In our system, each individual agent is represented as a simplified classifier system (Holland, 1992). Each agent has a collection of plans; each plan has a score that is updated after the plan was used; and the choice between plans is done according to their score. The main simplification when compared to a classifier system is that, at this point, our plans are not conditional on the environment. See for example Figure 3.5.2.

Specifically, a plan contains the agent's intended schedule of activities for the day, and the travel *legs* connecting the activities. An activity schedule specifies the following information for each activity:

- Type: what the agent wants to do (e.g. home, work, shopping, leisure).
- Location: x/y-co-ordinates within the simulated region and/or the network link id (i.e. street).

Agent	Plan num.	In-use	Score	Plan
1	1	false	462.2	sleep until 7:00 am; go to work at W1 for 8 h; go shopping at S1 for 30 min, ...
1	2	true	undefined	sleep until 8:00 am; go to work at W1 for 7.5 h; drink beer at B1 for 1 h, ...
2	1	true	1047.8	sleep until 6:30 am; take kid to kindergarten at K3; go to work at W2 for 6 h, ...
⋮	⋮	⋮	⋮	⋮

Figure 3.5.2 Example of information contained in the framework. It keeps all information contained within the agents' plans, with the addition of scores and other bookkeeping information.

- Timing information: how much time the agent wants to spend at the activity after arriving at its location, and/or absolute ending time of the activity. More detail of this is discussed in Section 2.3.

A plan also contains leg information for each pair of consecutive activities. Each leg contains the following information:

- Mode: what type of transportation to use.
- Travel time: estimated duration of trip.
- Departure time: estimate of what time the trip will begin.
- Route (certain modes only): the list of network nodes to traverse to get from the previous activity to the next.
- (Other mode-specific information).

The entity containing all agents' plans is called the *agent database*. Prototypes of the agent database can be found in Nagel (1994/95, 1996) and in Raney and Nagel (2004). Nagel (1994/95, 1996) describes a system where agents remember individual scores for different plans, but the plans were the same for different agents and the implementation was for demonstration purposes only. Raney and Nagel (2004) describe prototypes of the implementation also described in this paper, but concentrate on a completely different version. That version was not general enough to go beyond dynamic traffic assignment.

2.2 Iterations

Above, it was stated that a plan's score is updated after the plan is used. This corresponds to the dichotomy between the mental and a physical layer mentioned earlier. For a single agent, this simply means that the agent keeps repeating the following steps:

1 Select a plan.
2 Execute it and record the performance.
3 Update the score of the plan based on the performance.

In addition, from time to time plans that have a low score are replaced by new plans (see Section 2.4). Note that 'execution of a plan' means that it is submitted to the physical layer for execution. In our case, the physical layer is the mobility simulation. For a multi-agent system, one has in addition that all agents learn simultaneously. This means that a score for a plan is not necessarily stable over the iterations; in consequence, an agent needs to re-evaluate previously bad plans from time to time in order to check if the scores have improved.

The above is a generic design that should work for arbitrary multi-agent simulations. Some remarks are in order:

• It is important to have separate representations of the mental/internal and the physical/external processes. Sometimes, for example in robosoccer (e.g. Kim, 1997), it is possible that the physical layer is a real-world system, and then part of the challenge is to formulate plans such that they can indeed successfully execute in the physical world. For transportation simulations, a true physical model world will in general not be possible; instead, there will be a simulation of the physical world. However, plans should be designed in a way that they could also execute in the real world.

• The execution of the plan in the physical system can also be seen as interaction of the agent with its external environment and other agents, collecting 'sensory' input about its experiences, which it then uses to update its mental state (i.e. learn).

• Inside the framework, it would be possible to make plans conditional. For example, there could be a separate plan to follow if the agent was delayed on the way to work. Activity durations (Section 2.3) are a (small) example of conditional behaviour.

• A plan can be seen as a simple strategy from game theory. For a Nash equilibrium in game theory, an agent attempts to find a strategy that he or she cannot unilaterally improve.

• The framework as described so far is best suited for day-to-day (or more generally period-to-period) replanning. It can, however, be extended to within-day replanning. When doing this, one is confronted with some conceptual and some computational problems. These will be discussed in Section 6.

2.3 Conditional plans and activity durations

Some diligence is necessary in the treatment of activity durations. In principle, a daily plan is entirely defined by the given sequence of activities, the departure time from the first activity, and the durations of all subsequent activities. This can, however, lead to very implausible behaviour: An agent can, for example, shop beyond the closing time of the shop, or remain in the movie theatre beyond the end of the movie. In principle, an agent should not plan to do this; it may happen, however, because of unexpected delays earlier in the day. Since this is so grossly implausible, a first step toward conditional plans/strategies was implemented in our framework. Both the activity duration and the activity ending time can be specified, and the ending time takes priority over the duration if the agent's arrival time plus the duration would cause the agent to stay past the ending time. For example, say an agent wants to shop for 30 minutes starting at 5.30 pm, knowing the selected shop closes at 6.00 pm (specified as the end time of the activity). If the agent arrives late to the shop, at say 5.45 pm, the 30 minute duration would put the end of the activity at 6.15 pm, which is after the ending time. In this case, the ending time takes precedence and the agent departs at 6.00 pm instead. However, if the agent arrives early, at say 5.15 pm, it still stays for 30 minutes and leaves at 5.45 pm instead of waiting until 6.00 pm.

There is in fact a similar problem with the start of an activity. Assume that a shop opens at 8.00 am, and the agent wants to arrive exactly at 8.00 am and shop for ten minutes. Now assume that the agent arrives 15 minutes early. The plausible thing to do would be to wait the 15 minutes and then shop for ten minutes. Our current implementation will, however, let the agent wait for ten minutes and then let him travel to the next activity location. This nonsensical behaviour will probably need to be modified in future versions.

2.4 Generation of strategies/plans

The concept as described so far mostly discusses how agents maintain and use a larger number of plans; there is little discussion of how plans are generated. This is intentional since the precise methods of how strategies are generated do not matter to the overall design. One can for example use constructive algorithms (which construct plans from scratch), mutation (which locally modifies existing plans), crossover (which generates new plans by combining existing ones), etc. In particular, one can use externally existing programs that use the right type of input and generate the right type of output. The only two conceptual requirements are:

- The external module needs to 'think' in terms of agents. For example, an external route generation module needs to generate a path for a specific agent between two locations, rather than, say, a shortest path tree.
- There needs to be some commonality between what the external module attempts to achieve, and how the scoring is done by the agent database. The system will work as long as *some* of the plans generated by external modules are 'good' in the sense of the scoring function of the agent database. This is a considerably weaker design requirement for external modules than TRANSIMS has, where *all* of the plans generated by external

modules need to be 'good'. This is necessary in TRANSIMS because any previous 'good' (or 'bad') plan an agent knows about is overwritten by the new plan generated by the module.

2.5 Scores

The agent database needs a scoring function in order to give scores to plans that were executed. The primary candidate for the scoring function is the traditional utility function, but any plausible scoring function, for example one using prospect theory (e.g. Avineri and Prashker, 2003), can be used. Without much more implementation effort, concepts such as multicriteria decisions (De Smet *et al.*, 2002) could also be used.

An example of a utility-based scoring function will be presented in Section 4.7. As mentioned before, there needs to be some overlap between what the external modules compute and what the scoring function optimises.

3 Implementation of the framework

When implementing the above concept, one needs to make some decisions about the technologies to use. In our case, the most important criterion was that large-scale scenarios (several millions of agents) should be feasible, followed by the desire for flexibility and interoperability.

3.1 Agent database and external modules

The framework's strategic/mental layer provides the mental state of the agents and allows them to learn about their environment and make decisions about their behaviour. We divide this layer into a central *agent database* and several behavioural *modules* that model the different kinds of decisions that affect an agent's plan. For example, one module chooses activity durations, and another chooses routes. Figure 3.5.3 graphically depicts the relationships and interactions between these components. The agent database provides each agent with part of its mental state, and with a high-level decision-making ability. The modules provide the rest of the mental state and more detailed decision-making abilities.

3.2 Implementation of the agent database

The task of the agent database is to maintain, for each agent in the simulation, some number of plans plus their scores, to select plans according to their scores, to add new plans, and to remove plans with a bad performance. This looks like a standard database, and in fact our first prototype was implemented in MySQL, a public domain relational database (Raney and Nagel, 2004). A standard relational database is, however, not well suited to data that has hierarchies of variable-length objects. In our case, we have a large number of agents, each of which has a variable number of plans, each of which has a variable number of activities/legs, each of which has a route description of variable length. Since plans for a particular agent are added/removed one by one, this means that the plans of an agent are spread out in memory within the database, resulting in slow performance. In addition, the relational database approach is awkward to use, since once more agent information is not in one place.

In fact, one would need an object-oriented database, rather than a standard relational database. However, object-oriented databases are slow, which is a direct consequence of the problem to insert variable-length objects into linear memory. On the other hand, for our purposes many properties of databases, such as an always-consistent state also in under crashes, are not needed. It is therefore tempting to implement the agent database completely in software. Because of performance reasons, a decision for C++ was made, and the STL (Standard Template Library) was heavily used. This allows the program to implement a Person class, which contains one or more Plan classes. Each plan contains a sequence of activities and legs, and each leg contains the description of the route. Since the STL is used, it is straightforward to, say, add or remove a plan to or from a person. In addition, since the whole agent database is written in C++, it is straightforward to do computations such as plan selection based on a logit model. The number of plans that an agent database in software can hold is limited by the memory that a single process can address. In a 32-bit architecture, this number is 2 GB. Since in our current implementation one plan needs about 0.5 KB, our current implementation can hold about one million agents with a maximum of four plans each.

3.3 XML plans

The agent database needs to communicate with external strategy generation modules, and to send plans to the mobility simulation (Figure 3.5.3). All communication is done by using exactly the same plans format. This format uses XML; an example is in Figure 3.5.4. As one can see, the format is rather intuitive; this is in stark contrast to the TRANSIMS files. However, the main advantage of XML is its extensibility. That is, one can add fields to the format without breaking existing parsers. In particular, one can add fields only to a subset of agents, for example a format to describe a conditional strategy (Section 2.3). Such extensions would be very hard to do with TRANSIMS. It is important to note that the principal units of description are 'agents' and 'plans'. Any external module using the same principal units will be able to communicate with our system. Somewhat unexpectedly, file size is less of an issue with XML than expected. When compressed, XML files have about the same size as TRANSIMS files with the same information.

3.4 Events

A question remains of how to feed performance information from the mobility simulation back to the strategic modules (Figure 3.5.3). Our current solution is

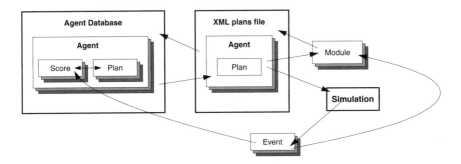

Figure 3.5.3 Components and data flow in the framework.

```
<person id="393241" income="50000">
  <plan>
    <act type="h" end_time="07:00" x100="697150" y100="232790" link="5834" />
    <leg mode="car" dept_time="07:00" trav_time="00:25">
      <route>1932 1933 1934 1947</route>
    </leg>
    <act type="w" dur="09:00" x100="700650" y100="233980" link="5844" />
    <leg mode="car" dept_time="16:25" trav_time="00:14">
      <route>1934 1933</route>
    </leg>
    <act type="h" x100="697150" y100="232790" link="5834" />
  </plan>
</person>
```

Figure 3.5.4 A typical plan in XML. This agent, id 393241, leaves home (on link 5834) at 7 am, and drives to work via a four-node route (five links) which it expects to take 25 minutes to traverse. The agent stays at work for nine hours, then drives home again via a two-node route. (The '100' on the x and y co-ordinate labels refer to the 100×100 metre blocks of census information. We do not know co-ordinates more accurately than that resolution).

that the entire output of the physical simulation consists of events, which are output directly when they happen. For example, a traveller can depart, can enter/leave a link, etc. That is, the simulation of the physical system performs *no* data aggregation; this is done by the other modules themselves.

At this point, we are still investigating if events should be in plain text or in XML format; there are some performance advantages to the former, but in the long run, this will probably be outweighed by the flexibility advantages of the latter. An XML events format roughly looks as follows:

```
<event time5".." type5"leave_activity"
agent_id5".." location5".."/>
```

Note that such a line is generated separately for each event.

The agent database, for example, will read through the events information and register, for each agent, events that are necessary to compute the score.

Since at this point the score depends on activity arrival and departure times only (see Section 4.7), these are the only events that the agent database will consider. In contrast, the router will read through the events and look for link entering/leaving events. If an agent enters a link, the router will store that information somewhere. If an agent leaves a link, the router will search for the corresponding link enter event, compute the link travel time, and enter that into some averaging mechanism for the link.

The advantage of events is that they are very easy to implement into the simulation of the physical system. In contrast, any data aggregation inside the simulation of the physical system in our experience is a continuous source of errors. This has to do with the fact that the team that writes the simulation is not truly interested in correct aggregation. Their main tool to check simulation correctness is the visual impression (and maybe some traffic flow considerations). In contrast, the team that is responsible for, say, the router or the agent database has a much higher interest in the correctness of the aggregation, since without that their module will not function. In our experience, seemingly trivial aspects such as this are rather important for the long-term robustness of the system.

3.5 Calling sequence

The modules need to be called in a certain sequence in order to make the system run. For example, choosing new activity locations will necessitate new routes to and from the changed activities, so the route-planning module should be called sometime after the activity location module is called. But routes and activity times do not (strictly) depend on each other, so it would be possible to make calls to either the activity time choice module or the router without calling the other one, or call them both in an arbitrary order.

At this point, let us assume that we treat period-to-period replanning only, and that each period corresponds to a day. Within-period replanning will be shortly discussed in Section 6. Let us assume further that the list of available modules is known, as well as the dependencies between them, and that the dependencies can be fulfilled without calling modules in a 'circular' order. Let us also assume that there is some initial plans file, in which each agent is contained, and each agent has exactly one completely specified plan. Such initial plans files can be generated with variations of the methods discussed in this paper, but the system is easier to explain if one assumes the file is already there. Finally, let us assume that the mobility simulation was run based on the initial plans file, and that it has written events to a file. This initial condition is now followed by many iterations, each composed of the following sequence of actions:

1   The agent database reads the events, interprets them, and updates the scores of each used plan.
2   The agent database, based on some behavioural model, and the information about what dependencies exist between modules, selects agents that are up for replanning on some level, and writes a corresponding plans file to disk.

The level of replanning needs to be matched to an existing external module, and any other modules that this module depends upon for plan information must have been executed previously in this iteration. The plans file written by the agent database can contain plans of arbitrary completeness, so long as all the information required by the module is available.

3 The external module is started, it reads the events information and the plans file, and updates the information that it can generate, by either overwriting existing information, or filling in blanks. Information not filled in by the module is left alone, or destroyed if it is invalidated by the new information provided by the module. For example, a route-planning module may over-write existing routes, but must not touch activity locations. On the other hand, an activity location planning module may update activity starting and/or ending locations, and must also delete those routes no longer connected to the new locations.

4 The agent database reads the new plans file, and stores the corresponding information. It then selects agents that are up for replanning on some other level, and the whole process with an external module is repeated. Within this process, the module dependencies described earlier need to be satisfied.

5 Once all module dependencies have been fulfilled and plans are completely specified, the agent database selects the plans that are to be executed in the mobility simulation. New plans, which do not have a score yet, are selected with a high probability. If an agent has not received a new plan, the agent selects between its existing plans, for example with a logit model. A specific version is discussed in Section 4.4. The selected plans are written to a file.

6 The mobility simulation is run based on the last plans file, and outputs events, as before.

As said before, this sequence denotes one iteration; many such iterations are run. To improve performance, the agent database stays alive throughout the whole process. This has the advantage that the several GB of data that the agent database has stored need not be written to file during the iterations.

3.6 Specification of external strategy modules

The specifications of an external strategy module are perhaps already clear at this point. The minimum requirements are:

- The external module reads an arbitrarily complete plans file.
- If the external module reacts to agent or system performance, then it reads the events file.
- The external module writes out an updated plans file, where any invalid information has been deleted.
- The external module needs to be reasonably fast; running it on 10 per cent of all agents should not take more than about one hour.

Note that this specification leaves the internal functioning completely to the module. In particular, the module is free to start anew with each iteration, or to accumulate information over all iterations. An example for the former is a route generator that uses link travel times from the last iteration; an example for the latter is a mental map that is built successively over the iterations.

3.7 Specification of the mobility simulation

The specifications of the mobility simulation are perhaps also already clear at this point. The minimum requirements are:

- The mobility simulation reads a complete plans file, with one plan per agent. Plans should be executed as chains, i.e. an agent can only depart *after* it has arrived at a location.
- The mobility simulation executes all those plans simultaneously.
- The mobility simulation writes events information to a file.
- There needs to be a mechanism to deal with all modes of transportation (see below).
- The mobility simulation needs to be reasonably fast; running the whole scenario once should not take more than about one hour.

In our experience, these specifications are not difficult to fulfil. They are, however, a significant departure from the way in which most current mobility simulations are written. They read OD matrices instead of plans, and they write link performance information instead of events. Writing events instead of or in addition to link performance information is relatively easy to implement. In contrast, making the simulation follow pre-specified plans sometimes necessitates a major implementation change. That change corresponds to the fact that in the agent-based approach all information is stored in the agent, whereas in many existing approaches most of the information (such as shortest path trees) is stored in the network. In addition, conditional plans files, such as discussed in Section 2.3, may make the simulation logic more demanding in the future.

Furthermore, future versions will necessitate a consistent way to deal with travel in different modes. It is clear that, in order to execute traffic with different modes, the use of these modes needs to be planned by the agent database and its external modules. However, as a simplification one could just assume that the execution exactly follows the plan – this would correspond to a system without congestion, without unexpected variability, etc. In that case, there are two options:

- The agent database itself takes care of modes that the mobility simulation cannot execute. That is, they are just not included into the plans file. The main disadvantage of this is that no corresponding events would exist, making, say, the consistent build-up of a mental map more difficult. For that reason, the following solution is preferred.

• The mobility simulation 'fakes' the execution of unknown modes. For example, let us assume that a plans file has the following information:

```
<plan>
<act type5"home" location5"ab" .../>
<leg mode5"walk" duration5"20min">
<route .../>
</leg>
<act type5"work" location5"cd" .../>
</plan>
```

A simulation that can simulate the walk mode would let the agent walk along the specified route. A simulation that cannot simulate the walk mode would just assume that the walk takes 20 minutes, as specified in the duration attribute of the leg tag, and move the agent to the next activity accordingly.

3.8 Scoring function

As mentioned elsewhere, the agent database needs a scoring function in order to give scores to plans that were executed. That scoring function needs to be entirely based on events information, and it needs to score the complete period (e.g. day). An example of a utility-based scoring function will be presented in Section 4.7.

An open problem is how to couple the scoring function used by the agent database to the scoring functions used by the external strategy generation modules. Because of stochastic effects, it is not necessary that they are completely consistent, but as mentioned before, some conceptual overlap is necessary. At this point, we solve this problem by manually defining the goals of the external modules. This is a subject of further investigation.

4 Verification setup

In order to test our implementation, verification scenarios were designed. Those scenarios are constructed in a way that they test the most important features of the framework. The features that are tested are: (i) capability to relax to an approximate equilibrium solution; (ii) capability to cooperate with more than one external module; (iii) capability to generate a meaningful solution even with an external module that just performs small random changes ('mutations') of existing plans.

A scenario consists of: (i) the network; (ii) the initial plans file; (iii) specific implementation details. These will be treated one by one in this section.

4.1 The network

The network used for this scenario can be seen in Figure 3.5.5. It consists of a circular arrangement where in one part travellers have multiple route options. Internally, all those routes have the same lengths and capacities, so that there is no bias toward one or the other. The expectation is that in the relaxed states all those routes are used equally. All roads are uni-directional; travellers need to follow the roads clockwise.

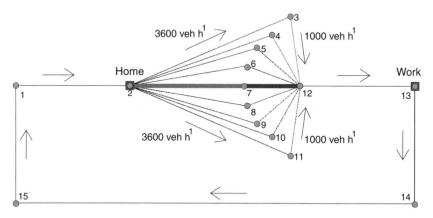

(a) Before replanning

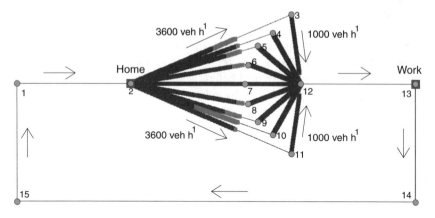

(b) After replanning

Figure 3.5.5 Diagram of the testing network overlaid onto example snapshots of the Routes Only scenario at 06.08 am, (a) before and (b) after many iterations of route replanning. After replanning, the agents have spread onto the different available routes between home and work. Link capacities are 36 000 veh/h except where indicated (the nine route options are identical).

4.2 The initial plans file

All scenarios need to start with an initial condition. In our case, we take as initial condition a plans file which contains 2000 agents, and one fully specified plan per agent. Those plans are the same for all agents. They specify that the agents leave the 'Home' location at 6.00 am, take the middle road (through node 7) to the 'Work' location, and work for eight hours. Then they take the lower part of the 'circle', through nodes 14, 15, and 1, to return home. The total free-speed travel time is about 54 minutes, with 15 minutes for the trip from 'Home' to 'Work', and 39 minutes for the return trip.

4.3 The mobility simulation

As the mobility simulation we use an improved version of a so-called 'queue simulation' (Gawron, 1998a). The improvements include an implementation on parallel computers, and an improved intersection dynamics, which ensures a fair sharing of the intersection capacity among incoming traffic streams (Cetin *et al.*, 2003). As pointed out elsewhere, the mobility simulation takes a plans file, executes it, and returns events information, such as when agents leave from or arrive at activities, or when agents enter/leave links.

4.4 Agent database

As discussed elsewhere, the agent database contains all plans for all agents, and manages addition, modification, removal, and selection of plans. The precise functioning of the agent database for our test scenario is as follows:

1   The agent database may be required to limit the number of plans stored per agent to N_{plans}. If any agent ends up with more than N_{plans} plans, it continues to delete the plan with the worst score until the number of plans is small enough. Note that in the steps following this one, an agent may obtain a new plan, which means it will have $N_{plans} + 1$ plans while trying a new one out, but it will have only N_{plans} to choose from when selecting from old plans.

2   With probability p_{times}, agents are selected to undergo times replanning. Each of these agents selects an existing plan from memory with uniform probability (not based on score) to use as a template for the new plan. This template is immediately copied into the agent's memory, to serve as a placeholder for the eventual new plan. The selected plans are written to a file, and the time replanner (see below) is called with this file as input. It writes the resulting new plans to a separate file. The agent database reads this file and overwrites the template in each agent's memory with the corresponding plan from the file.

3   With probability p_{routes}, agents are selected to undergo route replanning. As with times replanning, each of these agents selects an existing plan as a template and copies it into its memory as a placeholder for the new plan.

In addition, we set the router to be dependent on the times generated by the times replanning module, since the new leg departure times may offer better routes than the ones currently used. Therefore, all agents that underwent times replanning select their new plans for route replanning as well. Note that no plans are copied for these agents, since the plan with the new times already serves as the template for the new routes, and overwriting it will not change the new time information. All the template plans are written to a single file, the route replanner (see below) is called, the resulting new plans are written again to file, and the agent database reads those plans and over-writes the template plans with the new ones.

4   For each agent that has multiple plans, the plan to be executed in the follow-ing mobility simulation is selected.
   - All agents that possess a new plan select that new plan.
   - A fraction p_{rnd} chooses a plan at random from their memory, using a uniform probability for each plan, and ignoring plan performance. This is done to force agents to re-evaluate existing plans from time to time, even plans with a bad score.
   - All other agents select between existing plans, with probability

$$p_i \propto e^{\beta S_i}$$

where S_i is the score of plan i and β is a constant (see below). This is just a standard multinomial logit model (e.g. Ben-Akiva and Lerman, 1985). The value of β affects how likely agents choose 'non-best' plans. Higher values of β lead toward the best plan being chosen more often, while smaller values provide a more randomised choice. Since β interacts with the scaling of the scoring function, it is discussed in more detail there.
   - The selected plans are written to file; the mobility simulation runs with these plans and writes events information to a file.
   - The agent database reads the resulting events, computes corresponding scores for each agent, and adds those scores to the existing scores according to

$$S_i = (1 - \alpha)S_i + \alpha S_i'$$

where S_i is the stored score for plan i, S_i' is the newly calculated score, and $\alpha \in [0, 1]$ is a constant blending factor. This leaves the question of how plans are scored that have not used before. Plans from the initial plan set have no history, so there is no way to estimate their scores. Upon their first use, the agent simply gives it the new score:

$$S_i + \alpha S_i'.$$

However, when plans are copied as templates for replanning, score informa-tion is available from other plans, which can be used to provide an estimate of the initial value of S_i. This estimate can be calculated in many ways; at present, we set it to the score of the best plan in the agent's memory.

For this paper, we set the above parameters to the following constant values:

- The maximum number of plans per agent, N_{plans}, is six.
- The probabilities of an agent to perform time replanning, p_{times}, and route replanning, p_{routes}, are both 0.1.
- The probability of choosing a random plan, p_{rnd}, is 0.1.
- The plan selection constant, $\beta = 2 \text{€}^{-1}$. Section 5.4 describes what happens when we try different values of β.
- The score blending factor, α, is 0.1.

4.5 Routing module

An agent's plan must connect successive activities at different locations by travel legs that use the transportation network. Legs are described by their mode and mode-specific information. For example, a car-mode leg contains a node-by-node description of the vehicle's route through the network from the location of the previous activity to the location of the next activity. In principle, legs can be selected from different mode types, but at present we only model car trips. The legs have (expected) starting times, and the router needs to be sensitive to congestion so that it can avoid using already congested links.

We currently use a router based on Dijkstra's shortest-path algorithm, but 'shortness' is measured by the time it takes an agent to drive the route rather than distance. The fastest path depends on the travel times of each individual link (road segment) traversed in the route. These times depend on how congested the links are, and so they change throughout the day. This is implemented in the following way. The way a Dijkstra algorithm searches a shortest path can be interpreted as expanding, from the starting point of the leg, a network-oriented version of a wave front. In order to make the algorithm time-dependent, the speed of this wave front along a link is made to depend on when this wave front enters the link (e.g. Jacob *et al.*, 1999).

That is, for each link l we need a function $c_l(t)$ that returns the link 'cost' (=link travel time) for a vehicle entering at time t. This information is calculated from the events taken from a run of the mobility simulation. In order to make the look-up of $c_l(t)$ reasonably fast, we aggregate over 15 minute bins, during which the cost function is kept constant. That is, all vehicles entering a link between, e.g. 9.00 am and 9.15 am will contribute to the average link travel time during that time period.

4.6 Time choice module (time mutator)

In general, we want as a second module one that generates (or modifies) agents' activity schedules, which form the basis of their plans (Vaughn *et al.*, 1997;

Bowman, 1998). One can divide the task of creating an activity schedule into three parts: pattern choice, location choice, and timing choice. The *pattern choice* determines which activities to perform during the day, and in what order. For example, an agent might decide whether or not to go shopping, and if so, before or after work. The *location choice* determines where the agent will perform each activity. For some activities, such as home and work, agents make this decision very infrequently, while for other activities, such as shopping, the agent might choose a different location each time it wants to perform the activity. For example, an agent could go shopping at a bakery close to home or a grocery store near work. The *time choice* determines the duration of each activity, including when to leave home at the start of the day. A single module can make all of these decisions at the same time, or separate modules can be used to handle each one individually.

For this particular study, there is only a time choice module. This module takes the existing times of the plan and modifies them randomly. Note that there is no 'goal' with this module, that is, the module does *not* try to improve any kind of score. Rather, the module makes a random modification, and the plans selection mechanism in conjunction with the scoring will make the agents improve toward better scores.

The exact details of the time mutator are as follows. This module reads the plans file, and for each plan alters the end time of the first activity by a random amount r_1 uniformly selected in the range $r_1 \in [-30$ minutes, $+30$ minutes]. Values that come before 00.00 are reset to that time. It then alters the duration of each activity except the first and last by separate random values uniformly selected from the same range. The last activity does not need modification since it runs from whenever the agent arrives until 24.00. The modified plans are written back out to a file.

4.7 Scoring

The utility function we currently use is described in detail in Charypar and Nagel (2003). For the convenience of the reader, we summarise it here, though it is sufficient to recognise that performing activities is rewarded, and travel, early arrival, and late arrival are punished. The utility function essentially translates the layout of the plan into a numerical value, which can be thought of as a score or an actual value in monetary terms.

Agents have a 'typical' duration for each activity, represented by d_0. The utility for performing an activity ($util_{perform}$) is a logarithmic function of the duration of time spent performing the activity. It is calibrated so that performing the activity for d_0 (measured in hours) causes the marginal utility to equal a fixed value, $\beta_{perform}$, which is the same for all activity types. In addition, it sets the utility for performing an activity for d_0 to be (10 hours)$\beta_{perform}$. Mathematically,

$$util_{perform}(d) = \beta_{perform} \left[10h + d_0 \log\left(\frac{d}{d_0}\right) \right].$$

The result of the log function is that staying longer than d_0 always gains more utility, but each additional hour gains less utility than the preceding hour.

Note that there is no direct penalty for agents to have a duration larger than d_0 for an activity. This may seem counter-intuitive when looking at a single activity, but when agents must fit multiple activities into a limited amount of time (e.g. a single day), they end up having to trade-off the time spent on each activity in order to maximise their total utility for the whole plan. Assuming no other time restrictions, the optimal plan will be the one where all activity durations lead to the same marginal utility for duration. Charypar and Nagel (2003) sets $\beta_{perform}$ to $€+20h^{-1}$, though for this study we set it to $€+6h^{-1}$. The reason for this change is explained below.

As mentioned previously, we have only two types of activities: home and work. The preferred duration of work time is 8 hours, and the preferred duration of staying home is 16 hours, so that the agents have no free time; i.e. their day is 'full'. In addition to duration, we set the useful hours for performing the work activity to between 7.00 am and midnight, with the desired starting time to be exactly the opening time of 7.00 am. The home activity has no time constraints. The utility of an agent who arrives to work before 7.00 am must wait until 7.00 to start working. While waiting, the agent suffers a penalty defined by the marginal utility of waiting, β_{wait}, times the number of hours the agent waits, t_{wait}. Agents arriving after 7.00 am are assessed a lateness penalty, determined by the marginal utility of being late, β_{late}, times the number of hours the agent is late, t_{late}. The final component of the utility is the utility of travel, which is the marginal utility of travel, β_{travel}, times the number of hours the agent spends travelling, t_{travel}. We set the above parameters to the following values: $\beta_{wait} = €0h^{-1}$; $\beta_{travel} = €-6h^{-1}$; $\beta_{late} = €-18h^{-1}$.

Given a full day plan, the agent prefers to spend all 24 hours in the day performing some activity. Any time spent by the agent not performing an activity causes a loss of potential utility. The agent would obtain a perfect score if it spent exactly 8 hours at work and 16 hours at home, allowing it to earn utility every minute of the day. This would earn the agent $€60$ for each activity, for a total score of $€120$. In an actual day, the agent must spend some of its time travelling. While travelling, the agent does not earn any utility for being at work or at home, and is simultaneously losing utility for being on the road. This means the agent incurs a double penalty: the actual negative utility for the travel itself, and the loss of potential positive utility for not performing an activity. Similarly, if the agent arrives early to work, it is also not spending time working (or being at home) so it loses potential utility. Note that being late has a real penalty, but does not cause any loss of potential utility, since the agent begins performing the activity immediately upon arrival.

Therefore, there is an indirect penalty associated with arriving early to a location (waiting) and travelling. If the agent's activity durations are near the typical duration, this penalty is approximately $-\beta_{perform}$ times the number of hours spent waiting and/or travelling. Since agents will do their best to allocate time to the activities, we can assume that the durations are as near to the typical duration as possible. Given that the total travel time is on the order of one hour, this is a reasonable assumption. Thus, the effective values of the above parameters are approximately: $\beta_{wait} = € - 6\,h^{-1}$; $\beta_{travel} = € - 12\,h^{-1}$; $\beta_{late} = € - 18\,h^{-1}$. These effective values are selected such that, in rough terms, they model the Vickrey model of time choice (e.g. Arnott *et al.*, 1993). The desire to match the Vickrey model explains our choice of $€ + 6\,h^{-1}$ for β_{travel}; if it was $€ + 20\,h^{-1}$, the effective penalty for arriving early would be of greater magnitude than the penalty for arriving late.

As mentioned earlier, the β value used by the agent database to multiply agents' scores affects their selection of those plans. This value can be considered to be a scaling function, which maps utility in euro to unit-less values for the logit selection. In real-world applications, β will be estimated together with β_{wait}, β_{late}, and β_{travel}. This paper uses a value of $2\,€^{-1}$ as a baseline value for β, and then looks at deviations from that value in Section 5.4. In estimated multinomial logit models, it seems that values between $1\,€^{-1}$ and $10\,€^{-1}$ are normal.

5 Results

In this section, we describe the results obtained from three scenarios based on the modules, parameters, network, and initial conditions described above.

5.1 Routes Only

In the Routes Only scenario, we run the framework with the times replanning disabled, so that only route replanning may occur (i.e. $p_{times} = 0$). All agents are forced to forever use the initial activity time values, departing home at 6.00 am and staying at work exactly eight hours. This scenario demonstrates how well the agents distribute themselves among the available routes.

Figure 3.5.6 shows the relaxation/learning behaviour of the agents within this scenario, using two global performance measures: overall average score, and overall average travel time. One sees here that the average score relaxes to about €103.5 within 100–200 iterations, while average travel time relaxes to about 61 minutes within 20–30 iterations. Compared to the free-speed travel time of 54 minutes, the agents lose about 7 minutes due to congestion in this scenario.

Figure 3.5.7 shows the departure and arrival time distributions for this scenario, at iteration 0 (Figure 3.5.7(a)) and iteration 250 (Figure 3.5.7(b)). One can see from this figure that the work arrival time distribution (WATD) starts out at iteration 0 with an average of about 80–85 vehicles per five minute time-bin, corresponding to roughly $1000\,veh\,h^{-1}$, and lasting for about two hours. This makes sense, as the capacity of the bottleneck for a single home-to-work route is $1000\,veh\,h^{-1}$ and there are 2000 vehicles that want to traverse that route. After 250 iterations, the arrival rate increases to about 750 veh/(5 minutes), or $9000\,veh\,h^{-1}$, which corresponds to the total capacity of nine routes of $1000\,veh\,h^{-1}$ each. After 15 minutes, over 90 per cent of the agents have arrived at work, with the remaining arriving in the next ten minutes. This extra ten minutes comes from the incomplete equilibrium in the route distribution caused

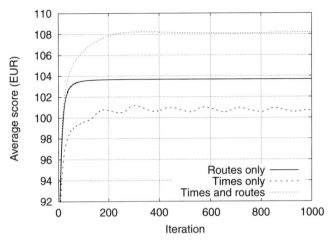

(a) Average scores

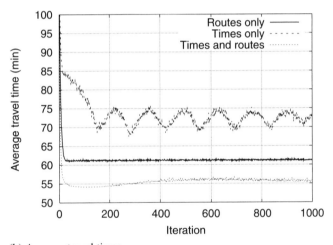

(b) Average travel times

Figure 3.5.6 Relaxation of score and travel times for all three scenarios of the baseline case. These plots display the average values of the (a) score and
(b) travel time collected over the entire population of agents during
each iteration.

by the 10 per cent route replanning, which is explained further below. Since
agents cannot change their work duration in this scenario, the work departure
time distribution (WDTD) is the same as the WATD shifted by eight hours, and
since there are no bottlenecks on the route home, the home arrival time distribution (HATD) is the same as the WDTD shifted by 39 minutes.

The only degree of freedom in this scenario is the route choice. Figure
3.5.8(a) displays the usage of the different routes as a function of iteration. This

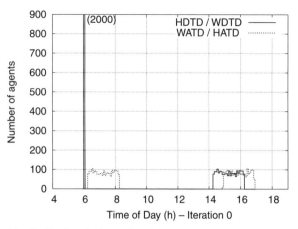

(a) Distributions before relaxation (common to all scenarios)

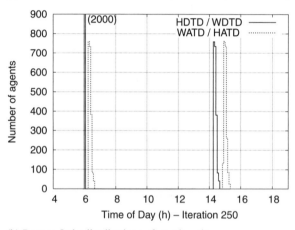

(b) Routes Only distributions after relaxation

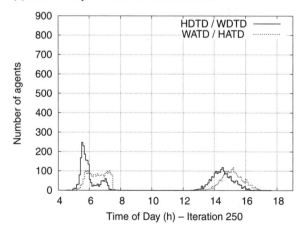

(c) Times Only distributions after relaxation

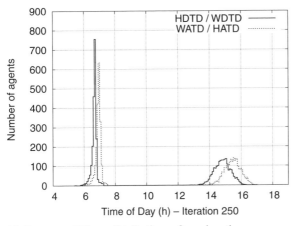

(d) Routes and Times distributions after relaxation

Figure 3.5.7 Histograms showing home departure time distribution (HDTD), work arrival time distribution (WATD), work departure time distribution (WDTD), and home arrival time distribution (HATD) of the three scenarios, before and after relaxation (250 iterations). The histograms are taken over five minute time-bins. For clarity, the range stops at 900 vehicles, though some of the initial departure peaks are above this value; these peaks are labelled with their actual values.

figure has several features. First, as expected, all agents start out using the initial route (number 7, 'middle'), while the other eight routes (represented in the figure by route numbers 5 and 9) start out with no agents. Second, the percentage of agents using the middle route decreases at approximately a negative exponential rate. This makes sense, since 10 per cent of all agents perform replanning each iteration. Some agents return to the middle route due to random plan selection, but most will stay on the other routes, lowering the percentage of agents using the middle route by roughly 10 per cent of its previous value each iteration, until the agents are using all routes equally. It takes about 40 iterations for the middle route to have about the same usage percentage as the other routes.

The third feature of this figure is that after equilibrium, most routes appear to be used on average by 10 per cent of the agents at a time, rather than the 11.1 per cent expected when nine equivalent routes are available. In addition, some routes appear to be used by 20 per cent of the agents during certain iterations. These phenomena are explained by the fact that 10 per cent of the agents perform replanning in each iteration, leaving the other 90 per cent to choose freely which route they want to use. These 90 per cent split up approximately evenly among the nine available routes, giving each a usage of about 10 per cent, and the 10 per cent who replan tend to choose the same route. This route will then have a total usage of about 20 per cent. Only three routes are displayed here; if all nine were displayed, there would be a 'spike' of 20 per cent route usage occurring for some route in each iteration. This extra group of agents

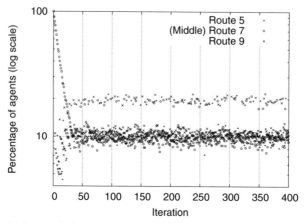

(a) Routes Only

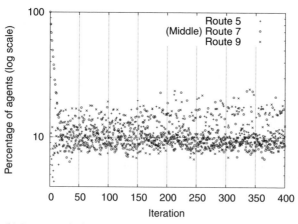

(b) Routes and Times

Figure 3.5.8 Route distributions for (a) the Routes Only scenario and (b) the Routes and Times scenario. The middle route has a distinctive curve since it is the one initially used by all agents. The other eight routes have qualitatively similar curves as Routes 5 and 9, only the 'spikes' occur in different iterations.

using one particular route causes that route to empty out later than the rest, extending the length of time agents arrive at work, as seen in Figure 3.5.7(b). Agents who replan tend to choose the same route because of the fluctuations in the usage of a route. During a given iteration, some routes will happen to be used least, and thus have the best travel time, so the router will use it for all (or most) of the replanned routes in the next iteration. These fluctuations are also driven by the fact that slightly more or less than 10 per cent of the agents may be replanned in each iteration, due to the probabilistic selection of agents for replanning. Note that it is not until near iteration 100 that the spikes appear to be in equilibrium.

The general interpretation of the above results for the Routes Only scenario is that the agents equilibrate to the different routes as best as they can, and once equilibrated stay in a very stable arrangement.

5.2 *Times Only*

In the second scenario, Times Only, we run the framework with the route replanning disabled, so that only times replanning may occur (i.e. $p_{routes} = 0$). Here all agents must forever use the middle route for their trips from home to work. This scenario demonstrates how well the agents distribute themselves through time; i.e. how they handle peak-hour spreading.

Figure 3.5.6 includes the average scores and travel times for this scenario. One can see that these measures contain a considerable amount of oscillation in comparison to those of the other two scenarios, though the oscillation appears to diminish as the iterations continue. We presume that the oscillations are due to the system being in a chaotic regime, though more investigation is necessary to learn the exact cause. For now, we only observe that they exist.

The average score oscillates around about €100.7, moving between €100.5 and €101.2, taking at least 200 iterations to reach this state. The average travel time centres around 72 minutes, oscillating between 68 minutes and 75 minutes, again taking about 200 iterations to get to that state. This scenario seems to find the worst scores and travel times of the three. It makes sense that the average travel times come out worse, since the agents cannot get around the $1000\,veh\,h^{-1}$ bottleneck of the middle route, while agents in the other scenarios can use nine times the capacity of this route for their home to work trips. This in turn explains why the average score is the lowest, because with more time being spent by the agents in travel, they have less time to spend working or at home, so they lose more potential score, which lowers their best achievable score.

Figure 3.5.7 shows the departure and arrival time distributions for this scenario, at iteration 0 (Figure 3.5.7(a)) and iteration 250 (Figure 3.5.7(c)). One can see that after 250 iterations, the WATD is still spread out to two hours and is still limited to $1000\,veh\,h^{-1}$. This is as much as can be expected when all agents use the same route. The main peak of the home departure time distribution (HDTD) is shifted to about 5.30 am, an earlier time compared to the 0th iteration, with a secondary peak around 7.00 am. Figure 3.5.9 shows a close-up of the distributions during the morning rush hour. In this figure one can see that about three quarters of the agents arrive in the 90 minutes before 7.00 am, and about a quarter arrive in the half hour after. This makes sense, because agents arriving to work early are effectively penalised $€-6h^{-1}$ while those arriving late are penalised at three times this amount. Therefore, an agent arriving 30 minutes late incurs the same penalty as one arriving 90 minutes early. Back to Figure 3.5.7(c), we see that the WDTD and HATD are much more spread out than the WATD, lasting about three hours.

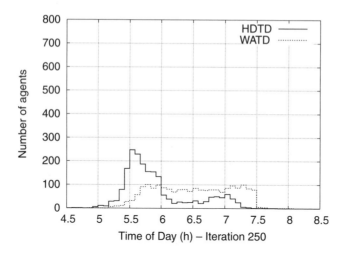

Figure 3.5.9 Histograms showing HDTD and WATD for the Times Only scenario, after relaxation (250 iterations). The histograms are taken over five minute time-bins.

The general interpretation of the results for the Times Only scenario is that even with a time choice module that simply mutates existing plans, the feedback mechanism and the agent database allow agents to learn enough about the system to find a plausible distribution of departure times.

5.3 Routes and Times

In the Routes and Times scenario, we finally allow agents to utilise both the routing module and time choice module to develop new plans. Agents who perform time replanning also perform routes replanning on the resulting plan, as discussed in Section 4.4. This scenario demonstrates the complete relaxation behaviour of the agents, where they may spread out over space and time.

Figure 3.5.6 includes the relaxation of scores and travel times for this scenario. One sees here that the average score is never perfectly relaxed, with what appears to be a slight oscillation with a period of about 800 iterations. However, after about 300 iterations the score seems to be rather stable, oscillating around €108. The average travel time initially finds the free-speed travel time within 100 iterations, then deviates from this value, eventually flattening out at about 55 minutes. The travel times may also have an oscillation, though it might also be a one-time 'bump'. More iterations would be required to find this out. It seems reasonable that this occurs because the agents are able to compensate for slightly varying travel times, meaning the travel time is not as important to them when they have more degrees of freedom to explore. In any case, this scenario finds a better average score and better average travel time than the other two scenarios, as expected given the larger number of degrees of freedom given to the agents.

Figure 3.5.7 shows the departure and arrival time distributions for this scenario, at iteration 0 (Figure 3.5.7(a)) and iteration 250 (Figure 3.5.7(d)). In iteration 250, the HDTD peak has shifted to about 6.45 am, a later time than that at iteration 0, or that at iteration 250 for the other scenarios. It makes sense that the peak is at a later time than that of the Times Only scenario, as the average travel times in this scenario are shorter. The time of 6.45 am makes sense as well, because most agents only need 15 minutes for the home to work trip. This is supported by the narrow WATD peak, which indicates that most agents arrive to work between 6.50 am and 7.00 am. The peak is nearly the same as the HDTD peak, only shifted by 15 minutes. See also Figure 3.5.10 for a close-up of those peaks. Naturally, both the HDTD and WATD peaks are wider in this scenario than in Routes Only, since the agents can explore alternate departure times from home. They are not as wide as those in Times Only are, since agents can also take alternate routes to avoid congestion, and do not have to spread out in time as much.

Figure 3.5.8(b) displays the usage of the different routes as a function of iteration. As with the Routes Only scenario, all agents start out using the middle route, while representative routes numbers 5 and 9 start with no agents. In addition, like in the Routes Only scenario, the percentage of agents using the middle route decreases rapidly while percentage of agents using the alternate route(s) increases. However, since 20 per cent of the agents are given the chance to change their routes each iteration ($p_{times} + p_{routes}$), the exchange of agents from the middle route to the other routes occurs more rapidly.

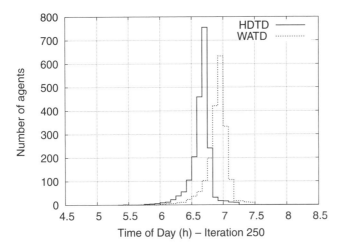

Figure 3.5.10 Histograms showing HDTD and WATD for the Routes and Times scenario, after relaxation (250 iterations). The histograms are taken over five minute time-bins.

This figure shows higher oscillations in route usage compared to the Routes Only scenario. In that scenario, route equilibration is the only option for agents trying to avoid congestion. Agents using some routes tend to 'notice' other agents using the same route, in the sense that their trip was made longer by the presence of the other agents. In this scenario, however, agents can also avoid congestion by choosing different departure times. So, agents using the same route may do so at totally different times, and may not notice each other at all, since they did not encounter any congestion from other agents along that route. Thus, they do not have much reason to try to switch routes, causing less of an equalisation among the route choices. Another way to put it is that the temporal spreading allows the routes to remain equivalent to each other, even if the number of agents using each route differs greatly.

The general interpretation of the results for the Routes and Times scenario is that both modules work together well to allow the agents to explore both spatial and temporal degrees of freedom to obtain better plans than possible with just one degree of freedom.

5.4 Varying β

Here we vary the β plan selection parameter to higher and lower values from the baseline value of 2€^{-1}, to see how selecting the best plan more or less often affects the score and travel time relaxation rates. We tried these values for β: 0.01€^{-1}, 1€^{-1}, 2€^{-1}, 4€^{-1}, and $\infty \text{€}^{-1}$. A value of $\infty \text{€}^{-1}$ means agents *always* choose the plan with the best score.

Figures 3.5.11(a) and (b) show the effect of β on the Routes Only scenario. The relaxed score and travel time averages are the same; only the rate of approach to those values differs. With a lower value of β, agents are allowed

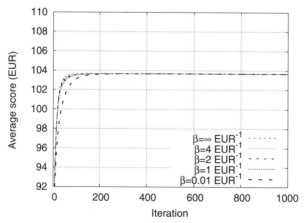

Figure 3.5.11 (a) Average scores for Routes Only

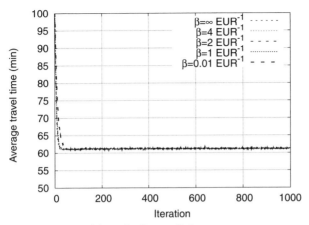

(b) Average travel times for Routes Only

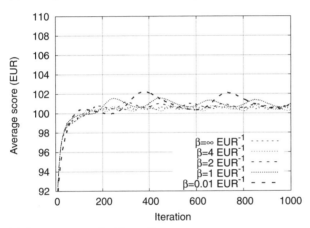

(c) Average scores for Times Only

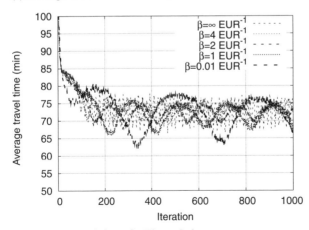

(d) Average travel times for Times Only

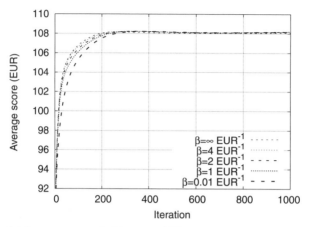

(e) Average scores for Routes and Times

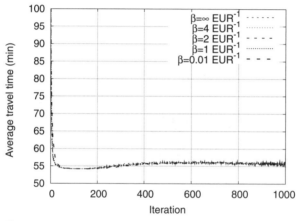

(f) Average travel times for Routes and Times

Figure 3.5.11 Relaxation of scores and travel times for the different scenarios, comparing the relaxation behaviour with varying β values. These plots display the average values of the score – (a), (c), (e) – and travel time – (b), (d), (f) – collected over the entire population of agents during each iteration.

more random selection among their plans, so the system approaches the steady-state at a slower rate, which makes sense. The infinite β, which causes agents to always choose the best plan they have, allows for the fastest relaxation of both scores and travel times.

Figures 3.5.11(c) and (d) show the effect of β on the Times Only scenario. One can see that the oscillations have a higher amplitude and lower frequency for lower values of β. For the scores, all the curves seem to have roughly the same worst score (lower bound) of about 100.5. However, with lower β the system is able to find better (higher) scores, though it cannot stay at those values. Similarly, on the travel time plots, one can see that the worse possible travel time (upper bound) does not change much, but better (lower) travel times are reached with lower values of β.

Figures 3.5.11(e) and (f) show the effect of β on the Routes and Times scenario. Like with the Routes Only scenario, the relaxed value of the score seems to remain essentially the same, but the different β values approach it differently.

Overall, it appears that the value of β does not matter very much for the scenarios with the routing module enabled. Perhaps this is due to the fact that the routing module makes decisions with some 'intelligence' behind them, allowing for an additional learning mechanism for the agents. Possibly, the Times Only scenario is affected more by the value of β, as the decisions made by the agent database are the only ones that have any effect on the learning behaviour.

5.5 Varying β_{travel}

Here we vary the marginal utility of travel time, β_{travel} from its baseline value of $\text{\euro} - 6\,h^{-1}$, to see how making travel time more or less important in the score calculation affects the score and travel time relaxation rates. We tried these values β_{travel}: $\text{\euro} - 0.06\,h^{-1}$, $\text{\euro} - 0.6\,h^{-1}$, $\text{\euro} - 6\,h^{-1}$, $\text{\euro} - 60\,h^{-1}$, and $\text{\euro} - 600\,h^{-1}$.

Figures 3.5.12(a) and (b) show the effect of β_{travel} on the Routes Only scenario. As expected, higher magnitudes of β_{travel} cause the average score to relax to a lower value, since all else being equal, the same travel time costs more to the agent. For all values above $\text{\euro} - 600\,h^{-1}$, the curves seem to have the same relaxation behaviour as seen in Figure 3.5.6. For $\beta_{travel} = \text{\euro} - 600\,h^{-1}$, the score takes about 200 more iterations to relax, while the travel time takes only 10–20 more iterations to relax.

Figures 3.5.12(c) and (d) show the effect of β_{travel} on the Times Only scenario. Here we see that different values of β_{travel} can also change the oscillation amplitude and frequency for the scores and the travel times. For $\beta_{travel} = \text{\euro} - 60\,h^{-1}$, the oscillation frequency is higher, and the amplitude is smaller, and for $\beta_{travel} = \text{\euro} - 600\,h^{-1}$, the oscillation is nearly non-existent. For the smaller two magnitudes of the marginal utility of travel, the score and travel times curves look qualitatively like those of the Routes and Times scenario in Figure 3.5.6. They improve at first, then slightly deviate from the best value obtained. This supports the idea that the behaviour of the Routes and Times scenario comes from the fact that travel time is less important to the agents when they are able to adjust their routes and their activity schedules simultaneously. In addition, as with the Routes Only scenario, Times Only takes longer to relax when the β_{travel} value is higher.

Figures 3.5.12(e) and (f) show the effect of β_{travel} on the Routes and Times scenario. Here we once again get basically the same relaxation behaviour, offset only by the different strengths of the travel time in the overall score. The scores for $\beta_{travel} = \text{\euro} - 600\,h^{-1}$ takes longer to relax, but all scores for the Routes and Times scenario relax to higher values than those of the other two scenarios.

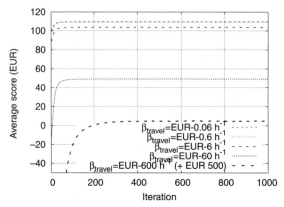

(a) Average scores for Routes Only

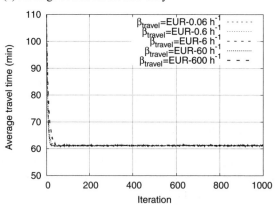

(b) Average travel times for Routes Only

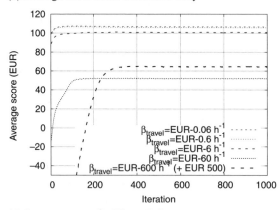

(c) Average scores for Times Only

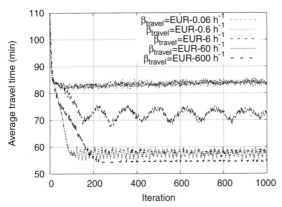

(d) Average travel times for Times Only

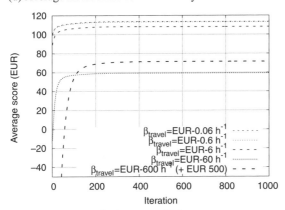

(e) Average scores for Routes and Times

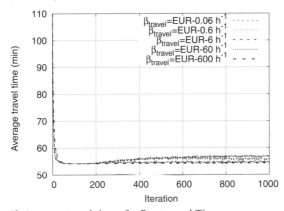

(f) Average travel times for Routes and Times

Figure 3.5.12 Relaxation of scores and travel times for the different scenarios, comparing the relaxation behaviour with varying β_{travel} values. These plots display the average values of the score – (a), (c), (e) – and travel time – (b), (d), (f) – collected over the entire population of agents during each iteration. For better comparison of the relaxation rate, we shift the average score curve for $\beta_{travel} = \mathbb{C}-600\,h$ up by $\mathbb{C}500$.

Furthermore, one can see that for the lower marginal utility of travel, the travel times stay flat at close to the free-speed travel time. The deviation from this level occurs more for higher values of β_{travel}, with $\beta_{travel} = \mathcal{E} - 6\,h^{-1}$ being the only one that deviates and appears to return to the lower value.

Overall, it appears that reasonable values of β_{travel}, as compared to the other marginal utility parameters, lead to the same relaxation behaviour (if not the same scores) in the scenarios with the routing module enabled. The Times Only scenario's relaxation behaviour is more affected by the value of β_{travel}, and it appears that a value of $\mathcal{E} - 6\,h^{-1}$ may represent an unstable case at the border between two more stable regimes: one where travel time dominates the decision-making, and one where it is not very important at all.

6 Discussion and future work

We have shown that the system can relax to an uncongested state using the present times mutator module; however, the relaxation takes many hundreds of iterations. We expect that a more goal-oriented module, which tries to return new activity time schedules that are better than old ones, would allow the system to relax faster. We are working on two versions of such a module at different stages of development and capability. Both of them use genetic algorithms (GA) to 'evolve' activity schedules by mutating or mixing existing schedules. One of these contains a global (for all agents) mental map of the traffic network for estimating travel times between proposed activities, but only adjusts the durations of the activities, leaving patterns and locations alone. Unfortunately, this module has some bugs in the mental map that have not been worked out yet, so it generates faulty schedules (Schneider, 2003; Raney *et al.*, 2003). The second GA-based model has no known bugs but is not yet integrated into the framework (Charypar and Nagel, 2003).

In addition, we plan to add a population generation module that would disaggregate demographic data to obtain individual households and individual household members (agents), with certain characteristics, such as a street address, car ownership, or household income (Beckman *et al.*, 1996).

As mentioned in Section 3.5, the agent database must be aware of dependencies between modules. At this stage, with only two modules, it is easy to hard-code this dependency. However, once we begin adding more modules, we will need to make this information configurable in some way. In fact, it might be desirable to have different 'module paths' an agent can carry out, with different execution probabilities. For example, an agent could be given the choice between calling only the activity time choice module, calling only the routing module, or calling both (perhaps even with different choices for the calling order). The combination and probabilities of the available choices could reflect behavioural aspects, such as the low frequency of changing work locations (with a work location choice module) compared to the high frequency of changing shopping locations or durations.

Currently a lot of time is spent writing and reading files to communicate plans between the agent database and the modules/simulation. We are working on including a message-based technology into the framework so that plans can be sent directly between the modules as needed, and plans and events can be sent to and from the simulation while it is running. This change will allow decision-making and simulation to occur simultaneously, meaning this change would allow us to implement within-day replanning.

As mentioned in the previous section, we intend to eliminate the memory size limitation imposed on the agent database by current 32-bit architecture by spreading it over many CPUs. The agent database on each CPU would maintain the plans and scores for a subset of the agents in the simulation and would utilise its own set of modules to update those plans. The different plan-sets would be merged when sent to the simulation.

7 Summary/conclusions

This paper presents a framework for large-scale multi-agent simulations of travel behaviour. The immediate goal is a replacement of the traditional four-step process for transportation planning; the longer-term goal is to have an agent-based system for all aspects of urban and regional planning. The core ideas of the system are:

- One should separate the simulation of the physical world from the simulation of the mental world of the agents. This is reflected by a design that strictly separates those two worlds. A mental/strategic layer generates strategies ('plans'); these plans are executed by a physical layer; and then strategies are adapted based on how they performed in the physical layer. In the specific case of transportation simulations, the physical layer is also called the traffic (micro-)simulation, or the mobility simulation.
- Agents should memorise more than one strategy. This gives them the option to try out all strategies multiple times, and thus to obtain average scores for them ('exploration'). When agents do not explore, then they exploit, by selecting strategies based on the score, possibly using some behaviourally justified model such as multinomial logit. From time to time, agents should also add new strategies to their repertoire, or delete strategies with low scores. All this functionality is implemented by a so-called agent database.
- As said above, agents from time to time add new strategies to their repertoire. These strategies need to be generated by some method. In our approach, the methods that generate new strategies can be completely independent modules. They read an XML file that specifies which pieces of an agent's plan are already known, and the external module adds or changes pieces. For example, one module could generate activity patterns, another one activity locations, a third one activity times, and a fourth one routes. The framework will call all those modules one by one and in the end have a completely new plan. The XML plans file uses exactly the same format for all those exchanges; and the same format is again used to send plans to the

physical simulation. This means that we have only one file format specifying agent plans.

- Performance information from the physical simulation is communicated back via an events file. Events are output every time something relevant happens, such as an agent leaving an activity, or entering a link. In general, the physical simulation performs no data aggregation at all; in consequence, something like link travel time needs to be constructed from link entry and link exit events. The two big advantages of this approach are: (1) it is straightforward to retrofit those outputs to any existing agent-based mobility simulation, since there is no data aggregation either along space or along time. Any event is just a simple print command inside the mobility simulation; (2) external strategy generation modules can also read this information and use it as they like. For example, an external module building a mental map for one specific agent will use the link entry/exit information in completely different ways than the routing module. If the simulation would aggregate link entry/exit information into link travel times, adding such a mental map module would no longer be possible.
- Strategies are full 24-hour day plans, and are evaluated as such. The strategy evaluation is based on the events, and therefore on actual individual performance of each agent. The evaluation is therefore immune against errors introduced by aggregation. One obvious candidate for the scoring function is the conventional utility function, but other systems such as aspect theory can be used. Since all agents are individually represented, it is no problem to couple those evaluations to individual attributes, such as gender or income.
- The approach is completely transparent toward parallel computing. Having a parallel mobility simulation needs some programming effort, but is conceptually straightforward since methods from the simulations of other physical systems can be applied. And making the agent database or the external strategy generation modules parallel is completely trivial as long as agents do not interact. One simply distributes agents (or possibly households) across CPUs. Only when interactions beyond the household level become important will more advanced computing techniques become necessary.
- The implementation was tested with three scenarios, one testing route equilibration, one testing times choice, and one testing route equilibration in conjunction with time choice. Route equilibration works as expected, in the sense that the system ends up with using nine equivalent routes equivalently. Also time choice works as expected, in the sense that agents adjust their daily timings in a plausible way.
- A curious aspect about the time choice test is that the external module that generates alternative timing schemes has no 'intelligence' at all. Instead, it just randomly mutates existing schedules of the agents. The interpretation of the new schedules is done entirely by the agent database and its scoring function. This means in practice that the correctness specifications toward external modules are significantly relaxed. In essence, it is sufficient if external modules generate meaningful solutions plus some variability.

Acknowledgements

The ETH-sponsored 192-CPU Beowulf cluster 'Xibalba' performed most of the computations. Marc Schmitt has done a great job of maintaining the computational system. Nurhan Cetin provided the mobility simulation. The work also benefited from discussions with Fabrice Marchal. Michael Balmer helped run the simulations from which the results presented here were obtained.

Notes

* Institute of Computational Science, ETH Zurich, CH-8092 Zurich, Switzerland, braney@inf.ethz.ch.
** Transport Systems Planning and Transport Telematics, Technical University of Berlin, D-10587 Berlin, Germany, nagel@vsp.tu-berlin.de.
1 Bottom (2000) adds a third component, the guidance map, which is relevant for ITS (intelligent transportation systems) applications.

References

Arentze, T., Hofman, F., van Mourik, H., and Timmermans, H. (2000) 'ALBATROSS: A multi-agent rule-based model of activity pattern decisions' paper no. 00–0022, Washington, D.C.: Transportation Research Board Annual Meeting.
Arnott, R., De Palma, A., and Lindsey, R. (1993) 'A structural model of peak-period congestion: A traffic bottleneck with elastic demand' *The American Economic Review*, 83(1): 161.
Astarita, V., Er-Rafia, K., Florian, M., Mahut, M., and Velan, S. (2001) 'A con n of three methods for dynamic network loading' *Transportation Research Re* 71: 179–190.
Avineri, E. and Prashker, J.N. (2003) 'Sensitivity to uncertainty: Need for paradigm shift' paper no. 03-3744, Washington, D.C.: Transportation Research Board Annual Meeting.
Beckman, R.J., Baggerly, K.A., and McKay, M.D. (1996) 'Creating synthetic base-line populations' *Transportion Research Part A – Policy and Practice*, 30(6): 415–429.
Ben-Akiva, M. and Lerman, S.R. (1985) *Discrete Choice Analysis*, Cambridge, MA: The MIT Press.
Bottom, J.A. (2000) 'Consistent anticipatory route guidance' PhD thesis, Cambridge, MA: Massachusetts Institute of Technology.
Bowman, J.L. (1998) 'The day activity schedule approach to travel demand analysis' PhD thesis, Cambridge, MA: Massachusetts Institute of Technology.
Bowman, J.L., Bradley, M., Shiftan, Y., Lawton, T.K., and Ben-Akiva, M. (1999) 'Demonstration of an activity-based model for Portland' in *World Transport Research: Selected Proceedings of the 8th World Conference on Transport Research 1998*, Vol. 3, pp. 171–184, Oxford: Elsevier.
Cetin, N., Burri, A., and Nagel, K. (2003) 'A large-scale agent-based traffic microsimulation based on queue model' in *Proceedings of Swiss Transport Research Conference (STRC)*, Monte Verita, CH: Swiss Transport Research Conference. Online. Available at http//www.strc.ch/ (accessed 15 September 2004). Earlier version, with inferior performance values in (2003) paper number 03-4272, Washington, D.C.: Transportation Research Board Annual Meeting.

Charypar, D. and Nagel, K. (2005) 'Generating complete all-day activity plans with genetic algorithms' in *Transportation*, 32(4): 369–397.

Daganzo, C.F. (1998) 'Queue spillovers in transportation networks with a route choice' *Transportation Science*, 32(1): 3–11.

de Palma, A. and Marchal, F. (2002) 'Real case applications of the fully dynamic METROPOLIS tool-box: an advocacy for large-scale mesoscopic transportation systems' *Networks and Spatial Economics*, 2(4): 347–369.

De Smet, Y., Springael, J., and Kunsch, P. (2002) 'Towards statistical multicriteria decision modelling: a first approach' *J. Multi-Cri. Decis. Anal.*, 11: 305–313.

Ferber, J. (1999) *Multi-Agent Systems. An introduction to distributed artificial intelligence*, Harlow: Addison-Wesley.

Friedrich, M., Hofsäß, I., Nökel, K., and Vortisch, P. (2000) 'A dynamic traffic assignment method for planning and telematic applications' in *Proceedings of Seminar K*, Cambridge, GB: European Transport Conference.

Gawron, C. (1998a) 'An iterative algorithm to determine the dynamic user equilibrium in a traffic simulation model' *International Journal of Modern Physics C*, 9(3): 393–407.

Gawron, C. (1998b) 'Simulation-based traffic assignment' PhD thesis, Cologne, Germany: University of Cologne. Online. Available at http://www.zaik.uni-koeln.de/~paper (accessed 15 September 2004).

Hensher, D. and King, J. (eds) (2001) *The Leading Edge of Travel Behavior Research*, Oxford: Pergamon.

Holland, J.D. (1992) *Adaptation in Natural and Artificial Systems*, reprint edn, Cambridge, MA: Bradford Books.

Hunt, J.D., Johnston, R., Abraham, J.E., Rodier, C.J., Garry, G.R., Putman, S.H., and de la Barra, T. (2001) 'Comparisons from Sacramento model test bed' *Transportation Research Record*, 1780: 53–63.

Jacob, R.R., Marathe, M.V., and Nagel, K. (1999) 'A computational study of routing algorithms for realistic transportation networks' article no. 6, *ACM Journal of Experimental Algorithms*, 4(1999es).

Jonnalagadda, J., Freedman, N., Davidson, W.A., and Hunt, J.D. (2001) 'Development of microsimulation activity-based model for San Francisco: destination and mode choice models' *Transportation Research Record*, 1777: 25–35.

Kaufman, D.E., Wunderlich, K.E., and Smith, R.L. (1991) 'An iterative routing/assignment method for anticipatory real-time route guidance' IVHS Technical Report 91-02, Ann Arbor, MI: University of Michigan Department of Industrial and Operations Engineering.

Kim, J.H. (1997) 'Special issue about the first micro-robot world cup soccer tournament, MIROSOT' *Robotics and Autonomous Systems*, 21(2): 137–205.

Loudon, W.R., Parameswaran, J., and Gardner, B. 'Incorporating feedback in travel forecasting' *Transportation Research Record*, 1607: 185–195.

MIT ITS Program (2004) 'MIT Intelligent Transportation Systems: DynaMIT', Cambridge, MA: MIT ITS Program. Online. Available at http://mit.edu/its/dynamit.html (accessed 15 2004) and http://dynamictrafficassignment.org/ (accessed 15 September 2004).

Nagel, K. (1994/95) 'High-speed microsimulations of traffic flow' PhD thesis, Cologne, Germany: University of Cologne. Online. Available at http://www.zaik.uni-koeln.de/~paper (accessed 15 September 2004).

Nagel, K. (1996) 'Individual adaptation in a path-based simulation of the freeway network of Northrhine-Westfalia' *International Journal of Modern Physics C*, 7(6): 883.

Nagel, K. and Marchal, F. (2003) 'Computational methods for multi-agent simulations of travel behavior' in *Proceedings of the Meeting of the International Association for Travel Behavior Research (IATBR)*, Lucerne, Switzerland: International Association for Travel Behavior Research. Online. Available at http://www.ivt.baum.ethz.ch/allgemein/iatbr2003.html (accessed 15 September 2004).

Raney, B. and Nagel, K. (2004) 'Iterative route planning for large-scale modular transportation simulations' *Future Generation Computer Systems*, 20(7): 1101–1118.

Raney, B., Balmer, M., Axhausen, K., and Nagel, K. (2003) 'Agent-based activities planning for an iterative traffic simulation of Switzerland' in *Proceedings of the Meeting of the International Association for Travel Behavior Research (IATBR)*, Lucerne, Switzerland: International Association for Travel Behavior Research. Online. Available at http://www.ivt.baum.ethz.ch/allgemein/iatbr2003.html (accessed 15 September 2004).

The Regents of the University of California. (2003) 'TRansportation ANalysis and SIMulation System (TRANSIMS)', Los Alamos, NM: Los Alamos National Laboratory. Online. Available at http://transims.tsasa.lanl.gov/ (accessed 15 September 2004).

Salvini, P.A. and Miller, E.J. (2003) 'ILUTE: An operational prototype of a comprehensive microsimulation model of urban systems' in *Proceedings of the Meeting of the International Association for Travel Behavior Research (IATBR)*, Lucerne, Switzerland: International Association for Travel Behavior Research. Online. Available at http://www.ivt.baum.ethz.ch/allgemein/iatbr2003.html (accessed 15 September 2004).

Schneider, A. (2003) 'Genetische Algorithmen zur Optimierung von Tagesplänen für Verkehrsteilnehmer' term project, Zurich, Switzerland: Swiss Federal Institute of Technology (ETH).

University of Maryland at College Park (2002) 'DYNASMART home page', College Park, MD: University of Maryland. Online. Available at http://www.dynasmart.com/ (accessed 15 September 2004).

University of Washington (2004) 'UrbanSim', Seattle, WA: University of Washington. Online. Available at http://www.urbansim.org/ (accessed 15 September 2004).

Vaughn, K.M., Speckman, P., and Pas, E.I. (1997) 'Generating household activity-travel patterns (HATPs) for synthetic populations', Washington, D.C.: Transportation Research Board Annual Meeting.

Vovsha, P., Petersen, E., and Donnelly, R. (2002) 'Microsimulation in travel demand modeling: lessons learned from the New York best practice model' *Transportation Research Record*, 1805: 68–77.

Wahle, J., Bazzan, A.L.C., Klügl, F., and Schreckenberg, M. (2002) 'The impact of real-time information in a two-route scenario using agent-based simulation' *Transportation Research C*, 10(5–6): 399–417.

3.6 A multi-criteria approach to the strategic assessment of advanced driver assistance systems

The role of sensitivity analysis and implementation strategy[1]

Cathy Macharis, [*] *Alan Stevens,* [**]
Klaas De Brucker, [***] *and Alain Verbeke* [****]

Abstract

This paper presents the results of an assessment methodology developed by the authors for the strategic evaluation of advanced driver assistance systems (ADAS). This type of methodology should permit to assess appropriately a variety of ADAS effects, especially effects on road network efficiency, traffic safety, usability, interaction safety, user acceptance, and the environment. Multi-criteria analysis (MCA) was used as the basis of this methodology, which synthesises information from both stakeholder evaluations and technical performance investigations. This paper focuses on the last two steps of the methodology, namely the design of mechanisms that permit effective sensitivity analysis and that address implementation challenges.

1 Introduction

This paper describes the results of an impact assessment for advanced driver assistance systems (ADAS) that was performed by the authors. The paper focuses on two issues critical to effective public policy-making, namely the sensitivity analysis and implementation scenarios. The results presented in this paper are based on the 'ADVISORS',[2] research project, which was commissioned by the Directorate General for Transport and Energy (DG TREN) of the European Commission under the Fifth Framework Programme.[3] The ultimate objective of this research project was to improve road safety in the EU through the introduction of new technologies. Do ADAS actually improve road safety, and are there any negative spillover effects? The authors' contribution to this research project consisted of evaluating and prioritising the different possible technologies from a strategic perspective, i.e. taking into account both their technical implementation potential and their value added to the objectives of a wide variety of stakeholders, and within the context of various scenarios (possible evolution of relevant parameters in the external environment). The results of this study should be viewed as an input for European innovation policy, which aims to stimulate the development of strategic new technologies, and can be usefully informed by the implementation priorities determined in this study.

Within the scope of this research project, a substantial number of stakeholder analyses were conducted, as well as a series of technical performance studies such as driving simulations and field experiments. Some of the key systems analysed included, inter alia, adaptive cruise control such as urban stop-and-go, intelligent speed adaptation, lateral support, driver monitoring systems, navigation, and lane departure warning.

Adaptive cruise control (ACC) is a vehicle system that automatically controls vehicle cruising speed and, if necessary, operates the throttle and brakes to maintain a safe distance from the vehicle in front. Stop-and-go systems constitute a special application of ACC. They enable the vehicle to adjust its speed automatically, and even to stop, in function of the position of another vehicle in front. Intelligent Speed Adaptation (ISA) refers to the automatic control of the maximum vehicle speed, based on specified speed limits or specific traffic characteristics. The ADAS for lateral control support aims to provide driver assistance with anti-collision purposes along the lateral axis of the vehicle. Moreover, it also assists the driver in situations of tiredness and distraction. The driver monitoring systems aim to evaluate the driver and provide a warning if his/her ability to control the vehicle is impaired (e.g. in the case of drowsiness). Navigation systems support the selection of the most optimal route(s) to a particular destination. Lane departure warning results in a signal given to the driver when the vehicle is moving out of a particular lane without the driver having signalled this intention. Other ADAS will be described further in this paper.

The final part of the research project consisted of evaluating and prioritising the different possible technologies from a strategic perspective, i.e. taking into account both their technical implementation potential and contribution to the objectives of a wide variety of stakeholders. Here, much attention was devoted to the context provided by various scenarios (possible evolution of relevant parameters in the external environment). The results of this study will hopefully contribute to the design of a new European innovation policy in the area of strategic technology development, building upon the implementation priorities suggested.

2 Common assessment methodology

Building upon the methodological approaches adopted in earlier projects, a common assessment methodology was developed that is represented in Figure 3.6.1.

The various ADAS submitted for evaluation (step 1) were screened through a risk analysis (step 2) in terms of their feasibility from a technical, environmental, legal, and economic point of view. Once an ADAS had passed this initial (pre-) multi-criteria screening test, it was evaluated through an MCA. The overall MCA approach was constructed as follows.

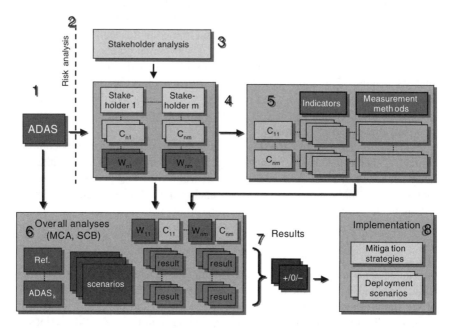

Figure 3.6.1 Common assessment methodology for ADAS (source: ADVISORS –
Competitive and Sustainable Growth Programme (2002a: 15)).

First, the various relevant stakeholders were identified as well as their key
objectives (step 3). The various stakeholder groups considered relevant were
pooled into three groups, namely:

- the ADAS users (i.e. individual drivers, fleet owners, etc.);
- society as a whole (local and national public agencies, other drivers, weak
  road users such as pedestrians, etc.);
- the ADAS producers/sellers (i.e. system manufacturers and car manufacturers).

Second, the objectives of each stakeholder group were translated into criteria
and then given a relative importance (weight) (step 4). In Figure 3.6.2, the criteria were stakeholder group are shown. The choice and definition of evaluation
criteria were based primarily on the identified stakeholder objectives and the
purposes of the ADAS considered. The users are interested primarily in the full
user cost, driver comfort, driver safety, and travel time duration. Society is concerned with public expenditures associated with ADAS introduction, the
environmental effects (impacts on emissions, noise, etc.), third party safety,
network efficiency, and acceptability. Finally, the manufacturers are interested
in the technical feasibility and the acceptance risk, as a proxy for the economic
viability of the systems considered.

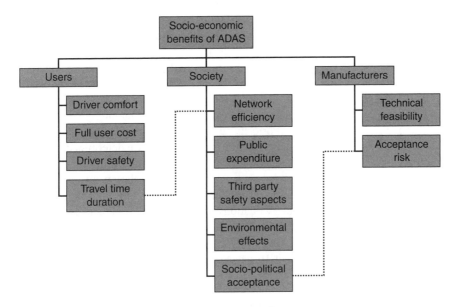

Figure 3.6.2 Hierarchical decision tree for the evaluation of ADAS (source: ADVISORS
– Competitive and Sustainable Growth Programme (2002b: 44)).

For each criterion, one or more indicators were constructed (e.g. direct quantitative indicators such as money spent, number of lives saved, reductions in CO_2 emissions achieved, etc., or scores on an ordinal indicator such as high/medium/low for criteria with values that are difficult to express in quantitative terms, etc.) (step 5). The measurement method for each indicator was also made explicit (e.g. willingness to pay, quantitative scores based on macroscopic computer simulation, etc.). This approach permitted the measurement of each ADAS' performance in terms of its contribution to the objectives of specific stakeholder groups.

Steps 1 to 5 can be considered as mainly analytical, and they precede the 'overall analysis' (step 6), which takes into account the objectives of all stakeholder groups simultaneously and is more 'synthetic' in nature. Here, an evaluation matrix is constructed that aggregates each ADAS contribution to the objectives of all stakeholders (step 6). The various ADAS had to be further refined in order to evaluate them properly. More specifically, it was noted that even a single ADAS can have different features. For example, one version of intelligent speed adaptation (ISA) provides information on speed and can modify the vehicle speed, but it can still be overridden by the driver, whereas another version has the capability to control the vehicle speed without the possibility given to the driver to override this. In addition, speed limits can be static or dynamic, depending upon whether external circumstances (e.g. traffic conditions) are taken into account. It was also necessary to consider the use of

ADAS on different road types and for different vehicle categories and user groups. Based on a long initial list, 22 distinct scenarios, linking particular ADAS with specific external circumstances, were identified and prioritised (a description of these 22 scenarios is given in Appendix 3.6.1. The MCA, more specifically the Analytical Hierarchy Process (AHP) method, yielded a ranking of the various ADAS scenarios (step 7). The AHP was developed by Saaty (1977, 1982, 1988, 1995) and is one of the most widely used MCA methods. It is based on three principles, namely (1) construction of a hierarchy (such as the one above in Figure 3.6.2), (2) priority setting; and (3) logical consistency. The relative priorities given to each element in the hierarchy are determined by comparing pair-wise all the elements at a lower level, in terms of their contribution to the elements at a higher level with which a causal relationship exists. The intensity of preference is measured on a scale from 1 to 9. In order to determine stakeholder priorities, several evaluations were performed, namely by experts, policy-makers, and users of the system. The inconsistency ratio for the evaluation of the criteria was 0.01. Saaty (1995: 81) has argued that the inconsistency ratio should not be higher than 10 per cent. If this had been the case, the pair-wise comparisons would have had to be revised. Inconsistency exists when the transitivity rule between the comparisons is violated. For example, if criterion A is considered to be twice as important as criterion B, which in turn is considered three times more important than criterion C, then criterion A should be six times more important than criterion C.

In Figure 3.6.3 the final ranking of various scenarios is given. On the x-axis, the overall score is given for each of the scenarios. The 22 scenarios are listed on the y-axis in increasing order of scores. The integrated scenario is ranked first, and well before the other ones. This implies that overall (i.e. taking into account all relevant criteria), this scenario is clearly the best as compared to all other ones. The two driver monitoring system (DMS) scenarios are in second and third place. The fifth version of the intelligent speed adaptation scenario (ISA5), which is the control scenario, is ranked fourth. Finally, the first adaptive cruise control system (ACC1) is ranked fifth.

The stability of this ranking can be assessed through a sensitivity analysis. The last stage of the methodology (step 8) included the actual implementation of ADAS. An implementation strategy can be described as all the steps that need to be taken to bridge the gap between the current situation/scenario (or the projected future situation without special action) and the desired future scenario. A further description of the MCA, as applied to intelligent transport systems in general, can be found in De Brucker *et al.* (2004: 151–179) and, as applied to ADAS in particular, in Macharis *et al.* (2004: 443–462). In this paper, however, we will focus on the last two steps in the methodology, which are crucial to the successful implementation of the recommendations.

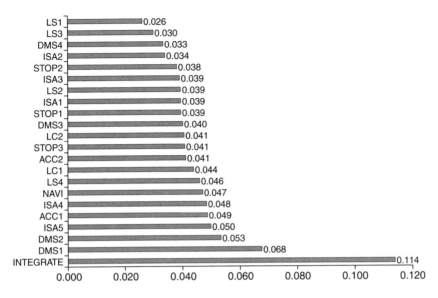

Figure 3.6.3 Result of the evaluation of ADAS (source: ADVISORS – Competitive and Sustainable Growth Programme (2002b: 86)).

3 Sensitivity analysis for the overall ranking

3.1 Significance

In the sections above, the results of an overall evaluation were described for a number of ADAS. These results were presented in the form of an overall ranking for the 22 ADAS considered, as illustrated in Figure 3.6.3. The five ADAS ranked first were considered to have the highest potential for implementation.

In this section, some insights are provided into the sensitivity of the final ranking. It is important to know whether a small change in the weights given to each criterion in the MCA could result in a different ranking. The sensitivity analysis presented here focuses on the alternatives ranked first. However, in order to take into account a wider spectrum of systems, vehicles, and road types, additional alternatives were added to the set. An extended set of scenarios, proposed by the experts in the ADVISORS group, was therefore subjected to the sensitivity analysis. DMS3 and DMS4 were added to the initial set so as to introduce the driver monitoring function of private vehicles in a warning and intervening mode. STOP3 was added in order to include the stop-and-go function. In order to extend the analysis of ISA, which was considered a priority, ISA3 and ISA4 were also included in the set. DMS2 was not selected, since DMS1 already refers to driver monitoring for professional vehicles. Lateral functions (LS and

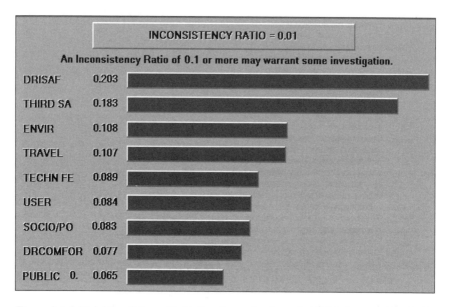

Figure 3.6.4 Weights of the criteria for the evaluation of ADAS (source: Macharis, Verbeke, and De Brucker (2004: 454) using ExpertChoice™).

LC) as well as the ACC scenarios were ultimately not taken into account. The set of ADAS analysed in the sensitivity analysis included therefore: INTEG-RATE, DMS1, ISA5, ISA4, NAVI, STOP3, DMS3, ISA3, and DMS4.

The weights applied to this set of ADAS are given in Figure 3.6.4 for the baseline scenario. These weights were obtained through the pair-wise comparison of the different criteria according to the judgement provided by several experts.

The choice described above is neither the only possible one, nor necessarily the most optimal one from the perspective of any stakeholder. Nevertheless it permitted the useful comparison of alternatives. Changing these weights then permitted us to assess whether the ranking achieved was sensitive to such an extent that it would result in, e.g., the alternative ranked last to become first or vice-versa.

The sensitivity analysis that was conducted consisted of three components, namely: (1) sensitivity analysis for each individual criterion, (2) scenario analysis, and (3) stakeholder analysis.

3.2 Sensitivity analysis for each individual criterion

As regards the sensitivity analysis for each criterion separately, it was tested whether the final ranking would be different if the weight of one specific criterion were increased or decreased, while the relative weights of the other criteria were to remain constant. In this type of sensitivity analysis, the 'trade-off points' were calculated. This means that one calculates how large the deviation or change of the initial weights should be in order to cause changes in the ranking of the actions or alternatives. The trade-off points mark an interval within which criterion weights may change without causing a reversal of the rank of the alternatives in the final ranking. Most often, the position of the alternative ranked first is given special attention. The actual calculation of the trade-off points was performed using the AHP software Expert Choice™ (Forman, 1998). That software package made it possible to visualise the incidence of changing weights on the final ranking for each criterion separately by means of so-called sensitivity graphs. In Figure 3.6.5, one example of such a sensitivity graph is shown for the criterion 'driver comfort'. This figure is shown here for illustrative purposes only, since the listing of the complete set of sensitivity graphs for all of the nine criteria studied would make this contribution too lengthy.

The present weight of the criterion studied (i.e. 'driver comfort') in Figure 3.6.5 is given by the intersection of the plain line with the abscis (7.7 per cent). The ranking of the various ADAS according to this sole criterion is given on the right ordinate in Figure 3.6.5. The final ranking taking into account all criteria, for the basic scenario, is given by the intersection of the (quasi) horizontal lines and the plain vertical line. This ranking may change when the weight of the criterion studied is increased or decreased as shown by the dotted line. An increase of this weight is simulated by shifting the vertical line to the right. A decrease of this weight is simulated by shifting this vertical line to the left. The new ranking

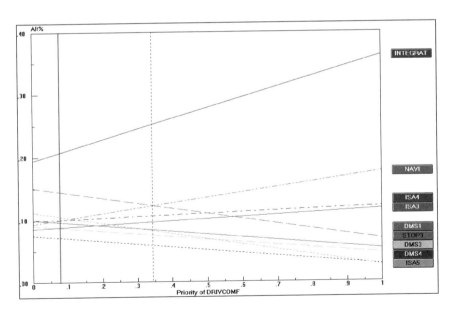

Figure 3.6.5 Sensitivity analysis for the criterion 'driver comfort' (source: Authors' own computation, using ExpertChoice™).

(i.e. the ranking that takes into account the higher or lower weight) is then given by the intersection of the new vertical line (dotted line) and the (quasi) horizontal lines.

All the other sensitivity graphs were established in the same way. These sensitivity graphs are not repeated here, since they are shown and discussed extensively in the final deliverable of the research project (ADVISORS – Competitive and Sustainable Growth Programme, 2002b: 95–106).

The sensitivity analysis for each of the nine criteria separately revealed that the position of the alternatives (ADAS) ranked first and second, namely INTEGRATE and DMS1 remain very stable. The position of the ADAS ranked last (DMS4) equally turned out to be very stable in all cases.

The position of ISA5 turned out to be stable for any decrease in the weight of the criteria, except the criterion 'third party safety effects'. When the weight of this criterion was decreased, the relatively favourable initial position of ISA5 worsened. In addition, when the weight of some criteria was increased, the position of ISA5 also worsened. Other ADAS then obtained a higher rank than ISA5. That observation, however, did not hold for the criteria 'third party safety effects' and 'public expenditure'. When the weight of those criteria was increased, the position of ISA5 improved significantly.

As regards the other ADAS, the so-called 'intermediate alternatives' (NAVI, ISA4, STOP3, ISA3, and DMS3), obtained similar overall scores. For a number of those ADAS, the sensitivity is rather low, while for other ones, the sensitivity is higher, depending on the criterion considered.

3.3 Scenario analysis

The second type of sensitivity analysis (namely scenario analysis), examined the extent to which the initial ranking changes when a different policy scenario is adopted, that emphasises other policy options. The emphasis on these policy options is simulated here by doubling the relative weight of the criteria related to that policy option. Five policy scenarios were identified, namely: (1) a scenario with emphasis on safety, (2) a green scenario, (3) a scenario with emphasis on the external effects, (4) a scenario with emphasis on risk, and (5) a scenario with emphasis on comfort. The weight sets corresponding to each of these specific scenarios are given in Figure 3.6.6.

In the scenario with emphasis on safety, the relative weights of the criteria driver safety and third party safety effects are doubled.

In the green scenario, the same is done for the safety criteria (driver safety and third party safety effects), as well as for the environmental criterion.

In the scenario with emphasis on external effects, both the third party safety effects and the environmental effects are given extra emphasis by doubling the relative weight of these criteria. The effects regarding driver safety are not given extra emphasis in this scenario since these effects are considered internal to the driver.

In the scenario with emphasis on risk, the relative weight of the criteria

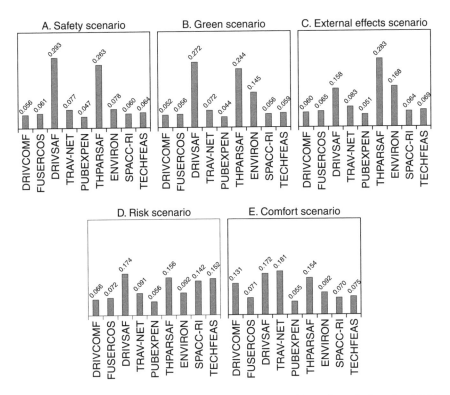

Figure 3.6.6 Alternative scenarios corresponding to specific points of view for ADAS evaluation (source: Authors' computation).

'socio-political acceptance' and 'acceptance risk' (SPACC-RI), as well as 'technical feasibility' (TEACHFEAS) are doubled. The first criterion measures risk from a socio-political point of view and the second one measures the same phenomenon but from a manufacturers' point of view. Both criteria are in fact bundled into a single criterion in the MCA (i.e. SPACC-RI). The last criterion (TECHFEAS) is related to technical feasibility and can also be considered to give an indication of the risk from a manufacturers' point of view.

In the scenario with emphasis on comfort both the criteria 'driver comfort' (DRIVCOMF) and 'travel time' and 'network efficiency' (TRAV-NET) receive a weight twice as high as in the basic scenario. The last two criteria are again bundled into a single criterion in the MCA. The results of the scenario analysis are given in Figure 3.6.7.

As regards the safety scenario, the position of the alternatives ranked first, second, third, and fourth (i.e. INTEGRATE, DMS1, ISA5, and ISA4), as well as the position of the alternative ranked last (DMS4), remained the same as in the basic scenario. The intermediate alternatives (DMS3, ISA3, STOP3, and NAVI)

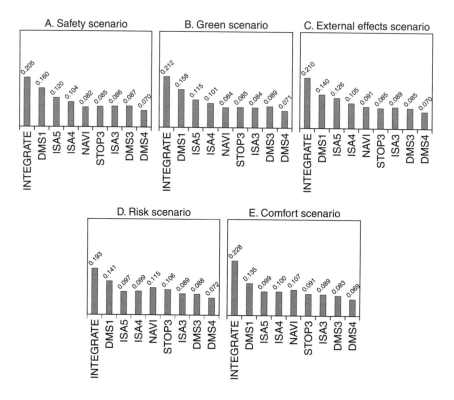

Figure 3.6.7 Results of the scenario analysis (source: Authors' computation).

did change position, but only among themselves and the difference among them remained very small.

The conclusions that can be drawn from the green scenario are similar to those of the former scenario (the safety scenario). The only difference is that the position of some of the intermediate alternatives such as STOP3 and ISA3 did not change as compared to the basic scenario. Here again, the differences among those ADAS remained very small.

The scenario with emphasis on external effects did not cause dramatic changes in ranking, except that the positions of ISA3 and STOP3 were inverted.

As regards the risk scenario, the position of the alternatives ranked first and second (i.e. INTEGRATE and DMS1), as well as the position of the three alternatives ranked at the end (ISA3, DMS3, and DMS4) remained the same as in the basic scenario. The intermediate alternatives (NAVI, STOP3, ISA4, and ISA5) did change position, but only among themselves.

As regards the comfort scenario, the position of the alternatives ranked first and second (i.e. INTEGRATE and DMS1) as well as the position of the various alternatives ranked at the end (STOP3, ISA3, DMS3, and DMS4) remained the same as in the basic scenario. Only the intermediate alternatives (NAVI, ISA4, and ISA5) changed position, and again, only among themselves.

The conclusions that can be drawn from the scenario analysis are, to a large extent, comparable to the conclusions drawn from the sensitivity analysis for each criterion separately. The alternatives ranked first and second (i.e. INTEG-RATE and DMS1) as well as the position of the alternative ranked last (DMS4) remain very stable as compared to the basic scenario, irrespective of weight changes. As regards the intermediate alternatives (ISA5, ISA4, NAVI, STOP3, ISA3, and DMS3), some changes may occur as illustrated in Figure 3.6.7. There, ISA5 and ISA4 obtain a less favourable position in the comfort scenario and in the risk scenario. They keep their position in the green scenario and in the scenario with emphasis on external effects.

3.4 Stakeholder analysis

In the stakeholder analysis, one examines whether the final ranking of the alternatives changes when the weight of a specific group of criteria is increased or even maximised (in this last case, the weight given to all other groups of criteria is zero). The criteria for which the weight is augmented or maximised correspond to a specific point of view of one specific stakeholder in the decision-making process. The criteria corresponding to the other points of view, i.e. the points of view of the other stakeholders, are ignored at that stage. As regards ADAS, three stakeholders were identified, namely: (1) users, (2) society, and (3) manufacturers. The sets of weights corresponding to the specific stakeholders' points of view are shown in Figure 3.6.8.

The users were primarily interested in the criteria 'driver comfort', 'full user cost', 'driver safety', and 'travel time' (Figure 3.6.8(A)). Society was primarily concerned with the criteria 'network efficiency', 'public expenditure', 'third party safety effects', 'environment', and 'socio-political acceptance' (Figure

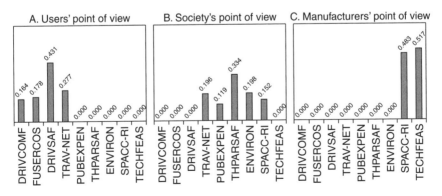

Figure 3.6.8 Weights corresponding to the points of view of specific stakeholders (source: Authors' computation).

3.6.8(B)). The manufacturers were interested in the criteria 'acceptance risk' and 'technical feasibility' (Figure 3.6.8(C)).

The results of the stakeholder analysis are given in Figure 3.6.9.

Regarding the stakeholder analysis corresponding to the users' point of view, the position of the alternatives ranked first and second (i.e. INTEGRATE and DMS1) remained the same as compared to the baseline scenario. The position of the other alternatives, however, underwent a more drastic change. ISA5 as well as the other ISAs earned the lowest scores in this new situation. DMS3, DMS4, and STOP3, however, obtained a much better position. The position of NAVI was not affected.

When focusing on the societal point of view, the ranking changed dramatically as compared to the baseline scenario. With the exception of the alternative ranked first (INTEGRATE), all the ADAS changed positions in the ranking. ISA5 and ISA4 became much more attractive from the societal point of view. DMS1 became much less attractive. ISA3, DMS3, and DMS4 were still ranked in the same order, but STOP3 earned a much lower preference. The position of NAVI was not affected. Regarding the stakeholder analysis corresponding to the manufacturers' point of view, the ranking was also very different from that in the baseline scenario. The only alternatives that remained in the same (unfavourable) position, were DMS3 and DMS4. DMS1 kept its relatively favourable position as compared to the baseline scenario. All the other ADAS obtained a completely different rank. According to the manufacturers' point of view, ISA5 is much less desirable than suggested by the baseline scenario. ISA4 and INTEGRATE were also considered less desirable than in the baseline scenario. The position of NAVI, STOP3, and ISA3 improved substantially from a manufacturers' point of view.

The results of the stakeholder analysis thus varied strongly, depending upon the point of view adopted, i.e. the weights given to each stakeholder group. The results of the stakeholder analysis were also different from those obtained through other types of sensitivity analysis. This implies that stakeholder interests are not aligned with the common interest. In the stakeholder analysis, only the

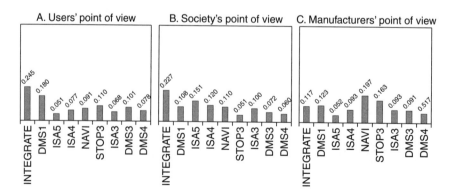

Figure 3.6.9 Results of the stakeholder analysis (source: Authors' computation).

criteria considered relevant by a specific stakeholder group were taken into account and their weight was maximised. The weights of the other criteria were set equal to zero.

Users appear not to be in favour of ISA5, ISA4, and ISA3, but rather prefer the INTEGRATE scenario, as well as DMS1, STOP3, and DMS3. Society appears to prefer ISA5 and ISA4, in addition to INTEGRATE. Manufacturers, however, are not in favour of ISA5, and adopt a position similar to that of the users. They rather prefer NAVI and STOP3. They do not particularly appreciate the INTEGRATE scenario, and ADAS positioned first in all former rankings (both in the basic scenario as well as in the various alternative scenarios). The conclusion regarding ISA5 (the controlling scenario in urban and rural areas) is that active government involvement may be useful. Both substantial incentives and a media campaign may be necessary to increase the perceived attractiveness of ISA5.

4 Implementation issues

The approach followed as regards the implementation of ADAS can be represented as a four-step process:

1 selection of specific ADAS for policy support;
2 choice of future 'state-of-the-world' configurations, which are different from the present configuration;
3 design of implementation strategies;
4 strategy validation (through workshops with stakeholders).

Step (2) identifies *what* situation is desirable, and this can be represented as a state-of-the-world configuration describing all the significant characteristics of the future situation, with a focus on those characteristics that are different from the present situation. The question arises whether specific ADAS can contribute to reducing the gap between the present and the desired, future state-of-the-world. This will critically depend on the impacts of ADAS implementation on the transport system, and on the quality of the knowledge of expected ADAS performance. Step (3) addresses *how* the future state-of-the-world configuration should be achieved, once a particular ADAS (or set of ADAS) is chosen. This will depend on the preferences and choices of the stakeholders involved in (or affected by) ADAS implementation, and this can be described through an imple-mentation *strategy*.

4.1 Strategy selection matrix

A tool to assist in ADAS strategy implementation was developed in the form of a matrix, shown in Table 3.6.1. Each cell in the matrix describes the shortcom-ings of the current situation and (in italics) a suggested approach to remedying these, so as to achieve the desired 'state-of-the-world' configuration.

Table 3.6.1 Strategy selection matrix

	Behaviour (Direct increase of adoption)	Structure (Indirect increase of adoption)
ADAS level	Technology is unreliable or inflexible. Range of application is inadequate. *Technical development to increase functionality and reliability*	Incompatibility between new ADAS and existing systems. Unclear interface definitions or inadequate tier 2 manufacturing. *Development of industry agreements and/or technical standards*
Consumer level	Consumers are uninformed of benefits or have suspicion and anxiety. *Information, demonstrations*	Inadequate means for consumers to access ADAS or derive benefits. *Driver training* *Loan, rental agreements* *'Bundled' services as OEM package (Original Equipment Manufacturer)*
Individual producer level	Poor product specification or presentation. ADAS use compromises safety or reduces market acceptance. *Consultation, guidelines, recommendations*	Market is insufficiently mature to differentiate between 'good' and 'bad' products and suppliers. *Industry code of practice or Government licence*
Market level	General climate of uncertainty concerning market viability. Industry unwillingness to invest. *Grants/research funding.* *Roadmaps, industry/government MoU (Memorandum of Understanding)*	Existing market players unwilling or unable to develop and exploit required ADAS. *Stimulate new players* *Lower entry barriers, e.g. by standards* *Selective sponsorship*
Institutional level	Policy-makers unaware or unsure of ADAS benefits and costs. *Inform policy-makers* *High-level demonstrations* *Identify euro best practices*	Uncertainty concerning liability and future government actions. Different national approaches. Requirement for mandatory approach. *European strategy* *Type approvals* *Clarify legislation*

Source: ADVISORS – Competitive and Sustainable Growth Programme (2002c: 46, adapted).

The matrix has two dimensions. The vertical dimension describes the target of strategic action. This may include:

- the ADAS itself;
- the stakeholders instrumental to achieving the desired state-of-the-world (i.e. users or consumers, individual producers, the ADAS market); and
- the broader institutional environment

The horizontal dimension distinguishes between two types of actions required to reach the desired future state-of-the-world configuration. These two types include:

- actions aimed at immediate behavioural change (how to improve adoption directly);
- actions aimed at improving system characteristics (how to improve system characteristics so as to facilitate adoption indirectly).

The matrix can be used to identify gaps between the current state-of-the-world configuration (or the future configuration without intervention) and the desired future configuration. Having identified this gap, the matrix provides suggestions that can be used as a starting point for designing implementation strategies. For example, if the desired state-of-the-world can be achieved through simple incentives that trigger direct changes in behaviour of one or more stakeholders, this implies only limited government intervention. Systemic changes usually require more 'invasive' intervention (and may also require behavioural changes).

4.2 Key questions to address

Four key questions were identified for strategy development.

Who? – Stakeholders and champions

Deployment of intelligent transport systems (ITS) usually involves complicated decision dynamics among multiple stakeholders, with none of them having total control (Tsao, 2001). Therefore, rather than designating a single 'deployer', there can only be, at best, a 'champion'. The champion may not have the full capability or authority for deployment, but acts in an organised way to push for favourable decisions by all the relevant stakeholders. It is not sufficient to define roles for stakeholders but it is necessary to develop ways to motivate them to fulfil those roles.

Where? – Geography and context

There are a number of issues to be addressed under this heading. Some activities (e.g. research, standards) may require an international rather than national perspective but other issues may be specifically national or regional. Deployment may be undertaken in a small geographic region or nationally. In addition to geographic considerations, it is also important to select the target market: e.g. privately owned vehicles versus the fleet market, passenger vehicles versus trucks.

When? – Timescales, roadmaps, and deployment

This concerns timing, co-ordination, and dependencies of the various actions that are part of the strategy and contribute to the objectives. Within this, developments can involve incremental steps (which in turn lead to intermediate concepts/scenarios) and 'big bang' changes. Strategies may be planned as deterministic or adaptive (and hence branch at decision nodes). Roadmaps have become a popular way of visualising a series of linked developments over time. Deployment scenarios can be described dynamically according to the results of the intermediate steps, and evolve over time into the future scenario.

How? – Implementation tools

Tools are specific devices or measures that can be used by one or more stakeholders. Some examples include legal instruments (such as type approval and contracts), influence tools (such as financial assistance and demonstrations), development tools (such as research and field trials), and support tools (such as standards and architectures).

4.3 Implementation strategy development

Since it is usually impossible to do everything at once or in parallel, an implementation strategy will, in general, be composed of a number of steps. These may overlap in time and may be related to one another in complex ways. A step (in a strategy) can be thought of as 'one or more closely related actions designed to achieve a specified impact such that the current situation moves closer to the desired, future state-of-the-world configuration'. Each individual action within a step is a specific undertaking by one or more stakeholders, usually over a specific period of time. The actions may make use of 'tools' such as financial assistance, demonstrations, or standards.

4.4 Implementation strategy examples

This section illustrates how specific state-of-the-art configurations were chosen that involve different ADAS and how implementation strategies were designed. In each case, the strategy selection matrix was used to diagnose the 'gap' between the present situation and the desired future situation, and to suggest actions. Then the key questions (stakeholders, context, timescale, and implementation tools) were addressed and the strategies developed. Full details can be found in the final research project (ADVISORS – Competitive and Sustainable Growth Programme, 2003 and 2002c).

4.4.1 Driver monitoring systems (DMS)

The development of a DMS desired state-of-the-world configuration considered all road and traffic environments. However, the first application is expected to be on highways, as this is technically more feasible and reduced vigilance is a particular problem for highways and rural roads (more so than in urban areas).

All types of motor vehicles were considered, although cost considerations might lead to a first application to professional vehicles, in particular from the heavy goods transport sector. The consequences of truck accidents are particularly serious and, from stakeholder analyses (ADVISORS – Competitive and Sustainable Growth Programme, 2003), it appeared that business firms are interested in DMS. Also, the application to trucks is more profitable and easier to realise from a legal and organisational point of view, than applications to the private automobile market.

For DMS, the main weakness is reported to be the general lack of maturity of existing systems. In the strategy selection matrix, this issue is highlighted in the ADAS/behavioural element of the matrix and the suggested remedy is further research and development as the main strategy forward. Consideration of the 'key questions' points to initial use by professional drivers as described in the preceding paragraph. The immaturity of the technology suggests an incremental introduction with initial use in a warning-only mode and then, as technology matures, development of intervention systems for – and product use by – the wider driving public. Adoption of a DMS would, hopefully, be viewed as useful assistance (assuming it works properly), and have high acceptance.

An implementation strategy concentrating on research and development (R&D) for the coming decade was developed with four steps:

- R&D professional warning only;
- R&D professional warning intervening;
- R&D all drivers warning;
- R&D all drivers warning intervening.

Table 3.6.2 gives an example of a strategy step descriptor taken from the DMS implementation strategy.

4.4.2 Adaptive cruise control (ACC)

ACC is already available on higher-specification vehicles and is marketed as a comfort rather than a safety system. The implementation strategy (in outline) concentrates on achieving a scenario whereby ACC can deliver safety benefits and become integrated with other ADAS.

Since the situations described at the 'ADAS level' of the strategy matrix do not apply to existing ACC, consideration focuses on the consumer level, where

Table 3.6.2 Example strategy step descriptor (for DMS)

Strategy title: Research and Development for Driver Monitoring

Step No: 1 Step title: R&D for professional driver monitoring system

Start event:	**Implementation timeframe:**	**Impact timeframe:**
Following AWAKE project	2006–2009	>2007

Step description:
In-vehicle sensors (including driver and vehicle behavioural sensors that are all unobtrusive) are required to detect hypo-vigilance with good reliability and low false alarms.

R&D is required to develop further the reliability of the sensors and associated algorithms/rules for detection of driver state impairment. R&D also needs to focus on behavioural effects such as complacency and offsetting the risk of low compliance.

Rationale:
Current technology is insufficiently mature to enter the market. Reliability is too low and variable. False alarms can be a problem. Behavioural effects and modes of adoption are under researched.
The focus of the truck as the first adopter is based on the considerable consequences of truck accidents.

Expected Risks:	**Mitigation:**
Reliability may still be too low and further R&D costly.	Public funding support
	Several parallel research efforts

Key actor (champion): | **Involvement:**
Relevant industry and research institutes | Research, research funding mechanisms, incorporation of transport companies as first system adopters

Other involved actors:
Policy-makers, car manufacturers, public funding bodies, transport companies

Expected impact:
Reduction of fatalities and serious injury accidents by 1–5 per cent.

Cost estimate: Not possible at this time.

Source: ADVISORS – Competitive and Sustainable Growth Programme (2002c: 61, adapted).

it appears some consumers are uninformed and behavioural effects of ACC are uncertain. Therefore a strategy of awareness enhancement and driver training is appropriate. It was also noted that current unstructured and multi-brand policies could impede ACC success and rapid market penetration. Therefore, consumer-oriented standards and systemic improvements, permitting integration with other ADAS on the right-hand side of the matrix also need to be promoted.

Accordingly, four strategies were chosen to improve the implementation of ACC:

* driver instruction and training;
* research on behavioural adaptation;
* technical development of integrated systems;
* standardisation and type approval.

In terms of key stakeholders, government agencies need to be involved in setting standards and solving driver-oriented challenges, and should partially fund them (especially the further research), but it is the corporate sector which has to perform most of the actions and, indeed, these are already being undertaken. The automotive industry is working on the technical development of driver assistance systems and research is underway on behavioural effects of ADAS. Furthermore, there are standardisation activities for ACC that have yielded a draft international standard for ACC, but currently, many points of discussion are left open and further research is needed, particularly on human factors issues.

4.4.3 Intelligent speed adaptation (ISA)

Five ISA scenarios were defined as shown in Table 3.6.3.

The ISA[A] system is already available in the market and no further implementation action is considered necessary. For ISA types [B] to [E], consideration of the current situation described in the strategy matrix implies a need for both ADAS-level and market-level actions to be undertaken. For legal and other reasons, and because of resistance from both users and the industry (identified during stakeholder consultation), mandatory ISA[D] should be the subject of implementation efforts rather than the mandatory ISA[E]. Consequently, the strategies chosen to improve ISA implementation are research and development, data collection and transmission to vehicles, and standardisation and type approval. Of these, research into criteria for setting speeds and issues of collecting data for transmission to vehicles were both considered extremely important and most urgent.

In terms of stakeholders, industry has to perform, or contribute to the steps but public agencies could facilitate introduction of ISA in a number of ways. Industry's willingness to invest could be increased by making 'infrastructure' available at low cost, e.g. static speed limit maps and dynamic traffic data (for increasing safe speeds). Governments can also assist through funding mechanisms and by continuing to inform public opinion on the detrimental impacts of excessive speed.

Table 3.6.3 Five ISA scenarios

ISA type	Description
ISA [A]	Warning and voluntary intervention Speed limit can be adjusted manually. Information or warning is given when speed exceeds the set limit, or speeding is not possible (except by kick down). Feedback type depends on the manufacturer.
ISA [B]	Static speed limits: *Informing, warning or intervening* This system conforms to the static speed limits of the roads (e.g. through on-board map). When the system is switched on, it can either give information or a warning when the vehicle is about to speed or it can intervene making speeding impossible. Fit for all road types. Possible coupling with in-car rain sensor for lower limits.
ISA [C]	Location sensitive: *Informing, warning or intervening* The system is based on the static speed limits ISA [B] but with maximum safe approach speeds for dangerous locations, e.g. curves, intersections, and railway crossings. When the system is switched on, it can just give information or a warning or can intervene. Fit for all road types. Possible coupling with in-car rain and light sensors for lower limits.
ISA [D]	Dynamic: *Informing, warning or intervening* This system is based on static speed limits ISA[B], safe approach speed of dangerous locations ISA[C] but also with speed modified according to dangerous road, traffic, and weather conditions. A service provider sends the dynamic information to the car. Fit for all road types. Possible coupling with in-car light and rain sensors for lower limits. Integration with navigation.
ISA [E]	Mandatory controlling ISA [E] is a mandatory controlling system and cannot be switched off by the driver. Fit for all road types.

Source: ADVISORS – Competitive and Sustainable Growth Programme (2002c: 50–51).

4.4.4. Scope for Integration

The state-of-the-world configurations discussed above have concentrated on implementing individual ADAS, viewed as functionally independent of other systems. However, in practice functional integration may be desirable, and, indeed, the 'Integrated Scenario' was preferred over all others. This desired, future-state-of-the-world combines the functionality of dynamic navigation, ACC, ACC with additional features for urban use, and ISA. Such an ADAS would fully cover the longitudinal control of the car and the next logical step will be its integration with lateral support aids to develop a virtual, electronic cushion around the entire car (Figure 3.6.10).

In terms of future scenarios, the first integrated applications can be expected to be on highways/motorways, as this is technically and organisationally simpler. The ultimate goal is the application in a rural, peri-urban, and urban environment, and seamless operation across different environments and national borders.

Such an integrated ADAS scenario could involve all types of motor vehicles,

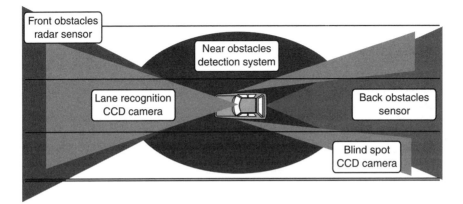

Figure 3.6.10 Integration of longitudinal and lateral ADAS for an extended integrated
ADAS scenario in the future (source: ADVISORS – Competitive and Sustainable Growth Programme (2002c: 61, adapted)).

though cost considerations might lead to a first application to luxury cars. An application to trucks might be easier from a legal and organisational point of view, but
any technical deficiencies may have a more serious impact in that domain.

Strategies to promote such a scenario include development (e.g. sensor fusion
and HMI integration) and work on interoperability and standardisation. Authorities can assist industry by providing the necessary infrastructure, or at least
provide incentives for its realisation (i.e. digital maps of high accuracy) and by
promoting subsystem standardisation. One specific area of focus needs to be the
driver interface and human factors considerations.

5 Conclusions

This paper has described the results of an impact assessment for advanced driver
assistance systems (ADAS). It has focused primarily on two issues critical to
effective public policy, namely the design of mechanisms that address, first the
challenges of appropriate sensitivity analysis, and second the choice of implementation scenarios. The strategic impact assessment developed by the authors
is based on a formal, analytical process, which includes both technical and
stakeholder perspectives. The main strength of a multi-criteria, multi-actor
approach is that it builds upon the stakeholders' own objectives in establishing
evaluation criteria, thereby facilitating the ultimate implementation of specific
technologies associated with high net benefits. The methodology was applied to
a set of ADAS that are likely candidates for commercialisation on a large scale
within the next decade. The ADAS ranked within the top five of this set were
considered to have the highest potential. These ADAS should therefore be given
the highest priority in government support policies, e.g. within the framework of
innovation policies favouring the development of such strategic initiatives in the

EU. The results suggest that the most promising ADAS include the integrated system, the driver monitoring systems, mandatory ISA, and ACC. However, these various systems are viewed attractive for different reasons: for example, mandatory ISA provides high societal benefits, whereas the ACC system results in lower safety or traffic benefits but is associated with a higher user desirability.

The extensive sensitivity analysis leads to the following conclusions. The first and second type of sensitivity analysis yielded results that were largely similar. Both in the sensitivity analysis for each criterion separately, and in the scenario analysis, the same two (and sometimes three) ADAS were consistently ranked at the top, and their internal position within the ranking always remained the same. These top ADAS are INTEGRATE, DMS1 and, to a lesser extent, also ISA5. This last ADAS, however, earned a less favourable rank in the comfort scenario and the risk scenario. Additionally, in both types of sensitivity analysis, there was also one ADAS that consistently ranked at the bottom, namely DMS4. As regards the other ADAS, the so-called 'intermediate ADAS' (namely ISA4, NAVI, STOP3, ISA3, DMS3, and DMS4), their ranking was less stable. The relative total scores they earned were positioned closely to each other. For a number of those ADAS, the sensitivity appeared rather low, whereas for others it was high, depending on the criterion considered.

The results of the third type of sensitivity analysis, namely the stakeholder analysis, were very different from the results of the first two types. In addition, the stakeholder analysis revealed that users appear not to be in favour of ISA5, ISA4, and ISA3, but rather prefer the INTEGRATE, DMS1, STOP3, and DMS3 scenarios. Society appears to prefer ISA5 and ISA4, in addition to the INTEGRATE scenario. Manufacturers, in contrast, have an attitude similar to the users, as far as not being in favour of ISA5 is concerned. They rather prefer NAVI and STOP3. They do not particularly appreciate the INTEGRATE scenario, an ADAS ranked first in all former rankings (both in the basic scenario as well as in the various alternative scenarios analysed in the sensitivity analysis).

The strategy selection matrix and related work intended to develop implementation strategies, provide a new framework to reflect on the complex challenge of ADAS deployment. The methodology, when applied to a number of favourably ranked scenarios, was considered helpful by a number of actors involved in strategic thinking on this issue. However, the time limits and resource constraints imposed on the completion of the research project (ADVISORS) precluded both the full development of the implementation proposals and a more indepth discussion on these proposals. The successful launch of innovative products usually entails a number of phases. These may include: research leading to innovation; testing; first application; market launch; mature use; decline; and replacement. The most promising opportunities to influence the content and focus of such products arise during the research phase, as well as during the transition between testing and market introduction. Those are the stages when scenarios and implementation strategies are developed. Those are also the phases in which most ADAS of interest are now positioned, which suggests fruitful avenues for business–government cooperation, especially at the European level.

Overview of ADAS scenarios

Scenario identification	Abbreviation	Road type	Traffic density	Penetration level	Communication features	Vehicle
STOP&GO scenario 1	STOP1	Urban	High flow			
STOP&GO scenario 2	STOP2	Urban	Lower flow			
STOP&GO scenario 3	STOP3	Peri-urban	High flow			
ACC scenario 1	ACC1	Motorway	High flow			
ACC scenario 2	ACC2	Motorway	Lower flow			
Lateral support scenario 1	LS1	Motorway		Assisting/intervening		
Lateral support scenario 2	LS2	Motorway		Warning		
Lateral support scenario 3	LS3	Rural		Assisting/intervening		
Lateral support scenario 4	LS4	Rural		Warning		
Lane change support scenario 1	LC1	Motorway		Warning		
Lane change support scenario 2	LC2	Rural		Warning		
ISA scenario 1	ISA1	Rural/urban		Information	Dynamic	
ISA scenario 2	ISA2	Rural/urban		Information	Static	
ISA scenario 3	ISA3	Rural		Assisting/intervening	Dynamic	
ISA scenario 4	ISA4	Urban		Assisting/intervening	Dynamic	
ISA scenario 5	ISA5	Rural/urban		Controlling	Dynamic	
DMS scenario 1	DMS1			Warning		Professional registered cars
DMS scenario 2	DMS2			Intervening		Professional registered cars
DMS scenario 3	DMS3			Warning		Private non-registered cars
DMS scenario 4	DMS4			Intervening		Private non-registered cars
Navigation and FM scenario	NAVI				Dynamic	
Integrated scenario	INTEGRATE					

Source: ADVISORS – Competitive and Sustainable Growth Programme (2002b: 129).

Notes

* Vrije Universiteit Brussel; Department of Business Economics and Strategic Management, Pleinlaan 2, B-1050 Brussels, Belgium, tel. +32 2 629 22 86, fax. +32 2 629 20 60, Cathy.Macharis@vub.ac.be.

** Senior Research Fellow, TRL; Nine Mile Ride, Wokingham, Berkshire RG40 3GA, England, tel. +44 1344 770945, fax +44 1344 770356, Web: www.trl.co.uk, astevens@trl.co.uk.

*** Professor VLEKHO Business School, Department of Economics and Management, Koningsstraat 336, B-1030 Brussels (Belgium), tel. +32 2 221 12 63, fax. +32 2 219 78 79, kdebrucker@vlekho.wenk.be; affiliated as a post-doctoral researcher with the University of Antwerp (Belgium), Department of Transport and Regional Economics.

**** McCaig Chair in Management, Haskayne School of Business, University of Calgary (Canada), Templeton College, University of Oxford (UK) and Vrije Universiteit Brussel, Department of Business Economics and Strategic Management, Pleinlaan 2, B-1050 Brussels, tel. +32 2 629.21.29, averbeke@ucalgary.ca.

1 This paper is based on a research project called 'ADVISORS' commissioned by the Directorate General for Transport and Energy (DG TREN) of the European Commission, under the Fifth Framework Programme. The project was carried out by the authors in collaboration with the Belgian Institute for Road Safety (Belgisch Instituut voor de Verkeersveiligheid – BIVV).

2 'ADVISORS' is the abbreviation of 'Action for advanced Driver assistance and Vehicle control systems Implementation, Standardisation, Optimum use of the Road network and Safety'. The project website is www.advisors.iao.fhg.de.

3 'ADVISORS' was a large scale, pan-European research project, co-funded by Directorate General of Transport and Energy (DG TREN) of the European Commission (EC) (2000–2002). It was set up to perform a comprehensive impact assessment of advanced driver assistance systems (ADAS) and to study implementation scenarios. The partners in the research consortium included various public agencies, publicly funded research institutes, transport and insurance companies, and automobile manufacturers from ten different European Union (EU) countries.

References

ADVISORS – Competitive and Sustainable Growth Programme (2002a) *An integrated methodology and pilot evaluation results (Deliverable D4/5.2 v8)*, Commission of the European Union, Directorate General for Transport and Energy, Brussels, contract no. GRD 1-2000-10047. Online. Available at http://www.advisors.iao.fhg.de Reports > Deliverables > D4/5.2 (accessed 16 September 2004).

—— (2002b) *Integrated multicriteria analysis for advanced driver assistance systems (Deliverable D6.1)*, Commission of the European Union, Directorate General for Transport and Energy, Brussels, contract no. GRD 1-2000-10047. Online. Available at http://www.advisors.iao.fhg.de Reports > Deliverables > D6.1 (accessed 16 September 2004).

—— (2002c) *Priority implementation scenarios, and schemes regarding equity, insurance policies, legislation, incentive and organisational consequences for ADAS deployment. Type approval and standardisation recommendations (Deliverable D7.1 v6)*, Commission of the European Union, Directorate General for Transport and Energy, Brussels, contract no. GRD 1-2000-10047. Online. Available at http://www. advisors.iao.fhg.de Reports > Deliverables > D7.1 (accessed 16 September 2004).

—— (2002d) *Actor interests, user awareness, acceptance, responsibilities and users' awareness enhancement (Deliverable 2.2 v1)*, Commission of the European Union, Directorate General for Transport and Energy, Brussels, contract no. GRD 1-2000-10047. Online. Available at http://www.advisors.iao.fhg.de Reports > Deliverables > D2.2 (accessed 16 September 2004).

—— (2003) *Final publishable report.* Commission of the European Union, Directorate General for Transport and Energy, Brussels, contract no. GRD 1-2000-10047. Online. Available at http://www.advisors.iao.fhg.de Reports > Deliverables > FPR (accessed 16 September 2004).

De Brucker, K., Verbeke, A., and Macharis C. (2004) 'The applicability of multicriteria-analysis to the evaluation of intelligent transport systems (ITS)' in E. Bekiaris and Y.J. Nakanishi (eds) *Economic impacts of intelligent transportation systems. Innovations and case studies*, Elsevier, Amsterdam.

Forman, E. (1998) *Expert choice.™ Advanced decision support software*, Expert Choice Inc., Pittsburg.

Macharis, C., Verbeke, A., and De Brucker, K. (2004) 'The strategic evaluation of new technologies through multicriteria analysis: the ADVISORS case' in E. Bekiaris and Y.J. Nakanishi (eds) *Economic impacts of intelligent transportation systems. Innovations and case studies*, Elsevier, Amsterdam.

Ministry of Transport and Communications – Finland (1999), *Guidelines for the evaluation of ITS projects*, Publication 24/99, Helsinki, pp. 443–462..

Saaty, T.L. (1977) 'A scaling method for priorities in hierarchical structures' *Journal of mathematics and psychology*, 15: 234–281.

—— (1982) *Decision making for leaders*, Lifetime Learning Publications, Wadsworth, Belmont.

—— (1988) *The analytic hierarchy process*, McGraw Hill, New York.

—— (1995) *Decision making for leaders, The analytic hierarchy process for decisions in a complex world*, RWS Publications, Pittsburgh.

Tsao, J.H. (2001) 'A framework for evaluating deployment strategies for intelligent transport systems' *ITS Journal*, 6: 141–173.